Occupational Placement

Occupational Placement

Its History, Philosophies, Procedures,
and Educational Implications

By ANNA Y. REED

Professor Emeritus of Education
New York University

Ithaca, New York

CORNELL UNIVERSITY PRESS

1946

PREFACE

THIS book is the second in a series of three which was planned by the author during the years when her university responsibilities claimed her entire attention and made it impossible to undertake a type of writing which required both research and concentration.

The first volume, *Guidance and Personnel Services in Education,* was published in 1944. It was focused on the educational aspects of personnel service and was historically oriented. The occupational world was brought into the picture only when mention of its processes, opportunities, requirements, and personnel procedures was needed in order to augment or explain the educational aspects of preparation for occupational life, or to show the relation between the various agencies—productive and distributive—which deal with the human factor. The accent was on youth.

This book reverses the emphases. It presents as its distinctive feature methods of distributing, rather than methods of producing, the labor supply, and it gives equal attention to youth as he enters the labor market directly from school and to the adult who seeks readjustments or replacements. Moreover, it has made a conscious effort to keep before the prospective reader the educational implications of productive employment, whereas, in the former volume, the occupational implications of education were stressed.

Since by both inclination and training the author tends to put high values on our inheritances from the past and since "provincialism in time" has characterized so many of the recent researches in the youth areas of employment and unemployment, this study also is definitely historically oriented. And it is believed that those who are sufficiently interested in the subject to read the book will realize how unfortunate it has been, both during the late depression and the war, that so many of our youth studies and programs have "started from scratch" without reviewing, as a basis for progress, the contributions of the past.

The purposes of this book are (1) to consider the social and economic needs which placement services, at different periods of time, have been instituted to meet, (2) to call attention to the various philosophies which have motivated the institution and controlled the operation of such services, (3) to present certain basic procedures which constitute the placement process wherever it may be in operation, and (4) to afford an opportunity for those who are not professional placement workers to become acquainted with the problems and procedures of placement services and with their close relationship to educational problems and procedures.

For many years there has been a demand for a treatise on this subject which would furnish all the technical information essential to the organization and operation of local services, whether designed to operate as independent units or to function as a part of federal, state, or municipal services, and at the same time would employ a method of presentation which would appeal to laymen and educators and might be used as a textbook in university classes. This book is an effort to meet that demand.

However, were there no demand for a more popular presentation on a broader social-economic background, there would be no valid excuse for another book. For, although scholars in the personnel field have, as yet, produced a very limited literature dealing with the placement aspect of personnel work—especially with its historical and philosophical background and its educational implications—there are available on the technical aspects of public employment services two excellent publications which are entitled to rank as classics in the field.[1] Both have been freely referred to in this book and are recommended to any who desire to follow the placement process as it has operated, and currently does operate, under public employment services.

Selection of a suitable title posed quite a problem. Neither placement nor employment properly characterizes a service comprising a series of procedures the end result of which is neither placement nor employment, but *referral*. Employment services, or placement services, terms which have been used synonymously in this book except when they denote mass or individual orders with acceptance of referrals guaranteed, are in reality *referral services*. This, along with other terminological problems in the personnel field, is left for future students of nomenclature in these areas. Ad interim, the best treatment of "Terminology in Employment Offices" is found in *Statistical Procedure of Public Employment Offices* by Annabel and Bryce Stewart, which is referred to in the bibliography to Part One.

Discussion of employment procedures in foreign countries has been omitted—for lack of space and because before the war much attention had been given to foreign development and there is an abundance of material available, some of which is outdated.

[1] Shelby M. Harrison and others, *Public Employment Offices: Their Purpose, Structure and Methods* (New York: Russell Sage Foundation, 1924), and Raymond C. Atkinson, Louise C. Odencrantz, and Ben Deming, *Public Employment Service in the United States* (Chicago: Public Administration Service, 1938).

References have been selected for accessibility, for general rather than local applicability, and as indicators of growth as well as reporters of current practices. Several of the references found in the bibliography of Part One are pertinent to topics discussed in later chapters.

It is hoped that the method of presentation chosen has resulted in clothing the indispensable skeleton of the employment process with enough human interest to lure the layman and the educator to study more intensively and more intelligently a social process of major importance to the welfare of the country; that continuous study of the problems involved in the effective distribution of our entire labor supply will broaden their vision and increase their knowledge of occupational experiences as valuable avenues for the education of youth and of educational opportunities as equally valuable avenues for the occupational adjustment and uninterrupted employability of adults. Above all else, it is hoped that it will result in a more sympathetic understanding of those youth who do not care to philosophize on the banks of the River of Time while awaiting permission to go in swimming.

Acknowledgments.

Several former students whose experience in personnel work has made them valuable members of the personnel departments of the Army or Navy have made generous contributions, in one way or another, to the preparation of this book. Since their present positions forbid personal recognition of their contributions, I acknowledge my obligation to them collectively and thank them for their assistance.

I also desire to express my appreciation to publishers who have permitted me to use copyrighted material. Their names will be found in the footnotes which identify the passages quoted.

Especial thanks are due to Dr. A. Gordon Nelson, Associate Vocational Adviser in the Office of Veterans Education, Cornell University,[2] for advice on and the reading of Chapter X, which deals with Veterans' Placement Services, and to my sister, Mrs. Nellie Y. Hamilton, whose research and editorial assistance has been of inestimable value not only in hastening the completion of the book but in improving its literary quality.

Anna Y. Reed

Boston, Massachusetts
October 1, 1945

[2] Dr. Nelson is now Assistant Professor of Education and Vocational Guidance at Cornell University.

CONTENTS

PART ONE

An Overview of the History and Philosophies of Placement and Employment Services

CHAPTER I
Methods and Media for Facilitating Employment

CHAPTER II
The Evolution of Public Employment Services

CHAPTER I

Methods and Media for Facilitating Employment

SINCE the major purpose of this publication is a practical one, what is presented on the history and theory of employment and placement must be regarded as a mere beginning—an initial effort to call the attention of educators in general, and personnel workers in particular, to the fact that modern placement services have a history; are a response to social and economic needs; and have gradually evolved a latent philosophy, which is awaiting crystallization and incorporation into our educational philosophy.

Everyone knows that a variety of practices, international in their usage, have come into being in different countries, at different times, and under different circumstances, to facilitate the exchange of employer and employee needs. As time has passed, even the most primitive of such methods has been retained provided it was adapted to the immediate situation. Also, everyone knows that certain employment and placement terms in use today were in use several centuries before Christ; that, in the main, interpretations of such terms have remained much the same; and that several practical employment and placement problems have been continuously troublesome throughout the centuries and promise to remain so throughout the centuries to come.

Documentary evidence from the Old Testament alone assures us that many centuries B.C. men were hired for wages and that neither oppression of hired servants nor delay in the payment of wages was approved by the law of the land.[1] Jacob's struggle to make good on his labor contract, coupled with his complaint that Laban had changed the basis of his wage agreement ten times, forms a part of one of the best-known love stories of all history and has appealed to sympathetic readers in every land. In the twenty-seventh chapter of Ezekiel, which is concerned with the fall of Tyre, 588 B.C., the city is described as a huge market where the interstate commerce of the day was carried on—a market wherein both merchandise and "the persons of men" were traded. There is, however, nothing to indicate that it was free labor which was traded, and one is probably justi-

[1] Lev. 19:13; Deut. 24:14, 15.

fied in assuming that this market was primarily a slave market for the disposition of conquered peoples.

Both the Old and the New Testament cite market places where, during the first century A.D. free labor and employers made wage-work bargains, or labor contracts, where services were exchanged for hire, where wage disputes arose and employer-employee relations were discussed.[2]

A very modern note is struck in John 10:12 where the hireling is characterized as lacking interest in the care of the sheep *because they do not belong to him*. And it is not difficult for the modern mind to visualize the "no small stir" which rose at Ephesus among the craftsmen when Paul's declaration that "they be no gods, which are made with hands" threatened to destroy the lucrative trade of the silversmiths, "so that . . . this our craft is in danger to be set at nought."[3]

The twentieth chapter of Matthew tells the story of the laborers in the vineyard. The householder found the *labor reserve* "standing idle in the marketplace." He appears to have *bargained collectively* for services at a "penny a day." Later in the day he employed other workers. At the close of the day the group which served for a full day protested, as an *unfair labor practice,* the payment of a higher proportionate wage to those who had worked the shorter day. The employer countered with: "Is it not lawful for me to do what I will with mine own?" Obviously, this labor reserve comprised free labor, and it will be noted that the principle that "the labourer is worthy of his hire" seems to have been accepted at this time.[4]

There is much evidence, in addition to the Biblical citations offered, to prove that labor markets, labor reserves, labor bargaining, labor relations, labor organizations, labor demonstrations, and labor disputes were early occurrences in the history of organized society, and that whenever and wherever each occurred, it was the resultant of some prevailing social or economic condition or need. Nor is it difficult for one to realize, as he reads, that technological change is not a modern invention; that shifting occupational patterns are normal accompaniments of the evolution of man in his social and economic activities; that labor demonstrations to protect the *status quo* were bound to intensify as the total occupational situation became more complex; and that labor markets did not enter the picture until there was a large enough labor reserve and enough demand for seasonal labor to produce a felt need on the part of both employer and employee.

[2] James 5:4; Job 7:1; 14:6.
[3] Acts 19:23–27.
[4] Luke 10:7; I Tim. 5:18.

Various methods have been used to facilitate the exchange of services for hire. In general, they may be classified in two groups, although there may be some difference of opinion regarding borderline media. The first and most primitive group comprises those in which contact between the two contracting parties is direct: there is no intermediary or organized middleman service. The second group, which was a response to the development of industry and the expanding geographical areas within which employment contracts were made, comprises media which provide a middleman who paves the way for personal contacts or who is authorized to close the contract for the absent party or parties.

Among those media and methods which fall into the first group are self-service exchanges, applications made directly to a business concern on one's own initiative or as a result of the suggestions of friends, "help wanted" signs, notices posted in conspicuous places, newspaper and trade journal advertisements, and the like. Some of these media, which are primarily methods of disseminating information relative to jobs open or workers available, may well be considered as using an intermediary, but hardly in the same sense as do bona fide employment agencies.

Whenever the conditions which fostered direct and unorganized methods of facilitating employment changed to such an extent that both business concerns and workers needed the assistance of organized, definitely located media through which services and positions could be cleared, employment and placement agencies came into existence under a variety of auspices such as employers' associations, chambers of commerce, fraternal organizations, labor unions, philanthropic and charitable organizations, individuals and corporations operating for profit, and the public represented by taxpayers.

Certain of the media and methods which are most closely related to realization of the purposes of this publication have been selected for discussion.

SELF-SERVICE LABOR EXCHANGES

Some of the Biblical citations have dealt with self-service exchanges. Obviously the labor reserve bargained directly with the master. History tells us that this type of labor exchange has not outlived its usefulness, although other types have supplemented, and in some localities superseded, it. The pooling of mobile labor reserves in similar self-service exchanges seems to have been the custom in France in the thirteenth century, where, in industrial towns, certain localities were set aside exclusively for the assemblage of workers of different trades. Masters in need of temporary or emergency employees went directly to these centers to secure them. In Sweden in the sixteenth century the "folk fairs" afforded an opportunity for agricultural workers and employers to meet and make labor contracts. In the United States this type of exchange was endorsed, if indeed it was not originated, by the City of New York when, in 1834, it passed an ordinance

appointing a place in every Market for the purpose of accomodating persons who want employment, to attend during Market hours, where persons who want to hire may also resort to be accomodated. That arrangement is now completed in the following Market Houses, viz. Clinton, Washington, Fulton, Catherine, Centre, Tompkins, and Jefferson. Hours of attendance for males, from 6 to 3, and for females, from 9 to 12, daily.[5]

Current examples, both rural and urban, are found in the designation, usually by mutual consent but sometimes by governmental action, of certain centers where those seeking work and those seeking workers may meet and bargain together. In small towns and rural communities a post office, a county courthouse, a county or state fair, or even a church may serve as a self-service labor exchange.

In the large cities where occupational districts are fairly well differentiated street corners are sometimes used for the same purpose. In New York City this writer has frequently watched the labor reserve for the fur industry as it congregated in the early morning hours on some street corner accessible to manufacturing houses, whose representatives went directly to that corner to look for help. And again, in another section of the city convenient for employing contractors, she has seen carpenters assemble with their tools, seen contractors drive up, make their bargains, and usually drive away with their new employees. The same practice has been noted with reference to women who work by the day. They assemble on some corner convenient both to their homes and to the homes of the housewives who usually depend upon day labor. Those in need of help find such corner exchanges very satisfactory sources of labor supply, especially in emergencies.

The major advantages of this form of exchange must be credited to convenience, to face-to-face bargaining without undue travel, to ease of abolishing the market or changing its location when the reserve dwindles or disappears or when the occupational center shifts, and to the fact that no expense is involved. But standing on the curb waiting for an opportunity to work was never a pretty picture, nor did it tend to improve the health of the workers. Therefore, when the long-continued custom was

[5] *New York Evening Post*, March 28, 1834.

recently spotlighted by the declaration of New York City's mayor that the city would no longer tolerate the "curb market" practice of employment agencies, nor would it longer permit daywork women to stand out in all kinds of weather in the open exchanges afforded by the street corners, the reaction was favorable. About 65 fee agencies, operating under middleman direction, moved into an employment agency building, and provision was made for the protection under cover of women workers.[6]

NEWSPAPERS AND TRADE JOURNALS AS EMPLOYMENT MEDIA

The posting of notices, in modern terminology, "help wanted" signs, has been mentioned in connection with journeymen's hostels during the middle ages and in connection with post offices, associations, and educational institutions in modern times. Usually it has been assumed that posting the reverse need, "position wanted," is a strictly modern practice; therefore it may be of interest to note that women, whose services were professional or at least semiskilled by present-day standards, were using newspapers as media for securing employment in New York City, and probably in other cities, during the eighteenth century. On May 21, 1753, the *New York Gazette and Post Boy* gave notice that the widow of Balthaser Sommers grinds all sorts of "Optic Glasses," such as "Microscope Glasses" and "Spying Glasses," at the most reasonable rates. Another advertisement gave the name and address of a woman who "covered umbrelloes" in the neatest and newest fashion. A third notice, from a third paper, the *New York Gazette and Mercury* of August 26, 1776, is similar to more recent occupational announcements:

Elizabeth Evans, Takes this method to acquaint her friends and the public that she is returned to this City, where she has been employed for several years, and given general satisfaction, in making up in the neatest manner and newest taste, all sorts of Upholstery work, such as festoon bed and window curtains, field or camp beds, Keety Fishers, wrought quilts, chair, sopha and settee cases; also ladies boned waistcoats and stays; all which she will execute with care and punctuality.

But most interesting of all and highly amusing as a servant's job specification for mistresses is the following notice taken from the *New York Weekly Journal,* January 28, 1733.

Here are many Women in this Town that these hard Times intend to go to service, but as it is proper the World should know our Terms, we think it reasonable we should not be beat by our Mistrisses Husband, they being too strong, and perhaps may do tender Women Mischief. If any Ladies want Servants, and will engage for their Husband, they shall be soon supplied.

[6] *New York Times,* March 17, 1942.

As economic conditions changed, the intermittent character of the demand for labor encouraged an ever larger labor reserve. Unemployment and unfilled demands for labor existed side by side. The recommendations of friends, help-wanted signs, and newspaper advertising brought hundreds of applicants to one "gate" after another in search of an opportunity to work. Statements relative to methods of securing help made by 750 employing concerns to the New York Commission on Unemployment in 1911 characterize the situation during the early years of this century; 459, or over 60 per cent, had no trouble in securing help and practically all depended upon selection from those who applied at the gate; 200 advertised in newspapers in addition to hiring at the gate; about 50 used employment agencies; and 10 depended upon trade unions.

Classified advertising in help-wanted and position-wanted columns is a very important current method of making known to one another the needs of employer and of employee. Its advantages and disadvantages and the extent to which the content, quality, and quantity of such advertising may be used by counselors as instructional material, and by placement functionaries and others as a source of information regarding immediately available positions and the current condition of the labor market, will be given consideration in connection with other presently functioning methods of securing positions and employees.

THE GUILD SYSTEM AND APPRENTICESHIP

Under the guild system each trade was a monopoly. No one was permitted to practice a trade unless he belonged to the guild. Apprenticeship was the method of recruiting workers. Contracts, of which there was a considerable variety, obligated the apprentice to serve his master faithfully, to keep his secrets, to obey his commands, and to protect him against damage. He might not absent himself without permission, visit taverns, ale houses, or playhouses, but in every respect must behave as a faithful apprentice should. The master was under contract to furnish food and clothing, to take responsibility for the apprentice's social, physical, and spiritual welfare, to teach him to read and write, to cipher "if he be capable to learn," and to prepare him for his occupational responsibilities. Contracts of this type were faithfully carried out, gave the apprentice the benefit of a personal service which included "all the arcs of the guidance circle," and left little opportunity for the disintegration of personality due to piecemeal dealing with the various areas of his developmental growth.

Employment was the end result and the ultimate goal of apprenticeship, and, when undertaken either by the master or by the guild, it brought a middleman of great importance into the picture, made the word "placement" meaningful, and might imply some assistance in employment adjustment. But the guilds did not always assume placement responsibilities even though they might contribute to the ease with which positions were secured. Records indicate that local self-service markets were in use; that welfare agencies sometimes aided in employment contacts; and that journeymen, wandering about in search of work, were aided by workers' guilds, which posted notices of vacancies in hostels—a custom which obtains in post offices, educational institutions, and elsewhere in this country today.

Apprentices, in this original and usually accepted sense, were a factor in the labor supply of the American colonies, which sometimes offered inducements to journeymen to settle in certain localities where tradesmen were needed.[7] But the documents of the period reveal a secondary, and perhaps an even more common, use of apprenticeship, which involved an entirely different type of placement. The poor laws in most of the colonies required the *apprenticeship* of children whose parents were unable to maintain them without public assistance, but there is nothing in the records to indicate that apprenticeship implied teaching a trade. Boys' contracts sometimes required instruction in reading, writing, and ciphering, but as late as 1771 ciphering was not included in girls' contracts—they were to be instructed in "reading and writing, if they shall be capable." [8] Overseers of the poor were in charge of such placements, with orders "to prentice upon the best Tearmes they can and with as little charge to the Towne as may be." The lowest bidder was an acceptable master.

This method of placing-out children was the custom of the day; the colonies inherited it from their old-world homes. It was approved and encouraged by both public and private relief organizations and must be judged by the standards of the time, not by present standards. As late as 1802 philanthropic societies are reported to have refused family relief unless parents would consent "to put out to trade or service children who were fit."

Laws regarding the placing-out of children, usually at ten years of age, varied somewhat from colony to colony. The New York order in council

[7] Thomas J. Wertenbaker, *The First Americans* (New York: The Macmillan Co., 1927), p. 18, states: "In 1658 Haverhill presented a house and land valued at 20 pounds to a blacksmith, John Johnson, in return for his promise to follow his trade there for seven years."

[8] Either of the following will give the reader thoroughly documented information of this subject: Edith Abbott, *Women in Industry* (New York: D. Appleton and Co., 1909) and U.S. Senate Document no. 645, 1910 (61st Congress, 2d session), vol. VI, App. A (data taken from Abbott's research).

of 1710 required masters "to clothe, victual, and use them well" and turn them back to the government when they were called for. A Connecticut act of 1673 provided for placing apprentices "into good families where they can be better brought up and provided for." Later the law was altered to permit magistrates to place children "where they shall see convenient." Undoubtedly much arduous child labor resulted from this juvenile placement system, and no possible claim for the all-around development of the child could be made. There were two objectives: saving community expense and teaching children habits of industry and thrift. The philosophy underlying both objectives was public service. Also underlying the latter was a firm belief that such training was of great educational value to children. Legally appointed public officials performed the middleman's services.

This juvenile placement system of colonial days with the principles upon which it was based was, after approximately two centuries, federally revived and carried on for several years under the aegis of the National Youth Administration and the United States Employment Service. The colonial child became the national youth; the juvenile placing-out system became a junior placement service, which, under legally appointed public officials, was charged with the provision of suitable wage-earning opportunities for youth. It was also sometimes expected, if not actually required, that the Service should "clothe, victual, and use them well." Again, there was a dual objective: the protection of society and service to youth. Again, public service was the controlling philosophy, but a somewhat riper philosophy of education which recognized productive work as an important factor in the education of youth was formulated and promulgated as the basis for future progress. It now awaits practical application.

METHODS OF DISTRIBUTING ALIEN LABOR

Since, with the exception of the American Indians, the entire population of these United States at any given time has comprised either immigrants or persons of immigrant ancestry, one would expect to find, and does find, that alien labor was an early colonial, and has remained a continuous national, problem. Sometimes the accent has been on recruitment, sometimes on distribution; sometimes on methods of protecting newly arrived immigrants from exploitation, sometimes on protecting citizen aliens from competition with more recently arrived immigrants who underbid them in the labor market. Periodically economic depressions and the attendant unemployment and relief have focused attention on the considerable number of both major and minor problems involved in immigrant labor. Were there time to do so, the entire gamut of such problems could legitimately be discussed under "Methods of Distributing Alien Labor," and every known medium for distribution would appear under one or more categories. Therefore, before considering the more general and the more familiar media for distributing all types of labor, two methods concerned rather specifically with recruiting and distributing alien labor must be mentioned—the indenture system and the padrone system.

The Indenture System. This system was primarily a seventeenth century method of recruiting labor for the tobacco planters in the southern colonies. Planters, through their agents, agreed to advance passage money for immigrants who were not able to pay for their own transportation but who were willing to contract to work out their passage after arrival. Increasing importation of Negro slaves, who were better adapted to plantation life, caused the discontinuance of the system. It had met a temporary need of both employer and employee; it had its advantages and disadvantages, both of which have been presented in the history of the period and have been generously exploited by writers of fiction. The practice was discontinued when it no longer served a useful purpose.

It must not be assumed, however, that this system was a response to southern colonial needs only. Walter Edmonds in *Erie Water* tells the story of the system in operation during the building of the Erie Canal. Contractors, especially those engaged on transportation projects, frequently secured workers under this system—sometimes with the assistance of padroni. In modified forms this "contract" system has been in more or less continuous use with reference to aliens who have entered the country as governesses or personal servants, as well as with reference to aliens who have been brought in by their employers to meet some specific need. For example, when the first herd of Holstein cattle was imported, several Hollanders, family men who were experts in handling such stock, were brought along under a very interesting "contract." The current and temporary importation of Mexicans and Bahamians under intergovernment contracts may well be regarded as a modified form of the earlier colonial system.

The Padrone System. This system is usually thought of by educators in connection with the importation of alien boys, mainly Greeks and Italians, to serve out apprenticeships as bootblacks in the larger coast cities. That was a common and lucrative method for the recruitment and placement of juvenile labor. The padroni were the masterminds of the system. They brought in young boys, frequently in violation of the immigration laws, apprenticed them to shoeshine-parlor bosses for a period of years and, by the most unethical practices, forced them to continue their service quite indefinitely, to the serious disadvantage of the boys but with considerable financial gain to both the padroni and the bosses.

But the padroni did not confine their attention or limit their nefarious practices to immigrant boys. They were a powerful factor in the distribution of adult immigrant labor, and they were often charged by contractors on public works and transportation lines with full responsibility for securing the number of workers required for a given project. In order to secure his quota of workers, the padrone frequently operated in collusion with transportation agents, hotel and lodging-house runners, and unscrupulous employment agencies; and he carried on all sorts of illegal and unethical practices which took advantage of aliens from the moment of landing, if, indeed, he did not reach back into the days before they left their homeland. Working with employment agencies, he sent thousands of workers to labor camps and to rural communities under misrepresentations and false promises. Oftentimes they reached their destination without funds and were forced to remain until they had earned enough to leave. Sometimes there was no work, while the municipal laws, if there were any under which employment agencies were licensed, had no jurisdiction outside the cities and the workers were too far away to enter municipal complaints. Fee splitting with foremen and superintendents was common.

In return for his services to contractors, the padrone

was given the privilege of housing the men and providing them with their commissary supplies at his own prices and in accordance with such standards as he himself might set. The laborer thus finds himself absolutely at the mercy of an unscrupulous padrone, who is under no supervision and who fears no law.[9]

New York State, early in the twentieth century, was actively interested in dealing with the abuses of this system. The *Annual Reports* of the Bureau of Industries and Immigration, established in the State Department of Labor in 1910, are excellent sources of information regarding the evils of the padrone system. The *Second Report* describes in considerable detail the extent to which abuses had developed and cites the causes of 1,112 complaints which had been filed during 1912 and the evils which had been uncovered during inspections. Among the latter were nonpayment of wages, overcharges and ill-treatment in labor camps, fraudulent representations regarding employment, importation of insane, destitute, and

9 *Second Annual Report of the New York State Bureau of Industries and Immigration* (Albany, 1912), p. 18.

undesirable persons, and white slavery cases charged against those whose business was that of procuring immigrant girls, "the trail leading directly to the activities of employment agencies." So lucrative had such practices become that in some instances they were carried on under the guise of *immigrant benevolent societies.*

Other states as widely separated geographically as New Jersey and California were facing similar problems and were interested in establishing bureaus under immigrant commissioners to safeguard the welfare of aliens within their states.

Although the padrone system operated over a considerable period of years, it flowered late and received comparatively little public criticism until the peaks of immigration in 1907 and 1914 focused attention on the antisocial practices of the padroni and of the "immigrant bankers" who controlled their activities. The system was a product of its time. Its practitioners kept in step with the changing demands of an expanding industrial economy and thereby created for themselves a most lucrative occupation. When the opening of the West, the rapid development of our national resources, and construction work of various kinds caused an inordinate demand for unskilled labor, the citizen padroni knew where to find recruits and how and where to distribute them. Through many different channels they kept agents in their homeland in touch with labor conditions in this country, and America's attractive occupational opportunities were widely broadcast.[10] Immigrants arrived in hordes—first the north Europeans, then the southern groups, and finally aliens from practically every country in the world.

The cessation of immigration practically destroyed the system. Ad interim, with the exception of those who had become stable workers, the unskilled immigrant was transformed into the unskilled migrant and continued to wander from place to place and to shift from job to job. A second generation of American migratory labor joined the original group. This type of labor, approximately half of which was reported to be citizens by birth, afforded an opportunity for the same sort of recruitment and distribution practices that the newly arrived immigrant had. Every large western center attracted its full quota of migrants. Minneapolis, Kansas City, Chicago, Seattle, and San Francisco are examples of cities which pooled for redistribution, according to the seasonal needs of the surrounding country, harvest hands, deck hands, construction workers, hop pickers, lumberjacks, miners, fruit pickers, cannery workers, and the like.

[10] Don D. Lescohier, *The Labor Market* (New York: The Macmillan Co., 1919), pp. 3–8.

Housing the temporary groups which invaded any given city was, and is today, a serious problem. Therefore, it is not surprising to find that practically every saloon which catered to migratory labor operated some sort of an informal employment office and usually practiced all the abuses credited to the padrone system. The serious predicament of unemployed men and women during the depression of 1913–1914 is affirmed over and over again in reports, surveys, and conferences. The Report of the First National Conference on Unemployment reveals that relief agencies and municipal lodging houses in a number of cities were turning away genuine seekers after work to sleep on bare boards at the docks, in the warehouses, and even in morgues.[11] *Unemployment in New York City,* reporting on 1913–1914 conditions, notes that many homeless persons slept in missions, employment agencies, and back rooms of saloons.[12] A Census taken by the New York police department on January 30, 1915, recorded approximately 25,000 homeless persons, of whom 135, including 7 women, slept in employment agencies; 341, including 1 woman, slept in the rear of saloons; and 23, including 3 women, had no shelter except parks and docks.[13] Lest we become too complacent and feel that all such happenings belong to an age that has gone and that such deplorable conditions can't happen again, the writer reports that in 1938 she was personally familiar with the cases of four unemployed college graduates who had no permanent lodgings. Night after night they wandered from parks to hotel lobbies, and from lobbies to railroad stations, always anxious to evade detection as "without employment" and always fearing recognition by friends.

Students who desire to continue their study of this most interesting topic, or those who are too young to remember the flurry of excitement from 1910 to 1918 caused by a certain type of migratory labor known as "hobo," will find abundant contemporary material from which to choose. Carleton H. Parker, who had first-hand experience with various types of migratory workers, has left us an excellent characterization of the "hobo" and his quasi organization, the Industrial Workers of the World, which he notes "can be profitably viewed only as a psychological by-product of the neglected childhood of industrial America." [14]

[11] John B. Andrews, "Introductory Note: Organization to Combat Unemployment," *American Labor Legislation Review,* IV (1914), 211.

[12] U.S. Bureau of Labor Statistics, Bull. no. 172, 1915.

[13] *Ibid.*

[14] *The Casual Laborer and Other Essays* (New York: Harcourt, Brace, and Howe, 1920). These essays apply the newer psychology to the study of labor problems. Lescohier, *op. cit.,* ch. 13, "The Laborer," and ch. 14, "Farm Labor," also affords a contemporary account of the recruitment and distribution of immigrant and migratory labor.

The goings and comings of the hobo were quite regular. A short period of work, 7 to 30 days, gave him a "stake" of about ten dollars with which he returned to his normal habitat—a hobo camp known as a "jungle." There he contributed his share toward the daily expenses until his stake was used up. Then he either took up his search for another job or degenerated into a "jungle buzzard." Periods of work and periods of idleness alternated until the work season was over, when, with a winter stake of thirty dollars, he sought some central distribution center where cheap lodging houses and saloons were waiting to provide temporary shelter and to act as his next employment agent.

It was during the winter of 1914 that Henry Pauly's picturesque group of hobo workers, who drifted into Seattle to spend their winters, became nationally known as residents of Hotel de Gink. There was plenty of soapbox oratory, and many rather clever words were set to old and familiar tunes and sung nightly with great gusto and pleasure for the edification of the public. The chorus of but one song is now recalled by the writer although she heard them many times:

> Hallelujah—I'm a bum:
> Hallelujah—bum again:
> Hallelujah—Give us a hand-out
> To revive us again!

Antiwar activities brought the I.W.W. into conflict with the Department of Justice. Their leaders were imprisoned, and shortly the organization either as an economic or as a political factor had passed into ancient history.

Although our country has, as yet, failed, either by education or by statute, to solve the problem of recruiting and distributing migratory labor with anything like satisfactory social and economic results, one is not justified in assuming that the migratory laborer, the hobo type included, is an entirely "forgotten man." John Steinbeck's *Grapes of Wrath* brings his story down to date and portrays him so vividly in word and film that the present generation cannot forget that migratory labor is still a social-economic problem and that padrone employment activities are still in vogue and are encouraged by certain environmental conditions. Occasionally the word *padrones* appears in current employment literature.

Bad as it was, the padrone system was not without a few constructive contributions. Its philosophy, based on avarice and expressed, either independently or in collusion with other agencies, in practices which victimized large numbers of helpless immigrants, was rather widely publicized and aroused a minority public opinion which was ripe for a new philosophy of employment—a philosophy which regarded the distribution of labor as a social-economic responsibility designed to accomplish two objectives: (1) to afford a middleman service which would be equally advantageous to both contracting parties, and (2) to distribute labor in the interests of the social and economic life of the community and of the nation. Throughout the country steps were taken to put unscrupulous agencies out of business and to license, regulate, and supervise all commercial agencies. Legal aid societies undertook to take up the complaints of workers who could not afford to pay for legal advice. Philanthropic and free public agencies increased in numbers, and before 1910 two efforts to establish national employment exchanges had been made—the Division of Information of the Federal Bureau of Immigration and Naturalization, July 1, 1907, and the privately financed National Employment Exchange of New York City, incorporated in 1909, with a program of service for the entire United States.

Public response to padroni activities in the juvenile and junior areas was expressed in child-labor and compulsory education legislation, in the establishment of philanthropic and education bureaus of vocational guidance, and in special provision by public employment offices for the distribution of beginning workers, or youth under 18 years of age. Each of these measures was a nail in the coffin of the padrone system.

Occupational Discrimination and the Alien. While protection of the alien against exploitation was receiving attention, there was, at the same time, a growing tendency to discriminate occupationally against the alien. Although in describing methods of recruiting and distributing alien labor, the abuses of the immigrant and social responsibility for his protection have been accented and will receive additional emphasis in the pages which follow, the impression must not be left that citizen interest in immigrant labor was purely unselfish and philanthropic. Citizens comprise many groups activated by different motives and combinations of motives, and the self-interest motive was omnipresent. Therefore, as was to be expected, when the economic situation changed, the attitude toward alien labor lost some of its humanitarian aspects and took on more specifically the characteristics of nationalism.

This shift in emphasis requires no detailed explanation. During the early years of our industrial expansion alien labor was an asset. The bars were all down—all who wished to come were welcome and many were urged to come. Widespread and genuine efforts, in which the humanitarian motive *seemed* dominant, were made to help new arrivals in their adjustments to American life, to aid them in securing employment, and to protect them against occupational exploitation. Gradually new factors entered the picture, among them periodic and severe unemployment coupled with a more conscious nationalism.

By 1819 statistics on unemployment were appearing in print, and relief measures were reported by most of the larger cities. Prior to World War I, cyclical booms were followed by severe industrial depressions in 1837, 1873, 1893, and 1907–1908, with minor disturbances in between. Sooner or later it was inevitable that questions should arise regarding the influence of the continuous influx of foreigners both on the total volume of unemployment and on the ability of citizens to compete with cheaper alien labor [15] for such jobs as were available. Factual evidence was cited to prove that, under certain conditions, foreign labor might be a liability rather than an asset. Although the fundamental employment philosophy, as cited, seems to have been fairly well established in theory, in practice nationalism superseded humanitarianism, and there was much concern regarding the competition of alien with citizen labor. Some states enacted legislation designed to reserve certain occupations for citizens.

Were one to make a thorough study of occupational discrimination with reference to aliens and to attempt to determine the true reasons for such discrimination, it would be necessary to begin with the restrictions which were written into the Constitution and have long been accepted as both legitimate and desirable. Undeniably, as the years have passed, legislative enactments and official rulings, business concerns, and organized and unorganized labor have all taken part in active and effective discrimination against the employment of aliens. Some of these discriminations were necessary or desirable; others were foolish, selfish, and hard to defend. At best it is difficult to draw a definite line between discriminations which are socially desirable and those which are antisocial and sometimes illegal. Nor is it possible to analyze the many motivating factors which dictate such restrictive measures.

What is easily ascertainable is that occupational discriminations began early in our national history and increased slowly after the War between the States until the peaks of immigration followed by unemployment resulted in state restrictions. World War I checked immigration, and labor in the United States became so scarce that again it was welcome

---

[15] Foreign labor has not always been in competition with citizen labor. When the development of labor-saving machinery, the subdivision of occupations, and the specialization of tasks called for unskilled, semiskilled, and skilled workers on a single project, the alien often furnished the unskilled labor which made employment for the other types of workers possible.

from any source. But war always foments nationalism: hence, after the war when the demand for labor markedly decreased and unemployment appeared imminent, increasing nationalism born of the war again became an active factor in militating against the employment of alien labor. The desirability of industrial discrimination on the part of labor, business, and the public was expressed in national restrictions on immigration and in renewed occupational discriminations on the part of individual states.

The extent to which legislative enactments and rulings by official bodies have affected equal occupational opportunities for aliens has been authoritatively presented by Harold Fields,[16] of the National League for American Citizenship. In a seven page tabulation, carrying citation of statute and date, Fields reveals that at the date of writing, 1933, restrictive occupational legislation was on the statute books of 48 states. A few statutes were enacted before 1900, but the dates of the great majority show a steady increase after 1900, with intensification of activity during periods of depression and unemployment. The occupations affected are classified under professions, public employment, trades, miscellaneous, and occupations for which licenses are required.[17]

Recent occurrences and current discussions familiar to all indicate that this country has not yet reached a satisfactory solution of its immigrant problem or of the problem of the occupational distribution of aliens. They also suggest that the ultimate solution, if there be one, will not be arrived at by way of legislative enactment—a suggestion which will be apparent again and again as other employment media which are used by alien and citizen alike are presented.

Such problems are not easy of solution. Business, labor, and social workers approach them from different viewpoints. Each presents a good case. Business after World War I frequently refused to employ aliens or to re-employ those who had not become citizens. There were many justifiable reasons, all centering more or less closely around self-protection, for it must be remembered that while occupational restrictions were being placed on the statute books so also were a considerable number of enactments designed to benefit and protect wage earners. These enactments placed certain responsibilities on employing concerns which made it impossible to employ illiterates or substandard workers from any source.

16 "Where Shall the Alien Work?" *Social Forces*, XII (1933), 213–221.

17 There was considerable difference of opinion regarding the essentiality of some of these restrictions (e.g., those which forbade the alien to fish for lobster, peddle, drive buses, own a dog, and the like), and, pending enactment, they were forcefully challenged. Nor was there always interstate agreement as to occupations in which the alien was dangerous.

Workmen's compensation laws, health and safety laws, minimum wage and hours-of-labor laws, and the like were all socially desirable, but they often forced employment departments to reject the applications of the old, the slow, the mental and physical defective, or of those with obvious personality difficulties. Habitually unemployed persons, whether citizens or aliens, are apt to degenerate into unemployables.

Labor, too, has its legitimate reasons for fostering certain occupational discriminations. And it insisted, as it does today with reference to Negroes, that it was restrictive legislation and the attitude of employers, rather than discrimination by labor unions, which caused the hardships of alien labor. Placement functionaries, whose personal sympathies might often be with the alien, were forced to distribute labor in accord with statutory pronouncements. They could not dictate or amend labor-union policies, nor could they ignore employer specifications when called upon for referrals. It required the exercise of sound judgment and much tact to steer a safe course between the Scylla of one supporting client and the Charybdis of another.

On the other hand, as the United States drew closer to war participation and mass production and job specialization made effective job placement increasingly important, employing concerns found it ever more profitable to pool their common educational and labor problems and to study them co-operatively. The National Association of Corporation Training, in 1915–1916, appointed a committee to study the occupational aptitudes of unskilled labor groups. Its first report, a prewar contribution, was concerned with the necessity for securing, educating, preparing for citizenship, and upgrading for promotion the best class of foreign labor.[18] Personnel work, at that time called *welfare work,* was designed to bring out the alien's and the Negro's best characteristics, and most of the educational workers were charged with the task of facilitating the job of distribution by means of education and through practical job tryouts.

The committee, at the 1921 conference, presented a most interesting postwar report entitled, *Racial Adaptability to Various Types of Plant Work.*[19] Sixteen concerns, employing large numbers of unskilled laborers, collaborated in the study. Thirty-six groups of workers, including American white and American Negro, and twenty-two occupations were included in the study. Nationalities best adapted to speed, precision, day or night shifts, and a number of different atmospheric conditions were considered.

[18] *Addresses, Reports, Bibliographies and Discussions, Fourth Annual Convention, The National Association of Corporation Schools,* 1916, pp. 741–760.
[19] *Ninth Annual Proceedings, The National Association of Corporation Training,* 1921, pp. 866–868.

Six "conspicuous conclusions" were drawn from the chart which tabulated the findings in such fashion that the relative-adaptability findings of various nationalities to various types of manual labor were shown. Five nationalities were reported fairly satisfactory, and two were reported preeminently so, on each type of work. With one exception, each nationality seemed to be especially well fitted for at least one type of work. Employers were reminded that in mass compilations individual exceptions to general conclusions always occur, *"and it must not be forgotten that personality means more than nationality."*

Of course, confirmed critics of the employing class attacked the study as an effort to effect speed-up or to exploit labor by assigning it to, and keeping it on, repetitive jobs. But fair-minded individuals, especially those who had read the reports of all the committees concerned with the education and work of the alien and were, therefore, in a position to consider the Association's program as a unit, found it a valuable contribution to the better understanding of the occupational aptitudes of different nationalities. Employment functionaries, within and without industrial plants, whose common purpose was the allocation of each worker to the advantage of both parties, found the average experience of others a helpful guide when the traits and abilities of individuals were known. Nor is it necessary to state that all studies of this type had educational implications for public day and evening schools whenever and wherever educators were aware of their existence and were alert enough to profit by them.

A number of cases resulting from restrictive state legislation found their way to the United States Supreme Court, whose decisions contributed to the total picture of the problems involved in the occupational distribution of aliens. Two decisions, rather widely separated in time and characteristic of the two dominant philosophies regarding aliens, are mentioned. In 1915 Justice Hughes in his decision on the Arizona law which required concerns employing more than five persons to see that at least 80 per cent were citizens, stated: "The right to work for a living in the common occupations of the community is of the very essence of the personal freedom and opportunity that it was the purpose of the (14th) Amendment to secure. . . ." To deny aliens the opportunity to work "would be tantamount to the assertion of the right to deny them entrance and abode, for in ordinary cases they cannot live where they cannot work." [20] Thus the Supreme Court appeared to give support to the philosophy of those who argued that law-abiding aliens, legally admitted, should enjoy the equality

[20] *Truax* v. *Raich*, 239 U.S. 33 (1915).

of opportunity which the Constitution of this country guaranteed to "all persons within its jurisdiction."

The second decision was made in 1926 when the Supreme Court upheld an Ohio law prohibiting aliens from operating pool and billiard parlors on the ground that the operation of such places by aliens had "harmful and vicious tendencies." Some felt that this decision was in direct conflict with treaties between certain countries and the United States which promised "equal opportunity in the ordinary occupations of commerce and trade" for other nationals legally admitted—treaties which had been upheld by the Supreme Court. The Ohio decision encouraged discrimination through state enactments and supported the less liberal philosophy of "caring for one's own."

No matter how widely the various interested groups may have differed in philosophy or practice, history warrants the assumption that a fundamental philosophy relative to the employment of aliens has crystallized—a philosophy which places a moral responsibility on community and nation for seeing that the legally-admitted, law-abiding noncitizens have a fair opportunity to share in the occupational life of the nation. This philosophy, with special reference to aliens, must be kept in tune with the two previously cited placement principles: (1) that employment officials who serve as middlemen so perform their functions that a service is rendered both employer and employee, and (2) that alien labor, as well as citizen labor, be distributed in the best interests of the social-economic life of community and nation.

PHILANTHROPIC PLACEMENT SERVICES

Relief, charitable, benevolent, and philanthropic agencies are very old. During the middle ages they frequently included placement services among their activities, but when they did so the services are reported to have been an incidental rather than a major activity.

The early years of the industrial revolution prepared the way for a rapid increase in philanthropic agencies, many of which were interested in placement and some of which made it a primary function. Students of social and economic history generally concede that philanthropic placement bureaus owe their origin to, and have developed as a part of, the world-wide humanitarian movement of the Victorian era. Therefore, those who desire to pursue their study of philanthropy as a factor in the evolution of placement services, and to understand more fully the part which such services have played in carrying the humanitarian movement forward toward fruition, may turn to some chosen source of information for an analysis of the social forces which immediately preceded, and were operative throughout, the Victorian era.

If legislative enactments be chosen, the complete story of the movement will be found in the statutes of the time. If fiction be chosen—and it must always be remembered by those who are dealing with social problems that fiction is an outstandingly effective medium for arousing the interest of, and conveying a message to, the general public—they will be able to follow the development of the lay interest which was aroused in the problems of humanity in the novels of Dickens, Kingsley, Charlotte Brontë, Mrs. Humphry Ward, and others; to note how unconscious beginnings gradually materialized into a conscious world-wide movement which found practical expression in many forms. And they will be able to determine the extent to which placement, by philanthropic agencies, was one of the forms in which the theory of the *unity of humanity and the brotherhood of man* found its practical expression.

Since no general study of the employment activities of such agencies has ever been undertaken, it is impossible to determine with any degree of accuracy when and where, in this country, philanthropy first instituted services actively interested in placement. Cook, who analyzed the sources covering this period very carefully, concluded that the panic of 1819 marked the beginning of *organized* relief by charitable institutions and that, although relief was mainly concerned with food and shelter, some agencies made earnest attempts to secure jobs for the unemployed.[21] Cook's conclusions are supported by such authentic contemporary sources as Benton's *Thirty Years' View* [22] and the *Niles' Weekly Register*.[23] Benton (p. 5) cites 1819 and 1820 as years of agony and gloom: there was no money, no price for property or produce, no employment for industry, and no demand for labor. The *Niles' Register* kept its readers informed on unemployment in the various cities of the country. In August, 1819, 20,000 persons were daily seeking work in Philadelphia; in New York 10,000 able-bodied men were reported to be wandering the streets looking for work while an equal number of employable unemployed women were pursuing the same occupation. Baltimore estimated about 10,000 intermittently unemployed, underemployed, or actually suffering for work. Most of the cities which reported were making some effort, usually com-

21 David W. Cook, *History of Public Employment Offices in the United States* (doctor's dissertation, New York University, 1935).

22 Thomas H. Benton, *Thirty Years' View* (New York: D. Appleton and Co., 1854), vol. I.

23 *Niles' Weekly Register*, August to October, 1819.

mercial or philanthropic, to provide labor exchanges or employment offices. Bread lines and soup kitchens were common.

Community agencies were frequently interested in servicing special groups. A disproportionate number of philanthropic bureaus, if preserved reports may be considered legitimate criteria, seem to have been established to service women, and, since other agencies including labor organizations were more specifically concerned with men, this seems logical. Boston, in 1850, at No. 2 Tremont Row was operating a free employment bureau for girls and was averaging 100 placements a day. In 1854 Brooklyn established an all-denominational Christian service where destitute females secured employment—not "alms." The Women's Employment Society of the Brick Presbyterian Church in New York City made its first report in 1869 and was still functioning and publishing reports when Cook made his study in 1935. In 1862 the New York Friends' Employment Society was established, and a report of its activities for 1921 is on file in the New York Public Library.

During this same period the Y.M.C.A. and the Y.W.C.A. began to include placement in their service programs. Both were philanthropically motivated, but here and there, if not universally, during these early years, their agencies were fee-charging. Both organizations have established, and will doubtless maintain, an honorable position in the placement area of personnel services. *Service* was their original *raison d'être;* they have met a definite need; and their practices have been legitimately, if not always effectively, conducted.

Another, and a somewhat different, example of placement as the practical expression of interest in the humanitarian movement is found in the documents which record the early history of the Emigrant Industrial Savings Bank, of New York City.[24] This institution, which was incorporated in 1850 and has been in continuous operation since that date, stemmed from the Irish Aid Society of 1816—a philanthropic venture with an office in Nassau Street from which, without charge, "strangers from Europe" were directed to employment in and outside of the City. In 1829 the Society changed its name to the Union Emigrant Society, and in 1841 it became the Irish Emigrant Society.

The objectives of the Society, which were stated in its by-laws, indicate that the founders had not overlooked the public-service motive. They hoped

24 Janet M. Mackey, Director, Business Development Department, Emigrant Industrial Savings Bank, responded generously to my request for information, copied essential documents, and has verified the data selected for presentation.

the more efficaciously to make the constant influx of strangers from Europe into the United States, and more particularly into this, advantageous to the immigrants themselves by affording them useful information, whereby they may be directed to situation where they may find permanent employment for themselves and families, and, at the same time, relieve the City from the burden of their maintenance.

The Act of Incorporation conferred very extensive powers, "to afford advice, information and protection to emigrants and generally to promote their welfare." That these powers were utilized to excellent advantage is evidenced by the early records of the Society, which are replete with references to the benefits received both by the "poor emigrants" and the general public.

The Savings Bank was the response of the same group of men to certain "pecuniary needs" which years of experience had revealed and which were making increasing demands on the gratuitous services of the members and on the facilities of the Society. The trustees of the Society became the trustees of the Bank; the President of the Society was the first President of the Bank. In an exchange of letters, in 1850, between the Executive Committee of the Society and the future first President of the affiliated organization, the relationship between the Society and the Bank is clearly revealed. The Executive Committee wrote:

It is our expectation and desire which we also know you entertain that the two Institutions shall be carried on in the same location and be conducted with entire harmony for the purpose of accomplishing to the fullest extent the benefits intended by each.

The President's reply referred to the Society as "in a safe and prosperous condition, not only sustaining itself but affording protection and pecuniary aid to many a poor and friendless emigrant, both young and old." He continued:

. . . to the able and efficient services rendered the Society by our present and late Treasurers—whose zeal, promptness and sound judgment in superintending the remittances to the Bank of Ireland are worthy of all praise, they have thereby nobly sustained and more firmly established the honor and credit of the Institution. It appearing to be your unanimous desire that I should resign my present appointment under the general government so that my sole attention be directed in carrying out the benevolent views of the Society by superintending its increased and increasing Bill Business, and also in connection with the New Emigrant Savings Bank of which many of you gentlemen are Trustees I feel myself bound to comply with your wishes and, therefore, tendered my resignation which took place on the 1st inst. . . .

His letter closed:

We have now, gentlemen, prospect of extending the benefit and usefulness of two benevolent Institutions, first in furnishing the means of safe remittances to the distressed people of Ireland and of distributing in charities whatever of profits may arise therefrom and, secondly, affording our people safe deposit for their hard earnings, thereby establishing in perpetuity two *Irish Americanized* Institutions, the success of which I do not doubt will form one of the highest pleasures of our lives.

There is much documentary evidence, in addition to that which has been cited, to suggest that the outlines of "One World" were taking shape in the early nineteenth century; that the New World was sharing with the Old, both in the effects of the Industrial Revolution and in the humanitarian efforts to alleviate its consequences. From 1819 on, many types of organized philanthropy responded to current economic depressions, panics, and unemployment, and, in their efforts to check the exploitation of "strangers from Europe" as well as of unfortunate citizens, a considerable number intensified their placement activities. Quite frequently such agencies serviced special groups, and a few instituted training programs to prepare the unprepared for positions.

The extent to which, during the post-Victorian era, placement has been a primary or a subordinate interest of philanthropic organizations has been largely determined by prevailing economic conditions. Shifts in emphasis have paralleled shifts in the status of the labor market. However, before the close of the nineteenth century organized employment services, under philanthropic auspices, were the rule rather than the exception in all of the larger cities.

Philanthropic interest in juvenile and junior placement services came later. During the early years of the current century philanthropy assumed the initiative in establishing placement bureaus designed specifically to serve youth, especially the public-school discard. Such bureaus were usually called "vocational guidance bureaus." Their functions included counseling and other activities as well as placement. Occasionally a public-school system assumed leadership and responsibility for a placement service, and a few public employment offices provided, or advocated, a juvenile department. But for the most part pre-World War I bureaus were instituted and operated under philanthropic auspices.[25]

Certain handicaps to success have usually been inherent in the objectives and administration of philanthropic bureaus. Hence their philosophy of placement has often conflicted with, and prevented them from

[25] Junior placement services are discussed in detail in Chapter XI.

participating in, the philosophy of placement which has gradually been gaining ground—equal consideration of the needs of employer and employee, always with due attention to the welfare of society. A considerable number of such agencies have been obliged to contend with one or more of the following handicaps: (1) A philosophy which required the *need* of the applicant to take precedence over the specifications of the employer, accompanied by the assumption that employing concerns were willing and financially able to operate as charitable or relief agencies. (2) Registrants have comprised a disproportionate number of unemployables or near-unemployables—the mentally or physically handicapped, the unstable or erratic, those who were unable to secure work in competition with others, and the like. Inferior applicants have attracted low-grade jobs and vice versa. (3) The stigma of charity has prevented high-grade workers from registering. (4) The cost per placement of applicants who require special personal effort has been excessive, even for charity. (5) Too many placements have been unsatisfactory. This has tended to react unfavorably on other aspects of the work of the same organization. (6) The large number of such agencies, each board of control taking pride in its own accomplishments, has led to undesirable competition, unwarranted duplication of effort, and to useless and detrimental decentralization of the labor market. (7) Pressure by wealthy contributors for the placement of special cases, or use of the agency to relieve themselves from refusing to employ needy persons. (8) Use of volunteer workers who were frequently the victims of frustrations or emotional disturbance, or who were not sufficiently familiar with the requirements and terminology of business to interpret job specifications correctly.

In spite of their numerous handicaps, throughout their entire history, whether operating as a single activity or as an adjunct to other services, philanthropic agencies have been an important factor in the distribution of alien labor and in counteracting the abuses of the padroni and of the type of fee agencies which exploited the immigrant, the ignorant, and the incompetent. That their early accomplishments were sufficiently effective to attract the attention of unscrupulous agencies is apparent from the fact that some of the latter agencies attempted, as has been noted, to conceal their objectionable character by conducting their activities under the guise of *immigrant benevolent societies*.

COMMERCIAL AND FEE-CHARGING AGENCIES

Commercial and fee-charging agencies have afforded another employment medium. The private enterprise system is largely dependent upon the alertness with which individuals uncover and take advantage of opportunities to institute services which are in harmony with, and often anticipatory of, public needs and desires. The continuance of any concern in its chosen line is largely dependent upon the degree of integrity with which its business is conducted and upon its ability to recognize that private gain and public service must travel hand in hand.

Commercial placement agencies *should be* a legitimate industry under the private enterprise system. They were operating in Germany in the early fifteenth century and spread rapidly geographically, increasing in numbers with equal rapidity. In every country their story has been the same. Their timing has been perfect. They have anticipated a growing but unmet need and have been first in the field—first to grasp the possibilities of both service and of financial gain. There was little expense involved in setting up an agency; and, since domestics and other personal-service workers, agricultural laborers, and hotel and restaurant employees were the main registrants, the volume of business was good and financial rewards were considerable.

During the nineteenth century the placement industry was practically monopolized by fee agencies, but in every country a certain proportion of entrepreneurs yielded to the peculiar temptations inherent in their business and before the close of the century their malpractice had so outraged public opinion that regulatory measures were undertaken. France, which after the Revolution had established fee agencies, regulated their fees, and given them a monopoly in the field, faced the same sort of complaints as did other countries. In 1852 she passed rather stringent regulatory acts, which remained in force for many years. Germany attempted to control such agencies by taxation, and in 1910 forbade the establishment of a private agency in any locality where the people were adequately served by public agencies. Switzerland required licensure in 1895. Experience with fee agencies in these United States has followed the same pattern as in European countries.

The commercial agency as a medium for the distribution of labor in this country has no authentic history. Its initial efforts are even more difficult to uncover than are those of philanthropy. It is, however, justifiable to assume that such agencies owe their existence to much the same social-economic conditions as did philanthropic agencies, that both responded to a demand for some systematic method of bringing the needs of employers and workers together, and that they began operations during the same period of time—about 1820.

Presentation of the activities of various types of fee-charging agencies in such fashion that the purposes and practices of the one type may be adequately differentiated from those of another is quite impossible. Nor is it possible to generalize regarding the purpose and philosophy, or the social and economic influence of fee-charging agencies as a whole: their variety is too numerous. For the immediate purpose a threefold classification is offered:

(1) The agency motivated entirely by profit which it strives to secure at all costs, ignoring the rights of its clientele and the antisocial effects of its practices.

(2) The agency operated for profit but entirely conscious of its social and personal obligations and willing or anxious to function in harmony with the accepted social philosophy of the time.

(3) The fee-charging philanthropic, or institutional, agency which is service-motivated but which feels that such services are a legitimate factor in the social economy of the time, that they should be financed as a business venture, and that after the initial expense they should pay fair dividends or at least become partially or wholly self-supporting.

To Group One are allocated that large number of agencies which have been mentioned as operating in collusion with padroni, foremen, contractors, hotels, saloons, and the like. They exploited the immigrant and the migrant, the illiterate and the substandard; made false statements as to wages and conditions of labor; practiced petty graft of various kinds; encouraged labor unrest, labor turnover, and unemployment; charged exorbitant fees, sometimes for no work, or unsatisfactory work; and fostered, in connivance with houses of assignation, the white-slave trade. Their numbers grew by leaps and bounds, and, as their nefarious practices became better known, an awakened public denounced them as a social menace and ultimately demanded their elimination or regulation. Municipal regulatory action was taken fairly early but proved ineffective because so many workers were sent beyond the bounds of municipal authority. Prior to the establishment of the first state employment services, Minnesota in 1885 and New York in 1888 passed laws which prohibited fee agencies.[26] Since no provision was made for the administration of the laws, they were a dead letter except insofar as they served as an index of public opinion.

Between the establishment of the first state employment services and World War I, efforts to control the establishment and practices of fee agencies went forward side by side with efforts to introduce public employment services. Both measures were regarded as promising legal methods

[26] See *American Labor Legislation Review*, IV (1914), 415.

of providing for the better distribution of labor and of lessening unemployment. At the same time it was assumed that they would eliminate by competition, regulate out of existence, or check the unethical practices of the type of fee agency under consideration. Various enactments designed to accomplish one or more of these objectives were passed.

The State of Washington, in 1914, initiated and passed by popular vote a law which declared it illegal for any employment agent "to demand or receive either directly or indirectly from any person seeking employment . . . any remuneration or fee whatsoever for furnishing him or her with employment or with information leading thereto." [27] This law, which abolished fee agencies of all types, was too sweeping in its provisions and was declared unconstitutional by the United States Supreme Court in 1917 on the ground that it was a violation of the Fourteenth Amendment. That it eliminated some antisocial agencies is undeniable. But it also ruled out some charitable and philanthropic agencies, and it denied agencies which operated as high-grade middlemen, satisfactorily serving both employer and employee, an opportunity to earn their living in a socially beneficial and in an entirely legitimate occupation.

The following year Idaho passed a law which forbade the operation of private agencies for profit but excluded from the operation of the law nonprofit agencies under religious, charitable, or benevolent auspices. It also excluded agencies classified as professional.[28] Wisconsin, influenced by the German imperial law of 1910, allowed the Industrial Commission to refuse licenses to private agencies if public agencies in the community were adequate to meet the demands.[29]

Although comparatively few states attempted to abolish fee-charging agencies, a considerable number passed legislation designed to control and regulate them. Specific provisions of such enactments were intended to remedy, or to prevent, the major abuses which had attracted attention. Among the various regulatory provisions were the following: (1) An annual license which gave the location of the office and was not valid for any other location had to be obtained. (2) Applications for licenses, accompanied by affidavits of good moral character, had to be published before licenses were granted. Bonding was generally required. (4) Registration fees and placement fees were limited, receipts had to be given, and provisions for refunds were specific. (5) Splitting of fees, false advertising, and violation of child-labor laws were forbidden. (6) Standardized

27 *Laws of Washington*, 1914, no. 8.
28 *Laws of Idaho*, 1915, p. 169.
29 See *Report on Allied Functions* (Industrial Commission of Wisconsin, June 30, 1918); also, *Laws of Wisconsin*, 1919, p. 178.

business methods including adequate records and reports were manda-
tory. (7) Inspection by authorized officials, and penalties for violations of
regulations, were universally required.[30]

In addition to these statutory requirements approved by many states,
several of the southern states enacted legislation for the sole purpose of
restricting, or eliminating, the activities of "emigrant agents"—persons
who recruited labor to work beyond the limits of the state.[31] Regulatory
measures comprised licensure based on occupational taxes—for the state
and for each separate county in which the agent operated—and on bonds
which guaranteed the return of laborers to their home state. Retention
of Negro labor in the South was the major objective. Alabama, in 1881,
and North Carolina, in 1891, passed such laws. During World War I the
demand for labor in northern industries brought a revival of interest in
such legislation and its enforcement. Press notices indicated that emigrant
agents were active in World War II and again caused agitation in the
South for the stringent enforcement of emigrant agent laws.

Those who have the time and the inclination to study in detail the
history of fee-charging agencies and the efforts which have been made to
control their activities will discover that this was a very absorbing topic
up to about 1920 when certain other phases of employment gained the
ascendency.[32] They will also discover that prior to 1920 two philosophies
regarding the best methods of dealing with fee agencies were competing
for approval.

The one favored the complete abolition of all fee agencies. It was endorsed by such men as Lescohier whose responsibilities had familiarized
them with the most vicious practices of unprincipled agencies and who felt
that eradication was the only remedy for their abuses. The *ideal* of employment services as a public monopoly was the keynote of their philosophy. In practice it was thought that it would tend to encourage the
development and effectiveness of public offices, guarantee nonpartisan
and fair treatment of employer and employee (always with due consid-

[30] Statutes of the various states, in which terms were carefully defined, are available
in pamphlet form. Other sources of information easily accessible are Frank Sargent's
Statistics of Unemployment and the Work of Employment Offices in the United States
(U.S. Bureau of Labor, Bull. no. 109, 1912), which describes (pp. 53–57) the Illinois
law of 1909 in detail; *Laws Relating to Employment Agencies in the United States as of
January 1, 1933* (U.S. Bureau of Labor Statistics, Bull. no. 581, 1933); and Harrison and
others, *Public Employment Offices*, pp. 83–88.

[31] Bulletin no. 581 of the U.S. Bureau of Labor Statistics gives the text of laws passed
prior to 1933 and discusses court decisions regarding them (pp. 5–7, 145–154).

[32] Dominant phases as they have come and gone are revealed in the literature of the
field, in the topics which appear on discussion programs, and in the annual reviews of
labor legislation.

eration of the public's interest), and that it would lessen the volume of unemployment by pooling supply and demand, thereby creating a single labor reserve.

This philosophy recognized the existence of the second and third groups of commercial agencies—those which were admittedly "giving reputable and reasonably efficient service," and those which were operating under educational and philanthropic auspices. But, its protagonists argued, all types of fee agencies were objectionable: one type because of its abuses; the other two as a matter of justice and public policy since it was "unsound in principle to compel a citizen to pay for a chance to get work." Supporters of this point of view were numerous, and strong enough internationally to put through, at the first International Labor Conference, Geneva, 1919, a recommendation that "all practicable measures be taken to abolish such agencies as soon as possible." [33]

A second, and less drastic philosophy, recognized that many agencies classified under the second and third groups were serving as efficient middlemen in the distribution of labor; that the longer the radius of the employing area the more both employer and employee needed some agency or organized and publicized means for assisting him to make known his needs. This was as true with reference to expanding urban areas where domestics, porters, hotel help, janitors, watchmen, and the like found it hard to locate positions while employers were equally at a loss to locate workers, as it was with reference to intercity and interstate distribution of labor of all types including nurses, teachers, engineers, and other professional workers who were employed on an annual basis and who paid employment fees based on annual salaries.

Without overlooking the evils of the antisocial agencies, supporters of this philosophy recognized the social potentialities of private exchanges and advocated their retention under such statutory regulations as would bear heavily on the undesirable agency without handicapping the introduction and operation of the beneficial type. Protagonists comprised, as did advocates of abolition, experienced and practical students of the influence of all types of agencies.

Bureaus operated by the Y.M.C.A., Y.W.C.A., and similar organizations, when they charged fees, fell into category three. The vocation bureaus, established by and for college women, and all institutional bureaus —including those operated by private colleges and secondary schools—if they charged fees, were classified in the same way and were subject to the same statutory regulations even though they might be operating under

[33] *American Labor Legislation Review*, IX (1919), 533.

subsidies or functioning at a financial loss.[34] That the multiplication of independent agencies—either philanthropic or fee-charging—no matter how well regulated, tended to intensify decentralization of the labor market was admitted. But, pending proof of the ability of the public services to centralize the market, those who opposed the abolition of private agencies felt that they should be given a fair opportunity to prove their worth.

Before the subject of fee-charging agencies is dropped, attention should be called to a unique private agency of the highest type which is somewhat differentiated from other such agencies by the character of its objectives, motives, and procedures, and by the fact that it introduced a new note into the philosophies of placement which had prevailed prior to 1909. The National Employment Exchange of New York City was incorporated and opened for business in 1909. Jacob H. Schiff, a practical philanthropist and successful financier, was its financial godfather. Its professional sponsor was Edward T. Devine, General Secretary of the Charity Organization of New York City, whose experiences with the distribution of alien labor, unemployment, and charitable relief had aroused an interest in the possibility of a nation-wide system of fee-charging labor exchanges. The story of this bureau and its outcome makes an interesting contribution to the various philosophies, and fragments of philosophies, which have controlled this country's employment practices and guided its efforts to apply European experiences to the solution of its employment problems.[35]

Schiff suggested an unofficial employment service covering the entire nation but benefiting primarily the unemployed in New York City. Its purpose should be usefulness; its motives philanthropic. It should operate as a business, not as a charity; should have a working-fund, or endowment, of about $100,000 secured by private subscription; should charge fees and be able to return a small profit on the investment. Devine was appointed to investigate and report on the desirability of establishing such an exchange. The report was favorable, and the program, as launched, followed very closely the original program outlined by Schiff: (1) that an exchange be organized under a board of trustees representing different occupational groups; (2) that a manager of great executive ability be appointed,

[34] The California law, effective July 21, 1919, stated very definitely that private schools which, for remuneration, assisted pupils to find employment were subject to the laws governing private employment agencies.

[35] See Bulletin no. 109, U.S. Bureau of Labor, pp. 110–113; Edward T. Devine, *Report on the Desirability of Establishing an Employment Bureau in the City of New York* (New York: Russell Sage Foundation, 1909); and *Annual Reports, National Employment Exchange* (New York: Russell Sage Foundation, 1910).

supported by a corps of assistants, interpreters, supervisors of men in transit—who would perform the functions so discreditably performed by padroni—and field workers who would look after employed men and re-distribute them with the least loss of time; (3) that fees should vary with the type of work secured. Common labor was to be two dollars, paid by the employer when labor was scarce, by the worker when jobs were scarce; mechanics, three dollars; clerks and professional workers, the first week's salary with six weeks in which to complete payment.

Once in operation, the procedures and problems were similar to those of other labor exchanges. Applicants were secured by runners sent out to solicit; job solicitation was unnecessary since demand exceeded supply; publicity comprised press notices, which were generous, and circulars, which were widely distributed and attracted considerable attention. Rec-ords showed about the same proportion of placements with reference to applicants and to orders received as was reported by other agencies. Many applicants were unplaced and many orders were unfilled. No branches were established outside of New York City but the majority of placements —36 different nationalities in 11 different states—were outside the city. Applicants refused to accept western positions because transportation was not often paid and because, as anyone who has attempted to place New York City residents west of the Hudson River knows, it is now and always has been most difficult to convince workers that attractive locations and desirable positions are to be found beyond the city limits.[36]

The project was a disappointment financially. Not only did the ex-pected profit fail to materialize, but in 1911 the exchange was not self-supporting. Its claim to a place in the history of the employment move-ment does not rest upon either its financial success or upon its volume of placement, but upon the following facts: (1) It was a major effort to organ-ize the labor market as a means of minimizing unemployment. (2) While its fee scale conformed to such permissive scales as had been established by enactments and licensure, it failed as a business venture. Therefore, con-sidering its philanthropic motive and the unchallenged character of its supporters, it did much to overcome the feeling that private-agency fees were exorbitant. (3) The educational implications of its inability to bal-

---

[36] The Des Moines Employment Association founded in 1918, later known as the Employment Bureau of Des Moines, Inc., was another attempt to provide a community placement bureau with a program for national expansion in view. For its objectives, plans, and accomplishments, see Hans C. Pfund and Ralph H. Faxon, *Manual for Con-ducting "Service at Cost" Community Placement Bureaus with a Plan for Nationaliza-tion* (Des Moines: Employment Bureau of Des Moines, Inc., 1926). Recently received word from Des Moines indicates that this bureau was not long-lived and did not expand beyond the community.

ance supply and demand better were made public, and analysis of the qualifications of unplaced applicants compared with job specifications for unfilled positions indicated a demand for considerably different abilities from those possessed by unplaced applicants. The manager suggested that were such findings to be translated into educational changes, public training programs would be better adapted to occupational opportunities. (4) The exchange, based on its hybrid philosophy, embodied in practical form the concept of employment exchanges as business enterprises in the nature of public utilities, or as semiphilanthropic services operated with the expectation of moderate dividends. (5) In its establishment it anticipated certain misgivings and brought into the limelight certain questions which were beginning to worry experienced placement executives and were later openly propounded by disillusioned advocates of the abolition of all fee agencies in favor of a monopoly under public auspices. W. M. Leiserson, Superintendent of Wisconsin Employment Offices, in 1914, stated the situation very succinctly:

Now it may be true that employment offices perform a public function, and that they are in the nature of public utilities, and yet the weakness of state activity may be such as to make it impossible for any American state to perform the service properly. Perhaps we ought to induce enterprising business men to organize the labor market on a large scale and then regulate them as we do our railroads and street car companies. . . . Perhaps we ought to rely upon philanthropists to invest in this business, as they have done in provident loan societies and model tenements, with the expectation of a moderate return on the capital.[37]

Although heated arguments pro and con the abolition of fee-charging agencies reached their peak about 1919–1920, contemporary literature from 1919 on indicated that by 1914 the tide was turning in favor of governmental regulation rather than statutory abolition. Supporters of abolition were challenging on their record the ability of public agencies to organize the labor market, and the value of the contribution of decentralized philanthropic agencies and of well-regulated fee-charging agencies was more generally appreciated. Meanwhile, the higher type of private agency, which resented its classification in the same category as the discredited type, became actively interested in clarifying public thinking regarding its characteristics and practices. Therefore, during the years when vigorous denunciation of *all* fee agencies was rife, associations for the protection of their mutual business interests were formed. Some were outspoken in their opposition to unethical practice, and sometimes, as for

[37] "Public Employment Offices in Theory and Practice," *American Labor Legislation Review*, IV (1914), 320.

example the Chicago Association in 1909, they joined with other agencies in fostering the enactment of regulatory legislation. Since about 1920 it has been rather generally assumed that private fee-charging agencies are a permanent institution in this country and that, in their relation to the public, they should be treated as a public utility.

Historically, it is most unfortunate for all parties concerned that, from the earliest times until comparatively recent years, it has been so easy to inaugurate such agencies, and that as a rule they proved such fertile soil for graft that very early in their history they were recognized as an attractive occupation for the lowest class of entrepreneurs, whose activities stigmatized the entire business. The highest type of middleman services have usually shared, at least by implication, the public censure which has been visited upon the unethical service. Since, under present conditions and probably for many years to come, commercial agencies will continue to operate, no personnel functionary who expects to render maximum service to his institution or to his clientele can afford to be ignorant of the disadvantages of the worst type of such agencies or of the advantages of co-operation with the best type. He must understand how to differentiate those which are unworthy of patronage from those which offer constructive supplementary services for his own personnel activities. And, if he be wise, he will not "throw out the baby with the bath."

CHAPTER II

The Evolution of Public Employment Services

BEFORE proceeding with the discussion of the development of public employment services, which were antedated by practically all other devices for bringing employer and employee together, it seems desirable to recall the grave dangers involved in attempting to understand any given social activity as an isolated force, or factor, without first having considered its relation to other organized social activities and without having arrived at some conclusion as to how other factors, or combination of factors, have influenced its form and progress, just as, in its turn, it has influenced the development of other related activities.

A recent publication [1] has indicated, in too much detail to warrant repetition, how, during the closing years of the nineteenth century, the time was ripe throughout the civilized world for the practical interpretation, in a variety of forms, of the theory of the *unity of humanity and the brotherhood of man*. This theory, in that volume, was applied to Guidance and Personnel Services, and Placement was considered as one factor in the type of guidance and personnel service which was the outgrowth of the application of this theory. Preceding pages in the present volume have suggested how the reader may trace for himself the social forces which, operative throughout the Victorian era, brought this theory to a focus on the social problems of the age, and may thus better understand that the development of philanthropic and public employment services rests on the same historical foundation as do other social movements.

Placement, whether it be regarded as a phase of personnel service or as an independent factor in the humanitarian movement, is approached, in the present publication, as the resultant of social forces influencing in common the scattered beginnings of a variety of service activities, which, in constantly increasing numbers, found expression during the nineteenth century and reached the crest of the wave on the eve of World War I. The legitimacy of regarding placement as a participant in the common historical origin and in the common philosophy which characterized the hu-

[1] Anna Y. Reed, *Guidance and Personnel Services in Education* (Ithaca: Cornell University Press, 1944), pp. 1–3.

manitarian movement is supported by the chronological development of placement activities in relation to other activities which owed their origin to the same philosophy.

For example, in these United States late nineteenth century interests in unemployment, in vocational guidance surveys and bureaus including those in colleges, in philanthropic services of various kinds, in concerted efforts to aid the alien in his adjustments, and in the establishment of public employment services traveled side by side, while the early years of the twentieth century registered many new practical expressions of interest in both the individual and the social aspects of the humanitarian movement. The growth of vocational guidance bureaus, which stressed *service to youth*, was paralleled by the growth of public employment services, which accented *the adult* without overlooking the employment problems of youth, or ignoring the deficiencies in public education which sent its charges into the labor market with no preparation for, and no understanding of, the work world, thereby complicating the effective distribution of the product and by-product of the public schools.

The National Association of Public Employment Officers, the National Association of Corporation Schools, and the National Vocational Guidance Association were organized during a single year, 1913. The findings of various municipal and state committees on unemployment resulted in the First National Conference on Unemployment, New York City, February 27 and 28, 1914.[2] This conference had two major themes—unemployment, and public labor exchanges as a means of alleviating the evils of unemployment. As would be expected, there was much duplication of leadership among these organizations, the roster of each carrying names of individuals who were early recognized as national contributors to social progress. Among well-known names one finds Henry R. Seager, John B. Andrews, Jane Addams, Edward T. Devine, Grace Abbott, Meyer Bloomfield, John R. Commons, Fred A. King, William M. Leiserson, Charles R. Henderson, Fred C. Croxton, Don D. Lescohier, Royal Meeker, Frances A. Kellor, Louise Odencrantz, and Charles B. Barnes.

One of the most interesting discoveries which awaits a person who has the time to study in detail the history of public employment services in this country is the fact that while there are comparatively few publications which deal exclusively, or even primarily, with the placement phase of public personnel services, those which are available have been authored by the type of research scholarship which gives assurance that their con-

[2] *Proceedings First National Conference on Unemployment, New York, N.Y., Feb. 27–28, 1914,* in *American Labor Legislation Review,* IV (1914).

tent contains authentic and impartial information on the theories and practices, and on the successes and failures, which have characterized public placement services from their beginnings in the early nineteenth century to the present.

Writers in this field have, admittedly, been more fortunate in their material than have those who have been concerned with some other areas of personnel service. Our colonial labor history is well documented, and many newspaper items which interpret such documents have been preserved. Together they furnish valuable sources of information relative to the employment theories and practices of the time. Later on, the texts of legislative enactments establishing municipal, state, and federal services, plus the reports of investigations, conferences, and debates which preceded and motivated enactments, are on record. Such documents throw light on the philosophy of different factions, reveal motivating influences, and permit readers to balance successes and failures with considerable impartiality. In addition, a vitally interested press and organization publications—not always impartial—have provided abundant food for thought as each proposed statute has materialized and has challenged the discriminating judgment of writers, who have made the periodic summaries which furnish posterity with the history of public employment services in this country. Only the briefest mention of the growth of such services, and of such problems and procedures as have historical importance for the immediate purpose, is warranted in this publication. Abundant references for the assistance of those who wish to accent the beginnings of public services are offered in the bibliography.

As was logical, public employment services followed a similar growth pattern in all sections of the United States. Municipal services usually preceded state organization, while state services preceded the first national service. Organization in the western states usually preceded organization in the east. Everywhere activity was motivated by similar social and economic forces and often traveled hand in hand with other programs for social betterment. The public was slow to give moral support and was exceedingly parsimonious with financial support—so much so that in a number of cases legislative enactments carried no provision for financial support, thus vitiating the statute.

The leading advocates of public services were inclined to concentrate their efforts on securing legislation which would curb, or destroy, fee agencies and substitute public services. And while so doing, they were prone to neglect two other equally important responsibilities—the education of the general public as to the purposes and values of public services, and adequate consideration of, and legislative provision for, the operational aspects of employment offices. Neglect of the former resulted in public ignorance or indifference; neglect of the latter permitted politicians, who are ever alert for "opportunities," to get in on the ground floor and set up standards of political rather than professional competence. The results of these early oversights were apparent immediately and caused many of the problems of public employment offices.[3]

MUNICIPAL EMPLOYMENT OFFICES

Although Ohio, in 1890, may be accepted as the first state to inaugurate an employment service, there is no similar assurance as to when and where the first municipal office was established. Doubtless were it possible to examine all the municipal records and newspaper files of the various communities which might have been interested in establishing local public exchanges, a considerable number of offices would be found to have been in operation prior to 1890. Two such exchanges were sufficiently publicized some years before that date to have attained historical status—one on the east coast and the other on the west.

The previously mentioned chain of self-service offices established by ordinance in the public markets of the City of New York in 1834 is the earlier example. Judged by the comments of the day, the city's action was motivated by an economic depression, unemployment, and a feeling on the part of the Council that the provision of free facilities for the exchange of labor was as legitimate a public responsibility as was the provision of facilities for the exchange of commodities. A second municipal bureau in New York City was established by State enactment in 1869 with an appropriation of $10,000. It was designed to serve "the poor and stranger, seeking employment and information," and was motivated by a desire "to remove the evils and abuses that had their origin in the numerous intelligence offices of the city." The report of an investigation of the bureau in 1873 indicated that the venture was not very successful and suggested many opportunities for improvement.[4]

---

3 W. M. Leiserson, "The Movement for Public Labor Exchanges," *Journal of Political Economy*, XXX (1915), 707–716. This article makes some rather caustic comments on the methods of reformers and social workers who during the last decade of the nineteenth and the first decade of the twentieth centuries carried the legislation through by slogan, but without thinking it worth while to provide for methods of selecting officials and operating offices effectively.

4 *Report of the Free Labor Bureau and Proposed Improvements of the Same* (Public Charities and Correction Commission, New York State, 1873).

The second municipal example was instituted in San Francisco in 1868 under private auspices, in order to combat "shanghaiing agencies." The office was sufficiently popular to win an appropriation of $500 a month for a period of two years from the 1869–1870 session of the State legislature. Two years ended its career as a public service. Further legislative support was refused, and it returned to its private status. Since, during its operation, there had been an appreciable decrease in the number of fee agencies, its sponsors felt justified in assuming that the establishment of free public agencies was an effective means of combating the abuses of fee agencies.[5]

STATE AND MUNICIPAL OFFICES, 1890–1914

Two tabulations afford an excellent background upon which to visualize the development and to summarize the procedures and problems of pre-World War I public employment offices.[6]

The first tabulation, *History of Public Employment Offices in the United States*, by David W. Cook,[7] covered the activities of public services from 1890 to 1906, both years inclusive—a period which witnessed two economic depressions. Cook's data are taken from state and municipal statutes, from contemporary reports, and from documents, including press notices and trade journals. Since the tabulation was not made until 1935, approximately thirty years of historical perspective had accumulated with reference to the period covered and several other tabulations were available for comparison. Each item or statement selected for inclusion is documented. On the whole, Cook's tabulation is the most comprehensive and convenient presentation of historical material to which one may turn for data regarding the origin and date of establishment, motivating influences, types of problems, policies, shifts in policies and methods, and procedures of public employment offices prior to 1907. His study also reveals

---

[5] Lucile Eaves, *A History of California Labor Legislation* (Berkeley: The University of California Press, 1910), pp. 339–340.

[6] Many tabulations concerned with the growth and procedures of public employment offices are available. Rarely does one find absolute agreement in their data. Discrepancies may be credited to a variety of causes, e.g., some include all offices authorized by law, others only those which received appropriations or were actually operating; some tabulate date of authorization, others date of opening. Variations in the use and in the interpretation of terms account for statistical variations. Such discrepancies, which are very annoying to research scholars who seek absolute accuracy, are of minor importance for the present purpose, since one or two offices more or less do not affect the general character of the data from which conclusions as to the past and suggestions for the future are drawn.

[7] Doctor's dissertation, New York University, 1935.

errors of judgment among early protagonists and provides the basis for understanding how politics gained the upper hand and for challenging, and frequently for appraising, results.

This tabulation covers 17 states operating 31 offices and 11 independent municipal offices, 42 in all. Column IV cites motivating factors: in 28 cases the avowed purpose was to combat fee agencies, five offices were interested primarily in lessening unemployment, four expressed interest in both ob-jectives, while five did not make their purpose clear. The example of Ohio is an additional influence which does not appear in the tabulation but which the author brings out in his comments on the data. The Ohio em-ployment service was well publicized, and its reports created considerable interest in several other states which based their pleas for legislative action on data secured therefrom.

Column V is concerned with annual appropriations for the support of the various offices. Twenty-four of the 42 offices were established by enact-ments which either entirely ignored the necessity for appropriations or definitely stated that no provision for financial support was included. Among the 18 offices which received specific grants, 5 were allowed from $300 to $500, 11 received from $600 to $2,000, and 2—New York City and Boston—were granted $5,000 each. Missouri, California, Iowa, and West Virginia made their original efforts in connection with the office of the state labor commissioner without either legislative sanction or financial support. On the other hand, the State of Connecticut affords an example of comparatively liberal financial support for the establishment of five offices for which there seemed to be no general demand and which re-ceived little patronage after establishment. The State Labor Commis-sioner, motivated by reports from Ohio, inaugurated the legislative campaign which terminated successfully in 1901. The report of the offices for the first year indicated, as the result of their combined efforts, the placement of 56 men and 49 women, and this in spite of the fact that dur-ing that year there had been an unusual demand for both shop hands and mill operators.[8]

The same report attributes this lack of patronage to employment meth-ods closely related to certain practices of the padrone system which, as has been noted, was flourishing during this period. Central employment de-partments in business concerns were the exception; therefore job solicitors and applicants for positions were referred by superintendents to depart-ment foremen, or overseers, among whom there was a widespread custom

[8] *Report of the Connecticut Bureau of Labor Statistics*, 1901.

of charging each applicant for his opportunity to work. In some localities the evils of this system were as severely criticized as were the abuses of the fee agencies.

In passing, it is well to recall that *selling an opportunity to work* was in vogue and openly practiced by highly respected concerns until very recently, and one may well question whether the custom has been entirely obliterated. Time brought changes in the original system: the treasury of the concern rather than the individual foreman received the fee, and the jobs to which the practice was applied were limited to personal-service occupations in which the worker received such generous gratuities that it was financially advantageous for him to waive wages and even to pay a moderate price for the opportunity to receive such gratuities. Minimum-wage legislation usually revealed the extent of such practices and the occupations in which they prevailed. Minimum-wage laws have tended to eliminate the practice, quite often at a financial loss to the worker.

A widely publicized and characteristic illustration of this custom attracted considerable attention a few years ago during the preliminary investigation for minimum-wage legislation in New York State. A highly esteemed and very popular restaurant chain catering to well-to-do patrons revealed that it sold its waitress positions, paid no wages, and always had a long waiting list of applicants. Restaurants in railroad terminals, theaters, night clubs, and many hotels have also reported that the value of gratuities not only made it worth while for certain employees to pay for the opportunity to secure positions but resulted in an average weekly "intake" far above any wage scale which could be either legitimately legislated or profitably paid. The purchase of opportunities for apprenticeship was also common at one time and was approved as *tuition* for educational services.

Teachers, counselors, and leaders of adult discussion groups who are looking for material for use in studying wage systems will find minimum-wage investigations a source of valuable data on the origin and effects of the tipping system and on the effects of gratuities in relation to the "take-home wage" of lower-level personal-service occupations such as Pullman porters, redcaps, waitresses, and chambermaids.

Column VI of Cook's tabulation deals with the attitude of labor unions toward public employment bureaus, column VII with the attitude of the bureau toward strikes. Although during the period under consideration labor unions furnished a more or less informal employment service for their members, they were for the most part favorable, neutral, or expressed no opinion as to the value of public services. In West Virginia they united with employers in enthusiastic appreciation. One union was so gratified with the bureau's success in eliminating fee agencies that it invited the office to act as its business agent. In Massachusetts alone was there open hostility.

Six of the 17 states which inaugurated services prior to 1907 issued directives governing activities in case of labor disputes. Therefore, one must assume that public employment services as a potential source of strikebreakers had received some consideration. Missouri, Connecticut, West Virginia, and Massachusetts expressed their policies in terms of nonintervention and neutrality, or they required that persons referred to positions be notified of the existence of a strike or lockout. Illinois and Wisconsin attempted legally to prohibit public offices from serving concerns where strikes were in progress. This prohibition handicapped development of the offices and was declared unconstitutional by the Supreme Court of Illinois in 1903.[9] Two discriminations were cited—one against employers and the other against workers who were willing to work in a struck plant.

Column X, giving the penalties for officials who accepted fees, is significant. One of the main purposes of public employment offices was to do away with fee-charging agencies and to end the fee-splitting practice of padroni and foremen. Forewarned seems to have resulted in being forearmed: 8 of the 17 states and 20 of the 42 offices wrote penalties for the acceptance of fees into the law. A fine of $25 to $100 and/or 30 days was the usual penalty.

The second tabulation which has been chosen to supplement Cook's and to carry forward the story of growth to 1914 is entitled, "Operation of Public Employment Exchanges in the United States." [10] It was prepared for the use of the First National Conference on Unemployment, New York City, 1914, and covered 19 states operating 54 active offices plus 15 municipalities operating 13 independent active offices [11]—67 offices in all. Whereas Cook's data were secured from contemporary documents and enactments, the Conference data were collected by correspondence with state and city officials, supplemented by statistical reports from the various offices. Whereas Cook's data were primarily concerned with the purposes and provisions of enactments and with controversial problems which arose during legislative discussions, the Conference data were confined to the status of employment exchanges during the year 1913 and to their operational procedures.

9 *Matthews* v. *People*, 202 Illinois 389, 67 N.E. 28.
10 *American Labor Legislation Review*, IV (1914), 364–371.
11 Three states and three municipalities each reported offices either inactive or not yet in operation.

The items included in the tabulation dealt with topics which were then, and are now, of basic importance: the number of applications for work and for workers; the positions filled; and the per capita cost of filling— which ranged from eight cents to $1.67. Under basis of referral, fitness received first place, with order of application, references, state residence, need, number of dependents, alphabetical order, residents with families, and family men, either singly or in combinations, mentioned as secondary influences. State appropriations ranged from $1,200 for one office in West Virginia to $50,735 for eight exchanges in Illinois. Los Angeles ranked first among municipalities with an appropriation of $10,000, while Everett, Washington, was lowest with $1,000. Departmentalization was in its infancy. The separation of men and women applicants was fairly common by 1913; a few offices separated the skilled and unskilled. Boys and girls were universally registered in adult offices. Los Angeles *reported* the only "juvenile" office, and Massachusetts was the only state which made special provision for the handicapped.

Items IX and X of the tabulation are worthy of special attention. The inclusion of item IX, "Is effort directed toward vocational guidance?" reflected the national enthusiasm for vocational guidance which was, at that time, at its pre-World War height.[12] An unqualified "no" was the almost unanimous response; Massachusetts alone appears to have been making genuine efforts to offer vocational advice. New York State, with a good but as yet inoperative law on her statute books, looked hopefully toward the future and replied "yes." Los Angeles, which on the same questionnaire had reported the only juvenile exchange, replied in the negative. This apparent inconsistency may, or may not, be attributable to failure to understand the function of vocational guidance in any junior labor exchange. From an educational viewpoint, the reply of Everett, Washington, was amusingly naïve, "Public schools attend to this matter." [13]

Item X, probably suggested by the dominant interest of the Conference, read, "Is effort directed toward industrial removal?" Replies indicated that there was little exchange of information, either interoffice or interstate, and that only the most casual efforts were made to clear jobs or to redistribute workers. On the other hand, applicants from without the state were usually allowed to register. A final item on the questionnaire dealt with "referral policy during labor disputes." Responses indicated

---

[12] Discussed in detail in Reed, *Guidance and Personnel Services*, Part I.

[13] During 1913 this writer was working on a guidance program for the Seattle Public Schools, but the schools were by no means "attending to this matter," nor were there any other schools in the state which were.

that the subject had become of increasing importance between 1907 and 1913. Seven state exchanges now refused to send out "strike breakers," while practically all of the other exchanges gave information as to strikes when making referrals.

Public-school placement bureaus were not very common in 1913, but wherever such a bureau did exist it was very important that it should understand and follow the best current adult-office practice with reference to strikes. Moreover, the operation of a junior exchange entailed other responsibilities with reference to strikes. As a counselor and placement functionary under the Seattle Board of Education in 1913, the writer early learned the importance and the difficulty of so conducting such a bureau that there was no possibility of involving the public schools in labor disputes. She also learned by experience that alert labor leaders kept a watchful eye on the comings and goings of junior applicants and that sometimes selected juniors were sent to ask for referrals to a struck plant. "Just to see what the bureau would do about it" was the explanation when the final showdown came. What was done about it *invariably*, whether or not there was suspicion that the request was not a bona fide application, was to require every minor to bring a written statement from his parent, or guardian, to the effect that he was aware of the strike situation, informed as to the possibility of personal danger under such conditions, but still wanted his son to work at the given plant, requested the referral, and took the responsibility. The referral was then made with "strike on" stamped across the front, and a duplicate was attached to the parent's request and filed.

Open versus closed shop was a live problem in the Northwest during these years, and strikes were common. A considerable number of the school product and by-product secured industrial opportunities through the general employment office of the Metal Trades Association. The school bureau was the intermediate counseling and referral agency. No boys were considered as applicants until they had cleared through the bureau; periodic reports on progress and promotions were made; and educational programs were discussed. No boys recommended by the schools were discharged without previous consideration, with the bureau, of the cause of dissatisfaction. It was somewhat of a surprise—upon inquiry as to the policy of the Association relative to placing school-recommended applicants —to learn that the names of all applicants cleared through the school office were withdrawn from the active file during strikes. "Otherwise we might involve the school in labor disputes" was the explanation.

INTERSTATE EMPLOYMENT SERVICES

While municipalities and states were organizing labor exchanges, a combination of circumstances was forcing into the foreground the necessity for some program which would provide for the distribution of labor beyond state boundaries. Since, from their very inception, a considerable portion of the work of commercial exchanges has been concerned with furnishing labor beyond the limits of the towns or states in which the specific exchange was located, it was inevitable that public exchanges could not compete unless they, too, were able to centralize information about jobs and workers and to develop a distribution system which would operate over more inclusive geographical areas. Originally, many of the out-of-town opportunities were for unskilled labor for railway and highway construction, mining, lumbering, and specialized agricultural services, but gradually mobility among semiskilled and professional workers increased. Labor unions had their "traveling members," and office workers, nurses, teachers, and engineers were increasingly in demand and were calling for assistance in locating beyond state lines.

Various methods of meeting interstate demand were tried. During the 1890's some of the state services were established primarily for the distribution of farmhands. Mail orders, with the post office as a medium of distribution, was the method, and interstate registration was permitted. The western railroads sometimes acted as media for both information and transportation, while agricultural station agents, serving in major crop areas, accumulated and passed back to some central agency information which was basic to the distribution of seasonal labor. The logical next step was co-operation among agricultural states.

The first definite effort in this direction, for which documentation is available, was the organization, in 1904, of the Western Association of State Free Employment Bureaus.[14] Organization procedures were initiated in November of 1903 as a result of the fact that, in that year, great areas of grain were unharvested because of insufficient seasonal labor. Interstate co-operation in the adjustment of surpluses and shortages of harvest hands seemed the only solution. Kansas City, Missouri, which was the natural center of distribution for the grain states, was designated as a clearinghouse. No further reports on the activities of this Association have been made public. Its major contribution to the history of public employ-

[14] The original report of the organization of this bureau, the states included, the objectives, and the program, by Don C. Despain, the President, 1904, is on file in the New York City Public Library in the form of a typescript on Association stationery. Cook, *op. cit.*, pp. 44–46, quotes liberally from this report.

ment services is found in the fact that it was the first step in interstate co-operation and paved the way for two later and more inclusive interstate organizations, the American Association of Public Employment Offices,[15] in 1913, and the National Farm Labor Exchange, in 1914, the purpose of which was identical with that of the earlier association.

FEDERAL EMPLOYMENT SERVICES, 1907–1917

The first federal effort to encourage wider co-operation in the distribution of labor was made during the panic year of 1907. The relief of the unemployment congestion in the eastern cities, due to the accumulation therein of newly arrived immigrants, was a major objective. Immigrant labor was stressed and the Division of Information, a unit within the Bureau of Immigration, was charged with the following specific responsibilities:

to promote a beneficial distribution of aliens admitted into the United States among the several States and Territories desiring immigration, . . . gather from all available sources useful information regarding the resources, products and physical characteristics of each State and Territory, . . . publish such information in different languages and distribute the publications among . . . aliens . . . and to such other persons as may desire the same.

Post offices were the media for the collection of information.[16] Questionnaires and inquiries were used. Manufacturers' associations, chambers of commerce, labor unions, state and municipal organizations, and individuals who were supposed to know if help were needed—what kind and where, wages, hours and conditions of labor, housing facilities, and living costs,—were sources of information. Newspaper notices regarding the establishment of new factories furnished clues to occupational opportunities and were immediately followed up.

Statistical reports, which included number of placements, nationalities, occupations, and states to which workers were sent, indicate a very moderate degree of success. But the effort marked the beginning of federal activity in the public employment field and it established a precedent for a second step forward when, in 1913, the Department of Labor was separated from the Department of Commerce and its purpose declared to be "to foster, promote and develop the welfare of wage-earners of the United States, to improve their working conditions, and to advance their opportunities for profitable employment." This declaration in the organic law,

---

[15] Now the International Association of Public Employment Services.

[16] *Annual Report of the Department of Commerce and Labor,* 1908. The final question asked of each employer was: "Do strikes or other labor difficulties exist in your jurisdiction? If so, kindly state cause of same."

coupled with the functions assigned to the Division of Information in 1907
—to distribute information to aliens and such other persons as desire it—
permitted the Commissioner of Immigration to broaden the scope of the
Division's activities and, in theory at least, to convert the immigration service into a nation-wide employment service for all wage earners.[17]

Certain events in 1914 encouraged this action: (1) War in Europe
caused the abrupt termination of immigration and left many immigration officers without employment. (2) This country was in the throes of
a periodic wave of unemployment, and, as usual, advocacy of public employment offices as a panacea was receiving public attention. (3) Reports
of several surveys of unemployment had been published [18] which were
unanimous in recommending the establishment of public employment
services as a part of their program for attacking unemployment. (4) International conferences on unemployment had been meeting regularly for a
number of years, and many municipal and state conferences had been
held in these United States. (5) The First National Conference on Unemployment in the United States met in 1914, and the report of its proceedings had created widespread interest in more adequate methods of
distributing labor. (6) Six bills providing for a national employment service were introduced during the 1914–1915 session of Congress. The Mur-
dock bill, which incorporated the tested experience of several states, was
most promising. None received congressional approval. (7) The American
Association of Public Employment Offices had been organized and was
vigorously attacking the problems involved in more effective administration of state and municipal offices. The time seemed ripe for the institution of a second national employment service, this time to be concerned
with the distribution of all types of labor and to be called an Employment
Service—a little later the United States Employment Service.

Between 1914 and 1917 several specialized services were introduced to
meet specific needs: Farm Placement in 1915 in co-operation with the
National Farm Labor Exchange; Marine Placement in 1915 at the request

[17] The *Annual Reports of the United States Department of Labor* for 1914, 1915, and
1916 describe the steps involved in this expansion of the 1907 service. No official order
was issued establishing this service as an independent organization, and the title was
not used on official reports until 1915.
[18] Among them *Unemployment in New York City* (U.S. Bureau of Labor Statistics,
Bull. no. 172, 1915); *Report of the Massachusetts Board to Investigate the Subject of
Unemployment*, House Document no. 50, 1895; *Report of Chicago Commission on Unemployment*, Charles R. Henderson, Secretary, 1914; *Third Report, the Wainwright
Commission*, New York, 1911; *The Report of the Mayor's Commission on Unemployment*, New York, 1914–1916.

of the Department of Commerce to recruit certificated seamen under the requirements of the Seamen's Act of March 4, 1915; two youth services in 1916, one for Women and Girls and the other for Young Men and Boys.[19] The purpose of these youth services is stated at some length and indicates that the federal authorities were familiar with, and in sympathy with, the current interest in vocational education and vocational guidance. The protection of women and girls from the abuses of certain types of fee agencies was not forgotten:

Every possible assistance should be extended to girls and young women to enable them to make suitable vocational selections with a view to proper vocational training in order to guide them in desirable industry and avoidance of occupations and places where evil conditions exist.

Another service which established a precedent for World War I was instituted in 1917 to place guardsmen returning from military service on the Mexican border. Members of the families of those still in service were included. More than 20,000 of about 50,000 who had returned registered, and 15,000 "were directed to jobs."

During this same period some important changes in organization were made. Plans were formulated for the establishment of federal employment exchanges on a national scale. The zone system with subbranches, each under an inspector from the Immigration Bureau corps, went into effect in January, 1915, and "mail order" registration through the co-operation of post-office officials and county agricultural agents was provided for. The Assistant Secretary of Labor had high hopes for this new venture. In an article entitled "Government Intervention in Idleness," he explained the program with emphasis upon the assistance to be given by post offices and by the Department of Agriculture. It was his opinion that the inauguration of the program would "promote labor distribution extensively and satisfactorily." [20]

Those who had been on the firing line for many of the twenty-five years since Ohio instituted the first state service held a different opinion. Practical experience had taught them that too many elements of failure were inherent in the program to warrant hope for success, and plans and procedures were at once challenged. Since no contemporary writer better understood the problems involved in instituting an effective public employment service, and no worker in the field had had a better opportunity to share in the vicissitudes which attend such an undertaking, Lescohier's

[19] *Annual Reports of the United States Department of Labor*, 1916, pp. 62, 322; 1918, pp. 199–200.
[20] Louis F. Post, *Survey*, XXXIV (1915), 270.

summation well represents the thought of leaders regarding this new movement for a federal employment service. Two pages were sufficient to characterize the three major features of "this pitiful federal employment service." Offices were distributed without reference to state size or employment needs. They were under the direction of immigration inspectors, sometimes called "superintendents of employment," although only by courtesy could they be considered employment officers. Operational procedures "violated most of the canons of good employment practice," and there was little effort to serve either employer or applicant. The character of the staff "made any real service impossible." [21]

The second phase of the plan—"to make every post office an employment office"—and its approval by so many people were regarded as "a striking tribute to American ignorance of the country's employment needs and of the fact that employment work, properly done, is a profession." The third major phase of the program—co-operation with other federal departments—brought limited results because "some of the federal officials were so concerned about who would get the credit for what was done that they never got to the work for which credit was sought. Interdepartment jealousy and suspicion crippled much of the effort at co-operation."

There are plenty of facts which substantiate Lescohier's characterization. No one today would consider the primitive activities of the federal government in 1907 and 1914 as employment services—information or intelligence services, both of which terms were sometimes used, are more appropriate. On the other hand, posting notices, collecting information on farm needs and opportunities by mail carriers, circularization of business concerns and organizations, and the preparation and distribution of material on occupational opportunities do tend, in any period, to facilitate employment, and each procedure is entitled to its proper place in the facilitating process. Such activities should not be dismissed as unworthy of historical consideration but rather be regarded as intermediate steps in the development of more effective placement services. Compared with some of the primitive types of exchanges and early methods of facilitating employment, they did not afford an opportunity for personal contact of prospective employer and employee as did the self-service exchanges, but they did furnish "take home" information for leisurely consideration and possible action.

So while another federal effort to establish a nation-wide public employment service must be branded a failure, it must also be counted as

[21] *The Labor Market*, pp. 174–175.

another steppingstone toward progress. Other federal attempts, other failures, and other steppingstones followed and without much delay, for between 1914 and 1917 there was a heavy demand upon these quasi agencies, their expansion was rapid, and, overburdened with the handicaps stated and implied in Lescohier's characterization, they were totally inadequate to cope with the increasing demands of war industries. However, before the war efforts to introduce a more effective federal service are taken up, it is well to consider to what extent the leaders, who were excoriating federal efforts, were equally critical of their own efforts with reference to state and municipal services.

Self-Criticism and Suggested Improvements. There is abundant documentary evidence that during this same period there was much self-evaluation going on. Leaders who had been active in pressing for employment legislation and had secured it were inventorying their accomplishments in the light of their objectives and the conscientious efforts which had been made to attain them. Among the most ardent critics of the some 70 public employment offices operating in 19 states were Don D. Lescohier, W. M. Leiserson, Fred C. Croxton, John B. Andrews, and Charles R. Henderson. Two of the major media through which they made known their dissatisfaction and discussed suggestions for immediate improvement were the American Association of Public Employment Offices, organized in 1913, and the two National Conferences on Unemployment held in 1914.

The 1914 conferences were open forums for the consideration of all phases of unemployment.[22] The February conference agreed upon five essentials for the solution of unemployment: (1) industrial training and vocational guidance, (2) a widespread system of labor exchanges, (3) regulation of business, (4) accurate labor market statistics, and (5) unemployment insurance. The December conference resulted in the publication of the details of a practical program for the prevention of unemployment. Its elaboration of four *musts,* comprising 26 pages, affords the best single summary of the social-economic situation immediately preceding World War I: *Public employment exchanges must be established; public works must be systematically distributed; industry must be regularized; adequate unemployment insurance must be established.*

Employment services were cited in the conference discussions as an important factor in centralizing the labor market—a means to an end. Discussion revealed quite general agreement regarding the prevailing status

22 The Conference reports are found in the *American Labor Legislation Review,* IV and V (1914).

of state and municipal offices, and it also revealed an increasing disillusionment and some discouragement regarding the future possibilities of
such services. Henderson, who was secretary of the Chicago Commission
on Unemployment which had just completed a two-year study on the
causes, prevention, and cure of unemployment, pronounced our public
agencies "inefficient to a very high degree. . . . We may say they are almost a failure." Leiserson felt that the administration of public offices was
in incompetent hands [23] and that additional offices should not be opened
until those already operating were made effective. Meyer Bloomfield
thought it better not to open offices if the usual type of officeholder were
to be put in charge, "men who could not earn their salt in private employment." Andrews regarded only a few offices as efficient, while Croxton, speaking of Ohio offices, hoped to increase their efficiency by a
uniform system of records "so that figures mean exactly what they are
intended to mean."

The first and second meetings of the American Association of Public
Employment Offices, 1913 and 1914, registered officials who were partially
responsible for the unsatisfactory operation of such offices. They gave their
undivided attention to the practical problems involved in the organization and administration of public services and in the course of the discussion laid down quite a number of desirable dos and don'ts for themselves.
Two topics on the agenda furnished the nuclei for a summary of the
thinking of employment officials with reference to their own problems:
"What is the matter with our free employment offices?" and, "What must
be done to make public employment offices more effective?" [24]

Replies to the first question, as brought out in the discussions, revealed
a variety of causes to which ineffectiveness might be attributable. Several
were directly traceable to the overemphasis which leaders of the movement had placed on securing legislation without giving due consideration
to the practical administrative problems which were bound to ensue.
Seven major "matters" were accented: (1) limited financial support,
(2) qualifications and character of the staff, (3) lack of a unified or centralized system, (4) control by political or other pressure groups, (5) neg-

---

[23] *The Springfield Survey*, published by the Russell Sage Foundation in 1916, was
made in 1914. It reported that the staff of the public employment office consisted of a
superintendent, who was formerly a mine manager, an assistant superintendent, who
was formerly a jail keeper, a woman clerk in charge of the women's department, a
stenographer, and a janitor. Only the stenographer and the janitor were required to
qualify under civil service; the others were appointed by the governor (see p. 95).

[24] At the second meeting, 1914, one of the topics was "The Wrong Way to Conduct a
System of Public Employment Offices."

lect of essential administrative procedures such as records and reports, (6) character of applicants, and (7) competition of private agencies.

Discussion on the second question brought out musts, point by point on each of the "matters" revealed:

(1) The public must be educated to understand what an employment service is, and, if it wants public offices, it must provide adequate financial support. Records showed no important advance in this respect since 1890. Efficient administrative officers who could compete with officials employed in private exchanges could not be secured for $1,200.[25]

(2) Better-qualified personnel must be secured. Politics and pressure groups must not be allowed to control appointments. In the Seattle municipal office, established in 1894, the personnel was required to qualify under civil service, but until 1906 the personnel of state offices was purely appointive.[26] Civil-service examinations, permanent tenure, and decent salaries were repeatedly mentioned as basic musts if public employment work were to attract and hold high-grade persons, encourage professionalism, and develop experts. The *in-service training* of personnel was suggested by Leiserson as an additional method of securing better-qualified workers. His experience as superintendent of Wisconsin offices had caused him to feel that in-service training was necessary and should be a responsibility of the state superintendents. This 1913 recommendation of Leiserson's was, in point of time, in harmony with the growing feeling that all aspects of personnel work were professional, requiring preparatory as well as in-service education. However, the first official recognition of the necessity for the training of employment personnel was delayed until 1918.

(3) A unified system of public employment offices must be established.

25 Harrison and others, *Public Employment Offices*, p. 452, cite a few salaries which had improved by 1920–1922. In the main, progress had been very slow. Atkinson and others, *Public Employment Service*, pp. 173–174, quote salary scales for principal positions in 45 state services in 1937–1938 and note that in many cases there were no employees at the maximum rates: state directors, $2,400 to $7,500; managers, $1,380 to $6,000; interviewers, $1,000 to $2,640.

26 Between 1906 and 1920 not over a dozen states introduced the merit system, although much publicity had been given to the improvement in the Boston and Milwaukee offices following its introduction. Under the Wagner-Peyser Act, in 1935–1936, state-federal agreements required the selection of state personnel under civil-service regulations, but the law exempted federal personnel from such requirements. Two books accessible in most libraries afford a complete account of the history of efforts to secure better-qualified personnel: Harrison and others, *op. cit.*, ch. xxiv–xxv, pp. 448–480, which suggests specifications for director general, state director, local superintendents, and interviewers (adapted from the *Report of the Congressional Joint Commission on Reclassification of Salaries*, 66th Congress, 2d session, House of Rep., Doc. no. 686, p. 793), and Atkinson and others, *op. cit.*, ch. x, pp. 152–175, which gives a very complete account of the history of the merit system in connection with public employment offices.

Local offices must be connected through state offices, and state offices must be unified by means of a federal service. Only by some such program of centralized control and decentralized operation of intrastate and interstate services could the labor market be organized on a national basis, the reserve be kept at a minimum, and research in procedures and problems and in the standardization of essential activities go forward.

(4) Appointments and policies must be removed from the control of political parties, employing groups, labor unions, or other special pressure groups. The management of an employment office is an administrative and technical matter. Officials should not change with each change in political administration.

(5) Employment services must be operated on a business basis. They were thought to be operating in a most unbusinesslike manner. Among the many essentials which required attention in any well-managed office, the following were accented: the location and character of the office, separate entrances for men and women, sections or departments for different types of labor, adaptation of office hours to business hours, absolute neutrality in labor disputes, referral of applicants on the basis of fitness alone, the improvement of forms and records, accurate statistical summaries, and more intelligent co-operation with other placement agencies.[27]

(6) Some way must be found to attract the better type of applicant. As long as the public offices continued to get the discard—both jobs and workers—the private agencies would skim the cream and leave the refuse. Hangers-on and loafers drove away the better class.[28] Office managers should get acquainted with hangers-on, study their records, and find out whether they can't work or won't work. Unemployables are not an employment office problem, and those who won't work should be driven out. There were too many immigrant applicants who pushed out seasoned workers and crowded them into the labor reserve. The better type of applicant resented the implication that employment was a charity; office managers could counteract it by refusing to send out the unfit and by preparing the kind of records which allowed them to determine who were the fit.

[27] Henderson's address at the 1913 meeting, "Bureaus of Employment in Europe," (U.S. Bureau of Labor Statistics, Bull. no. 192, 1914, pp. 16–23), discussed the adaptation to this country of the tested procedures of 15 European countries, taken from a report compiled by German statisticians in 1912, *Bulletin trimestriel de l'Association internationale pour la lutte contre le chômage,* July–September, 1913.

[28] Loafing in or about Missouri's offices was strictly forbidden. Applicants might call frequently but could not sit or stand about in offices. The purpose of the rule was not only to protect the reputation of the services but also to avoid discouraging applicants, who might be depressed by group discussions of unfortunate circumstances.

(7) Ability to compete with private agencies must be developed. Prior to 1907 statutory elimination was the advocated panacea. By 1913 and 1914 it was recognized that private agencies had come to stay; that, properly regulated, they had a social contribution to make; and that emulation of their most effective procedures was in order. It was conceded that private agencies were better staffed and better managed; that they attracted a better type of applicant and commanded the best positions. It was also conceded that if governmental operation of some offices and governmental regulation of others were to proceed side by side, operating officials and regulating officials would need to be honest, energetic, capable, and thoroughly familiar with all phases of the employment business. Some were optimistic enough to believe that if public offices were to employ equally well-equipped officials they would quickly eliminate private fee agencies.

Authoritative opinion at these various conferences and annual meetings was expressed on many matters in addition to those which received major attention. For example, it was conceded that both public and philanthropic interest in employment services had been motivated by unemployment and by the abuses of fee agencies, rather than by any primary interest in public employment services and its attendant evils; but it was the general opinion that public employment offices were not a solution for unemployment no matter how effective they might become. Unemployables [29] were recognized as an increasing problem but were rejected as a responsibility of public employment offices. Frances Kellor and Royal Meeker, the recently appointed United States Commissioner of Labor Statistics, stressed the importance of classifying the unemployables separately from the unemployed-employables and making them a charge against relief agencies rather than against industry. Meeker, immediately upon his acceptance of the Commissionership, advocated what is still being unsuccessfully advocated in 1945, a continuous survey of unemployment and employment conditions, which would keep the country informed as to jobs in existence and numbers of men employed, under-

---

[29] Occupational accidents and occupational diseases were increasing the number. Improved industrial standards and more careful selection of workers were branding others as "unprofitable." Some who had been allowed to grow up with no training for work, or who had no capacity for work and no ability to work, were also potential unemployables. Students of the problem were advocating state programs which would include vocational training for the young, rehabilitation for those who could be made fit under the new competitive conditions, even though it might be necessary to force under medical control those "who like freedom but cannot live the life of free men," and the segregation of abnormals in celibate colonies for three or four generations. Such measures they felt would reduce the number of occupational incompetents, while the more general acceptance of programs of euthenics and of eugenics would gradually prevent increase in their number.

employed, overemployed, and unemployed. Health and accident conditions should be included, and both unfit occupations and unfit occupiers of jobs should receive attention.

Other participants called attention to the waves of reform legislation which had periodically swept over the country since about 1890 [30] and indicated the necessity for public employment officials being familiar with statutes which controlled employment, so that placements might always be made within the framework of such legislation. Specific results, in terms of employment, of such enactments as the shorter day for women and minors under 16, minimum-wage laws for women and minors, accident compensation and insurance laws, and of employers' welfare programs, which included pre-employment medical examinations, psychological tests, health and safety programs, various types of insurance, and the like, were cited with case illustrations. Apprenticeship opportunities at a learner's wage of from $3.00 to $4.50 in semiskilled lines, such as chocolate dipping, which had provided employers with recruits at a cost of $50 to $75 each, were no longer profitable methods of securing workers and were no longer available in the industry. "From what source could employment offices secure trained applicants to meet such demands?" employment workers asked.

In the course of discussion many minor problems which have been continuously troublesome came out. Several placement officers were troubled about the placement of junior delinquents and of paroled prisoners. Walter L. Sears gave a practical reply: "Whenever we have an opportunity to place a discharged or paroled prisoner or a juvenile delinquent, we inform the prospective employers . . . of the facts about the applicants." He did not think it wise to attract attention to such applicants lest it lead the public to lose confidence in the office, but he felt that an office could

[30] While no voice decried such reforms whether they came about through legislative enactments or through voluntary action on the part of employers, experienced placement workers were not unmindful of the fact that every improvement in industrial standards forced employers to select workers more carefully and to reject as potentially unprofitable employees those who could not qualify under ever more stringent requirements. *The Report of the Committee on Standards of Living and Labor* (National Conference of Charities and Correction, Cleveland, 1912, p. 376) indicates that this situation was also rather generally recognized by social organizations: ". . . Restrictions upon employers set forth in this platform will lead them to refuse to engage any who fall below a grade of industrial efficiency which renders their work profitable. An increased army of industrial outcasts will be thrown upon society to be cared for in public labor colonies or by various relief agencies. This condition will in turn necessitate a minimum standard of preparation, including at least sufficient educational opportunity to abolish illiteracy among all minors and to train every worker to some form of industrial efficiency."

usually assimilate a few such applicants in connection with its regular work.

Filling, or refusing to fill, undesirable jobs was another troublesome problem. All officers reported both undesirable jobs and undesirable applicants. The work might be too heavy or the hours too long, the temperature too high or too low; wages might be unsatisfactory or payment uncertain; the location might be undesirable for a number of reasons; or the moral atmosphere might be questionable. Commission canvassing and several other factors considered to characterize undesirable jobs were mentioned. Every discussion brought out the difficulty of securing enough girls to fill housework jobs. How can more girls and more competent girls be secured? was a perennial question. A number of officials stated that whenever girls came to apply for work without knowing what kind of work to ask for, which happened very often, they suggested housework and made an effort to get the girls to try it because they thought the moral influence in the homes was better than it was in the factories.

Another common question was, How many referrals should be made to the same position? Officials seemed fairly well agreed that but one referral should be made unless more were asked for. The applicant who had registered first should be given preference if it were possible; otherwise the one with the best record and best suited to the job should be referred. Should an employment official tell a worker that he has not made good and why? Some did. The majority did not. What should be done about applicants who apply while holding a job? How can occupations and industries be classified so that there may be some uniformity in statistical summaries?

Those who are familiar with current employment problems cannot read the reports of these early-century conferences without being struck by the fact that there is hardly a problem of the present that did not appear in the discussions of yesterday; hardly a constructive proposal which was not anticipated by some participant in the employment services of 1913 and 1914.

Related Social-Economic Activities. The proceedings of the conferences on unemployment and of the Association of Public Employment Offices have indicated that the story of occupational placement services would be narrowly conceived were it to be based upon the pronouncements of only those agencies and individuals whose primary interests were in employment, and were the contributions of that large number of agencies and organizations, conferences, surveys, and individuals who had major interests in related social-economic activities, to be overlooked. A review of a few of the areas within which humanitarianism was increasingly prolific between 1890 and 1914 helps to keep placement services, which were but one factor in the total picture, in proper perspective. It also helps to keep before oncoming social workers the fact that a firm foundation for the majority of social reforms which were consummated by legislative enactments during the years immediately preceding World War II had been laid between 1900 and 1914, with peak accomplishments during the depression of 1907 and 1914.

Social agencies are one humanitarian area in which it is easy to trace progress. A considerable number of such agencies were functioning before 1900. Among them were the General Federation of Women's Clubs, which, through its industrial section, was expressing interest in the employment of women and youth, in vocational education, in education and labor legislation, and in the merit system in civil service; the National Congress of Mothers, later known as the National Congress of Mothers and the Parent-Teachers Association; the National Civic Federation; and the National Consumers' League. That the last-mentioned agency was fully conscious of the fact that it was sharing in the practical application of the theory of the unity of humanity and the brotherhood of man is documented by the statement of one of its founders that it was an affirmative response to the question, "Am I my brother's keeper?" [31]

Before 1910 the National Child Labor Committee, the National Women's Trade Union League, which was organized at the 1903 convention of the American Federation of Labor, the National Committee for Mental Hygiene, the American Association for Labor Legislation, and the National Society for the Promotion of Industrial Education were in the field each busily engaged in its own area.

By 1914 the National Council for Industrial Safety, the National Vocational Guidance Association, the National Association of Corporation Schools, the National Alliance of Legal Aid Societies,[32] the Society for the Promotion of Engineering Education, and local employment man-

[31] Maud Nathan, *The Story of an Epoch-making Movement* (New York: Doubleday, Page and Co., 1926). Well documented.

[32] Reginald Heber Smith, *Justice and the Poor* (Carnegie Foundation for the Advancement of Teaching, Bull. no. 13, 1919). This bulletin reports on a three-year study of the history of legal aid societies. Henry S. Pritchett, in the Foreword, states his belief that securing justice is a proper function of government but that in this area as well as in many others private initiative must lead the way. And then prophetically he adds, "New projects are continually suggested for improving the condition of the poor by the aid of government, and as to many of them there is a debatable question whether they come within the proper province of government and whether official interference will not in the long run do more harm than good to the beneficiaries and to the community."

agers' associations,[33] employers' welfare associations, and continuation schools were the resultants of experience and responses to recognized social needs.

During these same years several periodicals concerned with social, economic, and civic problems were launched; well-known literary periodicals included, and sometimes forcefully stressed, topics which tended to arouse and sustain public interest in social deficiencies and their possible removal. *McClure's Magazine* took the lead in publicizing the social, political, and economic sins of the nation and thereby inaugurated what came to be known as the Muckraking era—a name which has passed into history as synonymous with the Square Deal of Theodore Roosevelt. More radical and less responsible magazines, with writers of less authority and personal accountability and usually with less worthy objectives, followed *McClure's* lead. By 1906, when President Roosevelt made his *Muckraker Speech*,[34] the pendulum had swung so far to the left that he expressed not only his own opinion but also that of most thoughtful and fair-minded citizens, who felt that however desirable social reforms might be too much progress had been made in "purifying America in the interests of magazine circulation."

Books of various degrees of readability, written for a variety of purposes by authors of varying degrees of accuracy, intellectuality, and responsibility, but all more or less concerned with presenting social problems and the need for social reform in such fashion that some portion of the public might be aroused to action, appeared in considerable volume.[35] Ida Tarbell's *The History of the Standard Oil Company*, Upton Sinclair's *The Jungle*, and Lincoln Steffens' *The Shame of the Cities* exemplify types of publications which appealed to some people. Henry R. Seager's *Social Insurance*,[36] Alice W. Solenberger's *One Thousand Homeless Men*,[37] and Frances A. Kellor's *Out of Work* [38] appealed to others, who were inter-

---

[33] Meyer Bloomfield in "The Aim and Work of Employment Managers' Associations" (*Annals of the American Academy of Political and Social Science*, LXV, whole no. 154, May, 1916) gives the aims of the Boston organization in 1911, discusses its extension to other cities, and forecasts the national organization of 1918.

[34] Based on a character in Bunyan's *Pilgrim's Progress*.

[35] Parker, *The Casual Laborer*, p. 103, notes that by 1914 muckrakers had made a thorough job of agitating the public mind: "Few American analysts have realized what firmly held traditions have been established throughout all the working classes by the muckraking literature of the last twenty years."

[36] *Social Insurance: A Program of Social Reform* (New York: The Macmillan Co., 1910) p. 175, deals with the causes and extent of unemployment and summarizes steps which have been taken to solve the problem.

[37] New York: Charities Publication Committee, 1911.

[38] New York: Putnam's Sons, 1904.

ested also in the findings of a great variety of surveys which revealed social inadequacies in every area of life and in the numerous articles which advocated workmen's compensation, unemployment insurance or, as it was sometimes called, insurance against worklessness, economic security, retraining of the unemployed, and improvement in working conditions. Workmen's compensation legislation was passed during the first decade of the century, and unemployment insurance had long been a major topic for discussion. The *Annual Report of the United States Commissioner of Labor*, 1911, devoted some 500 pages to the subject, while the United States Bureau of Labor Statistics, May, 1908, published a bulletin entitled *What Is Done for the Unemployed in European Countries?* [39]

Throughout his entire administration Theodore Roosevelt had many opportunities, and created more, to raise his voice in defense of the "common man." Crusaders for human rights *versus* property rights enlisted under the banner of the Square Deal, and such topics as child labor, increased educational opportunities, unfair and unjust racial discrimination, protection for immigrants, public employment services, old age pensions, workmen's compensation, unemployment insurance, and safety and health regulations were thoroughly aired, and some were brought to fruition in legislation. When, as has been indicated, the pendulum had swung too far to the left, Roosevelt called a halt, differentiated constructive from destructive methods of reform, and branded for all time the activities of overzealous scandal mongers "muckraking." President Wilson's New Freedom carried forward more conservatively, but no less effectively, agitation for social reforms, and by 1914 additional humanitarian legislation was on the statute books.

The cumulative influence of the humanitarian appeal, whether expressed in conservative and scientific literature or in muckraking literature, the interrelation of the many social agencies which sprang up, their overlapping in objectives and in activities, and the factors and combinations of factors to which each owes its origin are not essential in order to understand their relation to employment services and to different philosophies of placement. But familiarity with these various agencies, all of which gave practical expression to current humanitarian thinking, affords a better background for accenting the fact that employment services were only a part of a broader and of a world-wide movement. Moreover, such agencies and activities determined to a considerable extent the framework within which the placement function was forced to operate, and the limitations of its effectiveness were, and still are, frequently due

[39] Bull. no. 76, 1908, pp. 741–938.

to some failure or activity on the part of one or more allied agencies.

The National Child Labor Committee, the American Association for Labor Legislation, the Consumers' League, and labor organizations had something to say about the type of positions to which applicants, might be referred and the conditions under which they might work. The National Vocational Guidance Association, the National Society for the Promotion of Industrial Education, and the National Association of Corporation Schools were concerned with the contribution which public education made to the readiness of its charges for occupational life. The philanthropic vocational guidance bureaus and the public employment offices which received the school product and attempted its occupational distribution were potential sources of helpful evaluative criteria, had school administration used them for this purpose. Sources of labor supply, methods of selecting employees, examinations for mental and physical condition and for specific aptitudes as well as for general qualities, reduction of labor turnover,[40] and the like were initial responsibilities of employment managers and the cause of their existence. Psychological laboratories brought new scientific knowledge to bear directly on the behavior of individuals and were promising, and to a limited extent making good on their promise, that they could help educators to understand the academic failure better, and foremen and superintendents to make their selection guesses and hunches more accurate.

Other agencies concentrated their efforts on the improvement of labor conditions. Alice Henry enumerated the labor-union interests as follows: raising of wages, shortening of hours, diminution of seasonal work, abolition or regulation of piecework with its resultant speed-up, maintaining of sanitary conditions, guarding of machinery, enforcement of child-labor laws, abolition of taxes for power and working materials such as needles and thread, and of unfair fines for petty or unproved offences, and recognition of the union. She also regretted, and cited cases to illustrate her point, racial and sex discriminations on the part of unions.[41]

Employers' welfare activities increased rapidly during this period. The introduction of improvements in lighting, heating, ventilation, toilet facilities, and safety devices, in supplying drinking water, dining rooms, rest and recreation rooms, and in special provisions for the health and

---

[40] Magnus W. Alexander, "Hiring and Firing: Its Economic Waste and How to Avoid it," *Annals of the American Academy of Political and Social Science,* LXV, whole no. 154, May, 1916.

[41] *The Trade Union Woman* (New York: D. Appleton and Co., 1915). This book tells the story of trade unionism in relation to the working women of the United States. The historical value of the book is enhanced by its elaborate documentation.

protection of women anticipated legislative enactments along the same lines.[42]

Charles R. Henderson, in *Citizens in Industry,* published in 1915 by D. Appleton and Company, made his final contribution to years of social service by leaving for posterity a summary of the many efforts which had been made to improve the condition of wage earners *throughout the world.* The activities of all agencies were included. Considerable attention was given to employers' welfare programs and the transition which was taking place as such activities passed from the realm of philanthropy to that of legislation. In this 1915 summary Henderson seems to have included almost everything of interest in 1945. There was a chapter on "Conditions of Home Life of Employees," and another on "Neglected and Homeless Youthful Employees." His choice of title and the interpretation which he put upon it was prophetic of the present:

[The title] describes the relation of employer to employed and of both to the city, state, and nation. . . . It intimates that the modern workingman never can be morally content and satisfied as long as his mind, will, and voice count for nothing in the direction of the industry and its product. He may not yet be adequately prepared for that responsibility; his ambition may outrun his education, but he is looking forward to it, and he chafes while he waits.[43]

Also prophetic of labor's attitude during World War II is Carleton Parker's interpretation of the split between the American Federation of Labor and the Industrial Workers of the World and of the many strikes which occurred during World War I:

This temper has not prevented the leaders of the American Federation from giving a traditional American patriotism to the present war. But no publicist of note has dared to analyze the spread of embarrassing strikes throughout the United States during the past two months, the most critical months of our war activities. A reasonable induction from the industrial facts would be that the American labor class is not participating in the kind of patriotic fervor that is in vogue among the upper middle class. It is not sufficient to say that their wage demands occupy their attention. Plus this ancient interest is a set of traditional and complicating forces which condition labor's war attitude. The recital of the war profits in steel, in copper, in foods, in medicines, does not fall on ordinary mind receptors. It falls on a labor class mind with a long cultured background of suspicion.[44]

[42] *Employers' Welfare Work,* U.S. Bureau of Labor Statistics, Bull. no. 123, 1913; *Welfare Work of the Metropolitan Life Insurance Company for its Employees* (New York: Metropolitan Life Insurance Company, 1923); *Report of the Tenth Annual Meeting of the National Civic Federation,* 1909. A considerable number of topics deal with labor conditions and employer-employee relations.

[43] Page xx.

[44] *Op. cit.,* pp. 109–110.

Thus again on the eve of World War I, motivated by immigration, unemployment, and private-agency abuses, public employment services were receiving renewed attention. The problems of yesterday, today, and tomorrow had been pretty thoroughly publicized, every social asset and liability had been discussed, every constructive proposal had been subjected to microscopic scrutiny, and a few "halting beginnings" in the direction of progress had been made. There was considerable reorganization in public employment procedures; new or revised statutes were enacted, for, characteristically, the country still turned to legislation as a panacea for unemployment. A few of the musts which had been brought out in conferences and annual meetings received attention. During 1914 New York City made a third attempt to operate successfully a municipal employment bureau—this time employees were required to qualify under Civil Service. Six states enacted laws instituting employment service. New York State employees were obliged to meet rather specific requirements under Civil Service; departments were provided for; and special services for juveniles were set up. Six bills providing for a national service were introduced during the 1914–1915 session of Congress. No action was taken.

FEDERAL EMPLOYMENT SERVICES DURING WORLD WAR I

Previous pages have sketched the outstanding characteristics of public employment services during the years 1914–1917. Conferences and surveys had revealed new problems and accented the recurrence of the old. Well-publicized reports of such activities had served to increase interest not only in employment services but in social reforms of various kinds and in the best methods of accomplishing them. As a result new organizations had come into being while older agencies had intensified their activities. State and municipal employment offices and their advocates had engaged in stocktaking and in self-evaluation.

In the meantime a series of events had been focusing the attention of federal officials on the necessity for a more effective national employment service and had led to certain initial steps in that direction. The outbreak of the European war, accompanied by the cessation of immigration, had resulted in a static labor supply simultaneously with an increasing demand for labor to man the expanding war industries. Unemployment ceased to be a problem; recruitment of labor became a serious problem. Agricultural labor shifted to war industries, and industrial workers shifted from job to job, upsetting production schedules and increasing the volume of labor turnover. Labor strikes became more frequent. Employment agencies—philanthropic, private-fee, and public—stepped up their services.

Industrial concerns sent their employment managers out into the high-ways and byways to bring back labor recruits. Pirating labor and hoarding labor became common practices. The specialization of recruiting services and the centralization of employment grew more and more important, and it was most fortunate that some initial steps had already been taken by the federal government before the United States declared war on April 6, 1917.

Few of the specialized services which had been established between 1914 and 1916 were retained in their original form after this country entered the war, but a precedent had been established and as new labor problems were revealed new agencies, some closely related to the old, were hurriedly brought into existence.[45] Among the most significant were: [46]

Shipyard and Marine Service. At the request of the United States Shipping Board, April 14, 1917, the branch offices of the unofficially titled United States Employment Service responded promptly and effectively to a call for assistance in securing a list of shipyard workers who were immediately available for employment in shipyards handling government contracts. Stevedores and other marine workers were also mobilized in such fashion that they could be distributed and redistributed as labor shortages and surpluses occurred in different localities.

Agricultural Services. The Farm Service Division was not established until December 13, 1918, but the earlier co-operation with states and interstate agencies was maintained. As the exodus from farms increased, considerable stress was put upon meeting the demand for an adequate supply of rural laborers. Under temporary suspension of the immigration laws Bahamians and Mexicans were imported.[47] They afforded agricultural relief and also provided essential maintenance-of-way workers for the railroads. Two farm-labor replacement services were organized in 1917: the United States Boys' Working Reserve, and the Women's Land Army, which was not a government agency.[48]

Two other war emergency services are within the purview of this book.

[45] These emergency services were financed by a congressional appropriation of $250,000 and by $850,000 from President Wilson's fund for National Security and Defense.

[46] The need to which each of these services was a response is of considerable interest in view of the recurrence of similar needs and the methods whereby they have been met in World War II. *The Annual Report of the Department of Labor* for 1917 and the *Annual Reports of the Director-General of the United States Employment Service* for 1918 and 1919 are the best sources of information.

[47] Authority to import Mexican labor was withdrawn and importers were ordered to return laborers to their own country on March 2, 1921.

[48] Organized in the spring of 1917, incorporated in New York in May, 1918, and affiliated with the United States Employment Service in December, 1918.

One was the *Negro Division,* which was created by the Secretary of Labor, February 2, 1918, but which was not put into operation until May 1, 1918. The combined functions of this Division and of the Division of Negro Economics were to make plans for the mobilization, employment and housing of Negro labor, to enlist the interest of Negroes in the war effort, to foster harmonious interracial relationships, and to investigate and report on Negro economic problems. Needless to state, some very difficult sectional problems were dealt with by this Division.

The *Women in Industry* unit was the forerunner of the Women's Division of the United States Employment Service, which was not created until January 3, 1918. This unit had been organized and carried on by the National League for Women's Service and was taken over by the government on October 1, 1917. Its purposes were to make surveys which would indicate where and to what extent women could replace men and to place women in essential industries. On April 1, 1918, the Women's Collegiate Section of the newly organized Women's Division was created, and in July Elizabeth Kemper Adams, who had been sent to Washington to represent the National Committee of Bureaus of Occupations, was appointed chief of the Section.[49] The armistice interrupted plans to amalgamate all professional placement service for both sexes into a single Professional Section. The Section as operating was abolished on April 15, 1919, but in the estimation of Miss Adams the efforts to co-ordinate women's professional services marked the beginning of a new era in collegiate placement work.

Very little organization on a national basis was undertaken by the Employment Service until after January 3, 1918, when it became an independent unit in the Department of Labor with a legitimate claim to the title United States Employment Service. Between that date and August 5, 1918, several efforts to perfect a working organization were made. Finally a plan was agreed upon which remained in use until after the armistice—three months later. The policies and purposes of the Service were more clearly defined. Five divisions—which absorbed the previously authorized services, sections, and divisions which had been instituted without much reference to relationships or nomenclature—were established: Control, Field Organization, Clearance, Personnel, and Information.[50] Three func-

---

[49] Elizabeth Kemper Adams, *Women Professional Workers* (New York: The Macmillan Co., 1921), pp. 393–406. The author, previously professor of psychology, Smith College, in one of the most scholarly books ever written in the occupational field gives an account of the Collegiate Bureaus of Occupations which, in 1917, organized the National Committee of Bureaus of Occupations.

[50] *Annual Report of the Department of Labor,* 1918, pp. 705–706.

tions which were assigned to the Personnel Division indicate that some of the advocated practices of the present were anticipated, at least in theory, during the hectic war year when the official United States Employment Service was born:

developing plans for and supervising the training of employees of the United States Employment Service; developing a classification of occupations and promoting the use of uniform terminology in the Employment Service offices; developing standard tests and supervising their use in the placement work of the Employment Services.[51]

The development of a training program for employment service personnel had been specifically suggested, in the following words, by the Secretary of Labor in his previous memorandum which dealt with the administration of this war emergency service:

There shall be organized a Division of Training of Personnel, the duty of which shall be to give the necessary training to the rapidly increasing personnel of the service. It is not intended that this division be permanent.[52]

However, until after the armistice the federal service was entirely dependent upon such training activities as were provided by state systems. After the armistice two abortive attempts to carry out the Secretary's directive were made: (1) A training section was established, and two-week conferences which registered about thirty selected representatives were held in conveniently located centers. Lectures, personal interviews, and group discussions covered the major phases of employment problems and procedures, and local representatives were supposed to carry the messages back to their colleagues. (2) A manual for the use of employment offices was drafted.

This writer participated in some of the conferences and in the drafting of the manual. The conferences were short-lived, and no manual, except that prepared by the Junior Division of the Service, was ever published. But some minor professional contributions resulted from these initial federal efforts. State reports indicated that they had been helpful in unifying procedures and in developing an *esprit de corps,* and that the conferences were being continued by a number of states.

The labor problems which have bedeviled the authorities responsible for the production of war essentials during World War II bring to mind the same type of problems, as they harassed officials during World War I,

[51] *Ibid.,* p. 706.
[52] *Annual Report of the United States Emergency Service,* 1918, p. 6.

and recall the numerous agencies [53] which crossed one another's paths as they struggled with "labor relations" twenty-five years ago. All of the problems of the late war period were present on a smaller scale. Hoarding labor, pirating labor, ill-advised labor policies were in vogue on one side; on the other side useless absenteeism, shifting from job to job, slow-downs, union pressure, and strikes. Some governmental policies in the former war, as in the recent, tended to increase rather than to decrease labor conflicts and to delay production. Parker's and Henderson's previously quoted comments seem to bridge the gap between 1917 and 1945 so completely that the framework within which war industries operated during the two war periods might well be interchangeable.

POST-WORLD WAR I SERVICES TO 1933

The decade or more which followed the close of World War I was a stormy period for the United States Employment Service. Perhaps it may best be regarded as a long transition period extending from the armistice to the Wagner-Peyser Act in 1933. Many factors operated against the improvement of the Service while few tended to push forward, or even to retain, the small constructive beginnings which had been made.

The Service had been instituted as, and was regarded as, a war emergency. Its program, formulated but three months before the close of the war, had been designed to recruit manpower for war industries. Overnight the Service faced a reverse demand. War contracts were canceled; [54] war industries closed down or turned their attention to reconversion and to peacetime activities. Thousands of war workers—men, women, and youth—were hunting new jobs. Soldiers, mobilized in camps in this country, were being demobilized and added to the number of job hunters. Servicemen returning from Europe intensified the problem.

Three major steps were taken to cope with the employment situation: (1) Another reorganization of sections took place. Wartime services which had served their purpose were abandoned, and three new units specifically concerned with demobilization were substituted—the Junior Section, the Handicap Section, and the Professional and Special Section. (2) Coordination of placement agencies was undertaken. A conference of public

---

[53] Among them were Training and Dilution Service, War Industries Board, Investigation and Inspection Service, Information and Education Service, Division of Conciliation, and Working Conditions Service.

[54] The efforts of governmental agencies to keep track of the effect of cancellation and to minimize the undesirable influence on the labor market is reported on by the *Annual Report of the Department of Labor*, 1919, p. 286.

and private agencies, all of which were interested in demobilization problems and some of which had operated placement bureaus over a long period of years, was held in Washington on December 2, 1918, and a committee was appointed to draw up a plan to meet the new situation. Under the committee plan, which was adopted, approximately 2,500 cooperative bureaus for soldiers, sailors, marines, and war workers were established. Three hundred of these conducted their work in the offices of the United States Employment Service.[55] (3) In March, 1919, arrangements were made for the distribution of occupational leaflets and for the registration of servicemen at embarkation camps in France. This method of registration was not a success.

The postarmistice financial situation of the Service was almost hopeless. Congress had lost interest and refused appropriations. An appeal to private organizations, states, and municipalities brought generous response in the hope that later on an appropriation of suitable size would be granted. But it was not. The enthusiasm of private contributors was dampened, and most of their support was withdrawn. By the summer of 1919 the remnants of the Service comprised a clearinghouse for information, the Farm Service, which had been in continuous operation, and the newly created Junior Division.

The quality of the available personnel was another postarmistice obstacle to progress. The Employment Service personnel had been composed of three groups: the dollar-a-year men, civil-service personnel transferred from other federal departments for the emergency, and recruits from civilian life, who received their positions either as rewards for some personal or political service or because of their ability to make some specific contribution to the Service. This writer went to Washington the day the armistice was signed to participate in the organization of the Junior Section. The central office personnel was still intact, and she was agreeably surprised to find the salaried members of the staff of uniformly high caliber. There were, as always, degrees of ability and competence, but there was no indication that the Emergency Service had suffered materially from an influx of personal favorites or political appointees. The field personnel was another matter. There were many grossly incompetent workers in employment offices, but the cause was more likely to have been scarcity of suitable functionaries rather than political pressure.

After the armistice the situation changed both in Washington and in the field. The dollar-a-year men went home. The cream of the

[55] *Ibid.*, 1918, p. 44. Placement work for soldiers and sailors was discontinued in the fall of 1919.

"on leave" personnel returned to its former positions. The alert, foot-loose employees read the handwriting on the economic and on the political walls and hastened to secure nongovernmental positions before the labor market was glutted and before a new administration was called upon to pay its political debts. The Director-General, as is the custom with all appointed officials, resigned when the Harding administration took office, March 4, 1921. Between that date and June, 1921, when Francis I. Jones was appointed Director-General,[56] a considerable number of political henchmen had, after being rejected as employees by other departments because they had no civil-service status, been assigned to the Employment Service, which was not under civil service, without reference to its needs or to their ability to contribute to its objectives.

Again, continuous criticism of the public offices forced the Service to waste considerable time and energy in self-defense. All the incompetencies which had been enumerated by the self-surveyors of 1913–1914 were repeated by its enemies during these transition years. Every time an effort was made to secure an enactment establishing a permanent federal service, or to obtain an appropriation, a barrage of defects was laid down and given wide publicity. Unfortunately, public employment services, which had not as yet won the confidence of the public, did nothing to win it during these critical years.

Finally, perhaps fortunately for the ultimate welfare of the Service, two waves of unemployment afflicted the country between 1918 and 1933. One was fairly acute by 1921,[57] and the other, well over the horizon in 1929, was of such prolonged intensity that once more, true to form, unemployment awakened the public interest in employment services. The long period of congressional procrastination came to a close, and the Wagner-Peyser Act of 1933 launched the United States Employment Service on a new period. But once again the Service was regarded as a means to an end rather than as a contributor in its own right to the solution of social-economic problems. This time it was charged with responsibilities in connection with the administration of the Social Security Law.

[56] The series of incidents connected with the appointment of Francis I. Jones, although by no means unique in the annals of governmental affairs, help one to understand the constant charges of incompetence which marked the decade of his incumbency. These incidents have never been made public.

[57] *Report of the President's Conference on Unemployment,* September 26–October 13, 1921, Herbert Hoover, Chairman (Washington, D.C., 1921), p. 178. The importance of community employment agencies was a major topic of discussion, and an Outline of a Permanent Employment System was drawn up and adopted by the Conference on October 11, 1921.

THE UNITED STATES EMPLOYMENT SERVICE, 1933–

The Federal Employment Service created by the Wagner-Peyser Act was the reward of fifteen years of persistent effort on the part of advocates of a national employment service. At last, with the help of another, and this time an inordinately prolonged, economic depression, the dormant interest of both the public and the Congress had been sufficiently aroused and long enough sustained to result in constructive legislative action. A central employment service, of the type which experience dating back to 1890 had indicated to be essential under normal as well as under emergency conditions, was established.

The general principles laid down in this enactment were not particularly new. They had been formulated some years before and were very similar to those contained in the rejected Kenyon-Nolan bill of 1919. The Service was charged with promoting and developing "a national system of employment offices for men, women, and juniors," with maintaining a veterans' service, a farm placement service, and a public employment service for the District of Columbia. A new and far better qualified staff took charge of the central office. W. Frank Persons, experienced in social welfare administration, was appointed Director-General. William H. Stead, who had directed the demonstration employment centers operated in connection with the Minnesota projects, was selected to head the Division of Standards and Research. Programs to be administered by the affiliated states under the supervision and with the financial assistance of the National Service were set up, and minimum standards for facilities, staff, and methods of operation were agreed upon. By 1938 forty-seven states had affiliated with the National Service.

In the meantime, in 1931 and 1932, during the period of watchful waiting while unemployment was increasing, while Congress was hesitating to endorse the Federal-State Service, and while the desirability of testing all phases of employment office procedure was becoming more obvious, three demonstration, experimental, or research projects to study employment office problems were undertaken. The projects varied considerably in scope, but their purposes were quite similar: to determine the legitimate place of public employment offices in our industrial economy, to test procedures and techniques, to improve standards, and to consider the best methods of organization and administration. Financial support was secured from various sources, public and private. Six different foundations subsidized one or more of the experiments.

The Rochester project, instituted in 1931, was conducted by and for the New York State Employment Service.[58] Its reports accented the value of the merit system in securing qualified personnel, stressed the importance of attractive office layouts, the use of modern office equipment and routines, and the introduction of carefully tested employment procedures. The Minnesota experiment, also instituted in 1931, comprised several projects carried on in co-operation with a number of public and private agencies. The Employment Stabilization Research Institute, of the University of Minnesota, was a major co-operator, and many reports covering a wide range of topics were published under its auspices.[59] Research was emphasized. Research in occupations, in individual diagnosis—industrial, psychological, and medical—and research in the use of such tools and techniques as case studies, occupational tests, and interviewing and placement practices. The Philadelphia experiment, instituted in 1932, was very successful in enlisting the co-operation of concerns employing large numbers of workers and in organizing employment work along the lines of major occupational divisions.[60] These three demonstrations, experiments, or researches, considered as a unit, carried forward most of the progressive ideas which had been suggested during, or prior to, World War I. Their findings and recommendations were reported in some detail and made a valuable contribution to dependable literature on methods of organizing and conducting public employment offices.

After the reorganization of the United States Employment Service under the Wagner-Peyser Act the staff of the Federal Service assumed leadership in several phases of employment research. Statistical procedures were studied and standardized.[61] A rather elaborate co-operative occupational-research program, designed to furnish the type of occupational information which had long been regarded as essential to the effective distribution of labor, was put into effect in 1934. This program, which received technical assistance and financial support from a number of local and national agencies, terminated in 1940. During the six years of its existence it accumulated a vast amount of factual information about occupations,

[58] Jess T. Hopkins, *The Emergence of a New Public Employment Service*, 1935, distributed by the New York State Employment Service, 124 East 28th Street, New York City.

[59] A complete list of the reports may be secured from the University of Minnesota Press, Minneapolis, Minnesota.

[60] Gladys L. Palmer, *Thirty Thousand in Search of Work* (State Employment Commission, Department of Labor and Industry, Harrisburg, Pennsylvania, 1933).

[61] The accepted plan was based upon the result of the experiments mentioned and upon the study made by Annabel and Bryce Stewart for the Committee on Governmental Labor Statistics of the American Statistical Association. See Annabel M. Stewart and Bryce M. Stewart, *Statistical Procedures of Public Employment Offices* (New York: Russell Sage Foundation, 1933), pp. 267-293.

which permitted the preparation of national job descriptions based on widespread coverage. These national descriptions pointed the way for the preparation of similar local descriptions, the making of which could be, and in some instances became, a continuous function of state employment services.

Another and more concise type of occupational information was offered in the *Dictionary of Occupational Titles,* which lists 18,000 jobs and defines their duties. Such standardized occupational data provide basic information of great value for placement functionaries, who are responsible for securing and recording facts regarding the requirements of available jobs and regarding the employability of registered applicants. It is also exceedingly valuable for the use of educational and occupational counselors. The development of selection techniques was included in the program. Two types of familiar placement aids received attention—trade questions and work-sample tests, and potentiality predictors. The former were similar in character and purpose to those developed during World War I and are commonly spoken of as proficiency tests; the latter, which are used to forecast probable success in an undertaking, are usually known as aptitude tests. A very complete and illuminating official report of this entire program—its origin, supporters, accomplishments, the utility of its results, and the extent to which it has made a contribution to the knowledge of *job equivalents* or *job families*—has been published [62] and will be found a helpful addition to counseling and placement libraries.

But the United States Employment Service did not have all smooth sailing during the years between 1933 and 1938.[63] In truth, these years were a period of terrible confusion and of many discouragements. Born, as the Service was, during an unemployment crisis, it was logical that its first major task should be concerned with the performance of such employment functions as would further federal efforts to alleviate unemployment. Large numbers of employable unemployed of all ages were seeking to market their services. Professional workers who had attained middle life in a single position, who had never considered the possibility of unemployment or of methods whereby positions might be secured, and who had usually assumed that an efficient worker could always find work now

[62] William H. Stead and W. Earl Masincup, *The Occupational Research Program of the United States Employment Service* (Chicago: Public Administration Service, 1943), also "Ten Years of Occupational Research, 1934–1944," *Occupations,* XXII (1944), 387–446.

[63] The best account of the vicissitudes of the new employment service from 1933 to 1937, and after 1937 when the Social Security Board entered the picture, is found in Atkinson and others, *op. cit.,* pp. 21 ff.

found themselves among the unemployed. Youth who were ready for the labor market at just the wrong time and had been denied even a toe hold in the occupational world were increasing in numbers and were being regarded as a potential social menace. Both groups were growing older. The one was adding the liability of years to the stigma of unemployed; the other was accumulating years of inexperience which counteracted the asset of youth.

Federal alphabetical agencies came into existence to deal with these problems. They strutted their day and were gone. At times they were born and died in such rapid succession that it was, and is, impossible to keep the record straight. Most of these agencies placed some responsibilities on, or called for co-operation from, the United States Employment Service. Therefore, it was constantly forced to make adjustments to new demands or to altered federal programs. There was little or no time to perfect a bona-fide employment service.

The recruitment of labor for public works under the National Industrial Recovery Act claimed the Service's first attention. The National Reemployment Service was created as a special emergency division of the United States Employment Service. It was liberally financed from emergency funds, and for about four years it monopolized the field, expanding in such fashion that frequently it duplicated the work of state employment offices which were operating in the same locality. When the Civil Works Administration was instituted in November, 1933, there was a demand for the rapid expansion of the Reemployment Service. New administrative personnel and new facilities were added. In the spring of 1934 the C.W.A. was demobilized, and an equally rapid curtailment of personnel and facilities took place.

Other agencies were created and took their respective places in the line. Each made some demand upon one or the other of the Services which were now in existence—the United States Employment Service, created by the Wagner-Peyser Act, which was co-operating with state services, and the National Recovery Administration, an emergency division of the National Service, which was operating a second system of national offices quite apart from state services. Permeating the directives which controlled the activities and dictated the practices of most of these depression emergency agencies, were some new and strange philosophies, some of which were beneficial and others detrimental to the progress of an effective public employment service, but all of which promise to have some influence on the future development of private as well as of public employment services.

The Social Security Act, passed by Congress in 1935, is the second major influence affecting the growth and development of the National Employment Service since 1933. Unemployment compensation, a need which had been obvious many years prior to this enactment, which had long been advocated by students of social-economic problems, which had been discussed at every conference on unemployment, which had been recommended in every unemployment survey report, and which had long since been responded to by the leading European countries, had at last received authoritative endorsement. The effective administration of unemployment insurance depends upon certain prerequisites. Local centers where the unemployed may register and file their claims must be provided. The same, or other centers, must act simultaneously as assistants to the unemployed in securing new positions with the least possible loss of time and as protectors of the insurance reserve against payments to malingerers, unemployables, and the occupationally superannuated.

Common sense suggests that a nation-wide chain of permanently established public employment offices is the most feasible co-operative agency for attaining compensation objectives. Nor is this a new idea. For many years each succeeding wave of unemployment had been accompanied by programs for dealing with its evils, and each program had renewed the preceding program's plea for unemployment compensation administered through the medium of public employment offices. The example of European countries had been the object of continuous study, and certain basic assumptions regarding the character and personnel of public offices, were they to assume responsibility for the administration of unemployment compensation, had been agreed upon long before the enactment of the Social Security Law.

Among the generally accepted assumptions were the following: (1) The location and equipment of public employment offices must be such that no unemployed individual need feel hesitant about going to the office to register. (2) Uniform and accurate records interpretable by other offices and useful for statistical analysis of the condition of the labor market must be maintained. (3) The quality of the office personnel must be vastly improved. Technical competence, resulting from training and experience, would not suffice. Knowledge of the sciences which dealt with human motives and behavior was essential to the proper application of the "work test" [64] and to the choice of such interview techniques as, without giving

---

[64] "Work tests" as here used always implied that philanthropic and public relief organizations had "jobs" of some sort available, refusal or acceptance of which tested the applicants' willingness to work. The woodpile was the old standard test.

offence to any, would help to differentiate the malingerer from the legitimate unemployed. In addition, the personality of compensation-employment functionaries must be such that it would appeal to all types of registrants—those of superior intellectual and cultural advantages as well as those of few or no advantages. (4) If public offices were to be used as re-employment centers for all types of workers, the co-operation of employers must be secured to such an extent that all types of vacancies would be reported to the offices.

The program in this country for carrying out the unemployment compensation provisions of the Social Security Act has followed the reasoning and the administrative precedents of other countries.[65] The public employment services have been assigned major responsibilities. The ultimate influence of these new and time- and effort-consuming tasks on the development of employment services has been somewhat disturbing to certain protagonists of such services who regard them as an independent enterprise. They recall how public employment services have always been relegated to subordinate positions; have never been actively supported except when they supplied the necessary string to some other social-economic problem's bow. They recall the number of instances when such services have been created to minimize the effects of economic depressions, and the long years in which they were advocated in order to frustrate the growth of private agencies. Also they recall how, beginning in 1913 and 1914, public agencies have been called upon in fairly rapid succession to reduce unemployment, to recruit labor for World War I industries, to minimize unemployment during the worst economic depression in history, to serve as a handmaid of unemployment compensation, and to act as a recruiting agency for labor for World War II industries. They are fearful of the effect upon the United States Employment Service and its state co-operators if the activities of the Service are permanently consolidated with the activities of the Bureau of Unemployment Compensation.[66]

On the other hand, equally active supporters of public employment service feel that close working relations with the agency administering

[65] An excellent and very complete presentation of the interrelation of the functions of the United States Employment Service and the Bureau of Unemployment Compensation, and of the implications of this relationship for employment services, is found in Atkinson and others, *op. cit.*, pp. 38–132.

[66] The President's Reorganization Plan no. 1, 1939, provided for the transfer of the United States Employment Service and all of its activities from the Department of Labor to the Social Security Board and it was consolidated with the Bureau of Unemployment Compensation to form a new joint Bureau of Employment Security.

unemployment compensation is a distinct advantage. They argue that the assumptions which have been mentioned with reference to any agency designated to carry on compensation activities serve as a challenge to employment offices—a challenge to keep their material equipment up to standard, to improve administrative and technical procedures, to make a greater effort to secure employer co-operation, to raise the quality of personnel so that it will appeal to individuals who heretofore have made no use of public offices, and to institute the type of in-service training which results in more factual occupational information, better understanding of applicants,. and the better use of such information both for counseling and for placement. If employment offices can meet the challenge, a number of continuously cited handicaps to their success should be removed, new and desirable sources of labor supply should be opened, and accurate statistics on the condition of the labor market including specific occupations in which shortage and surplus prevail should automatically be provided.

Before there had been sufficient time to test the effect of consolidation upon either the Employment Service or upon the Bureau of Compensation, the period of unemployment came to an end. Public works and public relief were shelved, and compensation claims materially decreased in number. Public employment offices were once again called upon to concentrate their energies on the recruitment of labor for war industries.

The future of the United States Employment Service, when the country once more resumes its normal occupational pursuits and economic conditions become more stable, is in the lap of the gods. There may, or may not, be danger that the administration of compensation will overshadow the importance of a genuine public employment service. But whatever the future no one at present denies that the enactment of compensation legislation and the consolidation of the two units has posed new problems for public employment offices, imposed new responsibilities, proposed new opportunities for development, and exposed them to new dangers.

SELECTED SUPPLEMENTARY READING

American Association of Public Employment Offices (now International Association of Public Employment Services, q.v.). *Proceedings, First, Second, and Third Annual Meetings, 1913, 1914, 1915.* Washington, D.C., 1916 (U.S. Bureau of Labor Statistics, Bull. no. 192). Many early-day problems which have been continuously troublesome are brought out in these discussions.

American Labor Legislation Review. Published quarterly since 1910 by the American Association for Labor Legislation, 131 East Twenty-third Street, New

York. An invaluable source of information on all types of labor problems. The bibliographies are especially helpful.

Atkinson, Raymond C., Odencrantz, Louise C., Deming, Ben. *Public Employment Service in the United States.* Chicago: Public Administration Service, 1938. Deals with the development of the United States Employment Service in its relation to the Wagner-Peyser Act of 1933 and to the introduction of unemployment compensation.

Beveridge, William Henry. *Unemployment: A Problem of Industry.* New York: Longmans, Green and Co., 1909. Called "the Bible of unemployment." Covers all phases including the reserve of labor, the personal factor, remedies of the past, and suggestions for the future.

Connor, J. E. *Free Public Employment Offices in the United States.* Washington, D.C., 1907 (U.S. Bureau of Labor, Bulletin no. 68).

Emerson, Lynn A. *Employment Services in the Young Men's Christian Association of New York City.* New York: The Young Men's Christian Association, 1931. The national scope of the Y.M.C.A. services is reviewed, and the local procedures are discussed in detail.

Employment Managers' Conferences. *Proceedings.* 1916, 1917, 1918. Washington, D.C., 1916–1919. (U.S. Bureau of Labor Statistics, Bull. nos. 196, 202, 227, 247). These reports are worth reading in the light of the problems with which we have been dealing in World War II. No. 247 suggests a number of employment service projects which have only recently been carried out, e.g., "We project; (a) a dictionary of occupational titles. This is now in course of preparation."

Harrison, Shelby M., and associates. *Public Employment Offices: Their Purpose, Structure, and Methods.* New York: Russell Sage Foundation, 1924. The first, and until the publication of the book by Atkinson, Odencrantz, and Deming, the only standard work on public employment offices. Will remain an important source of information on the history, procedures, functions, and problems of employment service before, during, and immediately following World War I. No other book is a satisfactory substitute in scope, and none of the more limited studies are as impartial and reliable in content.

Herndon, John G., Jr. *Public Employment Offices in the United States.* Washington, D.C., 1918. (U.S. Bureau of Labor Statistics, Bull. no. 241.) The study upon which this report is based was begun in 1915. It investigated all types of public and private employment bureaus including those operated by philanthropy, chambers of commerce, and state universities.

Hodges, Henry G. "Progress of the Public Employment Bureaus," *Annals of the American Academy of Political and Social Science,* LXIX (1917), 91–102. A very inclusive article which deals impartially with the problems of public offices and the relative effectiveness of public and private services.

International Association of Public Employment Services. *Proceedings* of the Annual Conventions. Variously published. Copies may be secured by addressing the General Secretary, Charles L. Hodge, Railroad Retirement Board, Washington, D.C. These proceedings contain very valuable material for those who wish to keep in touch with progress in employment procedures.

Lescohier, Don D. *The Labor Market.* New York: The Macmillan Co., 1919. The broadest in scope, most readable, and most generally available publication on the problems of public employment offices and related topics. Written by one who made a generous contribution to their development.

Moses, Mabelle. "The Regulation of Private Employment Agencies in the United States." *In* Persons, Charles E., Parton, Mabel, and Moses, Mabelle. *Labor Laws and Their Enforcement.* New York: Longmans, Green and Co., 1911.

National Archives, The. *Handbook of Federal World War Agencies and Their Records 1917–1921.* Washington, D.C., 1943. (Publication no. 24.) Gives the names of agencies, the allocation of extant records, "the niches occupied by those agencies in the structure of the Government, and something of their activities and objectives." The whereabouts of the records of most of the employment agencies are stated to be "unknown."

Red Cross Institute for Crippled and Disabled Men. *Employment Opportunities for Handicapped Men.* New York: The Institute, 1918–1919. (Publications, series II, nos. 4, 6, 7, 8, 9.)

Report on Conditions of Women and Child Wage-Earners in the United States. Washington, D.C., 1910. 19 vol. (61st Congress, 2d session, Senate Doc. no. 645.) Volume VI, *The Beginnings of Child Labor Legislation in Certain States— A Comparative Study,* pp. 9–21, contains a good summary of the apprenticeship system and juvenile employment in the early history of this country.

Sargent, Frank. *Statistics of Unemployment and the Work of Employment Offices in the United States.* Washington, D.C., 1912. (U.S. Bureau of Labor, Bull. no. 109.) A very complete and careful analysis of all types of employment services in the United States. A source publication of much value.

Smith, Darrell Hevenor. *The United States Employment Service; Its History, Activities, and Organization.* Baltimore: The Johns Hopkins Press, 1923. (Publications of the Institute for Government Research, no. 28.) A very brief, well-documented book.

Stein, Gertrude R. "Placement Technique in the Employment Work of the Red Cross Institute for Crippled and Disabled Men," *American Journal of Care for Cripples,* VI (1918), 148–157.

Stewart, Annabel M. and Bryce M. *Statistical Procedure of Public Employment Offices.* New York: Russell Sage Foundation, 1933. An analysis of practices in various countries and a plan for standard procedure in the United States made for the Committee on Governmental Labor Statistics of the American Statistical Association.

U.S. Department of Labor, U.S. Employment Service. *Annual Reports of the Director-General.* Washington, D.C., 1918–.

PART TWO

Organization, Administration, and Operation of Occupational Placement Services

CHAPTER III
Preorganization Investigations and Decisions

CHAPTER IV
External Organization and Administration

CHAPTER V
Internal Organization and Administration

CHAPTER VI
Placement Procedures—Securing Applicants

CHAPTER VII
Placement Procedures—Securing Openings

CHAPTER VIII
Placement Procedures—Referring Applicants

CHAPTER III

Preorganization Investigations and Decisions

PART One has offered an overview of the various methods whereby the occupational needs of two parties have been made known to one another throughout the centuries. It has indicated how the humanitarian movement, which owed its origin to the theory of the unity of humanity and the brotherhood of man, affected the thought of the civilized world and found its practical expression in a variety of ways including placement services. It has cited several types of employment media, each designed to respond to a social-economic need and each serving a definite purpose; and it has shown that whenever and wherever similar social-economic needs have arisen automatically, as it were, similar media of exchange have come into being. Some of these media such as self-service exchanges, news ads, and help-wanted signs have had sufficient survival value to remain in continuous use from ancient to modern times; all have been forerunners of the better-organized, better-administered, and more socially conscious media which came into being during the last decade of the nineteenth century and have developed to the point where, very tardily, even our educational systems are according them recognition as a final step in their dual responsibility of preparing youth for entry to occupational life and of affording assistance in occupational adjustments.

Part One has also indicated that during this same period, roughly embraced in the Victorian era, Old-World periodic social upheavals and unemployment crises resulted in emigration to these United States and that, throughout the history of our country, unemployment has traveled hand in hand with economic depressions and has been a major motivating factor in creating sporadic interest in the institution of private, philanthropic, and public placement services. This close relationship between unemployment, economic depressions, and placement services should be kept in mind lest it be forgotten that our presently functioning placement services have not developed as accepted social units in their own right— as a response to the need of a maturing economic society for some adequate method of distributing labor effectively and economically—but that their very existence has been dependent upon other factors, while their prestige has risen or fallen according to the degree of efficiency with which they have met unemployment crises and dealt with war emergencies.

It is hoped that Part One has furnished adequate information from which to cull the permanent values in the placement philosophies and practices of the past and to consider the extent to which present-day philosophies and procedures are worthy of inclusion in current personnel programs and of being regarded as forming an important articulation unit as youth enters upon occupational duties, or as adults pass from one occupational experience to another.

Placement is essentially a practical and a highly technical process. Its basic function has always been the pooling and distributing of workers and work opportunities. The outstanding characteristics of its currently dominant medium—placement services—are salesmen, middlemen, or placement functionaries, and satisfied customers represented by an employing and a working clientele. Placement involves marketing problems in an ever more complex civilization. It has its own peculiarities and problems, which must be given attention as ever better marketing methods are devised and put in operation. Or, to further elaborate, the major responsibility of a modern placement service is the assistance of individuals in analyzing and capitalizing on their experiences and personal assets in terms of successful induction into, and occupational adjustments during, their life work, paralleled by assistance to employers in securing, for their work units, those individuals who are potential contributors to the successful conduct of business projects.

But, as has been noted, secondary functions such as lowering the labor reserve, reducing the volume of unemployment, locating unemployables, administering unemployment insurance, enforcing labor enactments, providing a center for research activities, and the like have frequently denied public and philanthropic services the singleness of purpose which has been so advantageous to fee agencies; everything except the performance of major employment responsibilities has had priorities. This fact has tended to retard the growth of public interest in placement as a necessary social function in its own right. Cycles of interest rather than continuity of interest have prevailed. Inadequacies and deficiencies in the operation of public services have been highlighted every time a national emergency brought them into the limelight and, in spite of the caustic self-criticism of such services, even more caustic criticism from other sources has obtained.

The point has now been reached in the evolution of placement activities in this country where there is, or should be, general agreement regarding the desirability and feasibility of placement services operating under various auspices. Experience has proved that, no matter how many services under other auspices may be in operation, a nation-wide system of public employment offices is essential if this country is to meet its social obligations in the occupational areas of life; that only governmental agencies are in a position to collect and disseminate the type of statistical information useful to placement services as well as to allied agencies concerned with guidance and counseling, with programs for vocational education and for the retraining of technically displaced workers, with released war workers and servicemen, with the placement of the unemployed on public works, and with the economic administration of unemployment reserves. If, on a national basis, we are to effect a better balance between occupational supply and demand and afford centralized leadership in occupational research and in the publication of occupational information, if we are to test and standardize record forms, compile reports, and forecast population and occupational change, a National Employment Service is the only agency to which we may turn.

That fee-charging agencies under private auspices have traveled a thorny path has already been made clear. It has also been made clear that in competition with public services the better type of such agencies has afforded both employer and employee a more effective service—so much more effective that it was futile to attempt to abolish them by statute, regulate them out of existence, or freeze them out by competition. Commercial agencies, operating under governmental license and supervision, are today an acceptable and effective medium for the distribution of labor. Persistent efforts to eliminate such service, coupled with their recognition of their own deficiencies, led long since to their organization in order to protect their right to exist and to co-operate in the improvement of their policies and procedures.

Philanthropic services, which usually antedated both public and commercial agencies, have lost much of their early relief character and are operating more definitely on a business basis, while services in connection with educational institutions, with their unexcelled opportunity for social-economic service, are laggards in determining upon objectives, policies, procedures, and methods of evaluation which relate them definitely to other educational processes.

Part Two presents the types of problems which communities will face, and the types of decisions which they must make, before a placement service should be launched; it considers the external and internal organization of a community service; and it discusses in considerable detail the operational procedures which have been accepted as standard practice. In laying out Part Two only cursory attention has been given to federal, state, or municipal offices, or to commercial agencies as such. The accent has been placed on services organized and operated by communities within limited geographical areas, and general rather than special services have been stressed. Two types of special services, which it was thought might be of interest to those for whom the book has been prepared, have been included in Part Three.

Preorganization investigation and decisions comprise investigations and decisions on such questions as: (1) Is there a need for an initial or an additional placement service? (2) What should be its character—temporary or permanent, general or special, limited profit, free public, commercial, philanthropic, or some combination? (3) For what occupations, industries, and types of applicants are placement facilities lacking or inadequate? (4) What would be the probable applicant registration and what the potential sources of supply? (5) What would be the probable employer demand and from what sources would orders be received? (6) What is the status of the labor market with reference to decentralization? Will the introduction of a new service add another labor reserve and thereby tend to the further disruption of the labor market? Such preliminary investigations involve consideration of the possible and probable values of a service to society, as well as to business concerns and to workers.

Whether the inauguration of a placement service be under consideration as a private commercial venture, as a function of the public-school system, as a community project, or as an enterprise under other auspices, this type of preorganization problem must be given due attention and each question must be answered satisfactorily before individual, institution, or community can afford to advocate and encourage, or profitably institute, a new placement service.

The ultimate decision to establish, or not to establish, will depend upon many things, the influence of each varying with the type of community and its needs, the attitude of its citizens toward innovations in general and toward placement facilities in particular, the purposes the new agency is designed to serve, the estimated expense in relation to potential accomplishments, other competing or co-operating services which may be functioning, and the like.

If a community or an institutional service be under consideration, it should be wanted and should be supported by the citizens on the basis of factual evidence of need and with a planned program for administration, rather than receive endorsement as the resultant of a habit of following, in a random and uncritical fashion, the publicized activities of other communities. Much useless and ill-conceived social machinery, such as clinics of various kinds and guidance and placement services, has found its way into communities and institutions for no better reason than because some other community has found it good. All too often, after initial publicity, interest has lagged, and the service has been allowed to deteriorate or to pass into oblivion.

To be needed and wanted and to be desirable and feasible are very important, but such a combination of factors is not always present. Residential districts may be eager to install a placement service while facts may reveal that the demand for services would be too limited to warrant the expense involved; a one-, two-, or even a three-industry community may find a public placement service superfluous and a private venture unprofitable. A community with several employment centers may be eager to supplement its operating services with another general or specialized service, but, for the social well-being of the community, its citizens may conclude that, while its introduction would be feasible, the social effect of another center would be undesirable.

For thirty years there has been a theory that many communities need a center to which workers and employers may resort for information regarding the status of the labor market and for an exchange of employer-worker needs. Communities are increasingly debating the desirability of putting this theory into practice, and therefore the query often arises: How shall any given community determine whether or not the time is ripe for it to translate theory into practice? The all-inclusive reply is that the time has not come for any community to launch a placement service until it can justify its action by facts, and until it has received citizen endorsement. How then shall justification be determined?

Every locality will face two types of placement problems: those which are more or less common to all placement services and those which are peculiar to the community. A wise community, once its interest in placement is aroused, will undertake a series of investigations which will provide the facts for an intelligent decision. The first investigation will be concerned with a superficial overview of the extent to which similar communities or institutions have introduced such services. The results will furnish a general background of information regarding the objectives of such services, their problems, successes, and failures. A second type of investigation will be concerned with local conditions; will be outlined in detail and much more carefully made. It will seek factual evidence which will serve as a guide in determining whether or not there be a real need and a genuine desire for an initial placement service. If such a procedure seems unnecessary, it is well to recall that Part One cited instances where, because of public pressure, desire for private gain or social-philanthropic prestige, private, philanthropic, and public agencies came into being, not only without the slightest evidence of need, but with abundant evidence that they were superfluous, politically motivated, competitive, and actually disruptive of the labor market.

MAKING PREORGANIZATION INVESTIGATIONS

Community surveys have proved their utility for many purposes and have increased in popularity in recent years to such an extent that instructions for conducting them, with illustrations of a variety of types of surveys, are available from several reliable sources.[1] Among the topics which are usually included when placement services are being considered are statistical analyses of various groups, opinions relative to the desirability of the service, and estimated costs.

Data secured from statistical analyses of population, of employing concerns, and of the occupational distribution of workers are very important. The reports of the United States Census Bureau of the Department of Commerce, the *Directory of Manufacturers* compiled by the United States Department of Labor, and data available from the United States Employment Service, the United States Women's Bureau, the United States Children's Bureau, the United States Bureau of Labor Statistics, and the Vocational Division of the United States Office of Education are the best federal sources of information for such analyses. Private organizations which issue similar material include the United States Chamber of Commerce, the National Industrial Conference Board, the National Association of Manufacturers, the American Management Association, and the National Federation of Business and Professional Women's Clubs. Subdivisions of both federal and private agencies also issue analyses on state and community bases, and a considerable number of occupational surveys which deal with the distribution of special segments of the population, such as college and noncollege youth, mentally and physically handicapped persons, part-time and older workers, veterans, and others, are available.

The local school census and local plant surveys are indispensable sources of community information. Each of the sources mentioned not

---

[1] U.S. Office of Education, *An Outline of Steps in a Community Occupational Survey* (Washington, D.C., 1941), deals with survey methods as applied to communities of varying sizes and includes an annotated bibliography on survey methods.

only should make some contribution to an intelligent decision regarding the desirability of a service, but should point to sources of information with which, after its inauguration, the operating personnel should be able to keep abreast of population trends, shifts in occupational patterns, and the possible occupational influences of large migrations of workers such as have recently been perplexing communities attempting to forecast the postwar conditions of the local and national labor market.[2]

From such statistical analyses communities ascertain (1) their total population and its composition by age, sex, and occupational groups; the number of school and college attendants; the level of educational achievement prior to entry into full-time employment; where and what occupational preparation was made; what percentage of residents are absorbed by local industries; how, where, and what preparations for promotions are made; and the like; (2) how work opportunities are secured and the extent to which the wage-earning population might make use of a placement service; (3) the size, number, and geographical distribution of employing concerns; their methods of recruitment; their sources of supply; their preferred type of employees as to age, sex, education, previous experience, nationality, special training, residence, citizenship, and so forth.

A second type of local investigation comprises interview or questionnaire inquiries into the extent and genuineness of community interest, the prospect for continuous financial and moral support, and the possible and probable use of a service by employer and employee. Interviews with individuals and replies to questionnaires and opinionaires by employers and employees, by representatives of chambers of commerce and labor unions, and by educators and welfare agencies are logical sources of information. The extent to which similar services may have previously been tried and abolished, with the causes of success or failure, also contribute to this phase of essential information.

A third series of inquiries should be concerned with (1) an estimate of the expense involved, (2) the number and type of operating personnel required, (3) the organization procedures which promise to be most effective, and (4) whether or not extracommunity services are available and sufficiently accessible and satisfactory to void the need of a local service.

2 Just as the migration of "Okies" during the depression years of the 1930's caused serious social-economic problems, so the migration of war workers and the return of the servicemen have caused and are doubtless going to contine to cause ever more difficult problems. Communities, depending upon the extent to which war labor decides to stay, go home, or continue to migrate and upon the extent to which war industries decide to reconvert, close up, or engage in some other enterprise, are bound to face new education, housing, relief, and unemployment problems and the necessity of redistributing workers.

Information on such subjects may best be secured from a thorough study of the experiences of other communities. The existence of services in other places as an incentive to any given community to follow their example blindly, without factual data upon which to determine the desirability and feasibility of so doing, and without making the necessary distinction between factors which are common to all placement services and those which are peculiar to local conditions, has been mentioned. This error in judgment is easily avoided if, acting upon the inspiration received from other communities, the suggested investigations into local needs and conditions are made and then, in the light of their results, a more thorough study of other experiments is made. This is a legitimate method of determining probable costs, necessary operating personnel, and methods of organization and administration which promise to be effective, and of selecting for trial such tested tools and procedures as seem worthy of acceptance. Of course, those who are responsible for the selection of projects for investigation must distinguish meticulously between those which have attained functioning and evaluation status and those which are still in the paper-program and the publicity stage.

If the preorganization studies which have been outlined are carefully made and are broad enough in scope, they will furnish all the necessary data, not only to reach a valid conclusion as to the desirability and feasibility of a local placement service, but also to determine the auspices under which it should operate, the type of service—general or specialized, temporary or permanent—which will best meet community needs, and the location which will be most convenient for its anticipated clientele.

INTERPRETING PREORGANIZATION DATA

Collecting data and interpreting data are two different procedures, and before any given community may safely use collected data as criteria for or against the installation of a service, they must be correctly interpreted. Let us take, for example, the criterion of population. Under 50,000 has usually been regarded as too few to warrant the establishment of a public employment office—a decision which may be altered with the development of unemployment compensation. Moreover, population is but one factor, which varies in importance and influence when it is combined with other more or less dominant factors; 50,000 in a one-industry center or in a suburban residential center which absorbs a small portion of its residents in local occupations probably will not need a placement center. The same population in a community comprising several employing concerns may have located its plants in such close proximity to one another that both employer and employee have cultivated a preference for personal application, thus eliminating the desirability of establishing a service. On the other hand, a community with the same population, composed largely of the working class and of many small and diversified industries, widely scattered geographically and requiring a considerable number of seasonal and part-time workers, might need and want some center which would pool the entire labor supply and demand and which would respond promptly to calls for help and for positions, thus saving time, effort, and money for the principals, and at the same time lessening the social waste involved in useless labor reserves wandering about in search of work.

In the larger communities distance is always an important factor in the desirability of middleman service. So is the location of residential districts with reference to manufacturing and business districts, which are frequently widely separated geographically. In such cases workers find it impossible to keep track of vacancies, while they do not often see help-wanted signs or find it easy to co-ordinate transfers of residence with transfers of position. Strangers without occupational contacts coming into a city and all types of residents who fall into the category "difficult-to-place" turn automatically to middlemen for assistance in locating openings.

The findings relative to current methods of securing opportunities and employees are also subject to misinterpretation. It may seem perfectly logical to assume that wherever news ads, help-wanted signs, recommendations of friends, and applications at the gate have predominated, a pooling center for the distribution of labor will be a welcome community asset. But why is it not just as logical to assume that neither employing concerns nor workers will care to discard long-used and satisfactory contact methods for the new and the untried?

Another opportunity for misinterpretation of data lies in the danger of confusing community need for occupational information and occupational counseling with community need for a placement service. In residential districts where population analyses reveal that a considerable percentage of the public-school pupils go on to college or commute to near-by cities for vocational training or as wage earners, and adult workers are permanently employed or have other satisfactory facilities for re-employment, it will usually be found that a good public-school or community counseling service, co-operating with dependable placement services or with a business clientele in near-by occupational centers, will be more satisfactory than to attempt a placement service with one of its indispensable customers inaccessible for daily contact.

Deciding upon the Need for a Service

The application of whatever criteria may be set up for determining upon need must, if the establishment of a placement service is to be justified, result in affirmative replies to the following questions: Will it facilitate the securing of positions? Will it serve to segregate the unemployables from the unemployed? Will it benefit employing concerns by a preliminary sifting of applicants and by referring only those who seem to be potentially useful to such concerns? Will it render a social-economic service by pooling the labor supply and demand, thus lowering the labor reserves and maintaining a better balanced labor market? Are community desire for a service and the social desirability of a service in harmony, and is the need for a service reinforced by the feasibility of a service?

When one or more placement services are already in operation and there is reason to assume that another service—either general or special—is needed, preorganization investigations will parallel those which are prerequisite to the establishment of an initial service, but frequently they will be confined to a single segment of a city rather than cover the entire community. Again statistics will reveal the age, sex, and occupational groups which are in need of service and the type of service best adapted to their needs. They should also supply the information necessary to determine what occupational or other limitations should be imposed upon applicants and employers, the geographical boundaries within which the new service should operate, and its relation to other placement units serving both within and without the same geographical limits. Charts showing the location of employing concerns, residence sections, and placement facilities are very helpful tools in making decisions.

Supplementary or additional placement units are desirable under a number of conditions. Few of the larger cities, as time has passed, have escaped the demand for the expansion of general services or for the introduction of special services. It may be a service for an occupational group in the unskilled or skilled labor category, for a professional group, for handicapped persons, for part-time or older workers, for junior and inexperienced workers, or for some other group. For many years there was a growing feeling that the needs of such differentiated groups could best be met by subdivisions of general services. More recently questions have arisen as to whether or not the additional effectiveness resulting from such segregation has not reached the point of diminishing returns and is not tending to deny both employers and applicants certain other benefits such as those inherent in substitutions.

If preliminary investigations warrant the assumption that the time is ripe to institute either an initial or an additional community service, the committee in charge of the project will turn its attention to problems of organization and administration.

CHAPTER IV

External Organization and Administration

SINCE all types of personnel services under philanthropic and educational auspices have acquired an unenviable reputation for ineffectiveness in organization and administration, and since this book is designed to be helpful primarily to those interested in placement services operated by such agencies, attention is called to sources from which committees and individuals charged with either the external or internal aspects of organization and administration may familiarize themselves with the fundamental principles which are applicable alike to any business, industrial, educational, community, or philanthropic agency and therefore are worthy of study prior to the launching of any placement service.

The employment bureaus of business and industry are excellent sources of information on the organization and administration of the placement phase of personnel services, and to them this writer has habitually turned for many suggestions and illustrations which could be translated and applied to institutional services.[1] Public employment officials have given considerable attention to this matter, and, in spite of the difference in purposes, policies, and geographical scope of federal-state or community service, those who are desirous of securing helpful and up-to-date suggestions may profitably devote time to studying two or three of the books on public services which have been mentioned. Also worthy of study are several recent reports of the proceedings of the International Association of Public Employment Services.[2]

Part Five of *Guidance and Personnel Services in Education,* which was written after several months of detailed study of the fundamental principles of organization and their universal applicability, applied such principles to guidance and personnel services in educational institutions. The following discussion on the placement phase of personnel service follows, in the main, the rather elaborate procedures outlined in that volume.

[1] Paul S. Achilles, "Trends in Employment Procedures," *Personnel,* XIX (Jan., 1943), 609–617. See also "A Model Personnel Office," *ibid.,* 637–638.

[2] For reports of two panel discussions, one dealing with the "Organization of Large Offices" and the other with the "Organization of Small Offices," see *Proceedings of the Twenty-eighth Annual Conference,* 1940, pp. 19–36.

FUNDAMENTAL PRINCIPLES OF ORGANIZATION APPLICABLE TO PLACEMENT SERVICES

Among the outstanding principles which should be considered in connection with the organization of placement services are the following:

(1) The type of organization chosen should be in harmony with the total community or institutional setup. The preorganization investigation suggested in Chapter III will usually have been conducted and interpreted by a committee or by an individual, appointed by a public official or by a local agency or agencies for that purpose, and the same or another individual or committee may be designated to carry forward the external, institutional, or community phase of organization.

(2) The principles of organization and the principles of placement should be harmonized before the service is installed, and the functions to be performed should be determined on some thought-through basis.

(3) Placement services, institutional, community, or other, are a direct responsibility of the management of the agency under whose auspices the service is installed. It makes no difference whether management be represented by a superintendent of schools, a college president, a mayor or city manager, or other official, whether by an individual or by a group of individuals, this is a universally accepted principle and must be observed.

(4) The placement objectives and policies should be in harmony with the general objectives and policies of the agency which is to operate the service, and it should be so organized and administered that it will facilitate the realization of these general objectives.

(5) The director or superintendent of the service should be chosen because of demonstrated or potential ability to conduct it in harmony with the objectives and policies laid down by the organizing authorities and within the allotted budget. A well-informed board will attempt to secure as director one who possesses at least several of the following qualifications: (a) good executive ability and knowledge of how and when to delegate authority, (b) a practical working knowledge of economics, sociology, and psychology, (c) a practical understanding of the economic problems of management, of the objectives of labor unions, and of the attitudes and problems of workers, (d) ability to analyze and interpret labor laws, union regulations, and job specifications, and to use labor inspectors without assuming the functions of one, (e) sales ability—including the ability to express himself clearly and concisely orally and in writing, (f) tact and judgment essential to avoid the appearance of partisanship and the participation in controversial discussions which would react unfavorably on

the effectiveness of the service, and (g) ability to make such changes in placement procedures as have been indicated by wartime experience and as are essential during the demobilization and remobilization of service-men and war workers.

DIVISION OF ORGANIZATIONAL RESPONSIBILITIES

When these principles are applied to a placement service, it should be noted that responsibilities for the organization and administration of placement services usually fall into three categories: (1) those which must be assumed by the policy-making authorities, mainly external responsi-bilities; (2) those which should be shared jointly by the policy-making board and the director; and (3) those which must be delegated to the director—mainly internal responsibilities. There will, of necessity, be con-siderable overlapping in these categories varying from community to community, from institution to institution, and with the characteristics of the individuals who are available for the assumption of responsibilities.

Preorganization investigations will have supplied much of the data use-ful to a committee, board, or individual in arriving at decisions which will help in the distribution of responsibilities and will keep both the external and the internal aspects of the service in line with the funda-mental principles of organization.

The responsibilities of the policy-making board will include (1) deter-mination of the meaning of placement and of the objectives of the service, the auspices under which it should be conducted, and the desirability of boards—either administrative or advisory; (2) the type of service—general or special, free, mutual, limited-profit or private-fee; (3) the type of appli-cant to be registered and of employing concerns to be served; (4) policies with reference to co-operating and competing agencies and to integration with educational and vocational guidance agencies, business personnel de-partments, and other community activities; (5) policies as to clearance of information, applicants, and orders; (6) policies regarding the selection and qualification of operational personnel; and (7) decision as to the in-clusion of research activities, counseling, testing, employment supervision, and evaluation of results among the functions of the service. The selection of the geographical and building location and methods of raising what-ever budget may be determined upon are always functions of the policy-making board.

Obviously a policy-determining board composed of volunteers or of representatives of various organizations will be qualified only in the most general way to make valid decisions on some of the items which have been allocated to its domain. Hence it is quite customary to select the directors as soon as possible after the decision to organize, thereby giving the board the benefit of professional advice in meeting its responsibilities. The amount of such assistance needed, and wanted, will depend somewhat upon the type of professional experience supplied by the board members themselves.

Shared responsibilities might be concerned with such items as (1) location—geographical, building, and intrabuilding, all of which have an important budget and marketing implication; (2) type of organization—general or special, functional or departmental, and, if there be more than one office under the same auspices, centralized or decentralized; (3) type of service—temporary or permanent, groups of applicants to be served and employing concerns from whom orders should be received; (4) number, qualifications, and salary of subordinate personnel; (5) publicity—preliminary and continuous, which might include approved methods of recruiting applicants and of soliciting orders; (6) laws and ordinances which control the institution and the operation of placement services; (7) allocation of funds to the various departments, functions, and personnel; and (8) methods of appraising or evaluating the effectiveness of the service and the utilization of the findings for the revision of policies and procedures and for changes in personnel. There are also some controversial items which perplex boards and directors upon which joint decisions might be desirable. They include (1) referral policy during strikes, (2) personal items which should be called for on application blanks and on employees' orders, (3) spot placements, (4) refusals to register unemployables, delinquents, habitual quits or failures, and the like, or to refer applicants to substandard employment.

The responsibilities of the director, whose all-inclusive duty will be the execution of the policies and the supervision of the activities determined upon by the board, will be discussed in detail in connection with the internal organization of the service.

When the administrative authorities turn to their survey data for guidance in arriving at decisions on most of these duties, whether differentiated or shared, they will find them so closely interrelated that they will have difficulty in determining what should have priority of attention. For the immediate purpose the meaning and scope of placement has been given precedence. It is followed by type of service, auspices, administrative control, location, budget, operating personnel, general policies, and evaluation of results.

THE MEANING AND SCOPE OF PLACEMENT

There are many definitions of placement, and a considerable variety of functions has, at different times and in different situations, been allocated to placement services. Which definition shall the organizers choose? Is placement merely bringing unemployed workers and unfilled jobs together, or is it, as this writer decided years ago, the alpha and the omega of an educational system which includes vocational guidance? Is a placement service merely a center for the distribution of labor? Is it the drawing card of a commercial counseling program? Or is it an important aspect of a unified personnel service correlated at every stage and at every educational level with community services and occupational opportunities? Does it perform the single function of job placement, or, through the performance of this primary function, does it attain the broader objectives included under either incidental or planned research—research which reveals shifts in occupational patterns, in probable demands on future workers, and in temporary and permanent requirements of employing concerns, and which indicates desirable shifts in educational curricula or the necessity of instituting new ones?

TYPE OF SERVICE

After the meaning and scope of placement have been determined, the type of service which will best meet the needs of the community, institution, or agency may be taken up and should be approached from several angles. Shall it be a *general* service housed in one office and registering all types of applicants and all types of orders, or have the investigations revealed that a *special* service for some group of applicants is the pressing need? Communities which are instituting their first placement service or small communities which are planning to meet the needs of a number of concerns calling for workers with a considerable variety of qualifications will probably decide in favor of the general service. Such a service will pool the labor supply and demand, thereby making a more direct contribution to the organization of the labor market, reducing the labor reserve and utilizing it to better advantage, facilitating interoccupational mobility, and encouraging referral substitutions as between ages and sexes, physically normal and physically handicapped, and within job families. In arriving at a decision it is well to note that, after years of advocacy of specialization, consideration of the practical results of oversegregation of applicants is now causing a trend in the opposite direction.

This is a much more important matter for the social effectiveness of labor distribution than lay boards are likely to realize, and therefore it is worthy of emphasis. Twenty-five years ago this writer, then director of the Junior Division of the United States Employment Service but often placed in situations which permitted her to observe the practical workings of segregation of men, women, and juniors, noted that general services frequently permitted very satisfactory substitute referrals, whereas departmentalized services, if unable to fill the order, were prone to lose it, or to create interdepartmental animosities and jealousies if they attempted to fill it through substitution. Women and juniors were usually the worst sufferers, although sex and age segregation may work to the advantage, or to the disadvantage, of any differentiated group except such as are segregated on certain occupational levels and for whom age and sex requirements are so definitely fixed that substitutions are not possible. There is much difference of opinion on this subject and much room for research.

If a general service be in operation and the time seems ripe for the expansion of placement facilities, criteria must be set up to aid in determining which possible method of expansion will be most responsive to community needs. Statistical reports of the services already in operation should indicate why and where additional service is desirable. Perhaps growth of population, enlargement of city boundaries, or increase in number of industries calling for the same type of workers may lead to the establishment of a second general office located in the new industrial section. On the other hand, analysis of placement statistics may point to the need of a breakdown in types of applicants and occupations leading to departments for men, women, and juniors; to specialization for common labor on a sex basis or for white-collar workers on an occupational but not on an age or sex basis; and the like. As a generalization, neither departmentalization nor specialization are warranted until some given characteristic has become common to enough applicants to differentiate their needs from those of other applicants, and it should be the *dominant* variation of a group that is the deciding factor, e.g., the occupation of teaching would be a dominant factor and would supersede division by sex; stenographic ability would supersede both age and sex, and possibly physical handicaps. It is on the basis of dominant variations that some of us, especially since the raising of the age for entry into occupational life, have challenged age as the determining variant for registration in junior or in adult services.[3]

If segmentation of a general service be determined upon, then, follow-

3 Since junior services have received so much attention in recent years and are so important at all times, a later chapter has been reserved for this subject.

ing the findings of surveys, the details of departmentalization or special-ization will be worked out. All departments may be housed in one office under one roof, or in different buildings and in different localities. Among the many factors which might be dominant are sex, age, occupation, reli-gion, nationality, citizenship status, job status (i.e., whether full-time or part-time, seasonal or regular), educational status, and physical or mental condition. Many special or limited-service bureaus are sponsored by edu-cational institutions, philanthropic agencies, labor unions, clubs, etc. Churches and other religious organizations and labor unions may oper-ate services for their own members, colleges for their students and alumni; public and private services are instituted to serve the physically and men-tally handicapped, war veterans, older persons, and other groups.

Other types of service which demand preliminary consideration deal with methods of support and methods of control. How shall the service be supported financially and how shall the budget be raised? The early history of placement services in these United States has revealed general approval of free public services and marked disapproval of fee-charging agencies. But it has also revealed that public offices sometimes charged nominal fees,[4] that the labor unions which sponsored the public San Fran-cisco office (1904) endorsed a small fee; that the National Employment Exchange (1909) provided for fees on a limited-profit basis, and that Y.M.C.A.'s and other agencies with similar objectives have made reason-able charges. Mutual bureaus, of which the Employees' Mutual Benefit of Des Moines is a good post-World War I example, are another type of service in which cost is a control factor. Some of these types have charged employers; some have charged employees; and some, under varying con-ditions, have charged both. Some experienced placement workers feel that college and university services which assume the total expense of place-ment, especially repeat placements, are not only too generous with endow-ment or public funds but are encouraging applicants to depend upon service activity rather than on self activity in securing positions. They sug-gest a change to some partial-payment basis.

Quite a number of experiments, some successful and others unsuccess-ful, are on record for the assistance of boards or committees which must

[4] By 1918 the municipal office of Boise City, operating under the law of 1915 which provided for a fee of one dollar by any municipal office for each position secured for an applicant residing without the city limits and fifty cents for each position secured for city residents, was the only public service which charged a fee. Sometimes the fee was not collected, and sometimes, with the consent of the applicant, the employer deducted it from wage payments (U.S. Bureau of Labor Statistics, Bull. no. 241, [1918] p. 31).

determine whether a service shall be public-free, limited-profit, private-fee, private-free, or mutual. Each is a possibility, and any might prove to be the wisest choice under favorable conditions.

Whenever more than one office is operated under the same auspices, the question of administrative control must be met. What type of control shall be chosen—centralized or decentralized? Shall a single administrative board control the policies of all offices, with local administrators responsible for the execution of such policies in each office, or shall each office set up its own policies and carry them into execution? Excessive centralized control, especially if it be federal, is just now under a cloud, and there is often a justifiable fear that if a minimum of control be accepted a maximum of control will soon be assumed. Be that as it may, centralized control, which is concerned with certain standardized practices in connection with publicity, costs, selection of personnel, uniform records, clearance, research, and the like, accompanied by decentralized execution is considered a better type of organization than is complete decentralization of all responsibilities—so much better that centralized control and decentralized execution has been generally accepted as a fundamental principle of organization. Material on the value of this type of service is too abundant and too easily accessible to warrant further discussion.

Some authorities consider the decision as to whether the service shall be operated on a functional or on a departmental basis as another aspect of the type of service. It seems, however, to be more logically a type of internal organization and to be a major responsibility of the director of the service in each office. Departmentalization and the bases on which it may be made have been mentioned; functionalization, which is usually confined to large offices, is based on the breakdown of the placement process, each procedure—order taking, referral, etc.—being allocated to a different person. Under departmental organization the same person in each department performs all of the required functions.

THE OVER-ALL MANAGEMENT

The auspices or over-all management of the service under which it should be established and which should be charged with continuous oversight of the policies and operational effectiveness is another subject requiring preorganization attention—one which is too closely related to determination on location, policies, personnel, and procedures to permit its consideration without reference to these other topics. There are several possibilities. It may be an entirely independent service under a board of directors or an individual. A large part of the private, fee-charging, club, church, philanthropic, and fraternal agencies fall into this group. Their directors determine policies and select locations in harmony with their objectives, and so long as their practices and procedures conform to statutory and regulatory enactments they operate without interference.

It may be organized under governmental auspices—federal, state, or municipal, or under some combination of such auspices. In such cases the organizers will be obliged to conform to certain rules and regulations with reference to advisory boards or councils, selection and retention of personnel, registration of all applicants who are legally eligible for employment, use of certain record forms, compilation of certain reports, and the like. Application to the proper state or federal authorities will bring complete information, and conformity will be rewarded by financial and leadership assistance in some form—the franking privilege, use of printed forms, receipt of research reports in the shape of manuals of procedure, occupational information, and improved methods of interviewing and analyzing applicant qualifications. In recent years both federal and state governments have carried on extensive researches and experiments the reports of which are affording helpful information for all types of placement services. But there is, and always has been, some objection to, and considerable legitimate criticism of, the workings of the type of advisory councils which are included among requirements for co-operators.

A third possibility is organization under the auspices of some agency which is already engaged in other educational, religious, social, or economic activities. Under such circumstances policies, functions, and procedures must be determined within the framework of the parent organization, and the placement service must be allocated to its proper place in the superstructure of the organization. This is an important matter when instituting placement services in connection with a business concern, a Y.M.C.A., a welfare council, a college or university, or a public-school system. It has been discussed in some detail under the principles of organization in *Guidance and Personnel Services in Education* and has been ably presented from the businessman's point of view by Howard M. Dirks.[5]

Since advisory councils are common and at times very important factors in both institutional and governmental services, a few comments on their advantages and disadvantages may be helpful. The first point to

[5] "Wartime Organization of the Personnel Department," *Personnel Organization and Professional Development* (Personnel Series, no. 74; New York: American Management Association, 1943), pp. 20–31.

remember is that administrative councils and advisory councils are entirely different as to character and functions. An administrative council, board, committee, or officer may be responsible for the entire oversight of the service. Quite often, especially in small agencies, administrative, executive, and supervisory responsibilities will not be sharply differentiated, and the administrative authorities will perform all the functions involved in the formulation of policies and the evaluation of the effectiveness of the service, suggest changes in policies and practices, deal with and educate advisory boards, control publicity, advocate or discourage legislation, and the like. On the other hand, an advisory board does not make decisions on either policies or practices; it performs influence functions only; but if its composite knowledge and wisdom are sufficient, it may be of considerable value in guiding the judgment of administrators toward sound decisions and toward wiser formulation of policies.[6]

In view of the singleness of their purpose and the difficulty of securing satisfactory members and of confining them to the exercise of their legitimate prerogatives and functions, students of the practicability of such committees have long since challenged their desirability. Five kinds of people have been found to "get on" such committees: (1) those who are popular but have no knowledge or experience from which to make any advisory contribution; (2) those who for various reasons manage to force themselves on; (3) those who represent organizations which are invited to select a member because of their moral or financial support, or for propaganda purposes; (4) those who have not been able to secure attention in any other field; and (5) those who can and will help. This classification tells the whole story.

However, in spite of the fact that advisory councils have been variously characterized as of doubtful value, a nuisance, a handicap, and rarely an unmixed blessing, they are at times a necessary evil; and those who are not at liberty to reject them should learn how to make the best use of them. Therefore it behooves the organizing authorities to anticipate their possible advantages and disadvantages and to make the utmost effort to see that members are appointed with care. Minimum specifications for membership should be a genuine interest in and some knowledge of placement problems, also freedom from "complexes" and a desire to dictate regarding personnel or the referral of applicants, or to place personal

[6] Some authorities do not distinguish very clearly, if at all, between administrative, executive, and supervisory functions, and it is not always possible to do so in practice no matter how clear the distinction may be theoretically. See Leonard D. White, *Government Career Service* (Studies in Public Administration, vol. III; Chicago: University of Chicago Press, 1935).

favorites at the expense of other applicants and of employers. If all factions are equitably represented and a worth-while committee secured, the operating authorities may receive the benefit of considerable special knowledge and experience, of assistance in securing press support, and of expert salesmanship in securing the co-operation of community agencies.[7]

THE SELECTION OF A LOCATION

The location of a placement service is a business proposition and should be determined upon the same basis as is the location of any other retail business—a store, garage, bakery, or restaurant—for there is bound to be a definite relation between the site selected and the success of the service. Therefore, in the light of the objectives and character of the business the best geographical location will be the one which permits the service to be self-advertising to the largest possible number of customers, and to catch both types of customers as they pursue their daily routine—en route to trains, to work, to restaurants, to make business contacts, and to keep appointments of various kinds.

Individuals and committees who are called upon to select a site for a first service or either to expand or contract the geographical radius of services already in existence may receive suggestions from three sources: (1) the general rules for the selection of business sites which are said to operate with considerable mathematical certainty and are well known even to youth of tender years who "clock" purchasable corners for the establishment of newspaper or peanut stands or for other sales purposes; [8] (2) the data secured from preliminary investigations (these findings, which reveal the need for a service and the preferable type, are bound to include data which point to one or more desirable locations); and (3) supplementary investigations concerned with such items as accessibility to labor supply, employer demand, and transportation facilities, and rentals in relation to the total budget and the portion which may legitimately be paid

[7] Atkinson and others, "Advisory Councils," in *Public Employment Service*, pp. 144–151, is an excellent treatment of the problems involving appointing and using advisory councils in connection with public employment offices.

[8] The acumen of young newsboys in selecting locations is discussed in *Newsboy Service* (Yonkers, N.Y.: World Book Co., 1917), which reported on a 1915–1916 research by the present writer.

At one time the writer witnessed an interesting juvenile-court case in which a fourteen-year-old boy had hung around the same corner for so long that the police had insisted upon an explanation. The boy refused to talk and was brought into court where he again refused to talk except to the judge and in private. He had been "clocking" each of the four corners to determine the desirability of a "stand" on one of them, and he did "not propose to let the copper or anyone else steal my information."

for location, to the type of customer to be served, and to the reputation and efficiency of the service.

If choice must be made between a more desirable location and a less satisfactory interview, which shall it be? Will customers patronize the most efficient service irrespective of location? If free space is available in an undesirable location, under what conditions is it wise to accept? What elements in a location tend to attract loafers and cause the service to become a hangout? What tend to make it a popular meeting place for other than employment purposes? Each point mentioned and many others are worthy of consideration, and care must be taken that a desirable location is not overstressed to such an extent that more important considerations are neglected.

The selection of a building and of the location within the building is just as important as is geographical location. Public services frequently have no choice: space in some public building is available, and taxpayers expect the service to be operated as cheaply as possible. Philanthropic, college, and public-school services often suffer more or less from similar handicaps. Private agencies only are free to recognize and act on the knowledge that keen and skillful competition requires the selection of attractive offices in attractive and well-kept buildings. When choice is possible, basements are not likely to be selected, while decision as to street level, ground floors, or upper floors will depend on a number of variable factors such as type and volume of applicants and stairway or elevator service. The physical condition of the building, safety and sanitary provisions, heating, lighting, ventilation, suitable entrances and exits, and the convenience of internal arrangements are all of importance. The size and adaptability of space should be such that overcrowding will be avoided and the required activities carried on with ease.

THE BUDGET

The budget must be determined upon fairly early in organization procedures since so many other essential decisions are dependent upon financial allotments. But the history of placement services in these United States reveals that this obviously important responsibility has all too often been ignored. Not only have educational and philanthropic services been established without any financial outlay or any specific budget provisions, but legislative enactments authorizing public services have made no provision whatever for financial support. Space, light, heat, and furniture (often discarded by some other agency or by an individual) have been donated, and the service has been manned by volunteers or by personnel assigned from other payrolls. *When the per capita cost is reduced to zero, the effectiveness of the service is found to be commensurate with the cost.*

Such practices should be entirely outdated by now. The objectives of a service, its inclusiveness of functions, its probable volume of business, the number and qualifications of its operating personnel, and all other expenses should be estimated for the first year and revised thereafter on the basis of facts. Few services have published their cost analyses, and there is not much helpful data available for novices. Moreover, certain difficulties are inherent in the use of statistical analyses of the costs of other placement services as a guide to budget making in new services. What has been included in costs? To what extent have shared, or marginal, personnel functions been charged against placement? What guidance value have statistical analyses when no single basis of analysis is in general use? In one analysis total costs are related to the number of workers registered, in another to the number of referrals, and in a third to verified placements.

On the other hand, some data are available which, if regarded as estimates only and if interpreted for local use with full realization of the fact that the usual analyses of unit costs make no allowance for such variations as type of placements, kind of applicants, functions included, time consumed in the performance of each of the various functions, stability or instability of workers, number of employing concerns, and the like, may be useful in indicating the range of costs and variations due to different practices.

Soon after their institution public employment services began to analyze costs—on a variety of bases which were not always stated. As reported over the years, unit costs have ranged from eight cents to $6.68. Leiserson, in 1914, made a unit cost comparison, on the basis of verified placements, for the first and second years of the Milwaukee office.[9] During the first year, 1912, they were sixty cents; during the second year the volume of business increased forty per cent and costs were reduced to less than fifty cents. He attributed second-year progress to improvement in personnel and procedures. In 1937 the manager of the Cincinnati office of the Ohio State Employment Service reported: "It costs us $6.68 to put a person to work."[10] The most inclusive recent and easily available material on unit costs is found in the section on unit costs in *Public Employment Service in the United States.*[11] It is based on statistics for 1936–1937 for the 48

[9] *American Labor Legislation Review,* IV (1914), 324.
[10] *Proceedings of the Twenty-fifth Annual Convention of the International Association of Public Employment Services* (U.S. Department of Labor, Division of Labor Standards, Bull. no. 14, 1937), p. 105.
[11] Atkinson and others, pp. 208–214.

states, and combines those of state employment services with those of the National Reemployment Service. The average expenditure for the United States per gainful worker [12] was found to be forty-two cents, with costs per placement $4.23; the highest state cost per placement was $13.35 and the lowest $2.18. An analysis of the statistics led to the conclusion that the character of the service rendered, the number of placements per 100 workers, the density of population, and the type of placement were among the causes of cost discrepancies.

Comparisons of per capita costs to taxpayers for placements by public agencies with the cost to individuals for placement by commercial agencies and with per capita hiring costs to business concerns are interesting but have limited value and must be used with extreme caution. Commercial agency costs are, and should be, higher. As a rule they deal with a higher type of clientele, and therefore their contact men must be better educated, better informed, and higher salaried. Their rental, telephone, and telegraph costs will be higher; license fees are usually imposed; and they must qualify as profitable business enterprises or close their doors. On the other hand, their per capita placement costs may be lowered by the fact that they are not obliged to register any applicant whom they do not feel that they can place with both credit and profit, whereas the public agencies must register all who apply. Private agencies do not usually broadcast their operating costs; therefore any cost comparisons must be based on the cost to the individual placed, which is usually on a percentage-of-salary basis and varies with the type of position and salary received. Teachers' agencies rather generally charge 5 per cent of the first year's salary; agencies placing skilled, semiskilled, and commercial workers usually have a fee range of 10 per cent up to 60 per cent of the first month's salary.

A recent study of the cost of hiring by Chicago concerns reported in *Chicago Commerce*, June, 1943, gives $27.16 as the average cost when the company has to hire a replacement. Cost includes advertising, interviewing, medical examinations, personnel records, and induction.

A few cost statistics which are based on a broader interpretation of placement or which deal with the performance of functions which are marginal to placement may have budget suggestions for those who desire to approach the subject from a broader viewpoint than do either public or commercial agencies. One of the earliest efforts to distinguish between cost per placement which included counseling service and placement which did not was reported by the national headquarters of the United

[12] Number of workers who are potential users of the service, i.e., total number of gainful workers exclusive of those who are regularly self-employed.

Y.M.C.A. Schools in New York City, which, after World War I, were charged with the expenditure of a fund donated for the benefit of service-men. Guided by the previous experience of the organization, the disbursers of the fund allowed $5.00 for each veteran when counseling was included in placement and $3.00 for each who received placement service only. This was an estimated differential.

Two more recent studies of costs are available. One is found in *Men, Women, and Jobs,*[13] which stresses job placement; the other was reported on by the Adjustment Service of New York City,[14] which did no placement work but gave unit costs on practically every other phase of personnel service. Both reports contain rather detailed statistical analyses of cost items, including the time required for the performance of each function. The Minnesota statistics were reported on two bases: (1) The average cost per placement over a two-year period figured on the volume of placement without reference to the type of position or to the duration of employment was found to be $3.29. (2) The average cost per *transaction* was fifty-eight cents—applications, employers' orders, referrals, and placement were considered as basic transactions, and the overhead cost of expanding the service in order to conduct the study was included. When tests were included the expenditure for technical service and test supplies was, with an average of 4 tests in 1 hour and 45 minutes for women and 5 tests in 2 hours and 15 minutes for men, $2.95 per capita.

The Adjustment Service costs were also reported on two bases: (1) The total cost per client registered during the entire period of operation, February 1, 1933, to May 31, 1944, was $14.66. Cost included time spent in establishing the Service, selecting the personnel, making contacts with other community agencies, working out procedures, and preparing material for counselor use. (2) The total cost per client registered during January, 1934, when much of the initial overhead could be eliminated, was $7.97, of which $6.64 was allocated to professional services and $1.33 to supplies and routine services.[15] The time consumed in performing professional services was 8.26 hours, broken down as follows: administrators .22, technicians including doctors, psychologists, and statisticians .44, supervisors .42, counselors and information specialists 2.99, examiners 1.85, stenographers .81, clerks, scorers, and office boys 1.53.

---

[13] Donald G. Paterson and others (Minneapolis: University of Minnesota Press, 1936).

[14] The Adjustment Service of New York City, *Costs* (New York: American Association for Adult Education, 1935).

[15] Testing supplies and equipment, 14 cents; mechanical scoring of tests, 26 cents; clearance through Social Exchange, 10 cents; rent, maintenance, office supplies, telephone, etc., 83 cents.

THE EVALUATION OF A PLACEMENT SERVICE

The evaluation of the accomplishments of a placement service is an administrative responsibility—logically the final step which closes the annual cycle of responsibilities and prepares the way for the new year. The use of appraisal, evaluation, and measurement to determine the degree of success or failure attained by the guidance and counseling phases of personnel services have been rather elaborately treated in an earlier volume, and many of the same statements are applicable to placement. They are also subject to similar misuses and abuses if universally applied. Appraisals may be made not only of the end results of placement procedures but also of each step in the procedure, and of the contribution of each functionary. Evaluative criteria may be set up provided those who prepare and apply such criteria understand and act upon the fact that, while all placement offices are operated on the same basic principles and follow the same procedures, each office also has its own personality and its own distinctive features, which must be allowed for. This means, of course, that evaluation should be made on two bases, against a common standard and against individual objectives.

Those who set up evaluative criteria for determining the over-all effectiveness of placement services against which individual services may estimate, appraise, or evaluate their relative success will make use of statistical analyses for one type of criteria, of objective and subjective data on the quality of the work done for another type, and of authoritative opinion for a third type. Statistical analyses have been discussed in the previous section, and some of the dangers involved in the use of costs as a criterion of success have been revealed. As a rule, experienced placement workers feel that the costs should be included in standards of success, but they also feel that they should not be overvalued, since statistical analyses show wide variations in comparative costs. Moreover, when standards of relative efficiency are being set up, it is hardly possible to allow for variations in the meaning of placement and in the scope of its activities, i.e., in the amount of testing, counseling, verifying references, and the like; in the type of clientele attracted and held; in the occupations in which placements are made; in the duration of employment; in the proportion of positions filled with satisfaction to both parties; in the geographical location of positions and for the willingness or unwillingness of applicants to migrate; and for the reputation of the service in the community. All too often the largest number of placements with the lowest per capita costs are made by the least professionally effective services and by the most ineffective workers; indeed, an entire service may be operated with no more worthy objective than an increase in the volume of placements without reference to resultant labor turnover. Criteria which deal with employment duration, labor turnover, occupational promotions, and similar items based on statistical analyses derived from follow-up and employment supervision have considerable appraisal value, not only for placement offices, but also for educational institutions and employing concerns.

Appraisals of the kind and quality of the work performed by the service as a whole and by the various individuals, or evaluative criteria based on the items which are considered in such appraisals, are better indicators of effectiveness or ineffectiveness than is volume of placements or unit costs. Experiments with methods useful for this purpose have been under way for several years and are being developed. Some are very promising. The director of a placement service should be familiar with the best methods of appraisal and evaluation and should be able to furnish much of the data upon which the administrative board may base its conclusions.

A brief list of dos and don'ts for those who are charged with, or invited to share in, the solution of the external organization and administration problems of any type of placement service closes this phase of the discussion:

Dos for Administrators

(1) Be patient. It takes time to organize a service.
(2) Think through your purpose and the possible way to attain it.
(3) Prepare to face criticism whether it comes from within or without.
(4) Make your program perfectly clear.
(5) Stress proper performance of functions rather than number of functions or volume of work.
(6) Strive for co-operation. It is needed for success.
(7) Introduce the service on a carefully controlled experimental basis.
(8) Be scientifically impartial and critical enough to want proof.
(9) Be open-minded enough to discard preconceived opinions.

Don'ts for Administrators

(1) Don't be rushed, or pushed, into introduction. Some communities do not need a service.
(2) Don't introduce until a plan has been made and the cost estimated.
(3) Don't initiate a complete program. Let one grow to meet local needs.
(4) Don't be afraid of either labor or capital.
(5) Don't appoint advisory committees composed of unbalanced intellectual and professional uplifters.
(6) Don't appoint operating personnel for other than professional reasons.
(7) Don't fail to make a scientific appraisal of results.

CHAPTER V

Internal Organization and Administration

THE preceding pages have presented certain preliminary steps which must be taken by some individual, committee, board, or council *after* the decision to establish a service and *before* its installation. The responsibilities involved in such steps have been classified into three groups, and it has been suggested that the future operating executive can be, and often is, appointed while these preliminary steps are under consideration, so that he may act in an advisory capacity especially on professional matters and may, when the time comes to assume responsibility for the internal organization and administration of the service, already have been initiated in respect to many of the external phases of the service as they will influence the successful performance of his specific duties.

DUTIES OF THE DIRECTOR

Discussion of the responsibilities of the director in the different capacities in which he must serve is the function of Chapter V. Elaboration of two functions—publicity and the training of operating personnel—listed among shared responsibilities in Chapter IV has been carried over to Chapter V because, while they are important at every stage in the organization of the service, they require continuous attention throughout its life and therefore become a permanent responsibility of the chief executive. The director, in carrying out the policies of his superiors, will act in a variety of capacities determined largely by the size of the service and the number of assistants available. His duties in five major capacities are discussed: as a business manager, as a salesman, as a co-ordinator, as a functional specialist, and as an educator.

The Director as a Business Manager. As a business manager the director will be responsible for the layout and equipment of the office within the space and budget which has been provided for that purpose. (1) He will see that there are suitable signs on doors, offices, and desks, in building directories, and in classified directories issued by the telephone company; that entrances and exits are suitable and sufficient to prevent overcrowding; that stairways, if used, are wide and well lighted; and that safety and health regulations are enforced throughout the building. (2) He will lay out the space as conveniently as possible for practical use, making minimum and maximum provision, as the case may be, for clean, attractive, and comfortable reception rooms, for private and open interview facilities, for records and workrooms, for toilet and rest rooms for both employees and applicants, and, in some services, for private rooms where prospective employer-employee conferences may be held. Special services sometimes require a special layout.[1] (3) He will select the mechanical equipment for the office including such items as desks, chairs, counters, tables, files, pictures, posters, charts, shelves for magazines and books, office machines, and general office supplies. It is not necessary to purchase all the office equipment at once, but it is necessary to avoid the use of old and nondescript furniture which is donated but which is responsible for the appearance of some very unattractive offices. He will see that there are sufficient telephones and trunk lines to carry on the work of the service, and he will provide pay telephones for other than business use. (4) He will also purchase the professional tools which are essential to the conduct of placement procedures—registration blanks, employers' order forms, testing apparatus, occupational information, and the like. Probably he will have jurisdiction over the salary and publicity budget and will make out the payroll, vouch for office expenditures, and make other financial reports.

The Selection of the Placement Personnel may also be regarded as a business function. What training, experience, and other qualifications should the director have in mind when selecting applicants for recommendation to his appointing board?[2] Messengers and janitors may be by-passed; interpreters are needed in few offices; file clerks, record clerks, machine operators, and statisticians, if their duties are confined to noncompetitive and routine activities or to intraorganization research activities, require no especial attention beyond the information which assures competence in the performance of their duties. But the majority of place-

[1] There has been much improvement in the layout of placement offices from the day of the bank-window interview, no seats, and bulletin board announcements to current provision for open and booth interviewing. A wise director before laying out space will study, either by observation or from the printed page, the layout in other placement services and in business houses. Booths are not usually large and, with movable partitions, may easily be converted into open space. For a long time business concerns have been spacing interviewers' desks in one large room, and a few university faculties, where space is at a premium, have followed their example.

[2] This question does not assume that qualifications for placement workers are definitely known. There is no area of the personnel field in which qualifications for workers have been established, but progress is being made and some requirements are fairly generally agreed upon.

ment officials must qualify in personality traits as well as with regard to competence in the routine and professional aspects of their work. If the volume of business is large enough and the scope of its activities is broad enough, this category may include a number of telephone operators, reception clerks, interviewers, solicitors, plant visitors, home investigators, publicity experts, editorial workers, placement and referral clerks, office and employment supervisors, co-ordinators, counselors, research workers, psychologists, psychometricians, psychiatrists, physicians, nurses, and stenographers.

No matter how large or how small the office, and no matter how many or how few the workers, standards of selection should be set up and adhered to. Public offices may require appointees to qualify under civil service; school offices should be wary of retired teachers and philanthropic services of appointees favored by financial supporters. Specific qualifications for specific duties are best discussed later in connection with the performance of each placement function, but for all appointees who deal with the public, especially as interviewers, there are certain outstanding knowledges, technical skills, and personal traits some of which should be assured, or be promising potentialities, before appointments are made.[3]

On the personal side, qualifications may be summarized as follows: freedom from bias and a keen sense of values with reference to education and educational opportunities, to occupations and employing concerns, and to race, religion, sex, and age; a keen sense of fair play with the willingness and the ability to see that both employer and employee get a fair deal; a social vision which is broad enough to grasp the ramifications of the placement function and the myriad points at which it touches other areas of life, where it may function as either a disruptive or integrative factor in the personality of applicants; and an outlook on life which is at one and the same time sympathetic and scientific, practical and idealistic.

In the realm of academic knowledge, theorists as well as experienced placement workers have expressed many as yet undigested opinions, with the result that every possible preliminary preparation for a wide variety of undifferentiated positions is confusing directors, who would like to go forward with the professionalization of their corps. Take, for example, the subject of psychology, which is admittedly a basic knowledge or a background requirement. How much psychology is basic, and to the proper

[3] Lists of the qualifications which have been most frequently suggested, and perhaps most rarely secured, are found in the publications of the International Association of Public Employment Services—the only organization to which one may turn for professional discussions on placement activities.

performance of what functions? One person offhandedly replies, "Statistics, clinical psychology, the various subdivisions of applied psychology, tests and measurements, and even psychiatry"; another, equally nonchalantly, replies, "Enough to understand human nature and the fundamental workings of the human mind." But which functionaries need training in statistics and experimental methods, which need to be able to recognize physical and psychological symptoms which call for expert attention, which should be trained in clinical methods, and which will find one basic course sufficient?

It is very easy when the academic mind attempts to determine what constitutes a satisfactory theoretical background for any personnel functionary to become so involved in his own enthusiasm for the acquisition of knowledge that the meaning of *basic* is overlooked and the superstructure receives an unconscious emphasis.[4] However, if it can be agreed that, as a generalization, economics, sociology, psychology, biology, and perhaps anthropology are basic knowledges for all personnel workers— the next question is, Where shall such knowledge be acquired? In college courses, or via the road of experience combined with the type of education in theory which is secured by self-directed study, or by attendance upon some of the facilities afforded by adult education agencies? Confidence in academic degrees, diplomas, and certificates, which indicate variously the conclusion of attendance on courses, the accumulation of credit points, or, on some levels of education, the compliance with legal residential requirements rather than intellectual achievements, has perceptibly lessened during recent years. Therefore placement directors are growing to feel that a more dependable approach to academic qualifications would be to list the minimum pre-employment knowledge which may legitimately be considered basic for all candidates who expect to participate in the professional aspects of a placement service, and then leave the selection of sources from which knowledges are secured to the individual. Achievement tests could be used to determine the extent to which the essential knowledges were actually possessed. The same procedure might be followed in the selection of interns or apprentices.

What pre-employment experience should be required for successful candidacy? That, of course, would depend upon the size of the office, the number of workers, the extent to which each worker is expected to perform one or more functions and whether or not supervisory and training

---

[4] This tendency to spread all over the different areas of knowledge and into courses offered in business and educational personnel may be discerned in the course recently published for the training of counselors and placement workers for the veterans' service.

facilities permit the selection of inexperienced persons. For years there has been one point of agreement among placement directors: *there is no satisfactory substitute for training on the job*. As a corollary, recruitment of placement personnel is most effective when selectees for both regular positions and for internships are chosen on the basis of potentialities and are trained on the job.[5] This statement implies that supplementary knowledges and experiences will be continuously acquired during service.

College courses, and courses under other auspices, designed to prepare personnel workers for educational and business responsibilities were fairly common before World War I. They have been discussed in *Guidance and Personnel Service in Education*,[6] and their gradual increase in number accompanied by decrease in quality has been noted. Some such courses, if given by adequately prepared instructors, are very helpful—e.g., courses in labor problems, social and labor legislation, industrial relations, counseling, interviewing, and placement. Not all of the courses currently offered are needed by anybody; some are needed by all; and some are needed by nobody. It is interesting to note that few of these courses have dealt with *placement* as an independent topic, and it is safe to assume that even fewer have been given by instructors who have had practical placement experience. Progress in improving courses offered in university schools of education has been very slow. More progress has been made in the courses offered by schools of commerce and of business administration. Therefore, if a director desires to secure recruits who have combined theory and practice in their preliminary preparation, he will probably turn to the latter agencies.

The Director as a Salesman. As a salesman the director, unless the service be a unitary one entirely independent of any parent organization, will co-operate with the management under which it operates in the performance of its advertising and publicity functions. If placement be but one function of a parent agency such as a public-school system, a Y.M.C.A., a college, a municipality or a state, publicity for the various activities of the agency will probably be centralized so that there may be uniformity in policies and practices, proper timing of news releases, and equitable distribution of opportunities to share in the use of publicity media. In any case, the director should be familiar with the types and methods of publicity which are essential to the operation of a placement service, the different functions performed by the service which call for sales ability, and

---

[5] Various methods of apprenticeship training and the difficulties of effectively conducting such training are discussed in the reports of the annual conventions of the International Association of Public Employment Services.

[6] Reed, pp. 54–56.

the qualities of salesmanship which he has a right to expect from each subordinate. For example, during the initial stages of the service and continuously thereafter he, or someone to whom he delegates the responsibility, should be prepared to make addresses, prepare bulletins, circulars, house organs, and news items which will attract and hold the interest of the public and increase the patronage of the service.

Many illustrations of good and of poor publicity are available for the study of those who are novices in this area.[7] Although private agencies are apt to excel in this respect, some state services have issued very attractive publicity. The Intro Placement Service, a private-*free* agency, established jointly in the late 1930's by the Rotary Club of New York and the Institute for the Crippled and Disabled, for the placement of young persons disabled as the result of illness or accident, published a four-page bulletin at regular intervals designed as a sales medium for employers. *This 'n That for the Busy Man* contained a few news items, descriptions of a few cases available for employment, and replies to two or three legal or other questions which are always in employers' minds when they are faced with the employment of a handicapped worker.

The Greenewald Service of Philadelphia, a private-fee agency established in 1897, discontinued its house organ, *Picks* (the wheat from the chaff), during World War I but revived it in 1920. It offered a specialized service in restricted lines and registered only those who had "clean records and certified references." A long list of satisfied individuals and concerns, who had used it for years as a middleman, was excellent advertising.

On the other hand, no amount of general publicity of this type, no matter how clever it may be, will take the place of the type of publicity which circulates by word of mouth from satisfied or dissatisfied applicants to friends and employers, or from one employer to another. An employment service, for better or for worse, is advertised by practically every member of the corps. Receiving and interviewing applicants, taking orders and contacting employers, all involve a sales element, and all publicize the service in such fashion that they either add to or detract from its prestige.

Miss S. who was an interviewer in a public employment office always bought the afternoon papers as soon as they were on sale. She checked the "help wanteds" for contact early the following morning. From time to time with increasing frequency, she noted calls for bank messengers or runners and regretted that she

[7] Hopkins, *Emergence of a New Public Employment Service,* pp. 162–169, discusses various publicity methods. See also Atkinson and others, *Public Employment Service, passim.*

had no suitable registrants to recommend. One day she registered two applicants who seemed to have the necessary qualifications for such positions. Early the following morning she called for a desk relief and visited one of the advertising banks. After the presentation of her identification card she said, "I have noted your ad a number of times but I did not have a single boy on my list who was the bank type. Today I have two who seem very promising, and I came right over to see if you would like to talk with them." The banker was pleased, as who wouldn't have been? She had noted his needs, regretted her inability to meet them, but was unwilling to attempt a sale until she was fairly certain she could deliver the goods. After some inquiries as to what she thought was the "bank type" and why, and what sort of services the office was prepared to offer, he told her to send him both boys. He hired both, and within the week, on his recommendation, two other banks had become customers of the service.

Publicity, advertising, and the sales function permeate every activity of a placement service whether the activity be a responsibility of the director or of some subordinate. Their importance will be noted again and again in connection with the recruitment of workers, with job solicitation, and with plant visitation.

The Director as a Co-ordinator. As a co-ordinator the director will integrate all of the activities under his immediate supervision, and he will reach out and integrate his organization's activities with those of as many other community agencies as is possible. If he has charge of a unitary service, he will know that internal co-ordination should begin the moment more than a single functionary is employed, and that opportunities for such co-ordination are bound to increase as the growth of the service makes departmental or functional organization desirable. If he has charge of a group of offices, intraco-ordination responsibilities will remain and interco-ordination responsibilities will be added. Opportunities for external co-operation will vary from community to community. The most common and the most closely related agencies with which co-operative relationships should be established are educational services of all types, labor organizations, personnel departments of employing concerns, other placement services,[8] public libraries, philanthropic services, law enforcement agencies, health services, psychological clinics, and other welfare services.

The special aspects of a placement service which afford intraservice opportunities for co-operation differ with the situation. A unitary service which is organized on a departmental basis may co-operate in the use of applicant files and employers' orders and in job solicitation and field

8 A considerable number of public and other noncommercial agencies refuse to co-operate with commercial placement agencies.

visiting. But if it is organized on a functional basis,[9] the value of co-operation with respect to some of these opportunities would be less.

Clearance is the key word in connection with co-operation both within and without any given placement service: clearance of applicants, of opportunities, and of labor-market information with other placement services; clearance of educational and occupational information and returns on employment supervision with labor unions, personnel departments of employing concerns, public schools, and other educational agencies; and clearance of social information through a welfare council or a social exchange. No placement service, even a one-person office, if it has any appreciation of the broader social and economic implications of placement, can be entirely exempt from clearance responsibilities.

The Director as a Functional Specialist. The smaller the office the more important it is that the director have at least a minimum of qualifications as a functional specialist. His claim to rank as such will be demonstrated by his theoretical knowledges, by the way in which he makes practical use of them, and by his ability to avoid the misinterpretations, misuses, and abuses which so frequently occur in their practical application. If he is the only functionary in the office or the only one who could be rated as a specialist, he will be very careful not to undertake more special functions than his qualifications and time permit him to handle effectively. It is better to refer applicants requiring special services to other community agencies, if such are available.

It is very necessary that he or someone else in each placement service be familiar with all the tools and techniques used by education, placement services, and employing concerns for making job analyses and individual capacity analyses, and he should know to what extent it is justifiable for him to assume that records of tests and ratings administered by the placement office are likely to be accepted as substitutes for tests administered by individual employing concerns. Occupational information in many forms furnishes important tools for placement services. Knowledge of various types of personal handicaps and their probable relation to job success is another type of desirable special information. If a director is fortunate enough to have a number of functional specialists at his disposal, his major responsibility will be the over-all appraisal of the work of each specialist and the co-ordination of their activities in such fashion that

[9] The Cincinnati Employment Center was organized by functions, with separate units for administration, maintenance, registration, placement, research, records, promotion, and vocational adjustment. See Stanley Matthewson, "The Cincinnati Employment Center," *Proceedings of the Twenty-fourth Annual Convention of the International Association of Public Employment Services*, 1936, pp. 103–120.

the contribution of each is understood and maintained in its proper relation to the whole.

The Director as an Educator. As an educator the director not only will be responsible for the educational leadership and upkeep of his own corps, but he will have major responsibilities as a contributor to the education of the community as a whole, including employers, employees, teachers, counselors, and other social workers. This means that he will exercise many functions which lie within the field of adult education and that he must be familiar with the best current methods in use in this area. The quality and extent of his educational contribution will depend to a large degree upon the character and scope of his knowledge, and upon his ability to motivate the thinking of groups and of individuals along constructive economic and social lines with reference to employment problems and their educational implications.

The education of groups of casually interested citizens begins with pre-organization activities intended to arouse interest in the functions of a placement service and its community implications and to be of service in arriving at a wise decision relative to the introduction of such a service. In its initial stages this is a shared responsibility, but once the service begins to operate it is likely to become more definitely a responsibility of the operating executive. Addresses, house organs, newspaper items and stories,[10] bulletins, public conferences and forums, and under some conditions radio broadcasts and dramatizations are the usual educational media.

The In-Service Training of Placement Personnel was early recognized as among the most important responsibilities of administrators.[11] It was clearly and frequently stated that inferior geographical locations, unsatisfactory building location, and inadequate material equipment could all be made up for by a superior operating personnel, while no amount of expenditure for such items could make up for incompetent personnel.

If training on the job is the "one best way" to attain the status of "experienced," it is equally essential that such a status once attained should be maintained and improved through the medium of adequate control and constructive supervision. Each member of a placement service, the

---

10 In case stories are used, the utmost of care must be taken to see that, unless with their consent, neither applicants nor employers are recognizable.

11 In May, 1914, William M. Leiserson stated, "The first requisite of successful employment offices is that the people who manage them shall know their business." He did not feel that economists and sociologists should make up the office force but that ordinary people, appointed for merit and assured of permanent tenure as long as they attended properly to business, were satisfactory. He advocated in-service training and a system of salary and position promotions (*American Labor Legislation Review,* IV [1914], 322).

director most of all, requires a continuously growing and revised knowledge of industries and occupations, of shifting occupational patterns, of job classifications and job families in relation to secondary occupations, and of position substitutions, transfers, and promotions. Each member of the corps must be informed regarding newly validated tools and techniques which throw light on the current and changing character of the adjustment problems—physical, mental, social, economic, educational, emotional, racial, or religious—of various industries and businesses and of different groups of workers, and which suggest new and improved placement techniques. And again, if any given placement service expects to participate in shaping the program "of things to come," there must be, throughout the entire personnel, an ever-increasing appreciation of the broader social, educational, and economic implications of placement and an ever-clearer understanding of basic programs in education and in industry. Finally, each functionary, professional or routine, should acquire a reasonable degree of efficiency in appraising both his own accomplishments and those of the service as a whole.

During World War I some important contributions were made to the better understanding of employment problems, and practical training programs, mainly under governmental auspices, were developed to meet specific needs.[12] The immediate objective of such programs was improvement in methods of selecting, classifying, and distributing available manpower. Short courses designed to attain this objective were limited in scope to employment topics. Some were given for experienced workers, others for the inexperienced; and in some instances completion of such a course was prerequisite to employment. Literature describing these courses and reporting on their results was abundant, and, taken as a whole irrespective of their admitted weaknesses, they introduced a practical element into training programs which had been lacking, and which to a considerable extent has continued to be lacking, in so many university programs; and they stressed the importance of relating the placement functions of education more closely to those of employing concerns.

A number of tools and techniques are available for the assistance of directors in carrying out upkeep objectives. Even the one-person office can have some helpful information material—general occupational information and reading material, current local information on educa-

[12] See the Federal Board for Vocational Education, *Employment Management; Its Rise and Scope* (Employment Management Series, no. 1; Washington, D.C., 1919); *Personnel System of the United States Army* (1919), vol. I, ch. 30, and vol. II, ch. 3, 13; and *Proceedings of the Employment Managers' Conference*, 1918 (U.S. Bureau of Labor Statistics, Bull. no. 247, 1919).

tional and occupational opportunities and on community resources, material regarding labor, educational, and social legislation, and charts which show the location of employing concerns, lines of transportation, and lines of promotion in some concerns. Sometimes the bulletins, house organs, and manuals published by the larger private services and by federal and state services are available for smaller offices.

The bulletins issued by the National Employment Exchange of New York City illustrate one type of contribution which a private service may make to information regarding the current condition of the labor market. The Queens office, a public office also in New York City, a number of years ago issued a *Handbook on Queens* which was prepared by the office personnel and therefore accomplished the dual purpose of disseminating information and of providing in-service training. It included community information, a map, the principal labor laws, and a seasonal calendar showing hiring periods in different occupations.[13] Federal and state services have published manuals which are usually available for the use of other noncommercial services. Among the most helpful are those on interviewing and field visiting issued by the United States Employment Service and the series published by the New York State Service on various topics such as registration procedure, field visits, clearance, statistical procedures, junior services, and services for the handicapped. Such manuals supplement the general literature on the organization and operation of placement services which has been mentioned, but they do little to help the operating personnel understand their places in the organization, or the interrelationships which are essential in an effective service. The greatest deficiency in training and upkeep material is found on such topics, and on topics dealing with the objectives and scope of a placement service and the conduct of the various procedures involved therein—receiving and registering applicants, recruiting, making employer contacts, and establishing community relationships.

There are many other tools which are in practical use, some in one office and others in another, and which have definite value for training programs; in truth all the material secured by the most immediately available personnel techniques are desirable tools for this purpose. Prominent among them are printed forms of all types from registration blanks to statistical reports and case histories, validated tests for various purposes, rating forms and scales, interview aids, schedules, questionnaires and opinionaires, samples of occupational ability patterns for individual study

13 A calendar of seasonal variations in employment was also published by the Vocational Adjustment Bureau of New York City.

and comparison, and profile charts or summary records of individual diagnosis. Nothing, of course, takes the place of adequate, accurate, and up-to-the-minute occupational information, i.e., all the labor supply and demand data. This should be available in many forms, with all of which the personnel should be familiar, and all interviewers should be trained to use it with discriminating judgment. Surveys of several types—occupational, educational, statistical, and employment opportunity [14]—are useful in a placement office. Job classifications, job families or comparable jobs from which referrals may be drawn when qualified applicants within a particular classification are not available, and job specifications, including entry requirements and the more common lines of promotional specifications, must be understood in their relation to applicants.[15]

Providing a placement office with good tools is one thing; seeing that the personnel has the requisite skill and knows when and how to use each tool is another thing—another educational responsibility. It is called in-service training and it must be conducted by methods which are adapted to three types of workers—the intern or apprentice, the newly inducted employee, and the experienced worker. It is clear that not every method would be equally suitable for all three classes and that comparatively few services will maintain a large enough corps to warrant elaborate specialized programs to meet the differentiated needs of each group. Nor can the large number of one- or two-person offices, which to a great extent must make progress under their own steam, be overlooked.

The literature on in-service training, however scattered and scanty it may be, does contain much material which has proved its value for all three groups and for both director-controlled offices and self-directed functionaries. Some of these methods have been employed by the services themselves; others have been conducted by outside agencies. Both procedures have values. Methods in use without the individual service comprise courses given by universities and other agencies, conferences under various auspices, addresses, forums, conventions, and opportunities to participate in surveys or other methods of collecting and evaluating community data. All such group methods of upkeep have the advantage of bringing workers

[14] See Reed, *Guidance and Personnel Services,* pp. 71–144, and Howard M. Bell, *Matching Youth and Jobs* (Washington: American Council on Education, 1940), pp. 91–165.

[15] The United States Office of Education, November 22, 1943, issued a memorandum to State Supervisors of Occupational Information and Guidance describing the tools and procedures developed by the War Manpower Commission. The same agency has also developed conversion tables for use in placing Army and Navy personnel in civilian jobs.

into contact with others in similar situations, thereby affording opportunities to learn what problems are universal and what peculiar to individual services, and what methods and devices are being used for their solution.

Another upkeep method for experienced workers is grants of leave for definite periods of time to visit and observe procedures in some other office which is recognized as an effectively operating service, to attend a short unit refresher course, or to participate in a workshop. Individuals who are granted such privileges are usually expected to report back to their co-workers on whatever benefits may have been derived from their experience. Training and refresher centers are also used for the practical preparation of interns, and sometimes they are used as induction centers. If such centers have carefully prepared programs, exceptional material facilities, and superior supervisory personnel with sufficient time for instruction of assignees, there are some advantages in this method of training inexperienced workers; but there are those who feel that it is too expensive for general use and that the newly employed are preferably inducted in the center where they are to serve.

The type and quality of training which may be offered by individual services will vary according to their size, location, and facilities. In some offices methods may parallel those used by special training centers. Staff meetings afford the best opportunity for the upkeep and progressive development of experienced workers. Interns, or the newly employed, in addition to attendance at such meetings, may be assigned for more intensive training to some specially qualified person, or, if a suitable program has been set up, they may be assigned to work under different persons who are in charge of different functions or of different divisions. If training responsibilities can be delegated to those who possess the type of educator ability which knows how to help individuals plan developmental programs, to discuss accomplishments, strengths, and weaknesses, and to aid in understanding and interpreting community contacts and applicant problems, this is a good way not only to provide training-on-the-job but to uncover special interests and abilities and to suggest desirable later assignments.

All of these methods, individual or group, within a service, and most of those without, are predicated on the assumption that a successful placement service depends largely upon the efficiency of its nonsupervisory force; [16] that the first step in the direction of effectiveness is the selection

[16] In-service training and methods whereby the executive and supervisory force may be kept abreast of the times have both received attention in the meetings of the International Association of Public Employment Services.

of candidates for positions and the second is in-service training. Acceptance of this assumption implies that someone is qualified to select candidates, to plan developmental programs, and to see to it that novitiates are introduced in an orderly fashion to each aspect of the placement process so that at each step theory may be combined with practice and time enough may be allowed to understand their relation before another procedure is injected.[17] Beginning with its first conference, in 1913, the members of the International Association of Public Employment Services have maintained an increasing interest in the training of all three types of personnel mentioned, and it is in the annual conference reports of this organization that one finds the best-tested and the most practical suggestions for the training of employment office personnel.

Two or three examples, illustrative of the way in which pertinent employment tools and techniques may be used in a training program, are offered. They will suggest other ways, but it must be remembered that they are of a necessity general and suggestive rather than local and definitive.

Forms are one of the most generally used and one of the most important tools for the accomplishment of employment service objectives. They must be on hand the day the office opens, and the operating personnel must understand the purpose of each. Therefore, their selection and training in their use and in methods of appraising the extent to which each individual has contributed to the effectiveness of their use are of major concern in every service. What forms are essential for any employment service? Once again the reply depends to a considerable extent upon the volume of business and the type of customers served. Minimum requirements for a small office are suggested; those who are interested in a more elaborate equipment may use the suggestions found in reference material dealing with public employment offices.[18]

Generally speaking, every essential procedure involved in the placement process requires a correspondingly indispensable form. Registering an applicant requires an *application form,* the content and arrangement of which provides a permanent, cumulative record and a verbal picture of the applicant which differentiates him from other applicants: it individ-

---

[17] The danger of theory outdistancing its practical application was well exemplified in many of the induction or orientation *courses given for freshman college students.* The flood of unrelated information crowded into a brief period of time was hopelessly confusing, and much of it was forgotten before the student had a chance to make any practical use of it.

[18] See Hopkins, "Forms," *op. cit.,* pp. 104–118, 216–239, and Atkinson and others, *op. cit., passim.*

ualizes him for employment purposes and records his employment history. Receiving an employer's order necessitates an *order form*, the content and arrangement of which gives a complete and accurate picture of the opening to be filled and serves as a cumulative record of openings for which referrals have been accepted. A *call-in card* which, when an order is received, summons an applicant whose qualifications seem to fit the specifications, is a third essential form. If the individual responds and seems to be a potentiality, a *referral form* or an introduction card is issued and serves to make the employer-employee contact. A *verification form*, often a return postal form, is sometimes used to determine whether or not the placement process has been satisfactorily completed. Such forms may be mailed to the employer, to the applicant, or to both. *Reference letters* to previous employers and *follow-up letters* to ascertain the extent to which employed referrals are proving satisfactory are also in use.

These forms, which are basic in most offices, may in some offices be supplemented by cross-classification cards which permit the classification of applicants under more than a single or a preferred occupation, by index cards which help file clerks to locate material quickly, and by various record, report, and research forms.

Each training program will be concerned with the forms in use in its own office, and the extent to which each item is discussed and the quality of the discussion will be largely determined by the number, professional status, and experience of the personnel. For example, time spent on methods of using certain types of diagnostic tools in offices where no such tools are in use and where no one is qualified to use them, or where they are used by experienced psychologists, would be useless. But time given to training in ability to assemble, interpret, and integrate the results of expert diagnoses, to understand their limitations, and to read profiles might be well spent. The dangers of emphasizing objective measures per se, of placing too much reliance on mechanical devices, and of carelessly disseminating mechanistic counsel are very great, and may well be studied in any training program.[19]

As one essential form after another is taken up, its size, color, and arrangement and the number, spacing, and purpose of each item may be

[19] Comments on records for the use of personnel services and for a brief summary of methods whereby suitable forms for all types of services may be provided are found in Reed, *Guidance and Personnel Services*, pp. 207–213. Although the purposes of such records differ, the same fundamental principles apply to placement forms; and a single-person office, or a small office in the charge of a director of limited experience, will probably be wise to start with a minimum number of mimeographed forms and make revisions as experience dictates.

discussed, and the responsibility of each individual—clerical force and functional specialists included—for making his specific contribution to each separate placement procedure and to the total picture which results from the completion of the placement process may be accented. Such programs bring out the importance of each form and the purpose it serves in its relation to other forms, and they point out individual duties and stress administrative and intercorps relationships, as well as the relation between line and staff supervision.

Turning from the study of forms which accompany the performance of each placement procedure to the study of the more elaborate long-term records and research reports—data for which are frequently drawn from these primary forms—we may ask: What practical use may be made of such cumulative records and what is their research value?

Many topics which come within this category are suitable for training programs at the local office level, for example:

Employment Statistics drawn off from records and reports and analyzed and interpreted have a wide variety of uses in addition to the very obvious one of calling attention to the importance of accuracy on the part of all who contribute to statistical data. They may (1) indicate the relation between supply and demand, thereby revealing the necessity for recruitment activity or an increase in advertising, (2) indicate what per cent of the applicants qualify for the positions on order, (3) point out the sources from which different types of applicants are being drawn, (4) help to differentiate the difficult-to-place from the difficult-to-keep-placed and from the unemployables, (5) help to determine the value of vocational training and retraining, (6) suggest new educational curricula or the revision of the old, (7) supply one factor for evaluative criteria, (8) uncover data for the solution of problems, (9) suggest improvements in individual procedures, and (10) aid in guiding administrative practices.

Record Study, both the individual record (case material) and records en masse, gives placement personnel a chance to check the extent to which their current impressions and conceptions of individuals will stand the test of time; whether or not, as has been well said, they have an objective leg to stand on. It gives them an opportunity to understand how a too close "close-up" of applicants, employers, and placement problems may, by denying the perspective and detachment which results from the long view and the broad view, vitiate judgment and impair the intellectual integrity so essential to the sizing-up of persons and problems. The arrangement of record data in groups often helps the less experienced worker to find inaccuracies, contradictions, flaws, and gaps in the recorded information; to understand how such errors and deficiencies prevent the clarification of issues and the solution of problems; and to obtain practice in developing analytical habits of thought.

Why do some employers retain their employees over long periods of time while others are continually hiring and firing? Are there some employer characteristics, or some situational factors, which forecast such probabilities? Can explanations or warnings be found in one or more factors on the record? Why do some employees flit from one job to another while co-workers attain promotional and permanent status? Study of the records may reveal many facts which alone, or in combination, explain and influence a man's adjustment to employment. Do the records show that interviewers realize that certain measurable human capacities make for success on one job and for failure on another? Do they show that trade-test techniques are too "pat" and too inflexible, and do the tests tend in practice to supplement the interviewing technique, or do they narrow it to such an extent that interviewers lose, or cease to develop, their ingenuity, alertness, and imagination?

Looking for pictures behind the records, one catches a vision of possibilities for growth, for improvement in letter writing, in record writing, in methods of interpreting data, and in techniques of counseling and placement; and one uncovers suggestions for the revision of record content and form, for the integration of placement services with other community services, and for possible means of determining and increasing his own personal value to the service.

Field Visits—personal visits to employing concerns, educational agencies, and other organizations—are another suitable training program topic. They are useful for several purposes and are regarded as an important technique for establishing and maintaining the type of friendly, cooperative relationships which mean so much to the smooth and effective functioning of a placement service. Properly conducted, such visits are (1) a valuable means of promotion and a fruitful source of new employing clientele, (2) an authentic source of up-to-the-minute occupational information, (3) the best method of checking on previous referrals and placements, (4) a good, and often a casual, method of securing orders which might otherwise not have been given, (5) an opportunity to fill in gaps in job specifications, secure employers' appraisals of the service, and listen to compliments, complaints, criticisms, and suggestions under friendly conditions, (6) an opportunity to observe, without asking direct questions, machinery and various other equipment, types of workers, caliber of foremen and supervisors, and working conditions, (7) an opportunity to ascertain peak working seasons and major hiring season—data which may be utilized in preparing seasonal calendars or district maps to aid in scheduling and timing later visits, and (8) an opportunity to cultivate the type of vizualization which can be secured in no other way and which has incalculable value when selecting future referrals for the same concern.

Field visits furnish many subtopics for training programs and conferences. Among those most helpful to less experienced workers are their various purposes, the details of preparation for visitation, the characteristics of welcome visitors, the methods of approaching different agencies under different conditions, the timing of visits, and the desirability of central or intraoffice planning of visits and of central indexing of all visits and of all visitors—in order to avoid lost time, wasted effort, and the danger of antagonizing recipients by too frequent visits by too many different persons. Novitiates who have participated in such programs will be better prepared to meet criticism—fair or unfair—to secure desired information without asking direct questions, to observe intelligently and to interpret correctly, to read job specifications and entry and promotional charts, to understand the practical value of occupational dictionaries, job classifications, and job families, to translate into referral qualifications evaluative devices or criteria used by employers, to visualize applicants on various types of jobs both during the course of the interview and from study of the application blank, to evaluate the results of visitation, and to make intelligible reports.

Two lists of dos and don'ts for plant visitors which are the result of this author's personal experience are found in *Guidance and Personnel Services in Education:* one, on pages 123–125, is for those whose primary objective is the securing of occupational information; and the other, on page 320, is a brief supplementary list for placement workers. The latter is reproduced:

(1) Don't solicit so often that you become a nuisance.
(2) Avoid pressure selling.
(3) Don't expect special consideration for your referrals.
(4) Don't assume that social or family relationship will guarantee positions.
(5) If you are a woman, don't make a man of yourself. Businessmen respect and are inclined to favor womanly women.
(6) Don't engage in arguments regarding criticism of your referrals.
(7) Don't comment on wages, hours, or labor policies of your employing clientele.
(8) Don't offer gratuitous suggestions for the improvement of company personnel policies.

(9) Always stand ready to confer regarding the improvement of your referrals or to aid them in preparing for promotion.

(10) Learn to accept "heel cooling" as a part of placement procedure, and appear to accept it graciously.

Another conference topic which has always been fruitful of interest in university classes is the Value of Classified Newspaper Advertisements,[20] including the extent to which they serve as, or supplement, employment opportunity surveys. The influence of a decentralized labor market, involving a multiplicity of labor reserves, on the effective and economical distribution of labor has already been mentioned. No employment medium serves to focus attention more definitely on this situation than does the classified and display advertising found in the help-wanted and position-wanted columns of daily newspapers. Such columns contain reliable records of demand, but it is a segmented, not a pooled demand; it is representative of a small part of either the available supply or demand, and it comprises so many duplications and omissions that it is useless as an accurate estimate of either factor. However, it may usually be safe to assume that help-wanted and situation-wanted advertisements are indicative of the most urgent needs in both lines, at any given time, and in any given locality.

During the years of her university incumbency, this writer offered a course in placement which, while designed primarily for those who were preparing for placement work, registered all types of personnel workers. Ways in which educators, counselors, and placement workers could make practical use of classified advertisements was one of the course assignments. Several hundred studies were made in different localities for different purposes, and much interesting and illuminating material was exchanged among the group members, some of which was prepared for the use of school and college pupils.

Examples of values derived from such investigations are mentioned. (1) They are *general* indicators of the current employment situation. (2) Over a period of time they may help to reveal variations and trends in labor demand. (3) They usually reveal that five or six occupations carry the load while there is but scattered demand for many others. (4) As a rule, references are required only for positions on the upper occupa-

[20] Anne Bezanson, *Help-Wanted Advertising as an Indicator of the Demand for Labor* (Philadelphia: University of Pennsylvania Press, 1929). This is the only research on this topic with which this author is familiar. Its primary purpose was the construction of an index of help-wanted advertising; its findings are based on a continuous monthly analysis of help-wanted advertising in Philadelphia papers from April, 1923, through August, 1929, supplemented by less complete data from five other industrial cities; three periods of employment activity, broken by two recessions, are covered.

tional levels. (5) Placement services may use "situation wanteds" to locate applicants who are not available through registration. This is often done during a buyer's, or easy, market when employers tend to raise their training and experience requirements. (6) Blind ads and unscrupulous advertising received from different points in the country are not uncommon and should be guarded against. (7) Both pupils and adults may note the extent to which positions advertised are in line with those for which they are preparing, or are prepared, but care must be used in interpreting the findings since advertising usually reveals immediate needs. (8) The assets which employers consider of sufficient value to include in ads may be compared with the assets cited in "situation wanteds." For educational purposes they may be tabulated under assets which are called for in all positions and those which are applicable to specific occupations. (9) They indicate the type of job specifications which employers are likely to give placement offices. (10) They afford an opportunity for instruction in writing letters of application. (11) School and placement counselors find they have considerable guidance value.

Two rather unique uses of newspaper advertising are taken from this author's personal experience: one is concerned with "help-wanted," the other with "situation-wanted"; one tells the story of a commercial placement agency of the type which helps to discredit legitimate commercial agencies, and the other cites a very clever method of securing employees for an occupation which is frequently blacklisted in the minds of young women, its unpopularity being enhanced by the attitude of educators:

Miss C. was a commercial teacher in the public schools. Her school was organized on the two-session plan and she was employed during the morning hours. Fully cognizant of the scarcity of commercial workers, she conceived the idea of opening a placement service from 1 to 5 P.M. Cannily she followed, doubtless quite unconsciously, the preliminary program which has been outlined for the establishment of a placement service. She rounded up her "need" material and found it favorable; she considered publicity essentials and decided that her pupil clientele was all-sufficient as a source of applicant supply, and that newspaper advertising was an excellent substitute for employers' orders. Expense and personal convenience were the only items which influenced location, hence it was very easy to make an arrangement whereby desk space and use of office facilities were exchanged for clerical services. During free time in the afternoon the daily papers were studied, promising "leads" were contacted over the telephone, and their requirements were checked against pupil and alumni qualifications. Referrals were made without recourse to placement "forms," and defalcations on fee agreements were unknown. Cost per placement was practically nil, and when she first told her story she was more than doubling her teaching salary. Fortunately for both the teaching and the placement profession, this instance may legitimately be labeled "unique."

Equally unique and both legitimate and clever is the way in which Mrs. B., personnel director in a —— factory, used the situation-wanted ads to maintain a full quota of employees:

When asked if she had difficulty in securing women who were satisfactory, she replied, "I solved that problem very satisfactorily some time ago." Well aware that both the public schools and private commercial schools turned out large numbers of stenographers who could not compete in the labor market and would sooner or later find their occupational level in some other line of work, she scanned the ads for indications that stenographers of limited education and about two years of experience were available at beginners' wages. Persons so advertising she visualized as habitual stenographic failures, drifting from job to job, accumulating discontent and discouragement, and finally, perhaps with a little help, coming to realize that "white collar" was not as important as some other things. Letters to these women explained the work in her plant, told what it had to offer in terms of permanency and wages, cited co-workers who had deserted stenography to find satisfaction in the factory, and invited each to call and see for herself what the work was like. The response was good, and to the permanent workers already thus secured she added, in the same way, recruits as they were needed.

The internal organization of a placement service will be sufficiently completed to open its doors for business when the director has performed, or has made a beginning of performing, the functions which have been enumerated. Many of these functions, of course, are continuous responsibilities and will become increasingly important as the service develops. But the director will have acquired the necessary material equipment, professional tools, and professional and clerical personnel; he will have circulated information regarding the purposes and date of opening the service, made the preliminary community contacts, and conducted at least a few basic conferences on operational procedures.

As the work of the service goes forward, the director will be responsible for the performance of another very important function—the evaluation of the effectiveness of the service as a unit, and of each individual member of the force.

The Director as an Evaluator of the Effectiveness of the Service. Evaluation of the effectiveness of a placement service has been assigned to the administrative board, but in so doing it has been noted that much of the data upon which the board would base its decisions must be supplied by the director, and many of the suggestions for improvement which are derived from evaluations must be carried out by him.

On the over-all effectiveness of the service the director will seek to know (1) whether the information given out by the personnel has been adequate and accurate; (2) whether the tests used have been properly constructed, selected, administered, and interpreted; (3) whether the publicity has been adequate, in good taste, well-timed, and effective; (4) whether the attitude of the community toward the service is friendly, helpful and co-operative, tolerant, or unco-operative and hostile and whether it is deteriorating or improving; (5) whether the hours of service are meeting the needs of both types of clients; (6) whether the records are properly made for both practical use and for research; (7) whether the filing system is satisfactory and well located for convenience and time-saving; (8) whether ever more discriminating referrals are resulting in a higher percentage of placements and longer job tenure, and so forth.

In evaluating the effectiveness of each member of the force he will begin with executives and work down to the routine workers. Supervisors and executives may well be evaluated by principles which are basically the same as those used in education. Has supervision been instructional and inspirational, or has it been inspectional? Has leadership been a dominant characteristic? Have supervisors encouraged co-operation between offices, divisions, departments, and interviewers or have they fostered competition?

Turning to interviewers, the director will have at his command both subjective and objective methods of evaluation, and his use of the best methods will be one criterion of his own efficiency. (1) Does an interviewer know what information he needs and what to get first? (2) Is he tactful in securing information? (3) Does he exploit his interviewees in order to secure research material? (4) Does he attempt to give services which belong to experts? (5) Does he attempt to force job acceptance or employment? (6) What does rating of his interviewing or registration cards reveal as to the quality of his advice? (7) Has he stressed volume of placement at the expense of quality of service, or vice versa?

The director who would make fair and helpful evaluations will turn to the experiments in appraisal and evaluation which are being made by other agencies and select for his own guidance the best-tested and most promising ones.[21] If he desires "to rate" on the quality of personal per-

---

[21] Once again the reader is advised to make use of the *Proceedings of the International Association of Public Employment Services. The Twenty-fifth Proceedings* (U.S. Department of Labor, Bull. no. 14, 1937) reports a round-table discussion on "Evaluation of Training of Staff," which is well worth while. Business organizations also are making contributions to evaluation literature. Reed, *Guidance and Personnel Services*, pp. 440–450, discusses evaluation methods and results.

See also Lynn A. Emerson, *Employment Services in the Young Men's Christian Association of New York City* (New York: The Young Men's Christian Association, 1931), for the evaluation of placement under the auspices of the Y.M.C.A. in New York City, and J. A. and Florence Lee Fitch, C. S. Coler, and D. G. Paterson, *General*

formance and to utilize the entire or some part of the personnel as co-raters, he will remember that rating scales are supposed to be made by experts and to be applicable to each specific function, and that all who participate in rating others must be specially trained.[22] However, no matter how carefully rating scales are constructed and used, they should always be supplemented by other evaluative criteria.

Chapters VI, VII, and VIII will present the various procedures involved in the placement process.

Appraisals of the Adjustment Service, and L. S. Hawkins, Clients' Opinions of the Adjustment Service (Adjustment Service Reports, nos. IX and XII; New York: American Association for Adult Education, Teachers College, Columbia University).

[22] Books on psychology will usually give all the necessary information on the construction and use of rating scales. See also Reed, Guidance and Personnel Services, pp. 191–198.

CHAPTER VI

Placement Procedures—Securing Applicants

MANY of the data presented in previous chapters may seem to the reader to imply that a placement service may not be established without all the paraphernalia which have been discussed. Were this true it would be most discouraging, but it is not true. The great majority of services in operation would be rated "small." "Available space" would mean one room in which all the operational functions are performed; the "director and his corps" would be a single functionary who is responsible for all the activities of the service; there would be no functional experts; and whenever and whatever psychological or counseling service is offered, it would be given by the sole worker, or be secured from some co-operating agency. Functionalization and departmentalization, as organizational alternatives, would be by-passed, but functionalization would, of a necessity, be in continuous use; and, if the service were open to all types of applicants, departmentalization might also be in use even though its existence were recognized only in the files.

Some very superior work is done in small offices where there are never more than one to three employees. And there are some very good reasons why workers who are thrown on their own resources and are forced to act as their own directors, supervisors, and teachers frequently prove to be more resourceful and more alert than those who are connected with larger offices which provide upkeep facilities within the service. The small office lacks expert services, but it is less likely to be cluttered up with functionaries who sometimes get in one another's way and defeat their own ends; and the small office permits the unification of placement procedures, thereby giving the sole functionary that broad vision of the complete activities of the service which is usually denied workers in larger, and especially in functionalized, offices.

In view of these facts, before proceeding to the detailed consideration of placement procedures common to all offices, it seems desirable to focus attention once more on the community of problems which must be met by all placement workers and to note that there are some marked advantages on the side of the small office.[1] As the discussion proceeds, it will be assumed that each individual will be able to apply the methods and procedures suggested to his own particular situation.

The primary purposes of any placement service are to collect information on opportunities to work and on persons who want to work, and to use these two types of information in such fashion that placements result. A number of other ways of facilitating employer-employee contacts have been mentioned—self-service exchanges, applications at the gate, newspaper advertising, help-wanted signs, and recommendations of friends. None of these methods require both a fixed place of business and a third party who acts as an intermediary for the negotiating parties and, at the same time, assumes certain social responsibilities. This middleman, represented by the service personnel, is a very important factor in genuine placement services, the factor which allows the use of the terms *placement, placement office, placement service, placement problems,* and *placement procedures* in lieu of *labor market, labor exchange,* and the like.

A local office is the unit for a placement service, and each unit, small or large, must, in attaining its objective, utilize the same general procedures and must conduct them within the same general limitations. Workers must be recruited and registered, employers' orders must be secured and recorded, applicants must be sifted for referral, orders must be filled from promising applicants who wish to apply, and some method of followup is necessary in order to verify placements and to ascertain the extent to which both types of customers are satisfied.

Among the limitations which are imposed on all services are the following: No service can create either jobs or workers; it cannot enact, repeal, alter, or ignore laws; it cannot revise or ignore human nature—whether of employer, employee, or its own personnel; it cannot alter or override labor-union or professional regulations; it cannot force one party to accept, or the other to offer, a position against its will; it cannot dictate preparatory educational programs or labor conditions; it cannot control labor mobility; and it may not, with impunity, offend community customs. On the other hand, a tactful personnel may have an effective finger in almost any of these *verboten* pies. This will become more obvious as the discussion proceeds, while the fact that each unit office must follow uniform procedure and work within the same general limitations makes it

[1] Perhaps the reader may find it helpful to review the suggestions in *Guidance and Personnel Services* which deal with the equipment of small counseling services—Chapter VIII on filing occupational information, Chapter XII on records, and pages 429–434 on services for small towns or rural communities.

fairly easy for any placement functionary to adapt suggestions and methods of general applicability to his own needs.

Picture, if you will, a small placement office about to open its doors in any given community. It is designed to serve applicants of all ages, both sexes, all levels of education, all races, religions, and nationalities—only common labor and daywork women are excluded. Individual placements, more or less permanent in character, are considered its major task, but it expects to fill its quota of seasonal, temporary, vacation, and "spot" orders, and to carry its share of the load for the difficult-to-place and to-keep-placed applicants. It does not invite and hopes to avoid "mass" placements. The single room provided for all the activities of the service looks attractive and comfortable. There is one bookcase and a table suitable for reading material, and there are a few chairs and enough filing cases for a start. Good taste has dictated the selection of the pictures, maps, charts, and posters which are seen on the walls.

It was very difficult for those who laid out this office to determine how many desks were needed and who should occupy them. A review of pre-organization data did not help to draw the line between needed personnel and personnel which would clutter up the picture, but it did reveal that many unknown and unpredictable factors promised to influence the volume of activity, and that volume of activity and efficiency of service were both closely related to personnel.

A review of literature from other placement services indicated that much research was necessary before any reliable information on "proper staffing" would be available,[2] but a few scattered statistics allowed the painter of this picture to draw the conclusion that two workers might operate an office placing from 300 to 800 applicants per year. Therefore, two desks are found, and on each desk there is a telephone, one of which may be an extension. Since the community survey suggested that 60 to 80 per cent of the applicants would be men and boys and the other 20 to 40 per cent women and girls, at one of the desks, located close to the main entrance, a woman is seated. She has been appointed to act as the hostess and the housekeeper for the service, to interview women and girls,[3]

[2] For a good presentation of the problems involved in determining what constitutes "proper staffing," see Atkinson and others, *Public Employment Service*, pp. 246–251. Reports of philanthropic agencies, colleges, and other private services sometimes give statistical summaries which permit rough estimates of the number of personnel in relation to total applicants, orders, referrals, and placements.

[3] Obligatory assignment of interviewers on a sex basis is open to challenge just as is the assignment of counselors on a sex basis.

and to perform clerical tasks. At the other desk, far enough removed to guarantee privacy, a man known as the superintendent, director, or manager, who has general responsibility for operation of the service and who will perform the majority of the placement functions, is seated. The files are so located that they are easily accessible to both workers. The hours of service on the office door correspond to those which have been given out in circulars and in news releases. They have been chosen to meet the needs of the anticipated clientele as revealed in the local survey and are 8:00 A.M. to 1:00 P.M. to receive applications and orders; 2:00 P.M. to 5:00 P.M. for field visits, making records, filing, telephoning, and the like; and 5:00 P.M. to 6:00 P.M. to care for employers' emergency orders which are not known until after quitting time but which should be filled before nine o'clock the next morning. These hours may be changed after a few weeks of experimentation, and evening hours may be added if desirable.

The required work has been divided between the two functionaries, the extent to which testing and counseling shall be included in the service has been determined, and each worker has been assigned his hours of service. The picture is now complete and the service is prepared to open its doors and to perform the first procedure in the placement process.

RECRUITMENT PUBLICITY [4]

Three types of publicity are useful in connection with the development of a placement service; the ultimate object of each is to obtain clients and to retain their business. General initial publicity, designed to launch the service under conditions which will attract favorable attention and public support, is the first type. It has been mentioned as a responsibility of the policy-determining board, or individual, and it soon needs supplementation by the second type or announcement publicity, which is designed to catch the attention of individuals and organizations whom the office hopes to serve. One may not set up an office and then sit down to wait for customers to turn up. The existence and purposes of the office must be made known through all appropriate channels; otherwise, on the opening day, there may be neither orders nor applicants. In making the transition from initial to operational publicity care should be taken lest the lapse of time between promise to open and the actual opening be too great. Memories are short and interest once aroused must be sustained. Advertising the opening of a service before it has anything to sell is equally dangerous, while making a start with something to sell, without antagonizing either seller or buyer, has always been a problem. It is generally agreed that there

[4] Solicitation of employers' orders is discussed in Chapter VII.

should be at least a small pool of available applicants before an effort to increase employers' orders is undertaken, but the teacher who secured openings through newspaper advertising made sure of positions first.

Several methods of securing an opening-day nucleus of applicants and orders are in use. Each has its objectionable features. Circulars distributed among schools, colleges, clubs, and other agencies, sometimes accompanied by registration blanks, may result in registrations but also in the premature curtailment of education, in arousing hopes that cannot be realized on, or in flooding the service with applicants who cannot be registered or for whom there are no positions. If individuals are circularized, some are sure to interpret the circular as a personal assurance that a better position than the one currently held is available, and they quit, thereby increasing labor turnover and risking a period of unemployment. The best of judgment is necessary if announcement publicity is to be handled so that a reasonable supply of applicants and orders may be on file on the opening day without injustice or disservice to anyone.

The third and most specific type of publicity—recruitment or post-opening publicity—is a procedure legitimately included in the placement process. It is not only the first procedure in that process, but it permeates every other daily routine procedure in the process. The reception of callers, registration of applicants, referral of candidates—each has its recruitment publicity angle. Good service, courteous manners, accurate information, and discrimination in referrals have no substitutes as reliable and effective forms of recruitment advertising. Postopening publicity has an additional advantage in being able to cite actual accomplishments, whereas the other types of publicity are largely dependent upon promises. It is this third type upon which a service depends for a steady flow of orders and applicants, and for increasing first the one, and then the other, as market conditions fluctuate.

Many methods of recruitment aside from personal solicitation are known to placement workers. Some are useful in one situation, others in another. Sometimes they are selected and used with the utmost of discretion; at other times they are carelessly chosen and bring unfortunate individual and social results. Since each service maintains a separate labor reserve, one of its most difficult tasks is maintaining, as nearly as possible, a balanced supply of, and demand for, labor. Fluctuations in supply and demand accompany fluctuations in the general economic situation and are frequently accentuated by factors operating within the service. If either applicants or orders become too numerous, one type of clients or the other is likely to become discouraged and turn to another agency. If situation-wanted advertisements are used for recruitment purposes, care should be taken not to increase an already sufficient supply of workers who have the same qualifications and, if specific qualifications are essential to employment, this fact should be made perfectly clear.

If radio facilities, addresses, or other means of reaching large numbers of persons are used, there is always the danger that a considerable number of unemployables will accept the invitation and use up valuable time in registration only to have their applications placed in the inactive file. Recruitment of workers and of openings over the air has been common in recent years. Probably no other method would have been as productive of the volume of results, but it also caused some resentment and hard feeling toward the recruiting agency. For example, an appeal for additional war workers may have been illuminated by stories of various types of women, including grandmothers, who made remarkable records in war industries. Other grandmothers listened, and more than an occasional grandmother, or other unemployable, interpreted the story as a personal plea "to go to the nearest United States Employment Service and register."

Grandma A. accepted the challenge. She went to the nearest employment service all pepped up with the determination to "back the attack" which her grandson was helping to carry out on the Italian front. The walk seemed a little long, she was tired, and the "chit of a girl" to whom she told her ambition was casual in the extreme; rapid-fire questions poured out one after another: "Did you ever work in a box factory? Did you ever work in a gun factory? Let's see your hands. Did you ever work in an assembly plant?" "No!" "No!" "No!" said grandma, "but I think I could learn." "No you can't," retorted the young miss, "you're too old and nobody has time to teach you." Grandma went home, and other grandmas were very sympathetic; some were very resentful.

It is safe to assume that commercial agencies coincidental with their first appearance understood the necessity for, and incorporated in their procedures, recruitment of both applicants and employers' orders. Public offices, lacking similar motivation, long pursued a laissez-faire policy with reference to both, and, until the heavy labor demand of World War I followed by a period of unemployment focused their attention upon the necessity for recruitment procedures, their general assumption had been that if a public service was available, those who desired to make use of its facilities would make known their needs.[5] Private agencies were more aggressive; the sales character of an employment service was better understood; and a number of recruitment media and methods came into use early in their history. Some of these methods have come to be regarded as

[5] Atkinson and others, *op. cit.*, pp. 322–326, 431–433, give limited attention to recruitment of workers.

orthodox, or standard, for any well-conducted agency; others have been exceedingly unique, very clever, and well worthy of imitation; while a few, as has been noted in Part One, were socially undesirable and reaped their just reward.

Employing concerns also engaged in recruitment rather early. The economic history of New England reports the use of labor scouts, who were sent out from industrial centers into the smaller towns and rural communities whenever the demand for labor had consumed the local reserve. Families were frequently induced to change their residences and all of their members to join the labor force of the recruiting industry.[6]

The first general demand for the recruitment of workers came with the development of war industries during World War I. Every recruitment method and medium which could be devised was put into practice by manufacturing plants and by employment agencies. Decentralization of the dwindling labor supply accompanied by the "stealing" of labor from competitors resulted in an attempt to force all employers to secure recruits through the United States Employment Service. This effort was repeated during World War II, supported by the requirement that applicants for new positions must bring clearance papers from former employers. There were in 1918, and there are in 1945, several reasons why this logical and commendable governmental effort to force economy in the use of the available labor supply has not been very successful.

During the pressure for sufficient manpower to carry on war industries, orthodox or standard methods of recruitment were again supplemented by a variety of emergency practices. It is a truly fascinating study to trace the evolution of orthodox methods of recruitment from period to period and to note their supplementation by emergency methods which, when the emergency is over, are sifted in order to determine which have permanent values and should become orthodox and which should be discarded. Undoubtedly the recent experimentation with a diversity of recruitment methods will have a lasting influence on postwar policies in both industrial and employment practices. Also it is interesting to observe how, as time has passed, old methods and media of recruitment have been adapted to changed conditions and their use and popularity has fluctuated as the relation between supply and demand has altered. Glance backward at the old window sign, "help wanted," and then recall its recent window-display

[6] H. B. Coho, "Sources of Supply and Means of Getting in Touch with Them," *Proceedings of the Conference of the Employment Managers' Association of Boston,* 1916 (U.S. Bureau of Labor Statistics, Employment and Management Series, no. 4, whole no. 202, 1916, pp. 15–24). This is a forward-looking address which might have been made in 1945.

counterpart with photographic exhibits of plant facilities and with live workers performing the jobs. Read, if you will, the prewar "help wanteds," their content bristling with "qualifications," and then note the extent to which "persuasion" has been substituted for "qualifications." Or, if you prefer, listen to a radio program where recorded music has been used to attract an audience while spot recruitment publicity from several concerns is interspersed.

Those who wish to keep in touch with the great variety of recruitment literature issued by different business concerns and the content of their appeals as they are designed to attract one sex or the other may turn to such publications as the *Executives Service Bulletin* [7] and those issued by the American Management Association.[8] They will find examples of the use of the testimonials of satisfied workers as recruitment publicity, of the payment of given sums of money to present employees for leads which result in securing new workers, of an employment exposition, and of a puppet show in a public park designed to recruit women workers. One employer claims to have utilized all the techniques of attention attracting and persuasion which characterize high-power community selling—sky-writing being the only omission.

Of course there are dangers inherent in any method of recruitment—misrepresentation, overselling, and the like—but, if a placement service is to function, the recruitment of workers and of orders is essential to its success and, in one form or another, must be a constant accompaniment of every placement procedure.

RECEIVING PLACEMENT SERVICE CALLERS

Callers who visit a placement office include applicants or potential applicants, employers, teachers, social workers, law-enforcement officers, and other persons whose interest or business may bring them there. However, because so large a percentage of callers are applicants for positions, it has been the custom to speak of the reception function as though it were confined entirely to applicants, and to discuss it as the first step in the placement process, leaving the consideration of recruitment of applicants and of orders until later in the process. Either approach is legitimate, but it should always be remembered that neither procedure is confined solely to applicants. Also it should be remembered that, although it is only in com-

---

[7] Published by the Policyholders Service Bureau, Metropolitan Life Insurance Company. During the war this bulletin carried articles describing the recruiting, induction, and training policies of a number of concerns; e.g., the Jan., 1944, issue.

[8] *Management Review*, Sept., 1943, and Jan., 1944, are good examples. See also *Forbes*, 1943, "Tested Ways to Recruit Workers."

paratively recent years that the reception function has been deemed of sufficient importance to assign it differentiated responsibilities and to select personnel who possess specific qualifications for undertaking such responsibilities, it has been performed by someone ever since the middleman entered the employment picture and has grown in importance as time has passed.[9]

Two factors are partially responsible for this growth of interest in systematized methods of receiving placement office callers: (1) the increase in the numbers of applicants and the tendency of idlers, unemployables, and trouble makers to accumulate in offices and demand the time and attention which belongs to legitimate applicants and (2) the more general understanding, acceptance, and inclusion in the philosophies of all social agencies of the meaning and value of both human and public relations. Experience has revealed that the courteous reception of persons whose attention has been attracted by recruitment publicity creates a favorable first impression, draws a higher class of applicants and employers, and improves the general atmosphere and appearance of the service; that it reduces congestion, expedites service, conserves the time of interviewers, and keeps idlers and unemployables down to the minimum.

The titles, duties, and qualifications of persons who perform the receiving function vary with the size and character of the service. A large general service may have an official, called a receptionist or a floorman, whose sole duties are connected with the receiving and routing of callers to the proper interviewing desk or room. Or a small, general service, unless it is a one-person office, may have a clerk who performs the receiving function. And in between these two extremes will be found the receptionist clerk who performs a rather wide variety of functions the majority of which are designed to facilitate the placement process and to conserve the time of specially trained interviewers. The general duties of such officials are to greet callers and direct them to the proper persons, to prevent congestion, to maintain discipline, to distribute applicants among interviewers and see that each receives attention in his turn, and to relieve embarrassment if the service be operated for the opposite sex. Human nature being what it is, it may be well to include among these duties "speeding the departing guest" in such fashion that if, inadvertently or unavoidably, a feeling of dissatisfaction, injustice, or resentment may have arisen, the final word and act of the receptionist will blot it out, or so lessen it that the visitor will regain his original favorable impression.

[9] The administration of unemployment compensation by public employment services has greatly increased the routine duties of receptionists in some offices; in other offices compensation cases are referred to a separate desk.

There is a wide range of specific duties which may be performed by receptionists in connection with applicants for positions. They vary from the actual interviewing of applicants for registration and occupational classification, to the routine, preliminary, or assistant interviewing which saves the time of regular interviewers. Such duties are assigned by the manager or director in accordance with the most effective distribution of functions among the personnel, whether there be two or thirty employees, and they include supervising the filling out, or the filling out, of registration blanks; checking names and addresses with the central index file in order to prevent duplicate registrations; interviewing routine cases which involve neither new information nor personal problems; giving out information on occupations, educational opportunities, and community agencies; preparing introduction cards and, if no referral interview is necessary, delivering them to the proper parties as they arrive; and receiving and making contacts over the telephone. Among the clerical duties which devolve upon receptionists are receiving and opening mail, making out reports, caring for the files, forms, and correspondence, and serving as "housekeeper" for the service.

There is no general agreement regarding the qualifications and personality of those who serve as receptionists, and there is much less agreement in practice. Since some services have not yet realized that it is this official who creates the atmosphere, makes the first impression as to the standards and efficiency of the service, and frequently leaves the sole lasting impression, it is not unusual to find the youngest, the least gracious, the least experienced, and the least informed person assigned to this important task. Other services put high value on the securing of a mature, gracious, informed, and intelligent hostess whose personal appearance combines that of a "lady" with that of a high-grade businesswoman, whose social refinement is obvious in person, dress, speech, voice, and manner, who can greet as individuals and put at ease all types of persons—the welcome or the unwelcome visitor, the pleasant or the irate employer, the snooty and spying or the helpful law-enforcement official, the educator who comes to learn and to help, or the one who comes to complain and to criticize, the well-poised applicant whose outlook on life is wholesome and whose emotions are under control, or the angry, irritated, and emotionally disturbed.

A hostess who is qualified to assume such responsibilities is a valuable asset in establishing confidence and in removing any feeling of resentment or inferiority caused by the fact that the applicant is unemployed, or that he thinks he is the object of one or more "unfair employment practices" on the part of the government, an employer, or the placement office. By her very manner and her voice, which is cordial, friendly, and dignified, but never familiar, she creates an impression of equality of treatment, of no favorites, of no distinction between applicants or employees, but of a very real personal interest in each. Such a hostess will have at her command a good stock of information and the ability to use it in the right place and by the right methods.

During World War I this writer had occasion to visit a large general office in Minneapolis. A charming, middle-aged woman was in charge. The waiting room was full, and colored-numbered disks were used to distribute applicants to the right interviewer in the order of their arrival. Soldiers' wives and mothers, retired men and women, persons with physical and mental handicaps, and youth who had never worked were all hopefully waiting their turn. Cannily this experienced woman spotted the unemployables and interviewed them as they entered. Some, whom she was able to convince that Uncle Sam was very appreciative of their calling and of their willingness to help but the time had not yet come for them to make such a personal sacrifice, turned away happy to have received such prompt and gracious attention. Others, who were not willing to give up their interview privilege, were routed as were all other applicants, but the number on each disk was taken and, at a favorable opportunity, was slipped into the booth to which in his turn the applicant would go.

As the receptionist circulated about the large room, always keeping an eye on the entrance and exit doors, she paused for a pleasant word with first one and then another. Once she looked at the disk of a weary mother whose baby was growing restless and, turning to the other applicants, said, "I'm sure someone with a lower number will be glad to change with this mother whose husband is in the service and who has no one with whom to leave her baby." Several were very glad to do so, and one woman volunteered to care for the baby while the mother went to her interview.

During the postwar depression the same office was again visited. There was the same large number of applicants, the same charming, gray-haired receptionist and the same "atmosphere" so rarely found in public employment offices.

Another service which was rated very high in my report to the Director-General of the United States Employment Service was operated by and for Negroes. The receptionist was a scholarly, refined, and cultured college graduate whose cordial and dignified approach to visitors made a lasting impression and with whom in later years it was a pleasure to renew acquaintance.

On the other side of the ledger I have seen receptionists, not only in public placement offices but in private services, in business offices, in public school, college, and university placement offices, whose tongues were all too ready with such comments as: "A pity you didn't wait five minutes longer and I'd have been gone"; "Put your card down there and go on"; "What are you here for now? Why don't you sleep here?" "Don't keep pestering me or I won't try to get you a job." And, when my name was well known to the receptionist, I have been addressed as "girlie," "honey," "dearie," "say," "lady," or "miss," and I have heard much coarse language and many cheap stories passed out over the reception room counter.

There are two questions which fall midway between the domain of the receptionist and that of the final interviewer which may well be presented before taking up registration procedures:

(1) Shall all callers who desire to register be permitted to do so? Decision is a policy-maker, rather than an operating personnel, responsibility, but insofar as public offices and some institutional services are concerned the reply must be affirmative with reference to legally eligible applicants. However, by differentiating between application and registration, and by filing the registration forms of undesirables or unemployables in a separate, or inactive file, such offices sometimes avoid referral or placement. Private agencies, of course, are free to refuse to register any applicant who does not come within their purview, whom they cannot place, or whom, for some reason, they do not wish to take responsibility for referring. Some agencies, both public and private, refuse to register employed applicants—provided they know it. Receptionists, or interviewers, who are obliged to turn away would-be applicants are very careful to do so in such fashion that unpleasant incidents are avoided and a favorable impression of the service is left.

(2) Who shall fill out the application blank? There is no single answer to this question. Several equally satisfactory practices are in use, their desirability or undesirability being dependent upon such factors as type of position, education of applicant, method of registration—by mail or in person, volume of work passing through the office, personnel available for registration duties, and the purpose which the blank is supposed to serve. Among the methods of meeting, or of dividing, this responsibility are (a) The applicant may fill out the blank in toto. This is essential when registering is done by mail, and is recommended by some as a preliminary step when data are to be checked, corrected, and supplemented during a following interview. Others find it satisfactory for professional and clerical workers but do not recommend it for industrial and personal-service

workers. (b) A clerk may fill it out for all, or for some, applicants without comments or questions. This method guarantees legibility, uniformity, and accuracy in recording the data given, but, unless the content be carefully checked during a later interview, there will be bound to be gaps in the evidence. (c) A receptionist, or a preliminary interviewer, may fill out the form in part, leaving the remainder for the final interviewer. After World War I some busy public offices used interviewers' assistants, who filled out all items except those concerned with education and experience. (At that time not much attention was given to personality items.) (d) The entire blank may be filled out by an experienced and final interviewer. This, of course, is usually done in offices where the small number of registrants permits one person to complete the entire procedure.

Those who advocate the filling out of the blank in whole or in part by the applicant argue that it saves time, permits helpful inferences regarding the intelligence, education, and attitudes of the applicant, reveals the possession or lack of such qualities as neatness, accuracy, and ability to follow instructions, and, if questions which applicants are prone to resent are included, they feel that resentment is less if they are read rather than asked.

Those who prefer to rely on the use of a single well-trained interviewer argue that the record on the blank is a major placement tool, that making the record is a major employment function best performed by one who possesses a high degree of intelligence, a broad knowledge of occupations, and a wide understanding of human nature and human relations; one who will be able to weave into the bare facts of education and work experience information which can be secured in no other way but which will make an important contribution to correct occupational classification, reveal valuable personality traits, and suggest constructive follow-up service. They refute the assumption that legibility characterizes the records made by "educated" applicants by citing the difficulties frequently experienced in attempting to decipher the information put on application blanks by college graduates who not only cannot write legibly but cannot spell correctly, and who, judged by their failure to connect the proper reply with the proper question and to follow printed directions, are also deficient in reading ability.

REGISTERING APPLICANTS

Applicants for positions may register by mail or in person. Some services permit the use of either method; others confine their clients to one or the other. Usually when applicants register by mail, employers' orders will be received through the same medium, but it must not be assumed that registration by mail precludes a personal interview with a placement functionary on the part of both clients; usually it is encouraged.

Registration by Mail. The widespread and original use of the post office as a medium for the distribution of unskilled labor in various occupations, and the gradual increase in mail-order applications and employers' orders as skilled and professional workers were sought and desired to locate beyond their immediate geographical area, have been mentioned in Part One. Distance was a major control factor. Today taking orders and registering applicants by mail is practiced effectively by many commercial agencies and by most of the institutional bureaus operated in connection with colleges and universities. Mail-order services have worked out their own techniques; their practices vary considerably, and their effectiveness varies even more markedly. Of a necessity their major tools—application and registration blanks and employer-order forms—are very similar to those used in direct-contact placement. Recruitment may be initiated with publicity letters and bulletins and by visits to business concerns and educational institutions. The sending of case literature indicative of the type of applicants for whom positions are sought and the enclosure, in communications to former applicants, of blanks upon which to suggest prospective openings or applicants are common methods of enlarging clienteles.

College and university bureaus which regard their product as self-selling will usually confine their order taking to the receiving of voluntary orders. They will do no soliciting. When the initiative is taken by the employer, a more or less concise description of the essential and desirable applicant qualifications, accompanied by a more or less detailed description of conditions under which services are to be rendered—a job description or a job specification—will be received, and the service will be asked to send the credentials of one or more registrants who it feels should be given consideration. The application blank of the employing concern may then be mailed to such candidates as seem potentially desirable, and the remainder of the transaction may be carried on between the applicant and the employer.[10]

Registration by Interviewers. A previous chapter has indicated that registering an applicant may be either a unit or a split performance. If it be a split procedure, the initial steps will comprise receiving the applicant, conducting a preliminary interview, and recording, or overseeing the applicant as he records, certain routine data, while the more technical pro-

---

[10] Reed, *Guidance and Personnel Services,* pp. 309–327, deals with institutional placement.

cedures required to complete the registration will be carried on by persons especially trained to perform such functions. If the procedure be a unit, the entire task will be performed by one interviewer. The purpose for which the applicant registers is to get a job; the purpose of the interviewer is to help the applicant analyze his assets and limitations, and to so record all the data—routine and personal—that it may expedite the realization of his purpose.

The major technique for securing and evaluating registration data and for passing out to the applicant occupational or other information which will aid in determining upon his occupational classification, or classifications, is the interview. The tools most commonly used in this procedure are the application and registration blank, and such additional material and professional equipment as has been listed in Chapter V, especially dictionaries of occupations, employers' job specifications and job classifications which indicate lines of promotion and their requirements, and lists of educational opportunities and of community agencies. Equipment for the testing and rating of applicants is found in some offices.

The Purpose of Registration Forms. The application, or registration form,[11] is an instrument used by the interviewer to so portray each applicant that it will distinguish him from all other applicants; individualize him for immediate employment purposes; and at some future time permit either the same, or another, interviewer to withdraw the record from the files and visualize the applicant approximately correctly in one or more of the occupational units under which he has been classified. The making of such verbal pictures by one person so that they may be interpreted correctly by another is one of the most difficult of employment procedures— a procedure which may not be standardized, but one which a carefully constructed form may help to systematize, thus preserving the separate elements which contribute to the *presently prevailing picture.*

There is no uniformity in registration forms either as to size or content. They vary in size from cards five by eight inches to letter-size folders. The use of different colors for ease in differentiating various occupational age and sex groups is fairly common. Agencies limiting their service to professional and semiprofessional applicants and employing concerns usually prefer a longer form and one which includes more items than is customary in public offices, or in offices which register unskilled labor; agencies which place several occupational groups are inclined to include a larger number of generally applicable items than are those which register for specific

---

[11] Some consider the registration form a *re-employment interview guide*—not an application blank but a step initial to an invitation to apply.

positions. Most agencies and most employing concerns are tending to use longer forms than formerly and to include more items, especially those which call for personality ratings, test results, and observations of interviewers. Large offices sometimes number the items and subitems on their cards in order to facilitate coding and punching for various purposes including the selection of applicants for referral to positions.

The Content, Arrangement, and Spacing of the application form is of great importance. The first lead on this topic is found in the purpose for which these forms are filled out and for which they will be used—referral of applicants, counseling, statistical reports, and research—and in their relation to the application blanks of industrial and business personnel departments. Carefully selected items which are pertinent to the accomplishment of these purposes are assets on application blanks; useless items which serve to cloud the picture and conceal rather than clarify issues are liabilities. Therefore, each item and subitem should be chosen because it will make some definite contribution to a clear and accurate picture, and the arrangement of the items should be such that the different elements which comprise the picture may be quickly seen as each in turn becomes the dominant factor in some action or decision.[12]

The evolution of a registration form is an interesting subject—perhaps sometime it may be chosen as the topic for a graduate thesis. In the meantime readers who desire to know more about the development of this device and prefer to draw their own conclusions from authoritative sources may turn with confidence to the following studies: Harrison,[13] still an outstanding authority on public employment services, in 1924 summarized under eleven items the data compiled from 300 forms then in use by placement agencies of various types and by business concerns. Items usually required were differentiated from those less frequently required, or considered of less importance. Atkinson, Odencrantz, and Deming in 1938 referred to this summary as "the minimum standards of adequate registration . . . still considered the basic material." [14] An August 1942 study, dealing with the practices of 147 business concerns, included a question regarding the changes in procedures which had been made in the application blank during the preceding six months.[15]

These studies, covering a period of two decades, supplemented by studies of the forms in use prior to 1920 and those which have been subjected

12 The importance of item arrangement is even greater if a portion of the blank is to be filled out by other than the interviewer.
13 Harrison and others, *Public Employment Offices*, ch. 12, pp. 320–362.
14 *Op. cit.*, p. 284.
15 Achilles, *Personnel*, XIX (1943), 609–617.

to recent revisions, indicate, as is logical, that placement services have invariably followed the lead of employing concerns in the revision of application or registration forms, and that the items called for on registration blanks correspond closely to those found on employers' order forms. They also indicate a general tendency to shorten the forms used to register common labor and to lengthen those used for the more highly specialized workers, and to retain over a long period certain items which have attained the status of fundamentals. Two significant changes in content are revealed, both of which consist of additions: (1) items resulting from the use of new selective tools and techniques and (2) items due to social change. Additional space has been required for rating scale and test results, for the elaboration of personnel history, for additional reference data, for F.B.I. fingerprint records, for the draft status of male applicants, for social security numbers, and the like. In the future it is obvious that some special items will be demanded on veterans' blanks.

The first series of items on an application blank [16] comprises routine or identification data. It includes the following: (1) Information essential for any applicant in any occupational group—complete name, home address, home telephone number or one which may be used, and age; and sometimes date of birth accompanied by documentary proof may be added. (2) An expansion of such data to include certain items essential for some occupational groups but not for others—marital status, dependents, nationality, birthplace of parents, religion, status as to war service, trade union membership, and police record, if any (fingerprint identification may be required). Such items may be needed for identification, for selection for referral, or for the protection of society. (3) Questionable items, sometimes not distinguishable from essential items, while in other instances their questionableness is obvious and the only excuse for their inclusion is the use of a uniform blank, which, in order to be sure of essentials, interviewers are required to fill out in toto. Among items which are frequently challenged are ownership of home, stocks, and bonds, other sources of income, loans or debts unpaid, kinds of insurance, smoking of tobacco and use of alcoholic beverages, and use of leisure time. All identification data are concentrated at the top of the card where they may be quickly seen when needed for alteration, review, referral, or research.

Mention of the necessity for securing accurate replies to identification items may seem superfluous, but there are many chances for error, espe-

[16] Usually there is space at the top of the card for the date, the name of the interviewer, and the number of the applicant, if numbers are used.

cially if the registration procedure be split and the final interviewer makes no effort to check the preliminary data. Names make the most trouble. They should be recorded in such fashion that confusion with other applicants having the same name, or with the same applicant, who, if foreign, may spell his name in several different ways, may be avoided. Male applicants and single women should use their full name—their baptismal, legally permissible, usually used name, never pet names or nicknames. Married women are usually advised to register in their own names, but, for accuracy in identification, to add the initials of their husband's name, and if married after filing the original application to notify the service at once of the change in name. It is by no means uncommon for college women, who should know better, to register in their maiden name, apply for a position after marriage in their married name, giving references in the same name, and then wonder why the placement bureau is so dilatory and inefficient in placing them. Single women sometimes use initials in the hope that the concealment of their sex may lead to openings which would not be available for women; married women sometimes use their maiden name fearing discrimination against married women. Now and then such practices bring definite position rewards.

Other important items for which application blanks should make provision but which may not be discussed either in the order of their arrangement on the form or in the order in which it is desirable for them to be taken up by the interviewer are:

(1) *Education*—age of school leaving, grade status at leaving, degrees, licenses or certificates, subjects of specialization or major and minor subjects, correspondence and night-school courses, travel, special vocational training, internships or apprenticeships, and such special items as may be needed, e.g., ability to read, write, or speak foreign languages. Any given form should make provision for recording the educational information which is a legal prerequisite to the selection of applicants for the type of positions which the service purports to fill, or which comprises the minimum educational preferences, or requirements, laid down in employers' orders. Documentary proof of educational achievements may or may not be required.

(2) *Experience*—including information on occupational knowledge and skills and positions for which the applicant feels he is prepared and desires to apply. It may also include future ambitions and the steps which he is taking, or is willing to take, to prepare for promotion. The extent to which all positions, including vacation, part-time, and emergency relief,

or work under the Works Progress Administration,[17] should be listed varies considerably with age and with quality and quantity of experience. For some applicants vacation, part-time, or relief work may comprise their total experience; for others the placement value of any such experience may long since have been lost. Some placement workers advise recording work experience during the last ten years only, while others report that such a practice results in the omission of valuable data. But there seems to be general agreement that the form should provide the space necessary to complete the usual experience record, working back from last job to first job, and if additional space is necessary, a supplementary card should be used. Experience data usually include the employer on each job, kind of business, address, duties (exactly what did you do?), time on job, date left, salary or rate of pay, reason for leaving, employer worked for longest, and employer in the best job held. Under work desired and fitted for one finds positions desired, positions best prepared for, when able to start, own own tools, go out of town, and salary expected. Again inaccuracies must be expected, especially in reference to salary and reason for leaving. Space should be provided for recording the results of performance tests.

(3) *Physical and Mental Capacities.* The influence of workmen's compensation laws in focusing the attention of employers and placement services on the desirability of including the physical characteristics of applicants on registration blanks, and the physical requirements of positions in job specifications, has been mentioned. Workers were, at first, opposed to the inclusion of such items on application blanks—either those of employing concerns or of placement services—on the ground that they would result in the denial of opportunities to work. But it is now generally conceded that their purpose is the proper placement of each individual, an objective which can be promoted by job, or hiring, specifications which include minimum physical requirements, and by application forms which furnish comparative data for matching job requirements and applicant qualifications. Therefore, the majority of forms make some provision for physical data—subjective, objective, or both. Sources of information include the word of the applicant, records of various kinds, medical examinations by physicians, physical tests given by technicians, and the observations of the interviewer. Height and weight are easily secured objective data. Among the physical characteristics which interviewers may observe and record, either under the space set aside for such items

---

[17] Experience in WPA was not considered an asset. If of short duration, registrants were sometimes advised not to mention it; but if the period of relief had been prolonged, the time factor in the experience record made omission a dangerous procedure.

or under that reserved for observations, are poor posture, defects of speech, sight, and hearing, right or left handedness or ambidexterity, facial disfigurements, and loss of limbs or fingers.

The ability of scientists to measure mental capacity is increasing. The older mental ability or mental alertness tests are being supplemented, and may be superseded, by newer devices, some of which may be the result of Army experimentation. An increasing tendency on the part of some employers to require tests of mental capacity is reported. Here and there a testing bureau is attached to a placement office, and a considerable number of forms makes provision for recording the results of such tests whether they be administered by the recording agency or transcribed from the records of other agencies. At the present time one is not justified in assuming that such tests will be given in many employment offices; therefore, major reliance must be placed on the empiric judgments of the interviewers based on the accuracy of education and experience data, and on the mental alertness, ability to follow instructions, grasp situations, and take the lead in determining occupational classifications betrayed by the applicant during the interview. The decisions and observations of the interviewer should be recorded, but he should continually remind himself of the universality of the temptation to label people, of the danger of yielding to it, and of the impossibility of assuming that even the ablest technician can tag every human being accurately.

(4) *Personality Data.* There is a growing tendency in all types of placement and employment offices, except in those which rely mainly on physical strength, to expect interviewers to be able to recognize, and describe on the record, characteristics which are implied in the expression "type of personality." World War I encouraged research scholars to increase their efforts to provide devices for this purpose, to standardize items used, and to describe personal qualities in such fashion that more generally accepted meanings would make them understandable by others. A number of forms are currently used to secure this newer type of application information.[18] Tests, questionnaires, and inventories purporting to analyze, measure, or inventory personality traits are on the market. Some are more promising than others; none, as yet, have been accepted without reservations, but many placement workers feel that there are some which, if used with judgment and with full knowledge of their limitations, have value in determining an applicant's suitability for employment.

Personality ratings, or rating scales, are a very common form in which

18 Reed, *Guidance and Personnel Services,* pp. 187–203, gives considerable attention to personality tests, rating scales, and interviewer observations.

appraisal devices appear. The applicant may be asked to use one for estimating his own characteristics; the interviewer may use one for recording such of his observations and conclusions as will help to determine the applicant's qualities of both general employability and of special qualifications for given positions; and they may be used for securing definite and comparable statements on recommendation blanks. Usually they indicate the extent to which traits are thought to be possessed, or lacking; point out promising promotional material; reveal persons who may have reached the limit of their developmental growth and may be suspected of being of static or decreasing value as employees; and suggest applicants who might profit from counseling or retraining. Employers make use of ratings for selection, promotion, training, and discharge. Some employers use two types of progress rating; one during an initial or induction period comprising one to five years, and the other for the following years.

The list of traits upon which interviewers rate are designated as interviewer's impressions, interviewer's analyses, interviewer's notes, or interviewer's comments. The qualities to be rated vary in number; some include both positive and negative traits. A few from among the many qualities or traits which are found on rating lists are offered, and attention is called to the unavoidable interlocking of their emotional and intellectual aspects [19] and to the impossibility of avoiding overlapping in the present status of psychological advancement. *Personal Appearance or Physique* (observable physical characteristics): Explanatory items or subitems include facial features, distorted features, disfigurements, scars, shape and size of hands, height, weight, posture, eyesight, hearing, quickness, slowness, grooming or neatness, body odors, state of shoes, hair, hands, and fingernails and the like. *Comprehension and Insight* include such subitems as intelligence, mental alertness, perception, memory in varying degrees, reason, "brains," and ability to grasp situations, follow directions, and visualize. *Temperament, Mannerisms, and Attitudes* include such items as may warn of mental disorders: sociability or unsociability, confidence or diffidence, aggressiveness or timidity, affectation in speech or manner, attitude toward work, nervousness, nail biting, shuffling of feet, muscular twitchings of the face, uneasy eye movements, boasting, self-excusing, quarrelsomeness, jealousy, suspiciousness, talebearing, troublemaking, abrupt, discourteous, or unpleasant way of speaking, and many others.

A general placement service will usually seek information on more per-

[19] For a good presentation of this subject, see James S. Plant, "The Psychologist Looks at Today's School Child," *Educational Record*, XXIII, Suppl. no. 15 (1942), 69–82.

sonality items than does business, because it must be prepared to respond to the varied demand of many employers, whereas the individual employing concern knows upon what qualities it places most value and can eliminate the others. One of the simplest business scales in this writer's files at the present time allows for three ranks on each of seven items—appearance, personality, brains, drive, preparation, responsibility, and general fitness. The concern which constructed it has selected each item for a specific purpose, and its interviewers are trained to utilize each for the realization of that purpose.[20] The instructions for interviewers recognize, and help to avoid, the difficulties involved in rating on both personality and appearance without subitemizing either; they note that the subjective data called for under brains and preparation cut across similar data secured in the more objective sections of the application blank and explain how this duplication of approach may be used as a helpful verification method; and they point out that drive and responsibility are not to be rated in a vacuum but to be given careful attention in the light of the amount of each needed for occupational success in the position under consideration. Most important of all, interviewers are taught how to sum up all of the data on the blank, to study its interrelationships, and to so interpret it that they can visualize the general fitness of the applicant for employment in the concern which they represent.

Conclusions drawn from the data suggested are sometimes supplemented by items which focus attention on the status of the interview with reference to the immediate or future availability of the applicant. They are, of course, filled out by the interviewer. For example, (a) degree of readiness for employment—immediately, more training, retraining, (b) acceptable or unacceptable—rank 1, 2, 3, (c) status of interview. Was he offered a position—accepted—refused? Who is to make the next move—applicant, the service, or the employer?

(5) *References and Recommendations.* References and recommendations are a fifth source of both subjective and objective information which throws light on the employability of individuals and serves to verify information given by the individual. Provision for references is made on many blanks—more commonly on those used by private agencies and business concerns than on those used by public employment agencies. Even where this item is used there is considerable difference of opinion as to

[20] All modern placement services and the personnel departments of employing concerns are cognizant of the dangers involved in the use of ratings by untrained and underexperienced interviewers, or oral examiners, as they are sometimes called; and therefore some do, and all should, provide training or instructions and manuals for their use.

its value, since it is hardly to be supposed that applicants will furnish the names of those to whom they are other than favorably known. With the introduction of more formal and more inclusive registration blanks, improved record systems, objective tests, and the demand that ratings on both skill and personal qualities be accompanied by supporting evidence or trait actions, some feel that sufficient sources of recommendations are to be found in educational and experience data and that they will be more reliable than those secured from applicants. It is useless to assume that general services handling a large volume of work, those registering unskilled applicants or doing mass placement, will put this item on the blank with any intention of following up the references given, except in special cases or at the request of employers. It just isn't practicable or possible.

The *Employment Service News*, April, 1938, reported on a study made to determine the extent to which references were used in 37 state services.[21] Some did not use them at all; others tried to follow up all. In some offices only questionable data secured during the interview prompted verification efforts, while in others follow-up was undertaken only if employers asked for it. The study revealed some interesting points of view: (a) that the applicant should furnish written references, (b) that verification of references was an employer responsibility, (c) that follow-up of references was good publicity—that it indicated a desire to be informed with reference to potential referrals which created a favorable impression among employing concerns and focused their attention on the placement service as a desirable source of supply, (d) that follow-up has a desirable psychological effect on applicants, tending to make them more cautious in their statements if they know they will be verified, (e) that all placement services, public and private, should verify the qualifications and reliability of applicants, and (f) that reference replies do make a valuable contribution to information regarding the suitability of applicants.

When references are asked for on application blanks and are followed up, the recommendations, or opinions, of the reference may be sought by means of a form letter or by a rating scale. Usually an attempt is made to verify objective data given by the applicant and to secure information as to ability and character. It is rather common from employer to employer to ask for the willingness or unwillingness of the former employer to reemploy the applicant: Why or why not? In the same or in some other capacity? These questions, if honestly answered, may bring very illuminating information.

Hesitancy on the part of references, instructors, previous employers, or

[21] "Use of Applicant References in the Public Employment Offices."

others, to be honest in expressing their opinions, whether they be sought through the medium of a rating scale, a form letter, or free expression of opinion, are based on sound reasoning: (a) They fear to put in writing comments which may be so worded that they fail to express their real opinion or may be misunderstood and misused by placement workers. (b) They hesitate to give out unfavorable information, no matter how much it may be deserved, lest it may prevent the applicant from obtaining a position. On the other hand, they render a social and individual disservice when they give favorable ratings which are not deserved and which if assumed to be reliable are an ultimate disadvantage to all parties concerned. (c) They do not like to give a blanket or generally applicable recommendation which may be used to secure some unsuitable position or be placed in the files where another interviewer may find it and use it for even more unsuitable purposes. (d) They are cognizant of the genuine reluctance on the part of experienced placement personnel to attempt to translate general recommendations into recommendations for specific positions. (e) They do not, as yet, have sufficient confidence in placement agencies and, their operating personnel to risk the danger involved in putting certain types of "honest opinions or facts" in writing. Libel suits are not very welcome, and civil-rights laws are much in evidence at present.

On the whole, there seems to be a tendency to consider references and recommendations very important for applicants who are to assume financial or moral responsibilities [22] and to use them to verify actual statements as to family, education, diplomas or certificates, special preparation, experience, salary, and length of service, but to be cautious in giving, or in accepting at face value, ratings which deal with personal characteristics. As a rule the self-estimate of an applicant will be made at the time of the interview and will be included on the registration blank; the interviewer's comments, or rating, may be included on the same blank or may be recorded on separate sheets; while those secured from the follow-up of references will usually be on separate sheets attached to the blank or filed in the same folder. All of them, whether they be recorded on the same blank, or separately, have a common purpose—to help in understanding the applicant and in making discriminating referrals.

Other purposes for which space is allotted on application blanks are for a small photograph on the front page of blanks used by colleges and universities and by services catering to professional and commercial applicants, and for the occupational classification or classifications which may be determined upon during the interview.

[22] Bonding is frequently required.

Objections to Items on Application and Order Blanks. Items on almost any registration or order blank are open to challenge.[23] Sins of omission or commission, or both, can always be found. Employer, employee, placement personnel, and the casually interested public all share, to some extent, in the criticism, and constant revisions are in progress.

The recent challenging of several items usually found on application blanks and on employers' orders, which has been due to extensive discussion of unfair employment practices and to unfair discrimination in the referral of war workers, has fostered an already existent tendency to seek ulterior purposes in the inclusion of certain items heretofore thought by experienced workers to make an essential contribution to the accuracy of the picture which they have assisted applicants to prepare for referral purposes. Perhaps it may be illuminating for those whose experience with the content of application and order blanks is confined to the theoretical to examine some of these objectionable items and to question whether their use may not have a constructive as well as a destructive aspect. Among the items which have drawn fire during the current war are nationality, race, and religion.

Nationality is an old bone of contention. The reader is invited to verify this statement by rereading pages 14–19, which reveal how, on the one hand, by means of legislation certain groups attempted to protect their own employment opportunities against the inroads of foreign labor by denying such labor opportunities to work, while, on the other hand, the National Association of Corporation Training conducted a post-World War I study of the national characteristics of different foreign groups which had definite constructive value in furthering the better distribution and job placement of foreigners who were employed in industry.

Race discrimination also has both a destructive and a constructive aspect, but in this country the accent has been on the destructive aspect. It has been practiced to some extent with regard to all colored races. With reference to Negroes it is a logical aftermath of the outcome of the War Between the States, and, if the reader will again refer to Part One, he will note that many years ago labor unions took steps, by means of rules and regulations denying Negroes union membership, to protect their own members against the possible inroads of Negro labor—a practice which at that time did not invoke the universal approval of labor. The current development of practices with reference to the employment of Negroes and the ramifications of the controversy may be followed in the press and in

---

[23] This is as true of college, university, and social-club blanks as it is of placement service blanks and blanks used by employing concerns.

the activities of the federal Fair Employment Practices Committee and its state counterparts.[24] It seemed to be impossible to attack this very important problem of integrating the Negro into the occupational life of the nation with any hope of reaching a permanent, constructive solution while the war continued. We have been all too righteously indignant when any able and willing worker, because of race, religion, or color, was denied an opportunity to share in the defense of his country. Moreover, the immediate situation has been complicated by the fact that the unfair discriminatory practices which were reported were usually laid on the doorstep of the United States Government, represented by the Army, the Navy, and the war industries.

However, the present is a very opportune time for thoughtful citizens who would acquire a proper perspective, and who are interested in a permanent, constructive solution of the problem to glance backward over the history of employment practices—fair and unfair—in this country. They will find much factual evidence, quite often in the form of legislative enactments, which will help them in understanding the material factors and in interpreting the human factors which have brought about regrettable employment conditions in peacetime as well as in wartime. As their study reveals the true origins of such occupational discriminations as may be credited to race, nationality, and color, and reaches the present tendency to fix limitations within which occupational discrimination with reference to any person, race, nationality, or color may be exercised without violating the civil-rights laws, they may feel inclined to challenge the charge that the "vicious discriminatory practices of employers" and of placement agencies, and their collusion, are responsible.

For they may uncover much evidence to prove that the average employer of any considerable number of workers does not care whether an employee be of one race or another, or whether his skin be black or white, so long as he is, and remains, an effective worker in the work unit to which he has been assigned. But each work unit has its social as well as its occupational aspect, and this social aspect is controlled by co-workers rather than by employers. It is in-plant social attitudes rather than employers' preferences which dictate hiring specifications when they have social im-

[24] The extent to which discriminatory occupational regulations have been placed on the statute books of this country is truly amazing. Have those who are enthusiastically supporting "antibias" employment legislation reviewed such statutes in their own states to ascertain whether or not this new legislation, if enacted, will be in direct conflict with laws already in force? See L. Paul Miller, *State Regulation of Entrance into Occupations in the State of New York* (thesis, New York University, 1939). And for brief statements therefrom, see Reed, *Guidance and Personnel Services*, p. 112.

plications. Therefore, this may readily be seen to be a matter which requires re-education of the public in social attitudes rather than legislation, which only serves to intensify social prejudices and to increase irrational thinking on the content of application blanks and employers' orders, accompanied by efforts to eliminate therefrom items which have definite constructive values. Legislation is the easy way and the escapist's way, but it is not the road to social progress.

This is also an opportune time to look beyond the recriminations and trivia of charges and countercharges on the home front to the battle front where, without the help of legislation, jail sentences, and fines, in the cold, the heat, the mud and blood of slit trenches, foxholes, and life rafts, the brotherhood of battle leaped across the barriers of race, color, religion, and ideologies, and pointed to a new day in the brotherhood of man. The contribution which sharing the perils of war has made toward a more generous sharing of the advantages of postwar occupational life is well illustrated by the recently reported conversation between General Romulo and General MacArthur as they viewed the ruins on Leyte.[25] Romulo, as they rode together in a jeep, was thinking how in all the effort to defeat the enemy "there was no consciousness of race," and MacArthur, as though he were reading his thoughts, said, "Congress can give you political equality, Carlos, but no law could have given you social equality. That had to come another way." Romulo replied that he had been thinking about that and thought they had it, and MacArthur came back with, "Yes, you have it. You won it on Bataan."

Social preferences of workers, insofar as they influence equality of opportunity to participate in the occupational life of the nation, cause serious problems, for which there is no single solution, and the times call for caution lest even-tempered reflection give way to hysteria, intemperate epithets, and ill-advised legislation. Sometime, now that the war is over, full realization will come that international savants like Noguchi, whose services to humanity called for the supreme sacrifice, must not be recorded in the history of mankind as a "Japanese rat," or a "dirty little yellow man." Nor will the future historian fail to take cognizance of the courage, self-sacrifice, generosity, and camaraderie on the battlefield, in the air, and on the sea which made each man his brother's keeper no matter what his race or what the color of his skin. It is to be hoped, and expected, that those who owe their lives and freedom to men of another race will extend the right hand of occupational fellowship to one another, and that

[25] Robert van Gelder, "An Interview with Brigadier General Carlos P. Romulo," *New York Times Book Review*, Feb. 11, 1945, p. 4.

former occupational injustices may pass into ancient history as humanity starts on a new pathway together as "One World." The problem has many angles, perhaps more easily discernible in war, which brings issues into the limelight and gives a better opportunity to clarify them and change thought patterns, than in peace. But if the nation will take advantage of its opportunity to clarify, rather than to intensify and confuse, issues, the war will not have been fought in vain.

Personal Characteristics, some of which the applicant or the employer is asked to mention, while others are secured by means of tests, ratings, and observations, have received their share of criticism as items suitable for inclusion on application forms and order blanks. Insofar as criticism grows out of known injustices deriving from ill-advised tests, random ratings, and observations of irrelevant and unusual behavior under "staged" and oftentimes embarrassing conditions, every experienced placement functionary says an emphatic "Amen." Referrals, or refusals to refer, based on "half-baked" opinions will undoubtedly result in unfortunate and unfair discriminations in employment. Better no such items on the record. Let us put a stop to it with all the means at our command, but let us discriminate between the destructive aspect of such items and their constructive possibilities.

Height, weight, arm and leg length have no value for some positions, but they are control items in occupations which require a minimum arm reach, in which seats of uniform height and width are provided, or in which uniforms cut to standard specifications are worn. Discrimination on the basis of physical characteristics may result in work comfort for one, while lack of discrimination may mean discomfort and additional fatigue for another.

More than once this writer has been asked to send an office boy of the "right size." Perhaps some comments have been added about the variety of physical qualities found among sixteen-year-old youth and about some inappropriate referrals which had previously been made. Everyone realizes the octopuslike appearance of most sixteen-year-old boys, but not everyone visualizes these youths correctly in office-boy positions, and they wonder why *this* boy who needs the job so badly was discriminated against. More than once, in establishments where space was at a premium and the quarters for statisticians, accountants, and other clerical workers were very limited, the author has been warned to refer no applicants whose physical being could not be accommodated in the space available.

Even stranger to those who have had little experience with the great diversity of human specifications which must be given consideration when distributing workers are the check lists which appear on some order blanks —light, medium, dark, and now and then "red-head"—or again—color of skin, hair, and eyes. But the experienced worker knows that there are certain lines of work such as theater ushers and restaurant ushers, waitresses and hostesses where uniformity of appearance is very important and where uniforms are often furnished so that not only height and weight, but general coloring, may not be omitted on the application, minimized in the job specification, or ignored in making referrals. An excellent illustration comes to mind. A concern which was very popular among college women stressed uniformity of appearance in its job specifications; blondes of a definite height were provided with a gray uniform, a rather expensive and distinctive dress which would have been unbecoming in color to brunettes, who would have detracted from the general appearance of the layout. When college women did not meet these specifications, they were prone to feel that they had been discriminated against.

Mental and emotional qualities which appear on record forms in order to further the best interests of both employer and employee are open to the same charge of being used for unfair discriminations, and it is human nature, if a person thinks he qualifies for a job, to assume injustice on the part of another who does not agree with him.

Educational Information, strange as it may seem, has not come within the purview of critics of items on placement service forms. However, in this writer's experience, educational items have, for many years, been fully as potent a source of unfair occupational discrimination as have items of race, religion, color, or nationality. Therefore, she has chosen to include them without benefit of corroborative support. The situation has developed quite logically under the aegis of the educational authorities and has grown more serious as time has passed. Applicants have sometimes questioned, not the inclusion of such items, but the injustices which have resulted from the assumption, on the part of employers and referral personnel, that the information so secured is a legitimate means of separating the educated sheep from the uneducated goats.

The steady increase in the tendency of educational agencies to issue meaningless diplomas, certificates, and degrees as the sole, or the most dependable, criteria of educational achievement, or of educational knowledge and ability, has undoubtedly influenced occupational opportunities on every rung of the educational ladder from the lowest to the highest, which in some occupations is pre-empted by holders of the doctorate. Sometimes this influence has been destructive, sometimes constructive. It is true, of course, that certain occupations are open only to those who have attained a definite formal education status irrespective of how they have attained it, or what sort of academic baggage and mechanical skills they have collected along the road; but it is also true that failure to have secured this formal evidence of achievement has denied, and is denying, many of our ablest youth an opportunity to prove their occupational worth in competition with those who have secured it, even though all too often they are deficient in both native ability and in the type of knowledge and skill which they are assumed to possess because of the presentation of credentials officially authenticated by nationally known educators.

Were each item on employment forms to be subjected to microscopic scrutiny for evidences of unfair discriminatory intent it is safe to assume that none would escape unscathed. "Age" and "sex" have long been resented by those who have read handicaps to the furtherance of their own ambitions in their inclusion, while "religious preferences" has been fiercely attacked by many whose intellectual vision was not broad enough to realize its constructive value in making a happy as well as a financially satisfactory adjustment. If, in the heat of the present controversy over antidiscriminatory legislation, another "Noble Experiment" should be born, it will not alter the fact that placement services must utilize discriminatory referral procedures, based on data which permit constructive discriminations, if they are to be of service to either client, and that such discriminatory practices begin with the securing and recording of all the helpful data on application and order forms.

Further elaboration of these criticisms and the way in which they, if expressed in legislation, may invalidate the most desirable—both socially and individually—methods of occupational distribution, will be found in Chapter VIII, which deals with Referral, and in Chapter XI, which is concerned with Junior Placement.

Just now it would be a step in the right direction if all who are sincerely interested in the equitable distribution of occupational opportunities would remember: (1) That no uniform list of items will serve all purposes equally well. Always additions and eliminations will be desirable. Forms too long, too short, or too complex for one purpose may be exactly right for another. (2) That some items are bound to be resented by some applicants as "none of your business," "too personal," "impertinent," and the like. It is not uncommon for employers or applicants to refuse to give information on some specific item. The obligatory filing of income tax returns and of filling out draft forms are accustoming all of our people to a new type of personal inquiry which includes highly discriminatory items and may serve to remove the stigma from employment forms. (3) That there will always be some persons, not only applicants but often under-experienced, socially interested persons, who will be inclined to jump to the conclusion that certain questions are asked solely for ulterior purposes. If such persons could learn to wait for a close-up of occupational pictures, their social contribution would be more valuable.

Perhaps, since there are those who think there is something sinister about its use, a few words should be said regarding the ways in which coding is sometimes used on application blanks. One usage omits from the blank certain items—not necessarily the same on all blanks—upon which data are desired but carries them in code, and the symbols only appear on the blank. The advantages are obvious. Here and there an abuse has had a tendency to discredit the practice but by no means to obliterate it. A second usage does not code data on the blank, but it expresses in code the over-all conclusions of interviewers based on all the material contained in the blank plus any additonal data secured during the interview. This writer has used both practices in her own placement work and has found both desirable. From the latter, when it is used by a large number of employing concerns, she has secured much useful counseling material.

CHAPTER VII

Placement Procedures—Securing Openings

Leaving the interview with the applicant at the point where the application form is completed and ready to file, with such occupational cross references as may have been determined upon, and the applicant is ready, either during the same or another interview, and with the same or another interviewer, to discuss openings, we turn to the complementary placement procedure involved in securing and recording orders so that they too may be available for referral purposes.

An employer's request for help is the counterpart of the applicant's request for a position. No placement service can operate without a continuous flow of both types of requests. Therefore, the securing and recording of orders must be regarded as a procedure of equal importance with the recruitment and registration of applicants.

Preliminary efforts to pave the way for receiving immediately available orders, and for soliciting additional orders, share in the general advertising, publicity, or public relations carried on by the service, and are furthered by the use of the usual media. After the service is in operation, opportunities for employment will be received as orders, by mail, over the telephone, or by personal contact. They may be given voluntarily without solicitation, or they may be the result of solicitation by means of any or all of the media mentioned; they may seek a single worker, one or more workers for the same type of work, or one worker for each of several types; depending on the status of the market, they may involve "spot" placement, time orders—fill it when you get a good applicant—or standing orders—whenever you get our type of applicant give us a ring.

The right of a given service to place limitations on the acceptance of orders parallels its right to refuse to register certain types of applicants. If the order does not come within the purview of the service, a statement to that effect accompanied by the name of another service, which is known to respond to such orders satisfactorily, will be sufficient and will keep the good will of the order giver. But when the order does come within the scope of the service and, because of some known practice or condition within the employing concern, the service does not wish to refer applicants, then it is not always easy to sidestep the order without incurring the hostility of the employer; and, as a rule, public services may not refuse any order for legal employment. Methods for dealing with orders which are not desirable vary: (1) The order may be accepted without comment, be filed and forgotten. (2) It may be accepted with some comment to the effect that applicants who meet the requirements are few, and it may not be possible to fill the order. (3) It may be tentatively accepted pending a personal visit for the purpose of getting a better picture of the job requirements. (4) It may be refused with a statement of the reason why the service does not wish to fill it. There is some dynamite in any of these methods; the most explosive type is found in the last-named choice; the greatest chance for constructive social service is found in the third.[1]

Receiving and Soliciting Orders by Mail

Receiving and soliciting orders by mail, even when the clientele is local, will probably always be practiced more or less. As a method of general solicitation it is convenient, economical, and reasonably productive. But the use of the mail in connection with placement practices has already been sufficiently discussed, and therefore the accent in this chapter is placed on the two major media through which orders are received and solicited—the telephone and the personal interview.

Receiving and Soliciting Orders by Telephone

Registration of applicants over the telephone, except for renewals, is rare; receiving employers' orders over the telephone is the method whereby a large part of local, and a considerable number of long-distance, orders are received. It is the outstanding method. This fact at once suggests a very important deficiency in employers' orders which does not obtain with reference to applicants for positions and which must be compensated for whenever possible. Personal contact with the applicant, while the registration form is being filled out, affords an excellent opportunity to study his personality, to ask for supplementary information, and to fill in such gaps in the identification picture as may exist. Telephone orders forbid the making of correspondingly accurate pictures of positions; therefore they entail an obligation on placement services to visit, at the earliest moment, concerns to which they make referrals in order to remedy this deficiency.

Solicitation over the telephone, once satisfactory contacts have been established and a picture of the concern as a whole and of its various

[1] See Chapter XI which deals with Junior Placement.

departments, or work units, has been obtained, is a common and entirely acceptable practice. Any alert service will find some opportunities to solicit orders in connection with the performance of other placement functions, and it will create opportunities which allow it to base solicitation on employers' needs rather than on the needs of the service or on those of applicants. For example, if the service has been unable to fill an order and later a promising applicant has registered, it may reopen the contact to inquire if a satisfactory candidate has been found elsewhere, or if it shall send the new registrant for an interview. Follow-up of referrals, or of placements, by telephone affords many opportunities for incidental solicitation, while frequent reference to seasonal calendars indicates when rush periods in different occupations are due and suggests that employers may appreciate a ring to see if they care for assistance in anticipating their peak demand for workers. The more definitely an employing clientele is impressed with the fact that a placement service is interested in their businesses and wants to understand their labor problems and help to meet their employment needs, the more standing orders it will receive and the more confidence there will be in its sifting or referral ability.

Who shall be charged with the responsibility of receiving and soliciting orders over the telephone? Where the volume of orders is large and the service is organized on a functional basis, a special corps or a single person may make all telephone contacts with employers. If the service is organized on a departmental basis, this function may be allocated to different interviewers. In small offices the problem is much simpler, but capable of causing considerable trouble, if it is not carefully thought through and wisely handled. No generally satisfactory answer to this query has ever been given.[2] Perhaps none may ever be found, for there is inherent in the placement process a quality which forbids satisfactory solution. Placement is a unified process. Ideally the person who receives employers' orders should register, and classify occupationally, all applicants, thereby being prepared to relate order specifications to applicant abilities and personalities, and to refer only those who best conform to requirements. If the volume of work passing through the office permits the undertaking of many functions, the same functionary may also do the field visiting, thus adding to his repertory ability to look beyond applicant analysis and job specification and visualize the applicant in the plant surroundings and in the work unit to which he may be assigned. Some do not feel that division of labor, accompanied by the use of functional spe-

[2] Probably it is justifiable to assume that few, if any, of the larger individual services have ever found a satisfactory answer.

cialists, militates against such a unified view of placement; others agree that it does but realize that it is a practical necessity.

The pros and cons offered by protagonists of each method are summarized for the consideration of the reader. They have remained fairly constant as experience has accumulated, and it must be remembered that type of service and qualifications of the operating personnel are both important factors in controlling the successful outcome of either method.

Among the arguments for functional order taking are: (1) Time is saved by the division of labor. (2) Specialists are more likely to secure complete specifications. (3) It relieves interviewers of interruptions and allows them to concentrate on their job. (4) Constant repetition of procedures results in the development of experts. (5) Employers like to hear the same voice, and continuity of contacts makes for confidence. (6) Specialists acquire a general knowledge of what employers are apt to demand. (7) If a telephone specialist takes orders, verifies placements, and solicits orders, he soon grows to feel his responsibility as a middleman between employers and interviewers, and he learns from the criticisms which are made on referrals.

Those who prefer to have the regular interviewers make the telephone contacts with employers argue: (1) That no time is saved because one person can receive and record but one order at a time, while delay often results in serious loss. (2) That it wastes both time and money because of the fact that employment office business is very irregular, fluctuating over seasons, days of the week, and hours of the day. Specialization prevents shifts in the office personnel to provide for peak loads. (3) That employers prefer to give their orders to the person who is going to make the referrals. They grow to feel that they are talking confidentially with someone who is familiar with their problems and their needs and is making a personal effort to meet them. Solicitors grow to feel that repeated contacts tend to establish the sort of relationship wherein considerable information which is not necessary, but which helps to complete the picture, is given. (4) That experienced interviewers resent "order clerks" being placed in positions which automatically permit them to act as supervisors and appraisers of the activities of their superiors.

SECURING ORDERS BY VISITATION

Plant visitation is of various kinds and is undertaken for a number of purposes, among which is order solicitation. Commercial agencies have visited business concerns for this purpose from their very inception, but public agencies gave it little or no attention until after World War I when labor surplus succeeded labor scarcity to such an extent that some of the large offices, and some of the specialized offices for servicemen, experimented with "flying squadrons" as a means of recruiting orders. Early in the period of demobilization such a squadron composed of both volunteers and paid solicitors was utilized in New York City. It was not much of a success so far as recruitment of orders was concerned, and almost immediately its members and their activities became the butt of many verbal and printed jokes. Harrison, who wrote during this period, summed up the situation very well. He reported that the members of the flying squadron "flew" every morning from their headquarters and all too frequently alighted upon some concern which had already been visited by several other fliers. "What's the idea?" employers asked as they exhibited their collection of fliers' cards.[3] Antagonism, rather than orders, was the net result, and the practice was discontinued.

During the same period public services which employed one or more "agents," "procurement men," or "traveling solicitors," increased in number. Some solicitors were specially trained, others were not. Some services reported that they were very satisfactory and quite indispensable; others found them both unsatisfactory and expensive and were turning to the telephone as a valuable and satisfactory substitute.

In 1930 the economic depression brought another type of mass solicitation into vogue, which, under the auspices of Committees on Unemployment, was used in a number of cities. It is exemplified by the work of the late Governor Smith's Co-ordinating Committee on Unemployment, which, under the auspices of the Welfare Council of New York City, undertook a canvass of employers in Greater New York in order to secure openings for the unemployed. The avowed aims of such committees varied. Some confined themselves strictly to the business of solicitation; others wandered into the field of social-economic reform and confused the business aspect of employment with its philanthropic aspects. The New York Committee recruited a group of volunteer solicitors from nonprofit employment agencies and from other groups of interested persons, including graduate students in local universities. Obviously some were experienced workers in the employment field, others were not. All were trained in teams under team captains beginning on December 3, 1930, and on the same day the canvass, which was to continue for two weeks, began.[4]

---

[3] Harrison and others, *Public Employment Offices*, p. 263.

[4] The slogans used and printed on solicitors' calling cards—"Give a Job," "Make a Job," "Don't Discharge"—and presented by volunteer solicitors were a bad combination, and, had not the serious predicament of the unemployed made such a strong appeal, they would have been openly resented, as they frequently were *sub rosa*, as bad business for intelligent placement services.

Training was directed toward the accomplishment of four specific aims: (1) to familiarize employers with, and urge them to patronize, noncommercial services; (2) to solicit jobs; (3) to request employers to maintain current wage standards; and (4) to retain their working forces. It will be noted that the first two are very definitely legitimate employment service aims, while the last two fall into an entirely different category. Prevailing philosophies of placement did not, in 1930, permit the combination of such conflicting aims. By that date, it was generally agreed that selling a placement service and soliciting jobs is a business, not a charity, proposition; that, under normal conditions, it calls for tact, judgment, and high-class sales ability; and that during a depression, when employers as well as workers are struggling to preserve their financial integrity, it calls for the addition of considerable "nerve," without taking on the extraneous and unpleasant duty of asking those from whom jobs are being solicited not to lower wages and not to dismiss any of their employees. The first series of aims, difficult enough, could be accomplished with credit to the sponsoring agencies; the second, after the publication by the Council that it was "fully conscious of the difficulties that beset employers in times like these," seemed nothing less than philanthropic impertinence doomed to failure and bound to antagonize.[5]

There was little or no criticism on the programs of such of these committees on unemployment as confined their objectives to order solicitation. Everyone appreciated the economic situation and, whether or not jobs could be offered, solicitors were courteously received and their pleas listened to. But there were certain inherent features in the plan entirely aside from the confusion of aims in some cities, which, while they handicapped its immediate success, exercised a beneficial influence on the development of future methods of job solicitation. Among them were (1) the use of volunteers for one of the most difficult employment procedures;

[5] This writer was, at the time, offering a course on Placement Principles, Practices, and Problems in New York University. The Council's program and its aims were discussed in the class, and some who were willing to volunteer for the first series of aims objected to taking part in the second. A letter stating the objections to combining the two objectives was sent to the Council, and the following was received as a part of its reply. It is quoted because it is illustrative of the remnants of an earlier, and still prevailing, philosophy which does not differentiate the work of a public employment service from that of social reforms and charities: ". . . the Welfare Council feels strongly that the present standards and present working forces should be maintained. I am extremely sorry if you do not agree with us on this, for it seems to me a matter of very great importance that all possible emphasis be placed on these two important factors in the present situation. If we do not seek to maintain these two items, it seems to me we are undermining all of the past industrial history in this country" (Letter of December 10, 1930, to Anna Y. Reed).

(2) the use of any solicitors, volunteer or paid, whose training period had been limited to a few days; (3) the duplication of solicitation due to failure to organize the field and "clear" visits; (4) the antagonism which solicitors from nonprofit bureaus aroused when they attempted to combine conflicting aims, an antagonism resulting in loss of confidence in such services rather than securing support for them; (5) the use of such programs for the practical training of students.

This depression type of visitation for the purpose of job solicitation was never used by commercial agencies, and the social philosophy upon which it was based was severely challenged by the more experienced and more professional worker everywhere. A few leaders in the field before 1920, and many between 1920 and 1930, had rejected the idea that placement was a philanthropic function and had demanded its recognition as a business function. This more professional attitude toward placement was accented in the 1930's by the various subsidized experiments in placement and employment procedure which have been mentioned as going forward in Minnesota, Rochester, Philadelphia, New York City, Cincinnati, and elsewhere. As a result there is today a much better understanding of all the procedures of the placement process as business propositions, and plant visitation, one purpose of which is order solicitation, is now looked upon as a business function—a function which has its own techniques and which may be undertaken for the sole purpose of solicitation or may be combined with a number of other purposes. During the formulation of these conclusions attention has been given to each one of the five handicaps cited and methods of overcoming them have been suggested. Current practices, in the main, have incorporated these suggestions in their procedures, which are presented under six topics:

Choice of Contacts. Any placement service which expects to win and to hold the support of two types of patrons must choose its employer contacts to balance its openings, as well as is possible both as to quantity and quality, with its applicants. Therefore, from the first announcement publicity to its periodic personal visits it will give its major attention to concerns which seem to have the type of jobs for which its type of applicants qualify. A preliminary community survey such as was described in Part Two may have revealed potential opportunities for making desirable contacts. If no survey findings are available, lists may be compiled from various directories and associations. Original contact lists will be increased as new firms are established or as want advertisements and information from friends and applicants suggest the possibility of adding new patrons to the previously acquired list.

Who Shall Visit? Much the same factors are involved in this problem as were involved in attempting to determine who should solicit orders over the telephone, and consideration of the various possibilities results in much the same differences of opinion. One or more specialists are sometimes used in a functionalized service. In other services plant visitation is combined with telephone contacts, or is distributed among the interviewers. In small offices the director may make all employer contacts, while in other offices volunteers, apprentices, or newly appointed employees are used.

Before determining who shall undertake this responsibility, directors will do well to remember that job solicitation requires much tact and judgment, that it is primarily a salesman function, requiring special qualifications as a salesman, and that those who undertake it need a broad and sympathetic understanding of industrial and business problems, ability to observe accurately, question indirectly, and conceal their unfavorable reactions to anything they may see or hear. Moreover they should have been thoroughly schooled in the art of meeting destructive and constructive criticism on the service which they represent. As a rule such qualifications are not possessed by volunteers and are still to be acquired by apprentices and novitiates. On the other hand, it is hardly wise to advocate complete rejection of these inexperienced groups. Volunteers are sometimes the only persons available, and now and then they prove to be very satisfactory. Employment service recruits must be provided from some source, both to fill the vacancies which occur and to take new placement service positions; and the statement, "There is no substitute for experience," as a method of training, has been rather generally endorsed. So again, placement directors face a dilemma—no experience, no recruits; inexperience which antagonizes, no employers' orders.

Somewhere and sometime the in-preparation-for-employment-service personnel must secure experience in every phase of employmen⸍ procedure. Therefore, if it seems best to permit such persons to visit employers, it will lessen the chance of antagonism and of loss of clientele if (1) they are not sent out on "cold" contacts, but are assigned to carefully selected, or "easy" contacts, where the way has already been paved and friendly relations have been established; (2) they are not sent out unless, under careful supervision, they have made a study of the previous records of the business to be visited and have noted its hirings, discharges, retentions, and promotions, and their causes, and are thoroughly familiar with order forms and the items which they are expected to secure.

Some placement services train volunteers and beginners by sending them out for their initial experiences with an experienced solicitor. But "Go alone" has been an approved slogan among experienced solicitors for a long time. Employers whose confidence has been betrayed by the presence of a third party are loathe to discuss their business before strangers and are prone to reserve their most important contributions, for "sometime when you come alone."

This writer, before experience taught her better, attempted to help counselors and teachers increase their understanding of employment problems, and of job specifications in their relation to education and counseling, by taking them, one at a time, with her on her plant visits. In spite of the previsit emphasis which was put upon the necessity for silence and the concealing of unfavorable reactions when conditions of work or comfort facilities appealed to them as undesirable or inadequate, they frequently blurted out, so suddenly and so spontaneously that she could not soften the effect, "Are those all the washing facilities you have?" "How can anyone do that sort of thing all day?" In one instance the counselor exclaimed, "That girl over there is a graduate of our high school and she's too good to do that sort of work." The manager replied, "She has not done it so well, as yet, that we care to promote her." Later in the day he called the office and, after some brief comment, said, "Please come alone after this." The number of inexperienced women who make such blunders seems to exceed the number of inexperienced men who commit similar errors, while the number of older women exceeds the number of younger women. Perhaps men are more familiar with the work world than are women, and therefore are less surprised when they encounter the usual or notice variations therefrom; perhaps social-minded women who have reached maturity without first-hand knowledge of occupational life have manufactured a utopian picture of the business world which, as yet, time has prevented the younger woman from doing.

Some of the commercial agencies have a custom which, while not instituted for that purpose, gives educators an opportunity to keep in touch with the current and changing demands of occupational life. *Suitable* and *qualified* school counselors who have time to spare are engaged as solicitors on a commission basis and are furnished with a list of contacts. Among those who have reported on their experience, some "tramp all day and get no orders"; others "do fairly well and learn a lot"; while a third group do so well that they make more money in a day than they do in teaching. One woman who worked for an excellent agency and was an excellent school counselor was exceptionally successful as a solicitor and thoroughly enjoyed the work. She visited a variety of concerns and always brought back orders, sometimes for service personnel in hotels and sometimes for professional workers.

No matter who may be chosen for plant visitation, the function should never be performed hit or miss, never as an odd job by anyone who has a bit of free time in which to "run out and make a call." Someone, even in small offices, should be responsible for the planning and supervision of the task, and all who share in it should be carefully chosen and definitely prepared for it. Always the responsible party should remember that employers like to give their orders to those who are to fill them, and that too many different solicitors, or too frequent solicitation, are apt to antagonize, and he should so plan his program that it includes, so far as possible, compliance with the former and studied avoidance of the latter.

Preparation for Visitation. The first step in the preparation for personal solicitation of orders is the designation of some person who is charged with responsibility for outlining a program for visits, and for the training of every person who participates in carrying it out. The second step, if it has not already been taken in connection with other purposes for which field visits are made, is the grouping of concerns to be solicited by geographical location and by industrial and occupational classifications. Within these groupings, classifications may be made which indicate the frequency with which previous visits have been made and the time of the year, month, and day which has proved to be, or has been suggested as, most convenient for the employer and most productive of orders for the service.

The arrangement of calls by localities and the timing of calls are of equal importance. The former saves expense and travel time, and, since heel cooling is a common secondary (now and then a primary) occupation for solicitors, it may allow the solicitor, while he waits for one appointment, "to drop in while in your neighborhood" and secure an order or a report on a previous placement. Usually one cannot make more than two or three calls in a half-day. "Timing" spaces calls advantageously, assigns them to dates which are anticipatory of peak seasons when employers are more responsive to solicitation, and allocates them to times in the month when reports and other duties are less apt to interfere and to hours of the day when other demands upon the employing personnel are usually lightest. But planners need to remember that the best time for visitation for one purpose is not necessarily the best for other purposes. For example, one would not visit a restaurant during the lunch period to solicit orders, but it might be the most propitious time to study the preferred type of employee and the degree of efficiency required. Usually the early morning hours are needed for other duties and therefore are not considered very desirable for visitation.

The third step in preparing for visits is concerned with the "clearance" of programs presently to be executed. No service if it would avoid duplications and omissions may depend upon random visitation. The one-person office must clear with itself—check over its own records. If there are several workers in a single unit service who do soliciting, the clearance of programs among these workers is even more essential, while the clearance of both long-term and current programs as between the several units of the same service, or of co-operating services, are an indispensable part of a general clearance program for many other purposes.

The Approach to the Interview. Personal preparation for an interview with an employer involves securing full information regarding the firm to be visited and the name and rank of the person to be seen. If possible, this person should be the head, or chief, employing functionary. After that, the more subordinates, including supervisors and foremen, who participate in the employing function or under whom the applicants are going to work, with whom a solicitor becomes acquainted, the better he will know how to describe openings and visualize applicants for referral. On the other hand, he must be very careful not to overstep the regular lines of authority lest he antagonize those whom he has slighted.

There seems to be no agreement as to the better method of securing an interview—by appointment or by dropping in. Some very successful solicitors never make appointments, others always do, while a third group have no preference but use either method which seems desirable at the moment. If appointments are made, it is exceedingly important that the solicitor be prompt in keeping the appointment but that he show no resentment if he is asked to wait, as will very frequently be the case. In the larger concerns, where secretarial watchdogs guard their superior's time, it is sometimes impossible to see an upper executive unless an appointment has been made. In the smaller concerns where freedom of entry is allowed the employing executive may be found on the floor, and a caller can judge for himself whether or not it is an opportune time to approach him.

There are various ways whereby solicitors announce their arrival and the purpose of their call, especially if the concern is a new contact or if the caller is making his first visit. The presentation of a card, which serves as an introduction and has definite sales value, if in good taste, is a help to any solicitor even though, after first acquaintance, he may not care to use it. Perhaps he may be able to cite some specific reason for thinking that a call at this particular time might be helpful to the employer. For example, he may have learned that extra help was needed from a former or a present employee, from another employer, from a mutual friend, from newspaper advertisements, and the like. There are a number of reasons which might be very useful provided they are of such character that they may safely be used as introductions. The source of information and the judgment of the solicitor has to determine that. Sometimes the best approach is through the follow-up of referrals, or placements, with new orders being relegated to a secondary place.

The personal appearance, knowledge of business etiquette, and "attitudes" of a solicitor are very important since they are bound to be either assets or liabilities. Personal appearance must not be neglected, and gentlemanly conduct is essential. Helping one's self to a seat without an invitation, smoking in another person's office without some indication of its acceptability, asking to use a telephone, or using it without asking, and assuming that risqué stories are good icebreakers are hazardous methods of salesmanship. A display of labor or police insignia or betrayal of "wicked employer" or "exploited worker" complexes creates an impression that labor inspection, law enforcement, and "spying" are the real purpose of the visit and defeat the accomplishment of its legitimate purpose. If a job solicitor remembers that he is a salesman working for a highly competitive business, he will make his sales appeal in a dignified, businesslike way, stressing the fitness, never the need, of what he has to sell, and he will avoid the attitude of pleading or begging for jobs.

The Character and Content of the Interview. The sales character of the interview is its dominant factor, and its content should be built around the employer's needs and what the solicitor can do to meet them. A few points, both negative and positive, which tend to enhance friendly relations and to further the accomplishment of the objective of the contact are enumerated:

(1) Begin with some complimentary remark, or some question or comment which is apt to interest, and not likely to irritate, an employer.

(2) Don't ask questions if the information can be secured from observation or from authentic printed material. Confine questions to those which are helpful and essential. At all times avoid impertinent questions or reminding an employer of unpleasant labor experiences which he may have had.

(3) It is wiser not to comment either favorably or unfavorably on the employer's competitors or on competitors of the service—on commercial agencies when the solicitor represents a public agency, or vice versa; or on

other business concerns, especially if they are engaged in the same line.

(4) Observe everything, but confine comments and questions to "your own business." Don't pay any attention (openly) to law violations. Solicitors who do will lose their chance to perform their own functions. Every state has inspectors and they, not solicitors, should perform enforcement functions.

(5) Judiciously revealed knowledge of an employer's business, of his employment problems under prevailing conditions, or under prospective changes may appeal to him, but there are some employers to whom even the mention of social legislation, labor unions, or labor contracts are a "red flag."

(6) Get all the information, and get it as quickly and as tactfully as possible. *All the information* means all the data about the concern and the specific job which is necessary in order to select the most promising candidate for referral and to permit the applicant to determine whether or not he wishes to apply. Deficiencies in information which require calling back or returning in person to verify or supplement orders leave an unfavorable impression, provided the data were available and should have been secured during the first visit. Sometimes deficiencies, not immediately revealed, are the fault of employers who give orders so carelessly that the contact man is obliged to secure additional information or clarify that already given.

(7) The avoidance of sore spots when securing essential information is an art to be assiduously practiced. When resentment is caused by over-zealous solicitors who feel obliged to dot all the *i's* and cross all the *t's* on wages, job tenure, and advancement, it usually indicates that the solicitor is underprepared for his job and should fortify himself with certain types of additional knowledge before he makes further contacts. Take the question of wages and salaries; there are many occupations in which minimum wages are fixed by law. Solicitors who are familiar with these laws and the occupations in which they are in force do not need wage information on such occupations. They do need wage information in other occupations and they should get it, but they do not need to insist on it to the last dollar and cent. A reasonable wage range, with some explanation of the variables which control the allocation of different employees within the range, is quite sufficient. Unless so many employees are performing the same task that the salary has become standard, few employers care to fix an exact salary until they have had a chance to interview the person who is to receive it.

Another word which often rubs employers the wrong way is *advance-*

ment. When a solicitor sees alluring statements in advertisements and window signs, or hears them over the radio, in connection with common occupations with whose practices and possibilities he should be perfectly familiar, it is unnecessary and unwise for him to challenge the veracity of the employer, for he knows that "Choose your own hours," "Splendid chance for advancement," and "Big pay for little work," are just catch lines. Moreover, his experience will have taught him that advancement requires active preparation for promotion on the part of the employee as well as promises on the part of the employer and that employees are frequently more responsible than employers for failures to win promotions.

(8) Unfavorable comments, if unsolicited, on wages, jobs, or conditions of work are apt to put the employer on the defensive and may lead to the breaking off of contacts with the service which the solicitor represents. Examples of ill-advised comments are abundant: "My goodness, one man can't do all that list of things"; "What makes you think a college graduate is going to do matron's work?"; "That's the lowest salary we've ever been offered for an accountant"; "Which shall we send you—a janitor or an engineer?"; "No good stenographer will operate a duplicating machine." There is a tactful comeback to each one of the statements which caused these comments, and a solicitor who cannot find it on his own initiative should find an occupation in which his talents can be used to better advantage.

Closing the Interview. It is very important that each employer interview be brought to a close in an atmosphere of friendly co-operation, for it is by means of field visits, well-planned and effectively carried out, that placement services strengthen confidence in the quality of their service, widen their clientele, and increase their prestige. It is also important that the solicitor leave before he has worn out his welcome. The contact may or may not have resulted in an order, but time and attention given solicitors requires an appropriate expression of appreciation and thanks. Every solicitor hopes to receive an invitation to call again. If he does not, or if he is asked to make less frequent calls, or if, during the interview, he has received criticisms on the service or suggestions for its improvement, he will report back to his superiors and both will make use of the report in appraising and improving their efficiency.

RECORDING AND FILING EMPLOYERS' ORDERS

An order form is the instrument which parallels the application blank and serves to so describe the opening, or type of job, that it will be distinguishable from other jobs, or at least assign it to a job family. The record on the order blank should individualize the opening in the same way that the content of the application blank individualizes the applicant, and it should also contribute certain elements to the unified picture which will allow the referral interviewer to visualize the job for which a selection is to be made. This may seem to be a less difficult task than is making verbal pictures of individuals; perhaps there will be more facts and fewer variables; but it is no less important, for there can be no complete visualization of a worker in a work situation without it.

Record blanks used by different services vary as to form, content, and arrangement, but the same fundamental principles control, and the items will be much the same for the same types of positions and must correspond to similar or complementary items found on application blanks. A broad classification of items might include:

(1) Identification data which locates the business and supplies the routine information necessary for making mail, telephone, or personal contacts.

(2) Job requirements and rewards which indicate the physical and mental qualities, the knowledge, and the skill required for the work to be done, and the financial and other rewards [6] for doing it satisfactorily. Job specifications should be given in sufficient detail to cover all the requirements which the job makes upon the worker and the conditions under which the work is to be done, and they should be so written that they may be accurately read by any other official who needs to use them. To record only machine operator, drill-press operator, laboratory technician, engineer, or packer does not tell the necessary story.[7] There are many makes of machines, many kinds of operators, many engineering fields, each requiring special preparation, and numerous kinds of laboratory workers. What makes of machines are used in a garment factory, and does the operator make the entire garment or does she do section work? The solicitor may answer such questions for himself while in the plant, but when orders are taken over the telephone, it is necessary to ask for and record all such information.

Any special difficulties likely to be encountered on the job whether personal or mechanical in character are helpful data. Wages, hours, and probable duration of work are essential information. Whether salary data are given during a personal interview or are received by mail or over the telephone, whenever an employer states a salary he automatically gives

---

[6] Pensions, vacations, stock ownership, etc.

[7] See U.S. Employment Service, *The Dictionary of Occupational Titles* (Washington, D.C., 1939–1944).

an order taker, if he keeps abreast of the labor market, a fairly good idea of the type of ability, knowledge, and experience for which he is looking.

(3) Applicant qualifications which cover the qualities that the employer desires taken into consideration by those who attempt to help him in sifting applicants and which he expects to use in making his final selection. These qualities have already received considerable attention in connection with the discussion of application blanks. Among them are age, sex, race, religion, nationality, status as a citizen or alien, or as a veteran, general education, special education, experience record, physical, mental and emotional characteristics, and sometimes rather elaborate personality ratings. Preferences may be called for; wages expected will usually be asked; and when work can be begun is often a deciding item in employment.

There should be room on the order form to note how many applicants the employer desires to have referred and for how long a time the service may consider the order "exclusive." Good solicitors will usually want some provision for recording their observations on the material and personal aspects of their visit. Since such comments are largely subjective in character they should never be placed where they can be confused with objective data secured during the visit, nor should they be confused with the opinions or comments of firm representatives. Usually it is considered wiser to put them on a separate sheet, which, if the situation changes, may be removed from the files.

As has been implied, certain clerical duties devolve upon order solicitors which, unless they are assigned to other members of the force, should be performed immediately after a field visit. Every service, the smallest and the largest, should maintain a series of reports which are concerned with the results of field visits. A central system of such reports will comprise: (1) A report of the visit which contains information necessary for planning future visits to suit the convenience of employers, to catch peak loads, and to dovetail visits in such a way that the time of the solicitor may be saved, as well as all the information necessary for referrals. This report is the permanent record, and the data must comprise clear, pertinent, and concrete facts. After the report is made it should be carefully checked to be sure that its content can be understood and correctly interpreted by others. (2) A cumulative record of openings. (3) An employer's index card.

Filed in a convenient place, either alphabetically or by industries, employers' orders are accessible to all in the same office and may be cleared through a central office if several units use the same files. Fixed or movable colored tabs are often attached along the top of the card as signals. Their significance varies, and there are no special rules for their use, but frequently they indicate the geographical location of plants, suggest time for next visits, segregate occupational groups, and the like.

Two important topics connected with employers' orders remain to be considered: canceled openings, and conferences on the results of solicitation which serve the dual purpose of an appraisal method and a method of in-service, apprentice, or volunteer training.

CANCELED ORDERS

Orders once given may be canceled on the initiative of either the service or the employer. Some placement services have definite periods of validity for both applicants and openings at the expiration of which, unless there are renewals, they are transferred to the inactive files.[8] Other services carry openings in the active files until they are canceled by the employer or filled by the service, or until the service has admitted its inability to respond to the call and suggested that some other medium be tried. When cancellation is initiated by the employer, it may be due to one or more causes which it is very important for the service to know. There is little material in print on this subject, but what little there is is comparatively recent and has been the result of careful inquiry.[9]

The outstanding cause of employer cancellation is, "Order filled from some other source." This statement raises many questions. If no applicants were referred, Why? Were no qualified applicants available? Were qualified applicants unwilling to apply? Were applicants, who did not apply, referred? And so on. Undoubtedly every placement service will profit by a periodic survey which reveals the relation between orders received, orders filled, and orders canceled. Analysis of the reasons for cancellation will show the following (among those attributable to the employing concern): the employer secured an employee from some other source or decided not to fill, or some factor in the concern made applicants prefer to work elsewhere. Those chargeable against the placement service will center around such items as inability to make applicant contact, lack of qualified applicants, applicant not employed, applicant engaged but did

---

[8] Some services do not use inactive files.

[9] See Atkinson and others, *Public Employment Service*, pp. 341–343, who give a brief but inclusive summary on the Cancellation of Employers' Orders; D. V. Varley and Molly H. Wilson, "An Analysis of Cancelled Openings," *Employment Service News* (Dec., 1936), p. 7, who cover New York State Service and National Reemployment Service openings and cancellations in private industry during 1935; and Gladys L. Palmer, *Trends in the Philadelphia Labor Market in 1934* (Philadelphia: University of Pennsylvania Press, 1935), p. 11.

not report for work, slowness in making referrals, co-operating services competed and made the placement.

STAFF CONFERENCES

Staff conferences which appraise the entire procedure of order solicitation from planning a list of visits to challenging the extent to which orders are promptly recorded and quickly and satisfactorily filled are an effective method of improving placement services, keeping the entire staff alert and growing, and checking up on weak spots in operational procedures. Perhaps an interservice clearance system is needed, or new sources for the recruitment of applicants should be found; perhaps referrals have been carelessly made, or job specifications have been inadequate. No matter what such appraisals may reveal, the enumeration of the strong and weak spots in methods of securing, recording, and filling orders affords a liberal education in a very important phase of the employment process.

CHAPTER VIII

Placement Procedures—Referring Applicants

THE placement service has, up to this point in the placement process, been acting in the capacity of an assembling agency. It has collected and prepared for use complementary sets of data—orders from applicants and orders from employers. It is now ready to assume the responsibilities of a sifting or selecting agency, a function which must be exercised equally in the interest of employer and employee. This distributive aspect of placement is called "referral."

From a broad social viewpoint it involves procedures that must be carried on by functionaries who are thoroughly conversant with the characteristics of modern occupational life and with those of present-day workers—who know the demands which different jobs make on workers and the responsibilities which modern industrial and business organizations place on management. From a narrower point of view, it involves the selection of applicants whose registration records indicate that they are potentially desirable persons to fill the positions which employers' orders show to be open. Therefore, referral may be regarded as the effort which the service makes to respond to an employer's order. It opens the way for a sale, and a purchase, of services. Closing the sale is another matter.

THE SELECTIVE FUNCTION OF THE REFERRAL INTERVIEWER

The referral interviewer, if there be one and if not some substitute functionary, is charged with the performance of this phase of the employment process. He is the middleman. But he may not hope to render a constructive middleman service to employers unless those who service him provide him with adequate and accurate analyses of workers' capacities, knowledges, skills, ambitions, experiences, and their personality assets and liabilities. Nor can he hope to render a constructive service to applicants unless he has at his command adequate and accurate information as to the requirements of openings against which to check applicants' qualifications and desires. It is his job to refer *qualified* applicants, and *qualified* means those whose experience, education, and physical, mental, and emotional characteristics are such that they give promise of making the necessary adjustments quickly and easily.

In addition to employers' orders and applicants' orders, which are always first essentials, the referral officer may need, at different times, some of the other tools which have been mentioned in connection with the equipment of a placement service such as occupational dictionaries, tests of various kinds, company charts showing vertical and horizontal lines of promotion, transportation charts, and lists of special educational services.

The interview is universally conceded to be the key technique in all the major employment procedures. Nothing, as yet, has been found to take its place, although one or two services have reported the discarding of the referral interview in favor of selection of referrals directly from the record files. Endorsement of such a procedure assumes that all the information will be available on the record, that no worth-while supplementary data are to be secured during a referral interview, that the applicant has no right, or does not wish, to participate in deciding whether or not he shall be referred; and it places entire responsibility for the assignment of referrals on an official who may never even have seen the individual whom he is allocating to jobs.

Needless to state, this procedure is ultra impersonal and objective. For the immediate purpose it seems safe to assume that whenever the interview has been discarded, it should be credited to the wave of enthusiasm for objectivity which has recently swept through the ranks of social workers rather than to a green light from the experimental psychologists, who are continuously studying the developmental possibilities of the interview as an employment technique. Therefore, it will doubtless be more helpful to those of limited experience if referral is approached as an interview technique.

Before elaboration of the place of the interview in the referral procedure it is well to recall that three types of interdependent interviews, each having specific and somewhat different purposes, have been mentioned in connection with service to applicants. When all three of these interviews are conducted by the same official, immediately and consecutively in point of time, they may be, and usually are, considered as a single interview, even though, as in this book, they may be broken down for study and discussion purposes. But in the larger offices the interviewing function is more apt to be differentiated according to purpose, and "split" procedures, reception-registration and registration-referral, are common. The preliminary interview comes first and is assigned to a receptionist. In some types of services it may be very brief. Business personnel departments, which use it as a method of weeding out undesirable would-be applicants, are apt to make it rather elaborate. Some commercial agencies follow the same practice, but public agencies and institutional services are not usually in a position to do much preliminary sifting.

The registration interview comes second. The responsibility for collecting and recording all the necessary applicant information without causing friction or resentment is placed upon the official who conducts this interview. The satisfactory performance of his duties requires a wide range of occupational, educational, legal, and community information, familiarity with the tools used for employment purposes, and a keen psychological insight into human nature and human motives. The degree of efficiency with which this interview is conducted is a major determining factor of the degree of success which will attend the referral interview and its outcome.

The referral interview comes last. It functions as a method of selecting applicants for, and distributing them in, employment. It has been said, and is believed by some, that, barring the unemployables, for every job there is a type of individual who will never make good, one who will do fairly well, and one who will be successful. In a utopia, where functionaries always collect material which will definitely differentiate these types and where those who use it never commit errors of fact or judgment, it may happen that the first type will never be referred to a job in which he will not make good, while the third type will be accorded high selection priority. To strive to realize on this ideal postulate is the function of the referral interviewer. The extent to which he does realize on it is the measure of his service to the applicant, to the employer, and to the public.[1]

The experienced interviewer knows, what the inexperienced will soon learn, that he must work toward this ideal within certain limitations which are beyond his control. Some of these which already have been mentioned are the policies of the service as laid down by the administrative authorities, labor-union restrictions, the mobility of workers, the attributes of workers, the organization of industry and the conditions under which work is to be performed, legislative restrictions, and social traditions and prejudices. The influence of such limitations is frequently expressed in forms which tend to keep the labor reserve continuously decentralized on a nationality, religious, sex, age, race, education, or membership basis, and decentralization is always a handicap to the effective distribution of labor. Moreover, service agencies which purport to guide public opinion in the direction of constructive social-economic action are not always alert to the fact that two of the most influential handicaps cited,

[1] There has been some uneasiness among professional workers lest, under our scheme of unemployment insurance, the unfit unemployed be referred as a means of reducing insurance costs.

social traditions and prejudices and restrictive legislation, are directly controlled by the attitudes and activities of the general public.

In addition to the limitations within which referral officers must work, there is a considerable variety of problems which arise in connection with the daily performance of their selective function and with which they must be prepared to cope. Some will recur so often that eventually definite policies, or at least guiding principles, will have been worked out; others will occur infrequently, sometimes quite unexpectedly, and their wise solution will depend entirely upon the experience and resourcefulness of interviewers. Such problems are difficult to classify and perhaps are better presented as they are likely to occur in practice as the referral procedure goes forward.

CLASSIFICATION OF ORDERS FOR REFERRALS

Employers' orders of four types, emergency, standing, exclusive, and usual, require referral attention. An order which is about to be filled may fall into any one of the four categories.

If it is an *emergency order*, it will probably have come to the referral desk directly from the person who received it. It must be given immediate attention and may result in a spot placement, but rarely in a carefully selected referral.[2] Some services do not accept emergency orders on the ground that they are unnecessary, upset the regular work, and do not warrant the extra expenditure of time and money. Others feel that occasionally any business, even an educational institution, is forced to secure an employee on short notice and that hotels and restaurants and such professional workers as nurses are entitled to emergency services. If the service accepts emergencies, there is little or no time for selection and sifting. An applicant who is available and willing to accept may be located, consulted, and instructed where to report over the telephone. If no applicant is on hand, then clearance of the order, provided such facilities are available, is a possibility. Since this type of order permits little, or no, exercise of discriminatory ability, it may be passed over without further discussion.

If it is a *standing order*, referral will be dependent upon the appearance of just the right type of applicant, rather than on the fact that an order has been booked; therefore it too may be passed over with a minimum of attention. Standing orders are predicated on the assumption that the serv-

---

[2] For a good but brief discussion of emergency orders in public services, see *Proceedings of the Twenty-fifth Annual Convention of the International Association of Public Employment Services* (U.S. Department of Labor, Bull. no. 14, 1937), pp. 104–105.

ice to which they are given is so thoroughly conversant with the needs of the concern which gives them and so familiar with the type of employee which has heretofore been satisfactory to the organization that it will recognize the type in any applicant who may register. Not every place-ment service can command the confidence necessary to secure such orders, not every employing concern can profitably make use of them, and not every occupation warrants their use. But, if conditions are favorable, and if service officials can visualize a standard type of applicant as habitually satisfactory and satisfied in a standard situation, and if they neither overdo referrals nor use their clientele as dumping grounds, employers fre-quently prefer to employ, and carry until needed, a promising potential rather than to risk a less desirable selection when the need is more pressing.

Exclusive order [3] is a comparatively new expression in placement glos-saries, although this type of order has been in practical use for a long time. An order which is given with the understanding that the service which accepts it has the exclusive right to fill it for a stated period of time is called an "exclusive order." Such orders, properly handled, are advan-tageous for all three parties concerned. The applicant accepts his introduc-tion knowing that he has been carefully selected, has been invited to apply, and will receive the interested attention of the concern to which he has been referred. This gives him confidence, helps him to make a good appearance, and assists him to sell his services. The employer knows, from his own experience, that a placement service which can save him time, energy, and money in the preliminary sifting of applicants is a genuine "find," and he recognizes the injustice of giving his orders to several competing agencies with the ultimate necessity of canceling one or more after the expenditure of considerable unremunerated time and money in his behalf. The placement service which can develop methods of estab-lishing and holding a permanent exclusive-order clientele will enhance its reputation, establish its service on a higher professional basis, and protect and increase its profits.

The usual order is exactly what the term implies. The great volume of orders in most services is found under this category. Usually no time limit is set for filling orders unless asked for; doubtless many orders are regis-tered with more than one service; cancellations are common; and the employer takes no responsibility for preferential consideration of referrals. The necessity for speed in selection frequently forbids the care in selection

[3] Forest L. Miller, "Exclusive Orders," *ibid.*, pp. 66–67, 106, describes the exclusive order system of the Cincinnati Public Employment Service whereby employers make written contracts in solicitor's order books. A definite time is stated during which the exclusive right to fill the order maintains.

which characterizes the best placement practices. Since the majority of the readers of this book will have primary interest in usual and in exclusive orders, these orders will receive the accent in the presentation of the procedures which follow.

REFERRAL PROCEDURES

After an employer's order has been received by mail, over the telephone, or as the result of personal solicitation, the following steps are taken in the course of the referral procedure: (1) The job order is studied to make sure that the requirements are clear and thoroughly understood. (2) The applicant file is canvassed, and the records of those from which selection is to be made are removed. (3) One or more potentialities are summoned by means of call-in cards, telephone, telegraph, or special messenger. (4) A selection, or sifting, interview results in decisions "to refer or not to refer" and "to apply or not to apply." (5) The applicant is dismissed and his record returned to the files, or he is referred by means of an introduction or referral card.

Analyzing the Employer's Order. The referral interviewer approaches the employer's order from the point of view of one who is about to take the employer's place in the making of a preliminary judgment for him. Therefore, to the utmost possible degree, he must strive to put, and to keep, himself in the employer's position until the entire referral procedure has been completed. He must know the various bases upon which, under the same conditions, the employer would make the selection himself and the type of person whom he would think suitable for the vacancy. Possession of this guiding information assumes that the interviewer has interpreted correctly the psychology of the individual employer, and perhaps also that of the supervisor under whom the applicant will work, and that he is familiar with and will respect the employment philosophy of the organization with which he is dealing, no matter what his own philosophy, or that of the service he represents, may be.

History reveals, and Part One of this book has tried to indicate, that there has never been a single, or a static, employment philosophy. Conflicting philosophies and changing philosophies are important factors in social evolution and are bound to continue just as long as social knowledge increases and paves the way for new and different interpretations of society and better understandings of man in his activities as a social being. This makes it very important that referral officials understand the various philosophies of the employing concerns which they service. If a business organization does not deserve co-operation, it should not receive it: but if it does deserve co-operation in meeting its employment demands, it should receive the type of service which knows how to draw the line between a subjective attitude toward applicants who are in need of employment and an objective attitude toward fitness for work. An individual whose philosophy does not help him to see, and to make this distinction, between people who need work and people who qualify for work is thereby disqualified for placement work.

If the employer's point of view and his philosophy are understood and if his situation and his attitude toward employment problems have been correctly interpreted, translation of the items on the order blank into a concept of the ideal person whom the interviewer would like to select for referral follows. Each of the essential items is given attention. But which items are *essential?* That is a question which the interviewer must answer with respect to each individual order. Among the wide range of openings which come to various placement services many are of such a character that essential items are few, and checkups and selections for referral are quickly made. But in every order one or more items are apt to be so essential that they become the dominant factor in referral. The location of the work may be an essential factor in selection since men who own their own homes, have families, live at home, or object to transportation facilities will not accept an out-of-town position. The repetitive, or semi-automatic, character of some jobs in manufacturing industries may be an essential item, while the essentiality of such items as age, sex, salary, education, health, and religion for some positions is too universally recognized to require elaboration.

As the essential, more essential, and less essential items are being segregated one from another, challenging questions are bound to arise. Sometimes they will be answered. Why does this employer offer a substandard salary? Does he expect a substandard worker? Is the salary based on replacement cost? Does the organization promote from within and require a short trial period? Does it serve as a training school for competing concerns? The referral officer tries to understand salary as the employer sees it, and, no matter what factors may enter in, he knows that it must be fixed on a profit basis or there will be no position.

He turns to the qualifications enumerated on the order. He is accustomed to finding marked variations in *essentials* depending upon the prevailing condition of the labor market, but he is less sure than he once was that it is easier to meet employers' demands in a buyer's market when applicants are numerous and positions few than it is in a seller's market when the reverse is true. Each concern seems to have a list of preferred qualities which vary in importance with the character of the business and of the specific job to be filled. And they vary also as to the combination of qualities and the degree to which each should be possessed. The tenacity with which employers insist upon an applicant who possesses the full quota of specifications depends somewhat upon the labor market, but referral interviewers report that it is often easier to satisfy an employer when the reserve is small and he is willing to subtract an *essential* or two, than it is when the reserve is large and the multiplicity of applicants leads him to feel that all imperatives can and should be secured.

Sometimes the order is given in such general terms that much is left to the discretion of the interviewer; for example, send me a good stenographer at about thirty dollars, a good furniture assembler at ——, an experienced bus driver at ——. If the interviewer makes a satisfactory selection, he will doubtless be given future additional liberties in selecting applicants for the same concern.

When the service has no applicant who meets the specifications as given, what shall he do? There are several possibilities, all good practice under favorable conditions. The employer may be notified that the order cannot be filled in its entirety and certain item substitutions may be offered and may be accepted. This happens so frequently with reference to age, sex, education, and experience that it furnishes a strong argument against too many subdivisions of placement services on the basis of such factors. Clearance may be suggested, or tried, or the service may attempt to secure a suitable candidate from another placement service. If there is no hurry about filling the order, it may be possible to transfer it to the standing order file, more rarely to secure the promise that it shall become an exclusive order.

But the referral interviewer studies the employers' orders for a dual purpose. He wants to know what sort of an applicant will meet the employer's needs, but he also wants to know what sort of a job he must sell to a suitable applicant. What does the employer's record reveal as to labor turnover, promotion from within, opportunity to prepare for promotion, etc.? How many persons have already held the position under consideration? How long did they stay? Why did they leave? What's the matter? If the same service has made previous referrals to the same concern, he may turn to the applicants' file, or to the reports of field visitors, for help in replying to such questions. Before he canvasses the applicants' file for referral possibilities, he will have a clear-cut picture of the desirable and undesirable features of the position *as he sees them,* and of the type of applicant who may have a tendency to accent the desirable features and minimize the undesirable sufficiently to rate the position as desirable.

Selecting Applicants for Consideration. After the employer's order has been received and the job specifications mastered, the interviewer is ready to take steps two and three as outlined under referral procedure; ready to make a selection of potentials and issue call-in cards. Among the questions which he must decide as he enters on this phase of the referral procedure are: Should selections be made from applicants whose registrations are already on file or may they also be made from those who, at the moment, are in process of registration? Qualifications being equal, to what extent should priority of registration be a determining factor in selection? Is it wise to make selections from applicants who are, at the time, employed?

The temptation to select "the bird in hand" is very great, is frequently yielded to, and is sometimes justifiable. All the data are fresh in the mind of the interviewers; the personality, in the light of the situation to which it must adjust, is observable; and gaps in information which need to be secured in order to complete the picture are immediately available. There is no guarantee that "call-ins" will come in, thus threatening a delay in filling the order which may have unfortunate results, to say nothing of the wasted time and useless expense involved. But experienced placement workers usually feel that the selection of applicants for referral should be based solely on ability to do the job, and, if this requirement can be met from applicants on file, they deserve priority of consideration. To deny referral to an equally well-qualified applicant who has such priority rights because it is easier and quicker to select a person who is in the office is rated as "an unfair employment practice." Spot placements are justified in instances where the time element is so important that call-ins could not come in, and they are always justified for casual or common labor.

Some services will not, if they know it, register applicants who are permanently employed. Others do not find the practice objectionable, and nearly all realize that there are some perfectly legitimate reasons why forward-looking employees should be prepared for the type of emergencies which force them to shift positions on short notice. All reputable concerns condemn, as a decidedly unfair employment practice, the type of labor theft which, for a monetary consideration or through ignorance, encourages labor turnover and causes unrest and dissatisfaction among employees. Commercial agencies are the worst sinners when financial advantage is involved; educational institutions rate high in such practices when they are due to ignorance. This subject will be mentioned again under the section which deals with the placement of inexperienced and junior workers.

If the referral officer has decided in favor of selection from the files, he turns to the occupational classification from which the order logically would be filled. If the classification has been subdivided on the basis of age, sex, education, and so forth, signals and cross references will aid him in this preliminary sifting. Usually he will exhaust the primary occupational classification before he uses either the secondary classification or the job family lists, unless, of course, the order is a composite comprising so many duties that a specialist in a single line would be less promising than one who is less of an expert but more versatile occupationally. He takes from the files whatever number of applications he may think desirable for comparison with the order specifications which he is attempting to fill. He studies each application just as he has studied the order, item by item. He regards the record card as representing the applicant in his absence, and as the first assistant in helping him to attain his employment objective, but he does not forget the job specification with which he must correlate record data in order to determine its possible relation to success on the job.

It is difficult for one who is unfamiliar with the many variables and combinations of variables which have important bearings on job performance to understand what selection for referral on the basis of such variables implies. And it is quite impossible to convey to the uninitiated, by means of the printed page, any adequate conception of the problems and procedures involved. Experience alone can accomplish this. Therefore an item by item discussion of record content would not be sufficiently fruitful to justify the space required—especially when, were the same items to be considered in connection with another specification, they might be interpreted quite differently. In lieu of such an elaborate item analysis the reader is offered suggestive questions which the interviewer, as he challenges statements, weighs evidence, uncovers discrepancies, and tries to form accurate and impartial judgments as to whom to call-in, puts to the record. Has this applicant told the truth on routine items and on education and experience? Discrepancies overlooked at the time of registration may be suspected, but verification is frequently left until the record is challenged for selection purposes. Two illustrations of rather interesting discrepancies—one very common, the other uncommon—are cited:

During the early 1930's a man in the middle twenties was permitted to register in a university placement service anticipatory to the opening of the fall term, when he hoped to be occupationally located so that he could complete his college degree. He had filled out some items on his own blank; others had been filled in by a reception-registration clerk. He then went to the referral interviewer who, since it was not the custom of the service to register students until after matriculation, went over his application very carefully. There were several discrepancies which the applicant did not correct and could not explain—e.g., students who have attended the University of Chicago use that expression, not "Chicago University." "Matriculate," "tuition," "majors," and "minors" were meaningless terms. Observation of physical characteristics and personal appearance suggested outdoor manual labor. Gradually a well-laid plan to secure a loan from the student loan fund while "getting on my feet financially" was revealed. Of course it did not work out that way.

The second instance indicates more specifically the wide variety of experiences which are assets in understanding the many types of persons who take advantage, in one way or another, of the services of philanthropic agencies:

Mr. B., about thirty years of age, had quite a circle of friends who were variously interested in church, education, or social work. The tears rolled down his face every time he repeated the story of his broken home, the accidental death of its violator, and the penal term he had served in spite of his appeal to the "unwritten law." He had been a layout man before his misfortune and had a fine position. Would his friends help him to get a new start? Many placement services were appealed to; Mr. B. was referred several times in spite of the fact that he would not register; but he never accepted a position, and he always had a plausible explanation. From time to time he was given rather substantial financial assistance. One day he was sent by a church organization to a philanthropic placement service where the interviewer had had considerable experience placing parolees from federal and state penal institutions.

The man was hardly inside the door before the interviewer knew that he had never been in prison. His carriage and his lack of knowledge of prison and parole customs were confirmatory evidence. He knew nothing about the printing industry and could not recall his duties as a layout man. Still more incriminating was the fact that he would not fill out an application blank and evaded every attempt to get him to sign an application blank or leave his signature on anything. Long before the interview was over Mr. B. had been occupationally classified as a confidence man of no mean ability who should be reported to the police as soon as possible. This was accomplished fairly easily because of the fact that, although he had been decidedly cagey in handling certain aspects of his game, he had apparently underestimated the probability that sometime he was bound to arouse enough suspicion to cause arrest. He accepted the interviewer's suggestion that he attend the church club, as he had planned, on the following day. Plain-clothes men were also present and took him in custody, found his fingerprints on file, and rounded up a chain of confidence men who were operating in four states and for whom the police had been looking some months.

If the order calls for promotional material, what evidence is there that the applicant has learning ability and uses it to good advantage? What does his record show as to educational achievement in relation to educational opportunities, degree of intelligence, and mental alertness? Has he a goal? What progress has he made toward its attainment in relation to his age? What methods have been used and what seems to be the ultimate prospect of reaching it? Has he enough ability? Too much ability? Is it the right kind? On the whole, has he capacity for growth and willingness to learn, and is he potentially promotable? Careful consideration of such questions prevents the referral of superior persons to inferior jobs and of $25-a-week brains to $50-a-week jobs.

The referral interviewer knows that the extent to which family background items are essential and helpful in finding a satisfactory opening varies with different occupations, different employing concerns, and different applicants. He also knows that color, religion, nationality, and sex may one, or all, play an important part in employment selection and in satisfaction on the job, even though they may have no significance in employment efficiency. So he questions the application blank on these items in relation to the order items, and he does this both from the standpoint of an effective employment service which knows how very important it is to establish and maintain a reputation of no preference for any type of work or any employing concern, and of no preference for or discrimination against any type of worker, and from the standpoint of an experienced placement worker who knows that no service may overlook the fact that only in mass referral of common labor can such items be ignored with impunity. Several cases are cited in order to stress the practical essentiality of some of these controversial items and to indicate how many times their discriminative use is constructive in purpose as well as in effect.

Religion (Christian Science) was the control factor in filling this position.

An emergency order for ten clerical workers came into the office. "Send no applicants who are not Scientists," was one item in the specifications. Was it a legitimate specification? Did religion really matter or was it an "unfair employment practice"? Inquiry revealed that the employer was a Christian Science publishing house which felt that Scientists would be more interested and take more pleasure in their work. Many other equally well-qualified workers who were not Scientists were by-passed. Was it discriminating judgment constructively used, or was it unfair discrimination?

A combination of qualities was essential for referral to this position but all the indispensables centered around race, Jewish.

A call for a well-trained social worker at an excellent salary came from a mid-west city. A Jewish agency specified a Jew who must be able to speak Yiddish. It was during the 1930's and positions were scarce. The files were canvassed and the applications of two women were found, either one of whom would have qualified had she been a Jew. The organization was notified that the service had no Jewish woman who could qualify. Presently the better-qualified applicant came in to talk over prospects. The interviewer mentioned the social opening and said, "I thought of you, for had you been a Jew, you would have been an ideal candidate." "But I am a Jew," she replied, "and I speak Yiddish fluently." Everyone lost out. The service lost a sale, the applicant lost a position, and the social agency lost an ideal worker. Why had she not noted all her qualifications on her registration blank? She was afraid they would deny her a chance to work! The applicant had been guilty of unfair discrimination against herself.

And now we turn to a Catholic story which is highly amusing because it comes from a university bureau which did not ask for religious preferences:

President D. of —— University dropped in to have a chat with his old friend and incidentally to get his personal assistance in selecting a couple of new faculty members—one a woman for the home economics department. The placement officer brought a number of application blanks from the files, and the friend pronounced one very brilliant young woman, who had been in his classes while on sabbatical from another college, "a real find." "What about her religion? It does not appear on the blank," the president asked. "Does it make any difference?" the placement official replied. "Well, yes and no," was the answer. "We are a church-supported college and would not want a Catholic, nor would we make one happy for we are a long distance from a Catholic church." The officer was quite sure the applicant was a Protestant and very adaptable religiously, although she had no factual support for her decision. The president decided to offer her the position and went home pleased with his choice.

The call-in card was mailed. The applicant came in and laughed merrily when she found that the interviewer had recommended her to a Methodist institution as an *adaptable Protestant*. "I wouldn't be a bit happier in his institution than he would be to have me there," she said, "and by the way, lest the comedy of error go on, suppose you just write along the side of my blank *Roman Catholic*."

Since the referral officer is aware of the growing tendency of employers to demand the right type of personality as well as the right type of knowledge and skill, he next questions the rated items on the application blank. Does this applicant meet the usual personality requirements or where along the scale does he stand? Is he the physical, mental, and emotional type for this job? What specific qualities does he have which would be assets in this position? What are his personality liabilities? On the whole, how close does he come to the right degree of the essentials? Referral officers inflict a hardship on both employer and employee when they refer persons to positions in which the work causes an intense physical, mental, or emotional strain.

During the process of correlating application items with requisition items, the interviewer will discard applicants who fail to measure up to requirements, those who are thought to be "too good for the job," and those who for other reasons it seems useless to consider further. He will summon for a personal interview the number from whom he would like to make his final selection. The number will vary according to the position, the number which the employer has expressed a desire to see, and the probable number who will respond to the summons, prove satisfactory, and desire to apply. Call-ins may be sent out by regular mail, special delivery, messenger, telephone, or telegraph.

The fourth step in the referral procedure comes next.

The Referral Interview. When the applicant responds to the summons, the interviewer reviews with him the various items on his record, keeping the specific job in mind. If the items on the registration blank require supplementation in any one of several ways, this is done. Sometimes at the moment of referral a special test should be administered, either as an essential aid in arriving at a decision, or because the prospective employer has requested it. While the interview is in progress, both the applicant and the interviewer keep asking themselves questions. The applicant asks: What sort of a place is it? What sort of a boss, or superior, will I have? What will my co-workers be like? What will be my salary, my hours of work, and my prospects for advancement? Can I do the work? Do I want the position? Can I get it if I want it?

The interviewer continues and intensifies the questioning which he began when he was making selections for call-in, for he knows that the employer will ask some of these same questions, orally or silently, when the applicant is before him, and he knows that employment will depend largely upon the way they are answered: Is he the type? Will he fit in? What sort of a first impression will he make? How will he react to questions? Will he annoy and irritate, or co-operate with, his fellows? Can he do the work? Is he above the job? Will he be satisfied with the salary? Will he stay? Can he learn? What is his probable attitude toward work? Will he help to raise, lower, or maintain the morale of the concern? And finally, in the light of his family background, his educational advantages and the manner in which he has used them, his work record, his personality, and my own observations, is he a good employment risk? A good risk for referral to this opening? A good investment for this concern?

If these last three questions are answered affirmatively, the applicant has passed his referral test, and the referral may be completed as soon as he determines whether or not he wishes to apply. In reaching a decision he will probably wish to discuss a number of things with the interviewer, who, early in the interview, will have described both the desirable and undesirable points of the position but will have reserved certain items of information until a tentative decision has been reached. If the applicant's decision is negative, the interview will close without the revelation of the name of the concern and without mentioning certain other specific details usually reserved for potential employees.

If the decision is affirmative, the name and location of the concern will be given and the applicant will be allowed an opportunity to change his decision if he wishes. Few do. Withholding the firm name until after decision to apply is universally agreed to be desirable, but is frequently violated in practice, especially by inexperienced placement workers. If commercial services fail to observe it, they risk the dissemination among nonregistrants of free information regarding openings, thereby losing both customers and fees; if free services permit informal methods of giving out knowledge regarding vacancies, they lose their opportunity for the more scientific distribution of labor, cause annoyance to employers, and promote applications at the gate. There probably is no way to eliminate entirely the passing out of information on openings by registrants to nonregistrants. Commercial agencies are contending with the problem all the time, but the practice goes on. An excellent example of the results of carelessness in giving information to other than referrals was witnessed by this writer in the public service of a large city:

While she was observing placement procedure an order for an expert machinist came in. It was an emergency order. The files were hurriedly canvassed and a fairly satisfactory applicant was called in and referred. The plant was in the outskirts of the city with one bus transfer to make en route. Soon after the referral had left the office an expert in the same line came in to register. In a friendly and exceedingly casual way the interviewer said, "Gosh, why didn't you come in a couple of hours ago?" With amazing speed and cleverness the new applicant managed, without arousing the least suspicion, to get the name of the firm and the items in the specifications which correlated better with his own attainments than with those of the referral. With a "Good morning. You'll keep me in mind, won't you?" he was hot on the trail of the job. He hired a cab and, having timed his venture well, he reached the plant before the bus traveler arrived, announced that he had been told of the vacancy by ———, and went to work immediately. Ad interim, the referral appeared with his introduction and was not a little surprised to be told that the place had already been filled by a referral from the same service. The placement agency learned of its blunder from both the employer and the referred employee. The taxi applicant kept his own counsel and his job.

Not all the questions which arise during the final steps in the selection-for-referral interview are as close to the surface or as easily answered as is timing the revelation of the name of the employer. One to which no rule, except that of common sense, applies and to which there is no uniform reply is: To what extent shall the peculiarities and idiosyncracies of employers be told? If told shall it be in the form of a question as to the willingness of the applicant to put up with them, or as a warning of what to expect and how to meet it? A placement service recently referred a stenographer to the head of an advertising agency. The applicant inquired as to salary and promotional possibilities and was informed that the employer was very susceptible to flattery, "Keep patting him on the back; the more pats the more dollars." The applicant accepted the position, and the advice, and the dollars followed.

A chemical engineer, employed by a firm which had many orders for testing building materials, was assured by the placement service that the firm stood very high and enjoyed a fine reputation. After a few days he suspected dishonesty in test reports and flatly refused to sign one or two. The showdown came when he asked to be released from his contract, which had obligated him to appear in court cases arising in connection with the business. He was given a handsome bonus at leaving, which he regarded as an employer request that he "keep his mouth shut." The records at the placement service contained all the information necessary to have warned any professional man that the practices of this concern were unethical, but these facts were not even hinted at during the referral interview. This problem is constantly arising, and opinions differ considerably as to the best methods of meeting it.

To what extent shall the interviewer make comments which he believes will aid the applicant to make a favorable first impression on the prospective employer? Some interviewers never make suggestions except to inexperienced youth. Others, who feel that an opportunity to prove competence is often lost because of some trivial and easily remedied personal deficiency, always do whatever they can to further the employability of those whom they believe to be efficient workers. Granting that it is a bit embarrassing to call the attention of mature persons to deficiencies in dress and manners, this writer, after several unfortunate experiences, has been inclined to do so rather than to risk the rejection of applicants because of obvious liabilities. Two lost opportunities for service are cited:

Miss B. was about thirty years of age. She had every qualification for the position for which she was called in. As was her custom when an order and an applicant's qualifications correlated so highly that there seemed no question regarding employability, the interviewer expectantly awaited her appearance in order to make a quick, confirmatory onceover for first impressions. Miss B. was well-groomed as usual, but she was wearing a veil which was torn in such a way that it caused a sort of facial disfigurement, which was very noticeable. How easy it would have been, as the referral interview drew to a close, to have said, "I think you've had an accident with your veil en route and you may want to remove it." But it seemed a bit embarrassing and so Miss B., possibly without knowledge of the tear or how it affected her appearance, went to her interview and was not employed. Later on the employer reported. Everything was satisfactory except the torn veil, which, considering the importance of personal appearance, was a sort of character hint which made him afraid to risk employment.

And again:

A young college graduate, whose husband had had such a serious illness that she must secure a position, seemed highly promising as a receptionist since her dress was in excellent taste, her manners attractive, and her speech refined. When the right position opened she was called in. As she approached the desk her clothing exuded the stale odor of cooked food. It was easily explained and could have been remedied before referral. She and her husband had moved into a one-room apartment. It was an entirely new experience, and neither of them had ever thought of the necessity of protecting clothing against absorbing food odors. Moreover living with the odor had made her immune to it. She was referred but not employed.

Such illustrations seem trivial. To the uninitiated they seem to involve silly and unfair discriminatory practices on the part of employers. But it is often the trivial, rather than the big things, that add to, or detract from, the employability of applicants, and this writer long ago made up her mind that if it is worth while to refer an applicant, it is worth while to do the best one can, even if it be resented, to help him or her secure the position.

Will applicants resent it? Oh, yes, sometimes. Witness the college man who was told by the placement service of some personality trait which would be likely to militate against him and who replied angrily, "It's my personality, not yours. I don't care to change it. I like it as it is." Some people learn only by experience, and this young man is still learning that before he is likely to make an occupational success it will be necessary for someone besides himself to be pleased with his personality.

Another question, closely related to the previous one, is: To what extent shall an interviewer advise an applicant on the technique of marketing his assets? For a long time placement workers assumed that only occupational novitiates needed help in planning their sales program. A great change in this attitude came during the recent depression. Many very able men and women who had worked for but one concern, or who had operated their own businesses, were, when the wheel of fortune reversed its direction, occupationally stranded, with little or no experience in applying for positions either by mail or in person. Inquiry and observation revealed that frequently these competent and experienced persons with many assets to sell were quite ignorant of the techniques which expedite sales. Placement services lacked the time, and most of them lacked the ability, to be truly helpful to this type of applicant; hence, in response to an apparent unmet need, job clinics, man-marketing clinics and placement clinics were organized in various sections of the country and under various auspices. Those sponsored by business executives attracted the most attention and were probably the most successful. The December 6, 1939, issue of the *New York Times* described the methods of such a clinic which had been in operation for four years under the auspices of the Sales Executive Club of New York. Seven similar clinics were reported in operation at that time, and six more were in process of organization.

The demand for such services on a temporary basis ceased when war industries absorbed all the available workers, but the results of their experience should have a permanent influence on placement procedures in at least two specific ways: (1) They have demonstrated beyond a doubt the desirability of coaching any applicant who desires assistance in the techniques of preparing a letter of application or in planning a personal interview. (2) They have introduced such procedures on a higher professional plane than could have been expected from either public employment officials or educational workers, because as business executives they are more nearly masters of the know-how. Therefore, on the basis of what has been done, one is justified in replying affirmatively to the question under consideration and in adding—but only to the extent that the applicant desires help. And may the hope that when the applicant receives assistance it may be both worth while and ethical [4] be more than mere wishful thinking!

Interviewers find it difficult to determine the best course to pursue with reference to many other such questions as: Should referrals who fail to qualify in some *specific* respect be so told? Should a person who fails to qualify to such an extent that success is questionable ever be referred? If so, under what conditions? Should a referral be told that the interviewer questions his ability? If more than one referral is being made, should each individual know it? Both the fact and the number? All such questions

[4] Some of the printed material on "job getting" which appeared in the 1930's contained unethical suggestions. One book which this writer agreed with her seminar group should be condemned because of its "unfair employment practices" with reference to methods of approaching employers was C. B. Thompson and M. L. Wise, *We Were Forty and We Did Get Jobs* (New York: Lippincott Co., 1938).

usually receive qualified replies. The last, if affirmatively decided, frequently results in charges of unfair employment practices against both, or either, the referral interviewer and the employer; for always, no matter what the facts, some specific basis for the charges can be found by those who have been rejected. This writer has had several clashes with teachers as a result of referring more than one applicant, and she has seen more than one educational placement service lose the opportunity to fill a position because they refused to allow the employer any choice. "A take it or leave it" policy is very likely to result in a "leave it" decision.

Before the interview closes the referral should be told whether or not he will be expected to take a physical examination, or any other test. He should be informed regarding union regulations, license or certificate requirements, methods of wage payment, laws which must be observed by both parties, social security provisions, and, if uniforms are required, who provides them and looks after their upkeep. He should be given an introduction card and told to whom and when to apply.

However, telling, questioning, and informing is not all on one side. There are two clients to be served, each of whom must be served so impartially that when the final decision is made it will be a well-balanced decision based on all the information regarding both the applicant and the job, and the information given to both parties will have been equally free from bias either for or against the applicant and for or against the job. If questions arise regarding variation from the order specification or if the interviewer desires to make a substitution with reference to some such quality as age, sex, or education, the employer's permission may be sought by telephone—preferably not in the presence of the applicant.

The interviewer will meet many problems regarding dealings with employers similar to those noted with reference to applicants. If an employer calls at the office, should he be permitted to see the applicant's complete record? If transcripts are sent by mail, should all the information be given or should some items be suppressed? Suppose an applicant has paid the legal penalty for some law violation, or has been socially ostracized for some breach of the moral code, shall the prospective employer be told? What effect do civil-rights laws have on the reply to such questions? What effect, where such statutes exist, may be expected from the enforcement of the presently much publicized antidiscriminatory, antibias, or fair employment practice laws? More interviewers will face more such problems in the aftermath of the war.

Are there any answers? If there are, this writer does not know of anyone who has found them. She does know from personal experience that the custom, much too common in university placement services, of deleting from faculty reports any unfavorable comments regarding applicants is, in course of time, discovered, resented, and considered an unfair employment practice by employers, faculty, and applicants. But the placement service defends the practice on the ground that many faculty members furnish opinions and ratings designed "to take it out" on students who have been independent enough to challenge their opinions, or who have failed to show proper appreciation of their contributions to knowledge. The placement service regards the inclusion of known-to-be prejudices as an unfair employment practice.

This writer has also learned from experience that services which place certain types of mentally and emotionally disturbed individuals, those who have served time in penal institutions, those who are under police surveillance, or those who have nonobservable but known handicaps which are apt to result in overt acts, dangerous to either themselves or others, should make such facts known to those who employ them for their own protection, for the protection of their fellows, or for the protection of both. In some instances employers who are very willing to help in the occupational rehabilitation of parolees from penal institutions do so only on condition that they be given the facts, and that they be not asked to employ both men and women. Incarceration in any sort of an institution leaves a scar which rarely escapes detection by one who is fresh from similar experiences. One man may join another man in concealing a common secret, but the temptation for one sex to blackmail the other is very great, and employers prefer not to afford any opportunity for it.

As a general rule a bona fide prospective employer is entitled to all the factual information about a bona fide prospective employee which will throw light on the responsibilities he assumes for the satisfactory assimilation of the individual into the organization, and for his protection and that of the other employees therein. But when passing on information—favorable or unfavorable—which is based on personal opinions, a wise interviewer will keep in mind the elusiveness of the human factor and the wide discrepancies which are frequently found in opinions on the same individual expressed by different but equally well qualified raters, and he will be very careful lest he have too much confidence in his own judgment. Moreover, he may, if he have the inclination and the ability, eliminate, or soften by comparison, the halo effect which dominates certain faculty or employer opinions, or the equally objectionable use of demerits which characterizes the opinions of others. In this way he may be able to give the prospective employer a fairly well balanced picture of the prospective employee without practicing the wholesale deletion of unfavorable comments. Institutional placement interviewers have a better opportunity to exercise this sort of judgment than do those under other auspices because constant association with their colleagues gives them an intimate knowledge of their faults and foibles, and they have easy access to factual material by which to check on personal opinions which bear the earmarks of bias.

When the referral interview, or interviews, have been completed, decisions will have been reached by both the interviewer and the applicant; to refer or not to refer, and to apply or not to apply. Call-ins who do not wish to apply drop out of the immediate placement picture, and their records are returned to the file after such notations as seem desirable have been added. Those who may wish to apply, but whom the interviewer does not care to refer, require special consideration. Those who wish to apply and whom the interviewer desires to refer are given final referral attention under step five of the referral procedure.

The Introduction. The performance of two routine functions completes the referral procedure: the issuance of the introduction to the employing concern and the clipping together, until a report on the result of the referral is received, of the employer's order and the applicant's record.

A preliminary or temporary introduction may be made over the telephone if necessary and be followed by a more formal introduction, but the usual media are letters or double post cards. Final instructions as to hours of application and the person to whom the card should be presented are given.[5] If interviewers are careful in the selection of referrals, the value of these introduction cards will be recognized. Consistent refusal of introductions to the unfit and undesirable will increase the applicants' awareness of the sales value of their cards and will tend to secure larger numbers of exclusive orders from employers.

Not all referrals result in placements, but pending definite information as to whether or not a position has been offered and accepted it is necessary to clip together the order and the application form and put them in some specific place. After a decision has been reached, the forms are separated and filed in their respective places with filled or unfilled orders, and under applicants or placements.

How shall the interviewer explain the call-in to respondents who may desire to apply but whom he does not care to refer? Whenever a middleman passes selective judgment on a number of call-ins, there will usually

[5] Suggestions for conducting the interview with the employer will be found in Reed, *Guidance and Personnel Services,* pp. 323–327.

be some whom the application blank influenced the interviewer to feel were potentials who, as the interview proceeds, seem not to measure up to the specifications, or who, if employed, would seem to be underemployed in the sense that native ability and training qualify them for employment on a higher level. In the interest of both parties such applicants should not be referred. Either type promises to be, or to become, misfits, and misfits, no matter what the reason, neither render effective service nor are they happy in their work. On the other hand it is human nature for the applicant who wants a position to feel that he is qualified for it, and to rationalize his rejection as due to some personal prejudice or bias based on age, sex, nationality, religion, color of hair, skin, or eyes, and the like.[6] His friends, who may be totally unfamiliar with employment problems and practices, may join in an outcry against unfair employment practices.

There are various ways of meeting, or avoiding, this situation. It is not always necessary for a call-in to know that he is being considered for a definite position. The interview may be conducted as a reinterview, for the purpose of securing additional information for future use, rather than as a referral interview. If the tentative opinion of the interviewer be confirmed, at the right point in the interview the applicant may be told that an opening is available; if the interview fails to support the tentative opinion, it may be brought to a close without mention of other than future opportunities.

If the applicant knows that he is participating in a referral interview, experienced workers have found it desirable so to conduct the interview that, as soon as the selective judgment of the interviewer may be recognized as in error, the applicant may be brought to decide for himself that the job is not for him. The focusing of attention on any factual unfavorable aspect of the job, such as the constant physical strain, the woman superior under whom he will work, the limited transportation facilities, the unusual demand for overtime, the number of his best qualifications which do not correlate very well with the major job specifications, or the difficulty of fulfilling certain expressed ambitions if he accepts the position, may result in the applicant eliminating himself from further consideration. Self-elimination is always preferable to rejection by either the

---

[6] Such instances are on record but are not usual. This writer has had two interesting experiences: a well-known superintendent of schools ordered that no referrals be sent who were born south of the Mason and Dixon line, and an equally well-known businessman refused to consider red-headed men for executive positions. Both employers were convinced that these personal items were harbingers of failure. It is a very foolish placement service which refuses to comply with such personal idiosyncrasies.

interviewer or the employer, and it avoids feelings of resentment and charges of unfair discrimination.

When such a course is followed, the interviewer should be very careful that he does not leave the impression that the employing concern is an undesirable employer for any applicant. One hears and reads comparatively little about unfair employment practices as they militate against employers, but such situations as have been mentioned might unconsciously produce exactly that effect. Sometimes in the exercise of his referral functions an interviewer will, because of his personal distaste for it, discriminate quite unconsciously against an entire occupation. One illustration will be sufficient:

In one of our large cities which held a high position as a center of the retail trade, merchant after merchant applied to the women's division of the public employment service for store clerks. No applicants were referred. Several complaints were made to the community committee under which the service was operating, and this writer was asked to visit the city and see if there were any legitimate reasons, when the labor market was normal, why retail clerks could not be found. After a few minutes' talk with the council the reasons were so obvious that no further investigation was necessary. The woman who placed clerks regarded the work as highly undesirable, and her own personal distaste for it was expressed in her attitude to such an extent that she discouraged applicants who came to the service to apply for it, who were fitted for it, and who doubtless would have made good, and she never suggested it as a possibility for those who were looking "for anything." The committee was advised to redistribute placement responsibility in such a way that retail selling was assigned to someone who, whether or not she was enthusiastic about it as an occupation for herself, would be unbiased in her attitude toward it and would use some selective ability in referrals. The change was made, and soon the usual number of applicants were available for department stores.

SUMMARY

Part One has given a brief historical summary of the various methods and facilities which have been used by free labor and by private enterprise to exchange the personal services of the one for the financial rewards of the other. Part Two has given an account, step by step, of the usual procedures involved in occupational placement from the planning of a service to the recording of a placement. Those who have been sufficiently interested to read both sections will doubtless have arrived at much the same general conclusions. Among them:

(1) That the art and the science of occupational placement have been developing side by side, always within the framework of the social-economic milieu of time and place.

(2) That in methods and materials occupational placement has kept pace with the progress of other functions included in personnel service, and that its philosophies have been in harmony with—sometimes as a leader and sometimes as a follower—the changing philosophies which have dominated other areas of social activity.

(3) That public employment services are essential and desirable. That the outstanding handicaps to their development have been the utilization of their positions as party rewards for the services of political hacks,[7] and the tendency of socially motivated groups to use them as a clotheshorse on which to hang social reforms.

(4) That placement functionaries are, or ought to be, rated as professional workers. Their preparation, including internship, is, or should be, professional; their qualifications for appointment are, or should be, professional in character; their responsibilities to individuals and to society are commensurate with those assigned to specialists in other areas of public service; while their more inclusive duties obligate them to co-operate with educational systems in preparing youth for occupational life and in assisting adults to make occupational adjustments.

(5) That placement workers have established and maintained an organization the attitudes and activities of which entitle it to rank with other professional organizations, and they have been marvelously successful in retaining, from the very beginning through all the vicissitudes and discouragements of the years, a certain number of outstanding professional men and women who have never lost confidence in the ultimate success of the public employment movement.

(6) That placement workers have no predilection for, or sympathy with, age, sex, racial, religious, or other prejudices. But in the carrying out of placement objectives—to make placements satisfactory to both customers —they are obligated to take cognizance of community and individual prejudices as well as of the quality of employers' offerings and of individuals' qualifications.

(7) That the ideal of all professional placement workers, irrespective of the auspices under which they operate, is to select and refer to each available opening the candidate who most nearly approaches perfection, and, correlatively, to refer each applicant to a concern where work conditions are of the best, where opportunities for promotion are definite, and where there is sunshine all day long every day in the year. But they know that such ideals, desirable as they are, are "the stuff that dreams are made of," and that no matter how high their ideals or how humanitarian their

[7] The merit system has helped some in recent years.

views they must operate on the basis of objective data and hard, cold facts.

(8) That public and philanthropic placement services must find a way to meet all their combined responsibilities on a co-operative basis avoiding all possible duplication of effort and expense.

(9) That occupational placement services which even approximate the ideal are expensive. That their success must be appraised on more valid criteria than cost per capita on any basis. The desirability of cost as a factor in evaluation is not questioned, but placement services are eager to profit by, and to a very limited extent are contributing to, recent experimentation which is seeking to develop more satisfactory evaluative criteria.

SELECTED SUPPLEMENTARY READING

Achilles, Paul S. "Trends in Employment Procedures," *Personnel*, XIX (1943), 609–617. Based on a questionnaire survey of employment practices and trends among 147 business firms.

Anderson, H. Dewey, and Davidson, Percy E. *Occupational Trends in the United States*. Stanford University: Stanford University Press, 1940. Trends in all the major occupations from 1870 through 1940.

Atkinson, Raymond C., Odencrantz, Louise C., Deming, Ben. *Public Employment Service in the United States*. Chicago: Public Administration Service, 1938. Chapters 11, 15 to 18, and 20 to 23, which are concerned with employment service procedures, were written by Louise Odencrantz, who, over a long period of years, has made major contributions to placement practices.

Bingham, Walter Van Dyke. *Aptitudes and Aptitude Testing*. New York: Harper and Bros., 1937.

Bingham, Walter Van Dyke. *Oral Examinations in Civil Service Recruitment*. Washington, D.C., 1939. (Service Assembly Pamphlet no. 13.)

Bingham, Walter Van Dyke, and Moore, Bruce Victor. *How to Interview*. New York: Harper and Bros., 1941.

Crosby, Chapman J. *Trade Tests*. New York: Henry Holt and Co., 1921. Based on World War I experiments.

Dodge, Arthur F. *Occupational Ability Patterns*. New York: Teachers College, Columbia University, 1935.

Dvorak, Beatrice J. *Differential Occupational Ability Patterns*. Minneapolis: University of Minnesota Press, 1935. (University of Minnesota Employment Stabilization Research Institute, vol. III, no. 8.)

Dvorak, Beatrice J. "Occupational Testing in the Public Employment Service," *Employment Service News*, II (Nov., 1935), 7–10.

Garrett, Annette. *Interviewing; Its Principles and Methods*. New York: Family Welfare Association of America, 1942.

Gleason, Clyde W. "The Use of Job Families for the Physically Handicapped," *Psychological Bulletin*, XL (1943), 714–718.

Hopkins, Jess T. *The Emergence of a New Public Employment Service*. Albany: New York State Employment Service, 1935. Includes such topics as community surveys, advisory councils, interviewing, counseling in public employment offices, publicity, and staff training.

Howard, Charles H. "Commercial and Professional Placement Procedures in Public Employment Offices," *Personnel Journal*, XII (1934), 273–280.

International Association of Public Employment Services. *Proceedings of the Annual Conventions*. Variously published. These proceedings contain very valuable material for those who wish to keep in touch with progress in employment procedures.

Lobsenz, Johanna. *The Older Woman in Industry*. New York: Charles Scribner's Sons, 1929. A good reference on the problems involved.

Ordway, S. H., Jr., and others. *Oral Tests in Public Personnel Selection*. Chicago: Civil Service Assembly, 1943.

Paterson, Donald G., and Darley, John G. *Men, Women, and Jobs*. Minneapolis: University of Minnesota Press, 1936.

Pidgeon, Mary Elizabeth. *A Preview as to Women Workers in Transition from War to Peace*. Washington, D.C., 1944. (U.S. Women's Bureau, Special Bull. no. 18.)

Pintner, Rudolf, Eisenson, Jon, and Stanton, Mildred. *The Psychology of the Physically Handicapped*. New York: F. S. Crofts and Co., 1941.

President's Research Committee on Social Trends. *Recent Social Trends*. New York: McGraw-Hill Book Co., 1933.

Reeves, Floyd W. *Demobilization and Readjustment*. Washington, D.C., 1943. (Report of the Conference on Post-War Readjustment of Civilian and Military Personnel, National Resources Planning Board.)

Roethlisberger, F. J., Dickinson, W. J., and Wright, H. *Management and the Worker*. Cambridge: Harvard University Press, 1939. A final report on the series of research studies which began in 1927 and have become generally known as the Hawthorne experiment. Concerned with the intangible factors which affect morale and productive efficiency, Part II deals with the interviewing of 20,000 employees in order to secure personal reactions to working environment.

Salner, Edward, and Price, D. G. "Operating Tools for Employment Offices," *Employment Service News*, II (Nov., 1935), 4–5.

Scott, W. D., Clothier, R. C., Mathewson, S. B., and Spriegel, W. R. *Personnel Management*. 3d ed. New York: McGraw-Hill Book Co., 1941.

Shartle, Carroll L. *Worker Training and Job Families. Training Workers and Supervisors for War Production*. New York: American Management Association, 1942. (Personnel Series no. 56.)

Shartle, Carroll L., and others. "Ten Years of Occupational Research," *Occupations*, XXII (April, 1944). The entire number is given to an account of the various researches under the auspices of the Division of Occupational Analysis and Manning Tables, Bureau of Manpower Utilization, War Manpower Commission. An excellent bibliography is included.

Stead, William H., and Masincup, W. E. *The Occupational Research Program of the United States Employment Service*. Chicago: Public Administration Service, 1943.

Stead, William H., Shartle, Carroll L., and others. *Occupational Counseling Tech-*

niques; Their Development and Application. New York: American Book Co., 1940.

Stewart, Annabel M. and Bryce M. *Statistical Procedures of Public Employment Offices.* New York: Russell Sage Foundation, 1933. Pages 40–46 discuss terminology and definitions.

Strong, Edward K., Jr. *Vocational Interests of Men and Women.* Stanford University: Stanford University Press, 1943.

Symonds, Percival M. *Diagnosing Personality and Conduct.* New York: D. Appleton–Century Co., 1931. A standard reference.

Thompson, Lorin A., Jr. *Interview Aids and Trade Questions for Employment Offices.* New York: Harper and Bros., 1936.

Unger, Hunt H. "The Past-Employment-Reference-Inquiry Form," *Personnel,* XX (1944), 357–368. A survey of forms (Perifs) used by 35 companies is the basis of this article which deals with the history of references, the use of forms, and their construction, content, use, and probable future. A bibliography including authorities who favor "perifs" and those who consider them a selection tool of questionable value.

U.S. Congress., Senate. *Postwar Economic Policy and Planning.* Washington, D.C., 1943. (78th Congress 1st session, Senate doc. no. 106.)

U.S. Department of Labor, U.S. Employment Service. *Dictionary of Occupational Titles.* Washington, D.C., 1939–1944. Parts I and II.

U.S. War Manpower Commission, Bureau of Manpower Utilization. *Physical Demands Analysis Manual.* Washington, D.C., 1943.

U.S. War Manpower Commission, Bureau of Manpower Utilization. *Training and Reference Manual for Job Analysis.* Washington, D.C., 1944.

U.S. War Manpower Commission, U.S. Employment Service. *Selective Placement for the Handicapped.* Washington, D.C., Dec., 1943.

Viteles, Morris S. *Industrial Psychology.* New York: W. W. Norton and Co., 1932.

Yoder, Dale. *Personnel Management and Industrial Relations.* New York: Prentice-Hall, 1943.

PERIODICALS

Employment Security Review, The. (Formerly *Employment Service News.*) Published monthly by the Federal Security Agency, Bureau of Employment Security, Washington, D.C. Contains articles on population trends, unemployment, employment, employment security problems, job opportunities, and co-operative training.

Executives Service Bulletin. Published monthly by the Policyholders Service Bureau of the Metropolitan Life Insurance Co., One Madison Ave., New York City. Contains helpful articles on many topics.

Labor Information Bulletin. Published monthly by the U.S. Department of Labor, Washington, D.C. An important reference.

Management Review, The. Published monthly by the American Management Association, 330 West 42d Street, New York City. A good review of occurrences in the business world.

Mental Hygiene. Published quarterly by the National Committee for Mental Hygiene, Inc., 1790 Broadway, New York City.

Monthly Labor Review. Published by the U.S. Department of Labor, Bureau of Labor Statistics, Washington, D.C. Includes material on industrial relations, labor conditions, national income, labor laws, costs and standards of living, minimum wages and maximum hours, wages and hours of labor, employment offices, trends of employment, and pay rolls.

Monthly Vital Statistics Bulletin. Published by the U.S. Department of Commerce, Bureau of the Census, Washington, D.C. Statistics relating to the industrial, commercial, and governmental life of the nation.

Occupations—The Vocational Guidance Magazine. Published monthly, October to May, inclusive, by the National Vocational Guidance Association, 425 West 123d Street, New York City. Primarily for educators.

Personnel. Published bi-monthly by the American Management Association, 330 West 42d Street, New York City. Deals with the employment procedures, policies, and problems of employing concerns, but has many suggestions for public and educational placement services.

Survey of Current Business. Published weekly with annual supplements by the U.S. Department of Commerce, Washington, D.C. Studies of business trends.

PART THREE

Special Placement Services

CHAPTER IX
Some Types of Special Services

CHAPTER X
Veterans' Placement Services

CHAPTER XI
Junior Placement Services

Some Types of Special Services

THE origin and development of two types of placement services has been mentioned in Part Two: general services which are open to all types of applicants and serve all types of occupations, and special services which are designed to serve special groups of applicants and special occupations. Economic, social, and geographic factors have been important determinants as to when, where, and under what auspices either general or special services should be introduced, combined with other services, or dropped. The definitions of general and special services have not been changed much with time, although the bases for determining what shall be considered general and what special have changed as our knowledge of individuals, of occupations, and of the interrelations of the factors which constitute employability has increased. No sharp line may be drawn between agencies which have fostered the development of general and special services, but, as a generalization, there is documentary support for the statement that general services have been more likely to result from public interest and public activity, while special services have been more likely to be commercially sponsored, or to have originated in philanthropic interest and institutional needs.

Special services, under public auspices, usually resulted from the subdivision of a general service—a practice which has tended to multiply services, divisions, and departments and to split up the labor reserve, thereby intensifying the problem of substitute referrals. Commercial and philanthropic services have usually been organized to service some specific group. They also tended to multiply labor reserves. In the early years nationality and religion were major philanthropic control factors, commercial agencies determined specialization on the basis of business needs, and institutional services were a response to the demands of their constituencies. It is interesting, in this connection, to recall that the foundation of the recent charges of unfair employment practices on the basis of nationality and religion may be traced back to the philanthropic efforts of local groups of citizen-aliens to serve their own immigrant-nationals, or to adherents of some religious creed to render occupational assistance to their coreligionists. This was their only *raison d'être*.

The first bases for specialization were sex, citizenship, nationality, religion, and occupation. The many social and economic changes which characterized the first quarter of the present century,[1] some of which were recorded in legislative enactments, brought about changes in the bases for determining when and what special services should be instituted.

As an illustration, researches in the field of industrial health and safety encouraged workmen's compensation legislation and the establishment of employment bureaus for the physically handicapped. The special bureau established by the Charity Organization Society of New York City in 1906 exemplifies the best thought of the time regarding the desirability of special services for handicapped persons. The investigators emphasized the essentiality of a special service on the ground that the general free employment service was not equipped to give the time and personal attention necessary to understand the qualifications of, or to find openings suitable for, men suffering from physical and mental deficiencies. Nor, if general services were to retain their employing clientele, could they be expected to refer deficient men when competent men were available.

The *Report* of the Charity Organization Society for 1907 analyzed 596 special bureau applicants: 94 were handicapped by age, 56 by pulmonary tuberculosis, 13 by nervous diseases, and 8 by criminal records; 25 were partially and 2 were totally blind; 20 had lost a hand, 17 a foot, and 2 had lost more than one limb; 17 were mentally diseased; 4 were mental defectives; 2 were epileptics; 9 were inebriates; and 33 had more than one type of handicap. Most of the registrants had been on, or were about to be placed on, relief. Many of the 251 placements were in service occupations with wages ranging from $2.00 to $20.00 a week—an average of $8.36.

This report has a threefold significance for students of the development of special services for handicapped persons: (1) the inclusiveness of "handicapped" left little room for the expansion of categories, but much room for the subdivision of special disabilities; (2) the arguments for special services—those against were formulated later—were that regular interviewers had no time to study the needs and qualifications of handicapped persons or to solicit suitable openings for them, and that, were incompetents referred when competents were available, the service would acquire a reputation for substandard referrals and would lose its employing

---

[1] Part One contains a background summation of such changes, their resultant legislative enactments, and the influence of both on placement practices.

clientele; and (3) classification of persons known to be handicapped as *incompetents,* and those assumed to be mentally and physically sound as *competents,* characterized a philosophy no longer acceptable to placement authorities, to employers, or to handicapped persons themselves.

The happenings of the years between 1906 and 1945 have caused the rejection of this early attitude toward the occupational classification and the employability of handicapped persons. The prevailing philosophy was well stated by the War Manpower Commissioner, Paul V. McNutt, "Men and women must not be disqualified because of their disabilities; they must be qualified because of their abilities." This point of view has developed gradually and is now challenging the wisdom of providing special services for *all* handicapped persons. Would it not be better, some ask, to reclassify handicapped persons on the basis of the extent of their employability as (1) those who cannot do any work—unemployables; (2) those whose handicaps are so severe that such remunerative work as is possible must be done in their own homes or in special workshops; and (3) those who can qualify for regular and satisfactory employment under normal conditions, provided they be referred to, and employed in, positions suited to their education, preparation, and disabilities (or abilities)?

This third group, it is thought, should be divided. One subdivision would comprise those having disabilities of such a character that once they are clearly understood, if no special employment supervision is required, regular placement officials can make referrals which will permit satisfactory job performance without intensifying the disability. The other subdivision would comprise those whose deficiencies require more time, greater special knowledge, and more personal attention, both before and after placement, than the usual placement service is prepared to give. Personality characteristics, vocational aptitudes and interests, previous education, and any work experiences prior to incurring the disability may require detailed study. Methods of overcoming physical and other handicaps and of converting remaining abilities into salable vocational assets must be understood, and agencies which are available for assistance must be cultivated and used. This is a difficult undertaking. Each person requires individual study, and it is doubtful if the average placement functionary should be entrusted with such a highly specialized responsibility. All experienced placement workers advocate the use of specially trained interviewers for handicapped persons. Some would have these specialists function with and through a general employment service; others prefer a separate service. Both methods are in use.

SPECIAL SERVICES UNDER THE FEDERAL BUREAU OF IMMIGRATION

Special services only were operated under the Federal Bureau of Immigration. When its placement activities were expanded, 1914–1917, two services of special interest for the present purpose were added. The one, charged with the responsibility of placing guardsmen returning from military service on the Mexican border, established a precedent for the veterans' bureaus of World War I, and the other, including the placement of boys and girls, was the first national recognition of the desirability of special facilities for the guidance and placement of youth and for the organization of such service on a sex basis.

The departmental order [2] which established this youth service was decidedly modern in its philosophic tone; therefore it is comparatively easy to assume relationship between its avowed purposes and the purposes of more recent youth services. However, since no operational unit ever materialized, it is rather dangerous to assume that it established a precedent for the organization of later services. Its existence, even on paper, received little attention; it has not usually been included in historical accounts of youth services; and, except for its pronouncements as an indicator—perhaps an accidental rather than an anticipatory one—of a philosophy which was later to prevail with reference to junior placement services, it has little historical value.

SPECIAL SERVICES DURING WORLD WAR I

A number of special placement services came into being during World War I. Some served a temporary purpose and were discontinued at the close of the war while others, more specifically concerned with the reconversion to normal occupational pursuits, took their places. Military events moved rapidly. Placement services attempted to keep pace with the occupational demands which the military authorities made on industry, and to a considerable extent the services operated by the emergency federal employment service overshadowed the activities of services under all other auspices. These, then, are the services to which one must turn in order to secure a picture of the development of special services during the years included in and immediately following World War I.

The immigrant, who had been the objective of the first federal employment service, who had furnished the incentive for the institution of many local philanthropic services, and who, when the war broke out in Europe, ceased to emigrate, now became of prime importance to the war industries

[2] See page 47.

of the United States. The emergency United States Employment Service made a great effort, in co-operation with the immigration authorities, to meet employers' demands for foreign labor. Gradually it increased its occupational coverage until foreign-born men and women were employed in a wide range of occupations with special services organized to recruit and place a variety of national and racial groups.

To what extent were these immigrant services special services, and were special services needed for these groups? Some reports on the activities and methods of such services did not reveal any marked variation in procedures from those which were in use in general services. Others indicated the desirability of a different approach and somewhat different techniques if the psychology of the immigrant was to be interpreted correctly and his occupational needs to be met. "Immigrants will not fit into the processes by which labor is ordinarily marketed" well expressed this point of view.[3]

Among the special facilities which it was generally felt should be offered immigrants, even though they were placed through general offices, were: (1) interviewers who spoke their language, (2) offices located in immigrant colonies, (3) written directions for those who were referred to openings, (4) signs posted in foreign languages, (5) the use of the foreign language press to spread occupational information, and (6) a list of protective agencies, both public and private, to which immigrants who had problems other than occupational ones might be referred.

The need of immigrants for assistance in the solution of personal and family problems and for protection against many abuses and injustices was recognized, but it was also recognized that there were dangers in public employment services reaching out beyond their own field. Therefore it was generally agreed that such services should confine their efforts to acquiring an intimate knowledge of local work opportunities, to distributing employment information, to making placements, and to the wise handling of such educational work among employers as might lessen prejudice against any national or racial group and bring about a change in the characterization of what was then true of immigrant placement, "America takes little account of the immigrant's qualifications; they all go into the caldron of common labor."

As the industrial situation which had prevailed during the war period changed, the attitude of the public, of the employer, and of organized workers toward immigrant labor also changed—perhaps it would be more

3 J. W. MacMillan, "The Public Employment Service and the Immigrant," *Proceedings, Eighth Annual Meeting, International Association of Public Employment Services* (Ottawa, Canada: Department of Labour, 1920), pp. 40–47.

accurate to say that it reverted to its prewar status. Both the Bureau of Immigration, which had broadened its responsibilities to include leadership in formulating a national immigration policy as well as in developing its original plan for the wider distribution of aliens, and the public employment services, which had become interested in expanding occupational opportunities for different nationalities, encountered some serious difficulties.[4] Organized labor renewed its opposition to federal assistance for aliens on the ground that it would tend to lower the laboring man's standard of living, afford recruitment services for cheap labor, and foster the maintenance of the open shop. Motivated also by self-protection, business concerns refused to employ aliens or to re-employ aliens who had not become citizens.[5] Moreover, the many enactments which had been passed to protect and benefit wage earners made it impossible for business to employ illiterates or substandard workers. The general public expressed its approval of occupational discrimination against aliens when, by means of state statutes, it set aside certain occupations for citizens only. Long before the close of the war period national legislation was tending to restrict immigration, and discriminatory state legislation was aiding labor and other occupational groups to preserve for themselves the most desirable job opportunities.

Three other special wartime services should be mentioned:

The Negro Division, in conjunction with the Division of Negro Economics, was charged with the mobilization, employment, and housing of Negro labor. There are obvious reasons why, up to the time of the inordinate demand for labor in war industries, no special attention should have been given to placement services for Negroes. Special philanthropic services and the assistance of friends were, for a long time, their main avenues for employment. The southern states frowned on any activity which encouraged migration, and very drastic regulations controlled "alien agents" who attempted to draw Negro labor into the North. The comparatively few Negroes who sought employment assistance registered in the general public services. Special services were instituted during the war, and their desirability seems to have been determined purely on the basis of volume of business. If the number of registrants was large, special services were sometimes advocated, but there were thought to be no other reasons why Negroes should not be served by general offices. No special methods or

---

[4] The origin and development of these difficulties has been described in some detail in Part One, pp. 14 ff.

[5] The study of the occupational aptitudes of various alien groups by the National Association of Corporation Schools, 1915–1921, is exceedingly interesting in this connection. See Part One, pp. 17 f.

techniques were recommended, but location of services close to residential districts and staffing, so far as possible, by Negro personnel were suggested.

The Women in Industry unit developed into the Women's Division of the United States Employment Service, which, in turn, absorbed the privately operated Collegiate Bureaus of Occupations to form the Women's Collegiate Section. This section was short-lived, and the plan to develop a special service for professional workers of both sexes never materialized, although a number of professional and technical groups—teachers included—were given special attention under the war emergency employment service.

The United States Boys Working Reserve, a special service for junior boys, was organized primarily to serve agricultural occupations. Since it had a marked influence on the development of the Junior Section of the United States Employment Service and established a precedent for the organization and conduct of the same type of special services in recent years, its purpose and responsibilities and the methods and procedures which set it apart from other wartime services have been fully reported on in Chapter XI.

SPECIAL SERVICES, 1918–1940

Following the armistice several special war services were dropped, and others concerned with demobilization were substituted. The Junior Section introduced two or three innovations which have had a permanent influence; therefore it will be given detailed attention later. The Handicap Section was a response to, and an indication of, a growing national interest in the occupational rehabilitation and return to industry of persons who were suffering from any one of a variety of handicaps. For years special agencies, many of them private, had been in operation to service special groups of such individuals. The work of the Charity Organization of New York City and that of the Red Cross Institute for Crippled and Disabled Men have been cited as examples of such activity. The return of war cripples from the European battlefields added a new incentive. Between 1918 and 1921 [6] the federal government passed legislation providing for the rehabilitation of disabled persons. The Federal Board for Vocational Education was originally charged with the administration of these laws as they related to all persons, but, when the Veterans' Bureau was organized, the division for disabled soldiers was transferred to that organization. More or *less* co-operation between these rehabilitation services and the

[6] Massachusetts, Wisconsin, and several other states had, by this time, instituted some provision in certain local offices for the placement of handicapped persons.

various placement services which were in operation was maintained throughout these years.

The Handicap Division made no specific addition to the categories listed by the Charity Organization, and it made no specific mention of such persons as epileptics, inebriates, and parolees. It did mention specifically those handicapped by age and stated its intention to regard forty-five as the entry to the period when years may be regarded as beginning to be a handicap to employability and to warrant some special facilities and techniques. This interest in persons who found it difficult to secure employment because of age was pretty thoroughly publicized during World War I. It was revived, received even more attention, and the pros and cons of special services were again discussed during the late depression when positions were difficult to secure. It has continued to be of interest in 1945 when manpower of all ages has been in demand. Both war emergencies have focused attention on the waste involved in discarding workers in the prime of life and the experience of both wars has done much to indicate the extent to which retraining and refresher courses for those who have fallen into occupational ruts and become undesirable employees, or who have lost their positions because of technological change, can be returned to occupational life.

The Wagner-Peyser Act, of 1933, stated that services should be provided for men, women, and juniors, and that special services for veterans were to be maintained. Between the passage of this law and the opening of World War II a few significant changes were made in the classification or reclassification of handicapped persons and of special groups. The most concise presentation of data from which to summarize these changes is found in Atkinson, Odencrantz, and Deming, who in Part IV, Special Types of Employment Service, discuss five groups of persons for whom special services are desirable. Some of the classifications are much more inclusive than others: (1) the inexperienced, stressing the young who have not yet learned to find their way around in the occupational world and need considerable assistance in the know-how of securing openings, (2) veterans, (3) farm workers, (4) the hard-to-place, which is a very inclusive group comprising the types of persons whom, over a long period of years, employment office records revealed to have been continuously difficult to place. They include those who were older than the usual hiring age of large concerns, those whose loss of work was due to technological change or removals of industry, women who desired to re-enter the work world, those whose physical, mental, social, and personality disabilities curtailed their opportunities or caused employers to rate them as poor employment risks, and those whose nationality, race, or color forced the placement service, no matter how promising it might consider a worker, to place him within certain restrictions imposed by local custom or social prejudice, and (5) relief clients. This group is peculiarly interesting since its mention as a special service group is a recent departure in placement practice.

The explanation of this innovation is, of course, found in the severity of the economic depression, in its concurrent social problems, in a changing philosophy with reference to the unemployed, in the new relationship of the public employment service to the administration of relief and public works, and in the enactment of unemployment compensation legislation, which forced the service to distinguish between relief registrants and other employment service clientele. For practical placement purposes it revived the question as to what constitutes employability, compelled the placement service, or its co-operating relief agency, to differentiate between the unemployed and the unemployable, and posed a new problem regarding the extent to which those persons who may be classified as employables by a relief agency are actually placeable by an employment service.

To what extent should services organized for relief clients be operated as special services? Is "relief" a sufficiently distinctive variant to warrant the segregation of relief clients in a special placement group? Prior to the war emergency, which once again focused the attention of all employment services on the recruitment of labor and shifted many persons from the unemployable to the employable category, a program was crystallizing which may be reverted to and ultimately furnish a partial, or a tentative, reply to this question.[7]

The 1939 reorganization bill which created the Federal Security Agency again mentioned for special placement sections veterans, handicapped persons, Negroes, and juniors. And then, before the newly organized public employment service was fairly launched and its various functions in relation to other functions of the Federal Security Agency clearly defined, once again the normal development of public employment services was disrupted. This time by World War II. The War Manpower Commission, the United States Employment Service, and the Civil Service Commission, from time to time during the war, mentioned different categories of employees such as women, Negroes, and national minority groups, and in one

[7] Atkinson and others, *Public Employment Service*. The two final chapters, which deal with Placement Service for Relief and Public Works Programs, should be read by those who would understand how the happenings of the immediate prewar years changed the character of public employment services and who would anticipate how postwar employment problems may again change their character.

recent classification of handicapped persons made the serious error of including women.[8] The repercussions were immediate and effective. At the end of the war veterans' services are holding the spotlight.

What changes the postwar years may bring about in placement philosophies *in toto,* and how such changes may be expressed with reference to special services, is anyone's guess. Employment conditions may be so radically different that all preconceived programs will have to be discarded.

Therefore, insofar as special services are concerned, it is futile to attempt more than a brief summary of their development and present status as it reveals trends and suggests possible future policies:

(1) Special services have played some part throughout the entire history of organized placement services in this country. In the early years discrimination in favor of one group, involving, of course, discrimination against other groups, was a major reason for their existence.

(2) There are many special services in operation today under public, commercial, or philanthropic auspices. In some cases the basis of specialization has been types of persons, in others, types of occupations. Within these two broad categories there are many cross classifications and combinations of differentiating factors which have served as bases for special services.

(3) Historically speaking, the dominant variant upon which decision to organize a special service was based was sex, nationality, lack of citizenship, or religion. This was in harmony with the social philosophy of the time.

(4) Sex as a dominant factor in organizing special services has steadily declined in popularity. So, also, as public and commercial agencies have supplanted philanthropic services, have race, religion, and nationality. Extent of employability and degree of ability to sell one's occupational assets are gaining in importance as experience accents their value.

(5) In course of time the social effects of an increasingly decentralized labor market, plus the effect on the segregated individuals, who were thereby denied an opportunity to compete for all available openings, created a demand for the limitation of special services and for some criteria, or a criterion, to aid in determining upon the need for any special service which might be under consideration. Although this writer is not aware of any formal pronouncement of such a criterion, there seems to have been a

[8] The first edition of the Civil Service Commission's *Operations Manual for Placement of the Physically Handicapped* was entitled *Operations Manual for the Placement of Women and the Physically Handicapped.* The American Association of University Women protested "any classification of women as, or with, physically handicapped persons." The second edition contained no reference to women.

more or less general acceptance of the following principle: a special service is warranted if the character of the work, the qualifications of the workers, or the conditions and circumstances of the work need special facilities
and attention. Variations from the usual conditions of work, or from the
usual qualifications of workers, if sufficient to demand variations from the
usual placement responsibilities and procedures, was thought to warrant
the introduction of special services.

(6) That there is a field for special services is unquestioned; it is a changing, not a static field.

In view of this last statement, how may this book be of most service to
a community which is trying to decide whether or not to establish some
special service? One at a time, in order to determine which special services
might have most suggestive values for potential readers, the broad areas
within which the public and philanthropy have, over the years, instituted
special services, have been studied and compared. All services which cater
to professional groups and professional occupations have been eliminated.
They have already been pretty well publicized, and many of them are
operated under commercial, or organization, auspices. Important as they
are, it was thought that services dealing with farm labor, common labor,
and domestic service would not appeal to probable readers. They too are
omitted. Placement services for the "common man"—the man who requires no special attention and who is able to make such occupational
adjustments as may be necessary without assistance—have been discussed
under general services.

Two large and very inclusive groups for whom special services may,
under certain circumstances, seem desirable, remain. The first has been
mentioned both as the handicapped and as the hard-to-place, although
the terms do not designate entirely similar groups. The second comprises
juniors, or inexperienced persons; and again the two designations are not
entirely synonymous. Since war veterans are to be found in both groups
as well as in the "common man" category, and since juniors and inexperienced persons are also to be found in both groups, Veterans Services
and Junior Services have been chosen for special emphasis. From the point
of view of public interest and social implications both are timely topics
and are important because the time seems ripe to review, and perhaps revise, our thinking regarding their objectives, procedures, and the persons
to be served.

Since the placement process involves certain similar procedures no matter where, by whom, or for whom the service is operated, the universal
principles and procedures which have been discussed in some detail in

Part Two will not be repeated. Only such additional principles and procedures, tools and techniques as are peculiar to each special service will be mentioned. In order to facilitate reference to this previously presented material, the order of topics will conform to that followed in the preceding chapters.

CHAPTER X

Veterans' Placement Services

THE HISTORY OF VETERANS' PLACEMENT SERVICES

The history of special federal services for veterans begins with the services established by the government in 1917 for guardsmen returning from the Mexican border.

World War I witnessed a considerable development of special services for veterans under both public and private auspices. In the enthusiasm of the moment agencies competed with one another to provide centers for the advice and placement of ex-servicemen. Those who had firsthand knowledge of these agencies and those who listened to the experiences of men who had attempted to take advantage of their publicized offerings will recall, as we again face the same situation, the same problems, and the same dangers, the total inadequacy of the services available through the combined efforts of private organizations and of special and regular public services. Some services in both categories were better than others; a few were excellent; but in the main the country was totally unprepared to afford even a minimum of counseling and placement facilities for men who had served in the armed forces. The most elementary and fundamental types of information which ex-servicemen sought had not been collected and were neither in the heads of the half-trained or untrained personnel nor on the tables and in the bookcases of the office where men could find what they wanted for themselves. The tools and techniques for assisting men to make civilian adjustments and for conducting placement procedures were as Greek to a large part of the counselors who presumed to advise men, many of whom were their superiors in ability, education, and experience. Centers of information were badly needed then just as they are now. But it was common knowledge in the earlier period that few of the services set up for veterans commanded the confidence of their supposed beneficiaries.[1] There is much danger that, in this respect, the history of 1919 will be repeated.

[1] The *Report* of the Director General of the United States Employment Service for 1919 reveals that 517,902 servicemen registered and 321,007 were placed between December 1, 1918, and June 28, 1919. These statistics were widely quoted at the time to prove that the special services were not meeting their responsibilities. Statistics alone are insufficient evidence of ineffectiveness.

Special services for veterans lost much of their public appeal as the war receded into the background and peacetime economy claimed more and more attention. But politicians were not allowed to forget that ex-servicemen had special claims on whatever occupational opportunities the country afforded. The pressure of veterans' organizations led the Congress, in 1930, to grant an additional appropriation to the United States Employment Service so that it might maintain a special placement service for unemployed veterans. It wasn't much of a service while it lived, and its life was short. It was organized and administered directly by the federal government without reference to the offices under state services with which it might have co-operated, and the number of centers which could be financed under the appropriation was hopelessly inadequate and their material and professional equipment decidedly substandard.

Soon after the passage of the Wagner-Peyser Act this veterans' service was completely reorganized.[2] Separate offices were abolished and, under definite federal supervision, veteran placement became a responsibility of the regular state services. This was an advantage to veterans. It guaranteed a wider coverage, better-trained personnel, and more occupational openings from which to choose. The only special procedure required of local offices was that veterans be registered on application cards of a different color in order to facilitate selection when they were entitled to preferential referrals. This priority in employment was granted qualified veterans under the National Industrial Recovery Act of 1933, but was not renewed under the Emergency Relief Appropriation Act of 1935. As the depression intensified there was a growing feeling that it was an *unfair public employment practice* to discriminate in favor of veterans, and some placement functionaries resented the constant pressure exerted by federal veteran-placement representatives to secure advantages for veterans to which, under the law, they had no preferential rights.[3]

To what extent did the special placement services provided for veterans prior to World War II accomplish their objectives—superior services and preferential treatment?

Unquestionably the information centers set up after World War I were highly desirable in theory, irrespective of how badly they may have fallen

[2] For details of the organization, see *Report on Veterans' Placement Services* (U.S. Employment Service, 1933).

[3] Laws and regulations followed one another in such rapid succession that a chronological table is needed in order to keep events in their proper sequence. *Public Employment Service* by Atkinson and others gives all the alphabetical agencies concerned with the placement function, and it is suggested as a dependable reference for future students.

down in practice. The multiplication and duplication of services was wasteful of time, money, and personnel, and was very confusing to applicants. Lack of community organization encouraged these multiplications and duplications, while, at the same time, there were deficiencies in services which might have been supplied without additional expense had they been known. Well-meaning but untrained and frequently grossly, and at times dangerously, uninformed or misinformed personnel were designated "counselors." There was an inexcusable dearth of educational and occupational material and of information regarding community facilities from which ex-servicemen could obtain information for themselves. There was little knowledge of available rehabilitation facilities, or of the findings of special agencies regarding occupations open to the physically and mentally handicapped. There was even less knowledge of the various counseling and placement tools and techniques which had been developed by the United States Army [4] and by the United States Employment Service.[5] Job solicitors all too often exhibited the unwisdom of enthusiasts who appeal for orders on the basis of sentiment, or patriotism, rather than on the basis of recognized ability to perform.

All this was exactly as was to be expected. The country was entering upon an entirely new experience. It had never regarded its employment responsibilities very seriously and had no very secure foundation upon which to build. The education departments of universities were just beginning to include courses for school counselors in their offerings, while providing public placement functionaries was regarded as a political perquisite rather than as an educational responsibility. Nowhere was there even a small reserve of trained counseling and placement personnel upon which veterans' services could draw. Of course such services only partially accomplished their objectives.

The federal activity of 1930, which was due to political pressure, may be dismissed as of questionable value to veterans and as open to challenge as a wise expenditure of taxpayers' money. This writer has been unable to find any evidence that such services were needed, were of value, or that veterans could not have been better served had they been placed through the same channels as any other unemployed person. Perhaps the apparent ineffectiveness of this federal service was an important factor in the reor-

---

[4] *Trade Specifications and Occupational Index of Trades and Professions in the United States,* compiled by J. J. Swan (Washington, 1919); *Army Mental Tests; Methods, Typical Results, and Practical Application* (Washington, 1918); and *History of the Personnel System and the Personnel Manual, U.S. Army* (Washington, 1919).

[5] U.S. Employment Service, *Descriptions of Occupations* (Washington, D.C., 1918–1921).

ganization which took place in 1933. In any case, several changes, while far from all that were desirable, were obviously steps in advance. The special representatives of the Veterans Service who were allocated to local state offices were in a position to watch over the preferential referral of veterans to public works projects, and to keep the needs of handicapped veterans before employment interviewers and employers. They also made some contribution to the development of interest in employment services and to the securing of appropriations for their maintenance. They did not do much to increase veterans' opportunities in private employment, but their lack of accomplishment in this respect, once again, stressed the fact that success in private placements has always depended on the condition of the labor market plus the confidence which employing concerns have in the effectiveness of the local placement office. It is justifiable to assume that placement of veterans from the same office gave regular interviewers a better understanding of the handicapped, of war industries, tools, techniques, and training programs, and of methods of analyzing individuals and groups, all of which will doubtless have some carry-over value as public and private agencies plan employment programs for veterans of World War II.

A few real disservices to veterans and to the reputation of public employment services resulted from the special representative system. (1) Many physically sound, occupationally experienced veterans were, at the time the system was instituted, well below the upper hiring-age limit of most employing concerns. They should have been able to compete in the labor market with all other applicants on the basis of employability rather than as veterans. Each year an increasing number of such veterans automatically joined the group which was handicapped by age. (2) Handicapped veterans were, by this system, frequently denied the opportunity to profit by the knowledge and experience of the special services which, in the 1930's, some states and private organizations were setting up for the civilian handicapped. (3) Pressure by job solicitors for opportunities for veterans as veterans, and their referral to openings on the same basis, tended to create an impression that the placement of veterans, without reference to their assets, was the major function of the employment service, and to lessen its employing clientele.

To what extent have the experiences of post-World War I placement services—of veterans and others—been useful in determining upon the best methods of servicing the veterans of World War II?

Prior to the opening of World War II experience had indicated the desirability of certain changes in employment philosophy, in methods of organization and administration, in tools and techniques, in personnel, and in special employment procedures as they applied to servicemen. Leaders in the employment work, especially those who had made a profession of placement, recognized:

(1) That veterans without disabilities, who were still in the prime of life, should be allowed to compete in the labor market with nonveterans and should be placed through the same channels.

(2) That persons who were sufficiently handicapped to require special counseling service, or special consideration in the selection of openings— whether the handicap was physical, mental, emotional, or other, and whether it was congenital or acquired in industry or war—should receive the attention of specially trained interviewers. Even the most partisan of federal representatives agreed that the normal average veteran, until handicapped by age, needed no service other than that provided for other experienced workers. They also agreed that handicapped veterans could be better served by the special services which had been provided for the handicapped persons than they could be by the special-representative system.

(3) That the handicapped group—by this time very inclusive and frequently spoken of as the hard-to-place—comprised two distinct types of persons with reference to employability; those who needed medical care or retraining before they were ready for placement and those who were immediately employable. Special services of various types, including those under state bureaus of vocational rehabilitation, were available for the former and should be used. Special placement services for all handicapped persons were available to handicapped veterans, and to segregate the latter meant the narrowing of their range of selection and their opportunities for suitable referrals.

(4) That in the organization and administration of such special services the point to keep in mind was that *specially trained personnel must be provided*. Since local services differed materially in volume of work and in the number and qualifications of interviewers, there was no agreement as to the desirability of operating such services as separate units, as divisions of general services, or by the use of specially equipped interviewers in connection with general services. If specially trained personnel were available in general offices, that solved the problem. If they were not, then all handicapped persons should be referred to public or private services where they could receive information and counseling according to their individual needs.

(5) That practical demonstrations of the value of counseling, adjustment, and placement centers during the 1930's warranted the plea that such services be made available to, but not obligatory for, all registrants for employment—veterans or nonveterans.

(6) That the qualifications of persons charged with counseling and placement responsibilities must be raised. That wide knowledge of individuals and of personal adjustment problems, of community resources, of occupational opportunities and requirements, of the occupational significance of various handicaps, and of types of jobs suitable for the considerable variety of handicapped persons was indispensable.

(7) That changes in the avowed objectives of veterans' services were overdue. Twenty years before it was justifiable, and perhaps necessary, to set up as objectives the general promotion of interest in veterans' occupational needs, the enforcement of employment priorities, and a close liaison with veterans' organizations. At the close of the period the situation with respect to the employment needs of veterans had changed, and experienced workers had come to regard the objectives of veterans' placement services as one with the objectives of all other placement services—not to give preference to any group but to do everything possible to enable veterans to meet the requirements of business and industry, to be prepared to compete with nonveterans in the labor market, and to find their proper place in our occupational life.

This brief summary indicates that during the interval between World War I and World War II a number of dos and don'ts had crystallized on the basis of experience and experimentation and were available as warnings and guideposts were the country again to face the problems involved in demobilizing servicemen and war workers and remobilizing them in civilian occupations. Now that we do face these problems, it is well to ask if, and how, these previous experiences have helped to improve present procedures and programs.

Have the overenthusiasm, the excess emotionalism, the sensational publicity, and the lavish promises which, after the last war, led to many broken promises and ill-advised services warned political, economic, educational, and social leaders to keep their feet on the ground and their charitable impulses under control—to find appropriate and beneficial ways of expressing appreciation and gratitude without carrying their enthusiasm to the point where there is no distinction between a service and a disservice? The reply is obvious. It appears day after day in both spoken and written words. A warmhearted press and a very vocal public surfeited the country and the foxholes with all sorts of sentimental slush and with promises impossible to keep. At best, this is bad psychology. Veterans do not want to be smothered with kindness. They want a chance to develop and use their talents, and to compete occupationally with others on an equal footing. They want the public to express its gratitude by so setting the stage that they can accomplish their objectives. This is what they hoped and prayed for after the last war. They got it to a very limited extent.

What have our legislators learned, between the two wars, with reference to politically motivated and hurriedly enacted legislation? Many persons are questioning whether veterans' laws have been enacted primarily to serve veterans or because they are politically expedient. But, as usual, attempts to correct errors of political expediency need to be spoken in stentorian tones if they are to be heard. There is an increasing tendency for some groups and some individuals to speak in such tones. For, even before any large number of servicemen became veterans, experience had shown the desirability of challenging, and the necessity for revising, some of the enactments and programs which had been designed for their benefit.

Perhaps it is too much to expect that the lessons of experience will be more influential than political expediency. Custom tolerates, and at times encourages, the perversion of facts to political purposes, not only with reference to ex-servicemen but with reference to almost everything. An excellent illustration is a by-product of the political campaign of 1944, during which both political parties used the same untrue but vote-getting story as a springboard from which to assure the public, and especially the soon-to-be ex-servicemen, that under its protective aegis the extensive apple selling [6] which had been the occupational reward of veterans of World War I could never be repeated.

But determination of the extent to which the experiences of World War I have had a beneficial influence on the legislative enactments and

[6] This writer had personal knowledge and has personal records as to the date and object of apple selling in New York City. And she has an abundance of newspaper clippings which told the story of its nation-wide practice in October, 1930. It was not a boondoggling project for veterans of World War I, either in purpose or character. It was an advertising project, preparatory to the opening of Apple Week, of the Apple Growers Association. The Association offered, through the municipal employment office, to provide boxes of apples free to such unemployed *registrants*—veteran or nonveteran —as wished to engage for one week in the advertising project. Some of the unemployed who accepted the proposition selected desirable sales corners and continued to sell for several weeks, paying for their apples on a regular commercial basis. President Roosevelt, before the Democratic National Convention, and other speakers before the Republican National Convention, perverted this factual depression-years incident to appear to apply to veterans of World War I, and an emotional and uncritical public has not yet challenged the story sufficiently to prevent its periodic repetition.

programs which have thus far, or may in the future, characterize this country's efforts to serve veterans of World War II, is a job for retrospective, not for current, writers. Events are moving rapidly. The legislation of today is challenged tomorrow. Interpretations, revisions, amendments, and repeals follow. It is unsafe to assume that laws placed on the statute books one day will be reliable information for veterans and their advisors the next day. General programs have usually contained some excellent suggestions for veterans' services. As one example, the Baruch Report recommends (1) adequate machinery for job placement of veterans and war workers; (2) provisions for the resumption of education interrupted by war; and (3) only one place in each community to which returned servicemen and women need to go to learn all their rights and how to get them. The trouble with such suggestions is that before they can be woven into effectively operating programs they require much elaboration and interpretation, and it is the details of organization and administration, not the general statements, which harbor the troublesome problems that later arise to plague and confuse those who are charged with the responsibilities of organizing and administering the program.

Many of the problems which are bound to arise in connection with the demobilization and remobilization of veterans and war workers cannot legitimately be regarded as employment problems, nor can they receive very much attention in a book which is concerned primarily with occupational placement. On the other hand, personnel workers are talking too much about the organismic approach to the "human factor" and the integration of personality, and educators have proclaimed too loudly that guidance is a unitary function, that advisory services must be concerned with the whole, not the segmented life, and that adjustment in occupational life is the final step in the educative process, to assume that the occupational problems of either veterans or nonveterans can be separated from personal problems in other areas of life. Therefore, in presenting the current situation with reference to special services for veterans, while the accent must be placed on employment problems and such provisions as have been made, or could be made, for assistance in their solution, it is obvious that no satisfactory consideration of this subject, at this time, is worth while which does not recognize the over-all programs which the federal and state governments are planning. They are the framework within which community placement services must be set up, while their legislative enactments, for better or for worse, have imposed certain limitations within which local services must be organized and operated. Some of these programs and enactments are more closely related to employment than others, but all have some influence on the organization and administration of effective local placement services for veterans.

OBJECTIVES OF VETERANS' PLACEMENT SERVICES

In the light of the presently prevailing philosophy with reference to the objectives of all public placement services, and in view of the criterion which has been formulated as a yardstick for determining upon the desirability of instituting any special service, what are the legitimate objectives of a veterans' placement service?

The fundamental objectives of a veterans' placement service should be identical with those of any general placement service. Additional objectives were stated when services for veterans of World War I were instituted, and they have been repeated in the programs set up for veterans of World War II. These pronouncements provide a means whereby an appreciative public may express its gratitude to ex-servicemen by guaranteeing them certain special privileges such as priority in employment. It is these secondary objectives which differentiate veterans' services from all other placement services and warrant their classification as special services.

Naturally, the student of methods of effective occupational distribution will raise some questions: To what extent do special services for veterans meet the general requirements laid down by experienced workers as the criterion for the institution of special services? Is "veteran" a sufficiently distinctive variant to warrant the registration of veteran applicants in a special group? In view of the change in attitude toward the placement of veterans, which came about gradually as public enthusiasm for serving veterans of the previous war gave way to the considered opinion of those who attempted to carry out the secondary objectives of veterans' services, is it a service, or is it a disservice, to expect normal, experienced veterans, who desire to register in public employment services, to compete for openings with other veterans rather than in the open labor market? In the long run, does experience show that veterans, as veterans, have made any special and sustained appeal to either the public or to employers? When the one-year-retention-of-position guarantee has expired, will the veteran employees have been pretty well picked over, and, if there is a falling labor market, will only those who have promising potentialities be retained? This sifting process characterizes all successful business enterprises. How often will the patriotic appeal serve to secure another chance for occupationally substandard veterans? How many will be salvaged by our rehabilitation program? How long before a certain per cent will join the hard-to-place, and later on, the unemployables? What about unfair discrimination in employment? Already superpriority with reference to jobs for veterans is in open conflict with superseniority for union workers. As the war ceases to be a live issue, will class distinction for veterans become increasingly unpopular, not only as an unfair discrimination against other groups, but as an actual handicap to the occupational success of veterans?

This writer was in close touch with post-World War I veterans' services. As the years passed she watched with interest the shift in veteran placement philosophy which resulted from experience, noted the criticisms due to too many special services whose registrants did not have sufficiently common needs to differentiate them as a group from other groups, and recalled that since 1917 the federal government had maintained, more or less indifferently, employment services for veterans. She is now weighing, in the light of the past, the pros and cons of our current program for the employment of veterans. At best, this is bound to be a very complex task, based, as it is, on conflicting objectives and fostering many opportunities for disagreement.

But, no matter how logical anyone's replies to the suggested questions may be, no matter what story the facts may tell, there are very good reasons why many persons will endorse special public employment services for the veterans of World War II. Outstanding among them is the feeling that the immediate occupational needs of returning veterans do sufficiently differentiate them, as a group, to warrant special services and special privileges in competition with other groups. Unquestionably military service has disrupted, delayed, or spoiled the educational and employment plans of many veterans; it has denied others the opportunity to participate in the more lucrative war industries; and its cessation has brought some, and will bring many more, back to an occupational world to which they have become strangers or with which they have not yet become acquainted.

The country feels that it owes these veterans a favorable reintroduction and reorientation to this unfamiliar world. Current programs have expressed this feeling, and legislation in harmony with it has guaranteed veterans certain employment "rights." But these rights are, and should be, temporary. They must be cashed in on within a definite period of time. Therefore, may not some of the problems involved in the reconciliation of the primary and secondary objectives of veterans' services be resolved, or mitigated, by frankly admitting, political pressure notwithstanding, that the currently operating placement services for veterans of World War II are temporary services? Their objectives, then, would legitimately stress all the secondary objectives mentioned, while the fundamental objectives of all employment services could be relegated to second place until those whose occupational programs had been disrupted had made their adjustments. One year is a long enough period of adjustment for the average, normal, experienced man. It is also long enough for the orientation of the majority of occupational novitiates. Permanent services for veterans would then, preferably in co-operation with other groups which require the same types of service, provide for two major classes of persons: (1) those who can and should compete with others in the open labor market and (2) those whose disabilities classify them as *hard to place*.

PREORGANIZATION INVESTIGATIONS AND DECISIONS

The majority of the points mentioned under this topic and under External Organization in Part Two are applicable to veterans' services. Preliminary surveys should be made, community co-operation secured, committees set up, a budget prepared, publicity arranged for, location selected and office space provided, material equipment and professional personnel determined upon, and the like. Four topics may well be given special preorganization attention in connection with veterans' services— Legislation, Community Co-operation, Surveys, and Operating Personnel.

Legislation. All social legislation which is of interest to veterans is of concern to placement officials, but the latter's major responsibilities are found in connection with federal, state, and local enactments which deal with rehabilitation, additional education, vocational retraining, and placement. Of specific importance are: (1) Section 8 of the Selective Training and Service Act of 1940, as amended, which guarantees veterans certain re-employment rights. (2) The Federal Vocational Rehabilitation Law of 1920, with the amendments comprised in the Barden-LaFollette Act of 1943 (Public Law 113), which permits federal and state governments to co-operate in making available, to all types of persons, the various services necessary to make them employable and to help them return to, and retain positions in, the work world. (3) The GI Bill of Rights (Public Law 346—The Servicemen's Readjustment Act of 1944), which, among other provisions, grants subsidies for continued education and suggests methods whereby those who so desire may secure small loans. This legislation is generally conceded to have been unfortunately timed and too hurriedly prepared. (4) The Veterans' Preference Act of 1944, which outlines in detail the advantages to be given ex-servicemen and women in government jobs—a program whereby veterans of this and previous wars are going to have a virtual monopoly on new government jobs after the war.

These and other enactments not only provide the national framework and indicate the limitations within which placement services for veterans may be organized, but they influence to a marked degree their administrative and operational procedures. State and local laws and regulations often supplement them. However, in spite of their importance for information, counseling, and placement services, many of the provisions of such enactments have been, and now are, under fire. Dissatisfaction and criticism are rife, extending even into the much publicized field of discriminatory or unfair employment practices. Therefore, it is useless to analyze in detail, in their relation to the placement of veterans, legal provisions some of which will doubtless be so temporary that they will be wiped out, or revised, before this book can reach the market. The texts of statutory enactments are always available from federal and state authorities. Their collection and study is a first step in the preorganization activities of any given community. Keeping up with revisions and new enactments is also a local responsibility.

Community Co-operation. Lack of community co-operation has always been one of the outstanding criticisms on guidance and placement services in these United States. It was an acknowledged defect in the programs set up for veterans of World War I, and, in spite of all the warnings, conference discussions, and articles which have tried to focus sufficient attention on its evils to bring about reform, it promises to be one of the most serious handicaps to the organization of effective veteran services after World War II. For there is little evidence at present that any considerable number of communities are resisting the old temptation to decentralize and duplicate services, to avoid the appearance of charity, relief, or welfare, and to keep the single objective of veterans' needs in mind. Veterans of the last war became very impatient with the childish motives which prompted each clique to want to "put on its own show" in spite of the fact that their immature and ineffective performances resulted in no show being worth while. Veterans of World War II will not be less critical.

What can be done about this? No one knows. Everyone agrees that local agencies must assume major responsibility for the readjustment and reallocation of veterans and war workers and that they are ill equipped for this undertaking. They are handicapped, not only by local jealousies and lack of social vision and suitable operating personnel, but also by the diversity of governmental and private agencies, each of which has a finger in the rehabilitation pie. No less than eight national agencies are supporting contributory programs which read well, but which contain the seeds of many broken promises and which cannot be very effective until all of their activities are co-ordinated, harmonized with local activities, and woven into a single community service.[7] This requires an active, intelligent, and authoritative community council and is a preorganization must—a must which is already hoary with age. Why in any given community has such a council not been organized? Sometimes it has been—too often only on paper. Committees which are interested in community co-ordinating councils and in the organization of effective veterans' services will find it helpful to study some of the material which is available on the analysis and utilization of community resources.[8]

Preorganization Surveys. Chapter III has dealt with preorganization surveys in detail, and there is considerable material in print on the purposes, content, methods of making, and practical uses of surveys of educational and employment opportunities and of community resources.[9] The only surveys which require special attention in connection with veterans' placement services are (1) surveys which classify veterans and (2) surveys of special occupational and educational opportunities for veterans.

Surveys Which Classify Veterans may be patterned after population, or segmented population, surveys. They will tell the community how many of its members are entitled to classification as veterans and will characterize them, as well as is possible, from such sources of information as school and draft-board records, and in some instances from service records and reports from relatives and friends. A summary of their findings will reveal, just as will a summary of the characteristics of any other segment of the population, the various types of applicants which a veterans' service must be prepared to serve. It is safe to assume:

(1) That, in the large centers of population and within certain limitations, the veterans of World War II, on any basis one may wish to use, will constitute a cross section of the adult male population 18 to 50 years of age. "Fitness" variations from the total population should—allowance being made for those suffering temporarily from combat experiences—be favorable to veterans, since selection standards have ruled out of the

[7] Morse A. Cartwright, *Marching Home: Educational and Social Adjustment After the War* (New York: Teachers College, Columbia University, 1944), is a representative study which deals with this subject on the basis of a recent investigation by the Institute of Adult Education.

[8] See M. W. Zapoleon, *Community Occupational Surveys* (U.S. Office of Education; Washington, D.C., 1942), and the Bureau of Training, War Manpower Commission, *The Training of Vocational Counselors* (Washington, D.C., 1944). Pages 32–33 of the latter work contain a brief outline and bibliography on community organization; pages 48–64 describe eight federal agencies participating in services for veterans; and pages 74–77 outline in detail the Connecticut Program of Community Organization and Training, which is known also as the Gray Plan. See Carl Gray, "The Gray Plan for Post-War Reemployment," *Occupations,* XXII (1913), 3–9.

[9] Reed, *Guidance and Personnel Services,* pp. 71–132, covers these topics.

armed forces individuals who fall below or above certain age limits, or who fail to meet fixed educational, physical, mental, moral, and emotional requirements. In the small centers one or more dominant types of veterans may be representative of the community population. Either situation is an important factor in determining the sort of services which will best meet veteran needs.

(2) That veterans at induction comprise many types characterized by wide individual variations within types. This should warn the community that at demobilization it will be called upon to serve just as great a variety of types characterized by just as many individual variations. The personal peculiarities and idiosyncrasies which went to war with individuals may come back with them—minimized or intensified—or new needs, new experiences, new habits, and new viewpoints may have eradicated old characteristics and substituted new ones.

(3) That the entire group will not only be older in years, but richer in experiences, more mature in outlook on life, more self-reliant, more impatient with trivialities, more accustomed to regimentation, and better able to take care of themselves. Many will be healthier, more alert, and better prepared to live and co-operate with others. All will have changed in some respects. Some will classify as "more of a man," others as "less of a man." Changes within the individual may cause some to feel that the unchanged things to which he is returning are the things which have changed.

(4) That some of the home boys whom parents, teachers, and the community may have thought were pigeonholed for life as belonging to certain types will come back entirely different types of men as to interests, ideas, and attitudes. The community will need to be very careful how it approaches its boys who have become men.

(5) That many of those whose preinduction performances prevented their inclusion in any classification which theorists had prepared, and denied them the neat little prewar labels with which educators and social workers were prone to tag humanity, may be expected to return with enhanced abilities to evade postwar classifications and labels.

(6) That, after all the classifications and cross classifications have been made, an overwhelmingly large number of veterans will fall into that valuable, useful, and stable type known as the *common man*—the man who solves his own problems, makes his own adjustments, supports his own family, takes his own responsibilities seriously, and asks nothing of the public except that it so set the stage that he may return to normal community, occupational, and family life as quickly as possible.

Surveys of Special Occupational Opportunities will need to be supplemented by surveys of positions specifically reserved for veterans and by surveys of any special preparations which industry and business have made, or are making, to provide suitable openings for the various types of ex-servicemen and women who may desire employment. Opportunities reserved by law—such as civil-service positions—with full information as to eligibility requirements, the recent pledges of a group of Chicago concerns to set aside 25 per cent of their openings for veterans, and other similar reservations should be listed under the first category. Under the second category each community will list its own special openings, and, in the light of its geographical location, transportation facilities, and the needs, desires, and qualifications of its veteran population, it will include such opportunities in other communities as may be available to extramural applicants.

The number of opportunities reserved for both normal and handicapped veterans has caused those who recall the difficulties involved in the occupational integration of veterans after World War I to reinventory jobs and promises and, in view of the prospects for making good on their promises, to question whether both the government and private concerns may not have built up an overoptimistic picture of the absorptive power of the country and been overgenerous in their promises. The employing concerns of the United States have long been aware of the difficulties involved in remobilizing a "guestimated' 20 million ex-servicemen and war-industry workers in normal productive employment with the minimum amount of dislocation to individuals and to the entire civilian economy. Recently a more critical analysis of employment problems has been due to realization of the fact that their promissory notes must be paid off on demobilization day when demand for mass employment will be accompanied by a growing scarcity of jobs and keen competition for opportunities to work will dominate the labor market. Employers have been troubled, too, by the fact that plant surveys indicated that they will have major responsibilities to their nonveteran employees which must not be entirely set aside in favor of veterans.

In the same connection, they are challenging the "loose talk about psychoneuroses and combat fatigue," and the tendency of the authorities to refer for placement men who have suffered from mental upsets without giving those who employ them full information as to their type of disability. Furthermore, when they attempt to establish and carry out employment policies within the framework of the Selective Service Law, they encounter complications due to the different interpretations of the provisions of the law and the resultant competition between veterans and labor unions.

In spite of all the attendant difficulties, careful planning on the part of individual concerns and the co-operative efforts of business organizations, governmental agencies, and community councils have resulted in the institution of a number of programs to help in solving the multitudinous problems involved in veteran adjustment. Some are already in operation and others are in process of preparation. A few examples are cited:

The Peoria Plan [10] furnishes an example of an occupational survey plus a community information and placement service. Under the leadership of the Caterpillar Tractor Company, working through the Peoria Manufacturers' Association, every business establishment in the city was surveyed, and the entire community joined in establishing a center where any veteran—sound or handicapped—could secure any information he desired and where he could be referred to a job in harmony with his capacities. An organization chart and a list of activities carried on at the center are included in the description of the plan.

Three employment opportunity surveys on a nation-wide basis characterize the activities of associations and agencies. The Manufacturing Chemists Association of the United States has worked out and suggested to the War Manpower Commission a plan whereby a large number of veterans may have an opportunity to enter the industry. The Society of American Florists and Ornamental Horticulturists estimated that there would be opportunities for approximately 16,000 disabled men in light, quiet work in greenhouses and showrooms. The Smaller War Plants Corporation has been interested in assisting new "enterprisers," who indicate suitability, to establish their own businesses. Its program has been distributed to the 6,500 local selective service boards, and it has announced, as a basic rule, "no loan into bankruptcy." [11] The Standard Oil Company of New Jersey's proposal to spend five million dollars in building new filling stations, with up to $3,000 as a cash loan to each veteran who desires to go into the filling station business, is an example of private encouragement to small business. No strings are attached to the offer, and the station is not obliged to sell Standard's products.

A large number of industrial plants, retail establishments, and other

[10] H. A. Vonachen, "Business and Community Plans for Human Rehabilitation," *Executives Service Bulletin*, XXII (1944), 3-4.

[11] The loan provisions of the GI Bill of Rights should be considered in connection with establishing an independent business. Veterans and their counselors will also do well to heed the warning by Leo Cherne, "So You Want Your Own Business," *Magazine Section, Boston Herald*, April 1, 1945.

employing concerns have made surveys for various purposes, all of which are concerned with forecasting employment demands and estimating employment opportunities. Sometimes a company may seek to know how many former employees expect to return, what new skills each has acquired, and what each has to suggest regarding re-employment. The purpose is to ascertain how many men will be available for each job classification. The surveys made by retail stores have revealed no eagerness on the part of former employees to return to their previous occupation. If this situation continues, it suggests possible openings for veterans, or nonveterans, who may not, as yet, have determined upon any occupational preference. A number of concerns have made surveys in order to determine the types of jobs on which physically and mentally handicapped persons may be employed safely and productively. Some of the findings are accompanied by charts showing the jobs which can be handled by those who have experienced such common disabilities as loss of limbs, fingers, toes, eyesight, hearing, nervous disorders, heart ailments, and back injuries.

The Ford Motor Company is, of course, recognized as the pioneer and outstanding illustration of the ability of industry to absorb handicapped workers advantageously to the individual, the industry, and society. In March, 1945, the Company reported that there were 12,000 men and women with physical impairments on its payroll, that 3,000 veterans had returned, and that preferential consideration for all veterans had been adopted as its policy. The Ford Company does not reject persons who are handicapped by prison records. Another recent and interesting survey is concerned with opportunities for the victims of epilepsy—a disease which some have acquired as the result of war-incurred injuries. Prepublication news notices indicate that insurance companies are presently employing a considerable number and that they "may be employed in any business or industry, provided their position is not one which would endanger themselves or other persons." [12]

Since knowing how and where to refer handicapped civilians implies knowing how and where to refer handicapped veterans, every placement service will need the information collected by the Special Services Division of the United States Employment Service. These very complete files cover practically all employables and mention companies which employ

[12] W. W. Johnston (safety consultant for an insurance company and consultant for the Ordnance Department of the U.S. Army) in the *Boston Herald*, May 22, 1945. Mr. Johnston's findings were to be submitted at a congressional hearing in Washington by the American Epilepsy League, Inc.

various types of handicapped persons.[13] For example, one firm will employ deaf mutes, hernia cases, heart cases, and men with one eye; another can employ those having leg injuries, mental cases, and the deaf. Special attention is given to the placing of epileptics.

A long and constantly increasing list of occupations in which the blind have proved satisfactory is available for counselors and placement workers, while several public employment offices report themselves unable to respond to the orders for deaf employees. Women veterans are entitled to all the benefits accorded ex-servicemen, and some surveys have been made to ascertain to what extent handicapped women have proved satisfactory and in what occupations they may hope to find postwar openings. For example, the United States Women's Bureau in a recent study of 513 handicapped women found them engaged in 110 occupations: 62 per cent in clerical and sales work and 38 per cent in widely diversified occupations. This sort of information is very helpful. Of course, most surveys of opportunities for all types of handicapped persons have been made under war conditions when labor was at a premium. Counselors and placement workers would seem to be justified in being hopeful as to postwar openings, but they would probably be wise if they are not overoptimistic.

Surveys of Educational Opportunities and complete information regarding the conditions under which veterans may take advantage of them are also a part of the essential equipment of community counseling and placement services. Governmental programs have been in operation during the war, are under way on different educational levels for men while they are awaiting transportation to return home, and are instituted in Army and Navy hospitals as soon as injured men are able to respond. Apprenticeship and vocational training programs, as well as other educational programs, were operating in industry, with or without co-operator assistance, before the war. Some types of programs, which in co-operation with governmental agencies have been enormously expanded during the war, will doubtless continue for the retraining of veterans, and some new opportunities may be offered as need is shown.

In addition to the usual preorganization surveys of educational opportunities, which are essential equipment for all counseling services, agencies specializing in services for veterans will need to be familiar with legislative enactments, federal, state, and municipal, which deal with the postwar

---

[13] Provisions of workmen's compensation laws, especially those which require an employer to pay the entire compensation if an already partially disabled person becomes totally disabled because of a subsequent injury on the job, make employers hesitant about employing handicapped persons. Alterations in such laws are being made, and local services should be informed as to the provisions in force in their own states.

training and education of veterans, and to collect complete information on special opportunities on all levels of education and under both public and private auspices. Two acts of Congress provide for free education at public expense for such veterans as meet the requirements: Public Law 16, The Vocational Rehabilitation Act, "To restore employability lost by virtue of a service-incurred disability . . . ," and Public Law 346, "To continue education or training impeded, interrupted, delayed or interfered with by reason of entrance into service, or to provide a refresher or retraining course."[14] Administrative responsibility for both statutes is placed on the Administrator of Veterans Affairs, who may use other existing agencies in carrying out the purposes of the enactments. Decentralization of authority to regional areas has taken place.

The Vocational Rehabilitation Law seems to have been fairly satisfactory, probably because its main provisions have been in operation since 1920 and have been carried out effectively. In any case, Public Law 346, popularly known as the educational provisions of the GI Bill of Rights, has borne the brunt of the criticisms and has created considerable commotion in college circles. Although choice among a wide variety of educational and training institutions, including on-the-job training, is permitted under the law, publicity has accented collegiate opportunities to such an extent that they have tended to overshadow all other opportunities.

The college subsidies include tuition, books, and a subsistence allowance of $50 per month for single persons and $75 for those who have dependents.[15] Some college authorities, while more than anxious to open to veterans every educational opportunity from which they can profit, are fearful lest such subsidies will invite "intellectual hoboism," and they call attention to the fact that the generosity of the federal government has resulted in many smaller subsidies in the form of competitive scholarships —as for instance the 1,200 New York State scholarships good for four years in any one of a large number of institutions—being without bidders. Others predict that acceptance of its offer will delay the entry of many to occupational life until they are beyond the age for successful induction and have reached an educational level upon which they cannot realize.

[14] The provisions of these two laws, set up in parallel columns for comparative purposes, may be found in the *Ladies Home Journal*, LXII (May, 1945), 143, in connection with an article by William Waller, "Which Veterans Should Go to College?" See also Arthur C. Johnson, Jr., "The Federal Program for the Vocational Rehabilitation and Education of Veterans," *Guidance, Practical Arts and Vocational Education*, I (1944), 39–40.

[15] This allowance has now been increased by Public Law 268 to $65 a month for single, and $90 a month for married, veterans. Veterans with dependents other than wives receive additional amounts.

Whatever the advantages or the disadvantages of the law may be, colleges are making elaborate preparations, either independently, or in co-operation with the Veterans Administration, to set up counseling services and to adjust educational routine and programs to veterans' needs. Therefore college surveys should include information on whether the program is to be administered as a separate, or in connection with a regular, administrative unit, and such data as eligibility requirements, registration periods, subsidies, review courses, deficiency courses, noncredit courses, advisory services, and possibilities of credit for military experience and for courses pursued under the Armed Forces Institute.[16]

Also included in the surveys should be the considerable number of postwar educational programs of less than college grade which are being offered under both public and private auspices. Each program, unless its value is already established, should be evaluated according to accepted criteria for judging such programs. Public institutes, or "area schools," on the junior-college level have been established in Michigan and New York, and several large cities are expanding offerings at the secondary level.

Two training projects which have been undertaken by industrial concerns are mentioned as illustrations of the way in which good business practice, service to veterans, and contribution to our postwar economy may be combined. The Henry Ford Trade School has opened Camp Legion in Dearborn, Michigan, as an occupational rehabilitation center. Veterans receive three dollars a day and room and board while they prepare for machine-shop work and learn farm practices. The Bulova School of Watchmaking was chartered by the Board of Regents of the State of New York, April 21, 1944, and ground was broken for the school in New York City on May 15, 1944. Its purpose, expressed in the inscription on the cornerstone, "To serve those who served us," is to train physically handicapped veterans and to place them in positions through the co-operation of retail jewelers throughout these United States. Seven hundred jobs were immediately pledged for graduates.

Veterans' counseling and placement services will find a list of the training-in-employment opportunities in their own geographical areas a very important addition to their educational data.[17] Some concerns have maintained programs of this type for years; others have inaugurated them

---

[16] The Armed Forces Institute, established by the government as the Army Institute in April, 1942, includes both in-service programs and programs of general education which are intended to bridge the gap between military activities and the resumption of normal educational experiences.

[17] Reed, *Guidance and Personnel Services*, pp. 99–105, covers this topic.

as a war necessity. Some which combine the rehabilitation objective with the training objective will be open to veterans whose disabilities allow them to return to normal employment conditions immediately. This sort of information is helpful also to veterans' counseling services, where interviewers are finding that college education has been oversold to such an extent that too many men, who are easily recognized as potential failures in formal educational programs, are applying for subsidies under Public Laws 346 or 16.

Experienced counselors recognize many factors which militate against a successful college career for certain types of veterans and regret that more opportunities for job training are not available. The educational program of the government includes training-on-the-job, and the Veterans Administration is supposed to supply "training officers," one of whose functions is the solicitation of opportunities for this type of training. There seem to be at least two major obstacles to the successful prosecution of this phase of the program: (1) lack of a sufficient number of properly qualified persons who are willing to accept training-officer positions and (2) the unwillingness of employing concerns to go through the red tape required by the Veterans Administration before a training-in-employment program can be approved. The latter situation seems to be improving.

Placement clinics, if the location of the service be such that veterans can take advantage of them and if their character be such that they are worthy of recommendation, should be listed among educational opportunities.[18] Sometimes "how to sell one's services" is the sole type of education in which a veteran or nonveteran is deficient. Perhaps it is superfluous to suggest that, as society under various auspices establishes ever more lifesaving stations for those who seek assistance in making occupational adjustments, placement officers should know where they are and for whom operating so that, while taking advantage of every service which helps to develop more placeable applicants, they may discourage the existence of commercial "mousetraps" whose sole objective is to catch and squeeze the purses, if not the lives, of the unemployed.

What type of service shall the community institute?

On the basis of the data revealed by various surveys, each community will be able to make a tentative decision regarding the sort of services which it should set up and the qualifications of the personnel necessary for it to function satisfactorily. Will returning veterans, in the main, desire information on their rights, privileges, and opportunities under the laws?

[18] Some of the men and agencies who conducted depression-period clinics are again active in behalf of veterans who need the same type of assistance.

Will they expect a counseling service with a personnel sufficiently informed and experienced to help them interpret the available information
and advise with them on its personal implications? Will they want help
on entering, or re-entering, occupational life?

Whether they need one, or all three, the community should be prepared to provide them. But this will not necessarily imply new units of
service. No new unit should be organized until all of the presently operating community services have been co-ordinated and possibilities of duplications ruled out. For example, a suburban residence community may
find that most of its younger veterans expect to complete educational
programs, while most of the older men desire to return to occupational
pursuits as soon as is possible. If the public schools support a counseling
service which is daily called upon to furnish its pupils with similar types
of educational information and counsel, it can easily expand the range of
its activities to include the needs of young veterans, many of whom were
doubtless formerly members of the school. And if there is a placement
service operating in the community, or if employed residents have previously depended upon services in near-by urban centers, it would be gross
stupidity to open another unit for which there was no demand.

Survey data, especially if supplemented by authoritative material suggested by such organizations as the National Committee for Mental Hygiene, should do much to check the growth of the psychoneurosis fad,
which is sweeping the country, and to counteract false impressions gained
from literature accenting the trials and tribulations which veterans, their
relatives, and friends may be expected to experience on demobilization
day. Helpful also should be the nation-wide series of conferences on "The
Community and the Returning Veterans" under the auspices of the con-
valescent training section of the Army Air Forces, the first of which was
held (May, 1945) at Athens, Ohio, in co-operation with Ohio University.
These conferences and the films shown are expected to aid communities
to evaluate more intelligently the fiction, magazine, and newspaper articles, radio soap operas and the cinema, all of which have had a share in
educating the public to expect veterans to return as sort of emotional
monstrosities.

A third way in which the findings of surveys may be beneficial is in
pointing out the type of operating personnel which is essential to carry
out the objectives of the service. The qualifications of the personnel
should vary with the functions they are expected to perform. Of course,
no ordinary veterans' service should be expected, or should be allowed,
to perform technical rehabilitation services; that is not their function

and other agencies are better prepared to perform such functions. The usual community services should confine their efforts to information, general counseling, and occupational placement, and their officials should be thoroughly prepared to perform such of these functions as are included in the program, to detect signs of need for reference to more highly specialized services, and to be fully cognizant of the disservices performed when they attempt to assume psychometric responsibilities or utilize therapies which are dangerous tools in the hands of laymen.

Operating Personnel. Operating personnel is the fourth topic which has been mentioned as requiring preorganization attention. The difficulty of securing qualified operating personnel for counseling and placement services is not peculiar to veterans' services. It is universal.[19] But, because of the immediate, excessive, and probably temporary demand for such functionaries in connection with the demobilization of the armed forces, the difficulties of the veterans' services are magnified, and some communities are yielding to the temptation to substitute quantity of service for quality of service. The result is that many would-be veterans' services are manned by second- and third-rate personnel or by well-meaning volunteers. Is any counseling better than no counseling? Experienced personnel workers say "No." They agree that counseling and placement services for ex-servicemen, to be other than an insult to the service which they have rendered us, must be manned by thoroughly informed men who have at their command a wealth of educational and occupational information suited to meet calls which may come from all levels of education, all degrees of intelligence, and all types of occupational experiences; men who know that adjustment to civilian life is primarily the veteran's problem, that it is he who, in the final analysis, must do the job. They must be his helpers, and the community is responsible for seeing that he gets the right kind of help. Nowhere has this point of view been more forcefully expressed than in the statement presented by Horace E. English at the fifty-second annual meeting of the American Psychological Association and adopted by unanimous vote.[20] Large urban centers, and counseling

19 Reed, *Guidance and Personnel Services,* pp. 417–434, deals with the selection of directors for counseling services in educational institutions.

20 "The American Psychological Association at its Annual Meeting in Cleveland, September 12, 1944, took account of two influences adversely affecting the vocational, educational, and personal counseling of men and women being returned from the armed services to civilian life: On the one hand there is a serious stultifying duplication of counseling which is certain to diminish its effectiveness; and on the other hand (and partly as a result of the duplication), too many of the counselors are most inadequately trained.

"The Association therefore instructs the Council of Directors to take active steps,

services operating at collegiate centers under the authority of the Veterans Administration, will be more fortunate in securing qualified personnel than will small centers. The majority will probably employ psychometricians, or clinical psychologists, and possibly psychiatrists in connection with their counseling services.

In order to remedy this general deficiency in operating personnel the War Manpower Commission sent out an S O S and hurriedly arranged for the preparation of training course outlines which could be used by such colleges and universities as desired to prepare vocational counselors for veterans' services.[21] As usual, unit contributions were secured from a number of persons each of whom attempted to prepare a suitable unit for a balanced training program. Each contributor, in such cases, automatically, and probably quite unconsciously, stresses his own major interest and selects topics and reference material adapted to the age and educational level of the group with which he habitually deals. The final result is a collection of short units and long units, overemphasized and underemphasized topics. One unit is adapted to the needs of secondary-school counselors, another to the needs of industrial-relations counselors; a third is given to the functions of psychometricians, statisticians, and clinical psychologists; while others deal, in more or less detail, with mental abnormalities, various therapies, labor relations, employee services, and the like. Such programs lack the unity which comes from determining upon a definite, clear-cut objective, selecting primary and secondary objectives, and determining what teaching or informational content should be used to construct an overview of the picture of the general field and what must be given the major emphasis in order to afford the best initial preparation for the specific functions to be performed.

Other training programs promulgated by governmental agencies have been mentioned in Part One, and their effectiveness may well be reviewed in connection with this most recent effort in the interest of veterans. This writer has had some small part in each of the programs designed to service adults and major responsibility for two which were attempted in the interest of juniors.[22] From her point of view, none has been a success. In view of the character of the responsibilities for which they prepare and the

---

by making the appropriate representations to the Federal Government and the several agencies concerned and in any other way which shall seem effective, to minimize both these evils" (*Psychological Bulletin*, XLI [1944], 739).

[21] Bureau of Training, War Manpower Commission, *The Training of Vocational Counselors* (Washington, D.C., 1944).

[22] See Chapter XI.

essentiality for successful counselor performance of such qualifications as continuous study on a broad background of basic knowledges, maturity of judgment, and long and fruitful experience, she is inclined to feel that all such programs should be relegated to the in-service, or upkeep, of trained personnel.

When the preorganization steps have been completed, there will be a clear understanding that a veterans' service is a business, not a charity, proposition, even though gratitude may have been a motivating factor. When it has been determined whether the service shall be a public or a private enterprise and co-ordination of activities and responsibilities has been provided for at each different level—national, state, and local—so that duplications and conflicts may be avoided; when the scope of the service—information, counsel, placement—and the extent to which counseling shall include testing and other expert services has been determined; when the housing problem has been decided not only with reference to location and expense but also in view of the possible results of oversegregation on veterans and nonveterans; when the surveys have been completed and their findings have been prepared for use and supplemented by similar material used in the usual employment office; when the director has been appointed and his responsibilities clearly understood, including the training of such volunteers as may be selected to assist in the service, then the doors may be opened and the various functions which have been determined upon may be put in operation.

Placement of some type or types of individuals is the purpose of all placement services. Placement of veterans is the object of a veterans' service. The procedures involved in attaining its objective are exactly the same as those of any other placement service—the registration and classification of applicants, and the referral to openings of those who are prepared for employment. A secondary responsibility may be imposed if a screening process has not previously taken place or if, irrespective of how carefully it may have been made, the registration interview reveals unreadiness for employment. All procedures should be carried on in harmony with federal and state statutes and activities, and the placement service should be so organized and operated that it serves as an important articulation unit in the total reconversion program, at the same time observing to the utmost extent the social obligations which present-day employment philosophy imposes with reference to the increases of labor turnover and the multiplication of labor reserves.

PLACEMENT PROCEDURES

The Reception. The reception interviewer will have responsibility for assuring the service that it is dealing with a bona fide veteran. Elaboration of this point is not necessary. It would, indeed, be strange did no individuals attempt to take fraudulent advantage of the special occupational opportunities available for veterans; therefore some method, or methods, of identification should be decided upon. This is not difficult if preliminary interviewers are even reasonably alert, since veterans, to a greater extent than any other group except those fresh from educational institutions, are supposed to bring their identification data with them in the shape of discharge papers or other documentary proof of service. Sometimes such data will have reached the local office before the veteran calls. The over-all federal program for the demobilization of veterans [23] provides for a number of documents which are valuable aids in assisting them to make their transition from the armed services to civilian life, whether it be as an immediate employee in private business or under civil service, as an entrepreneur under the loan program, as a candidate for some form of rehabilitation or education, or as an unemployed person eligible for compensation.

One of the most important documents in this demobilization program is the separation classification known as "form 100." It is the result of the counseling interview which completes the cycle of Army personnel work and paves the way for reabsorption into the nation's civilian economy. Its entries show civilian and military training and education, job experiences, and many other items. Were these documents, properly filled out, always available either as introductions to employers or, if registration in a public employment service or in a veterans' counseling service were the next step, to counseling and placement interviewers, they would be exceedingly helpful. But any assumption that they are always, or even usually, available for counseling and placement services is refuted by the personal testimony of interviewers in such services, while any assumption that counseling at the point of demobilization is offered by qualified counselors is denied by the testimony of veterans when, and if, they are ever fortunate enough to come in contact with a properly qualified counselor. Moreover, any assumption on the part of the Army that such documents contain all the information essential for the adjustment assistance of ex-servicemen is

[23] Discussed in some detail by Col. George R. Evans before the Industrial Relations Conference of the American Management Association, Hotel Pennsylvania, New York, Sept. 25–26, 1944.

far too optimistic. The most that can be claimed for form 100 is that when it is available it is sometimes a helpful supplement to the work of an experienced interviewer.

There is so much duplication of functions among governmental agencies, so much competition to offer counseling services, and so many different agencies doing placement work that it is too much to expect that any reception interviewer will have a clear-cut picture of the activities of each agency, or be sure that any given procedure, if recommended to a veteran, will eventuate in satisfactory reabsorption into civilian life. It is his business, of course, to be able to give veterans the most accurate information possible provided other agencies are better prepared to service him than is the employment service. He should know (1) that at the national level the Re-employment Division of the Selective Service System is charged with the responsibility of assisting veterans to secure their old positions, while at the community level the draft boards are supposed to take the initiative; (2) that the Civil Service Commission has jurisdiction over placements in federal civil-service positions; (3) that the Veterans Counseling Services advise disabled veterans referred by the Veterans Administration under Public Law 16 and such nondisabled as are eligible for vocational guidance under Public Law 346—in the former case advice is obligatory, in the latter optional; (4) that the United States Employment Service is responsible for new placements for veterans, for the placement of war workers, and for all other persons who seek to use its facilities—including those referred by Rehabilitation Services.

It may also be useful to remember that the Veterans Administration, the United States Employment Service, and the Office of Vocational Rehabilitation, with the War Manpower Commission acting as the coordinating agency, are assisting the Army and Navy to conduct a pre-discharge program for disabled men during their period of hospitalization. It includes education and counseling and registration for employment, and is intended to facilitate the employment of discharged persons. The registration cards are made out by an interviewer from the United States Employment Service and are accompanied by any medical information which may have a bearing on employment. The cards of men who wish to return to their homes are forwarded by the United States Employment Service to appropriate local offices. At demobilization each veteran is classified as to his immediate desires and plans. If he wishes a position and one is available, or if he owns his own business, he goes to work. If he has no position or business, and so desires, he may consult with the counseling service regarding a formal education program, vocational training, or immediate employment. If his preference is employment, the placement service takes over and a registration interview follows.

The Registration. Veterans register in local offices on special cards provided by the veterans' employment representative whose responsibilities include (1) supervising the registration and placement of ex-servicemen and women, (2) keeping informed on openings in private concerns and on public works, (3) interesting employers in the employment of veterans, and (4) co-operating with veterans' organizations in developing opportunities and improving working conditions.

Some, or all, of the following should be available to services which register veterans: preinduction school record, draft-board data, the Army classification card,[24] a case history or duplicate of the service record accompanied by demobilization interviewer's comments and a copy of the soldier's qualification card showing his last employment and the results of tests given at demobilization. The registration interviewer, whose function in a small office may combine interviewing for other than purely registration purposes, should, if even a small part of the documents enumerated are at his command,[25] have considerable informational data to start with and should, therefore, be obliged to conduct fewer of what have previously been mentioned as "cold" interviews.

Any person who is qualified to conduct interviews based on data derived from such sources will know enough to challenge them at every step for accuracy and reliability. He will know that some items are likely to be more accurate than others and that all personal comments and opinions on service records, or made by military counselors at points of demobilization, and all ratings for service promotions require the same microscopic investigation as do corresponding civilian data.[26] He will realize that the most effectively publicized in-service program is just as apt to be a paper program with its counselors going through the motions of counseling without accomplishing any constructive results as are the numerous programs with which he is familiar in civilian society. He will use his interview opportunity to observe, question, challenge, and compare; and then, after analyzing and interpreting it all, if he feels the need of additional data which will throw light on the immediate problem to be

[24] Harold Siegel, "Army Classification in Post-War Vocational Guidance," *Occupations*, XXII (1944), 248–250, gives a brief, clear-cut statement of the purpose of the classification test, its limitations for guidance in civilian occupations, and the importance of careful interpretation of its results. The article is a good one for counselors.

[25] Reports indicate that to date interviewers have not received many of these data. Have businessmen? Have educational institutions? Have rehabilitation services?

[26] See Reed, *Guidance and Personnel Services,* pp. 151–153.

solved, he will take steps to secure them. He will know that the Army tests were sometimes given under unfavorable conditions and were improperly administered, and, unless other data plus interview findings corroborate their results, he may consider it advisable to see that a new series of tests are administered by qualified psychologists.

The interviewer may have some difficulty in establishing the rapport which is so important in productive interviewing. Obstacles will vary. He must be able to forecast the main obstacles and understand how to overcome them. His client may have left the service with an unfair-discrimination chip, real or imaginary, on his shoulder. He may resent being asked to fill out another form, for he has already been asked at every way station from induction to discharge to fill out many and cumbersome ones.[27] He is tired of it, and by the time he reaches the local placement office he may be expected to be pretty outspoken both as to the number and the content of these forms. Again, he may be so thoroughly disgusted with the spurious counseling which he has been forced to listen to that it may be difficult to convince him that any counseling is worth while. If he is interested in securing the benefits of Public Law 16, he will visit the Veterans Counseling Service,[28] fill out the forms, and take the prescribed tests, only because it is an essential step in securing the desired benefits.

When all the available data on each person have been collected and transmuted into a case study, the record will provide the basis for a counseling interview. When a sufficient number of cases are accumulated, their various items may be drawn off and used to elaborate a broad pre-organization and anticipatory characterization of future veterans and to give a more complete picture of types of veterans with whom counseling and placement services may be expected to deal.

The veterans' registration data available at present and of most value for the purposes mentioned permit rough classification on several bases:

(1) Classification on an educational basis will reveal that the status of veterans ranges all the way from those who lack the fundamentals of an

27 The detailed forms which federal agencies usually require are potent sources of irritation to both applicants and personnel functionaries. Revisions and eliminations of useless items are making some progress. Ad interim counselors and placement workers who understand the type of inhibitions and resentments which these forms create are using their ingenuity to comply with the requirements of the Veterans Administration without making their counseling procedures more routine, mechanical, and clerical in character than is absolutely necessary.

28 This is layman terminology. Washington has recently stated the procedure as follows: The veteran goes to the Vocational Advisor in the Veterans Administration Guidance Center, where certain functions, such as checking his credentials, are performed. He is then turned over to a Vocational Appraiser who "appraises" his desires in the light of his personal qualities.

education to those whose education is far superior to that of those under whom they have served. Some of those who fall in the lowest classification on the basis of performance may possess diplomas, or other credentials, which rate them liberally educated. Others, who possess no such credentials, may have demonstrated their possession of a liberal education. At every rung of the educational ladder there will be found credentials which represent little or no education, and educated persons who have no academic credentials. Test results may have revealed that the mental capacities of those who, according to documentary evidence, have attained the same educational status vary greatly, extending from below to above average. Interviewers will doubtless have discovered that among persons of the same educational status some are narrow-minded, unreasonable, and illogical, while others possess opposite qualities and are mentally alert.

Records will reveal that, in many instances, war has acted as an incentive to education. The Armed Forces Institute, the Army Specialized Training Program, the Officer Candidate Schools, and the exploratory courses which modern combat offers noncommissioned officers to try out their abilities have all had inspirational value; have resulted in the revelation of intellectual interests and abilities and of previously unsuspected qualities of leadership.

(2) Classification on an occupational basis will reveal that some should be classified as untrained, inefficient, misplaced, maladjusted, underemployed, or frequently unemployed in their previous relations to occupational life, while others will fall into just the opposite categories. The records of some will show that they have never held a steady job, that long and frequent periods of unemployment have characterized their prewar work history. A certain number of these will qualify as true Micawberites, always waiting for something to turn up. The records of others will show that they have never worked except under compulsion, that they have become professional idlers, and are now awaiting endowment as such. Some will be found to have fallen into a rut on their prewar job and to be returning to civilian life with seniority rights but with nothing to indicate seniority abilities. The records of others will indicate that, from the day of their induction, they have taken advantage of every opportunity for self-improvement. Interviews will reveal that they have acquired a new consciousness of themselves and their potentialities, that they have learned new trades and want to use them, that they have a new feeling of social importance due to their service promotions and think that correspondingly important executive positions in civilian occupations should be

open to them. Negroes and whites will both fall into this category, and both will find occupational adjustment difficult.

After all the more or less troublesome occupational classifications have been made, the records, supplemented by the results of registration interviews, will reveal a very large group of men who have never lost their civilian occupational bearings no matter how the service may have affected their temporary status. Whether such veterans return to their old jobs or to new ones, they have been, and will again be, satisfied and satisfactory workers and important contributors to the development of the nation's economy. This is both fortunate and encouraging.

(3) Classification on the basis of physical and mental data will reveal some registrants with physical and psychological deficiencies and the extent to which and under what conditions they must be regarded as occupational assets or as liabilities. There is a good deal of comparative data available on physical disabilities and their relation to occupational placement and success. The occupational possibilities of psychoneurotic cases and of those suffering from minor emotional and personality handicaps are attracting much attention, but, as yet, there is little specific information as to their various types of disability in relation to job placement.

A new practice on the part of the Washington authorities with reference to furnishing the United States Employment Service with data on physically and mentally rehabilitated persons has been instituted. It is in perfect harmony with our newer philosophy relative to the occupational efficiency of handicapped persons, but its influence on the placement of rehabilitated persons whose handicaps are not observable remains to be seen. Whatever such influence may be, it is obvious that it denies the referral functionary access to *all* the data which have a bearing on the making of a satisfactory placement, and it assumes that the mechanical matching of a "physical demand analysis," which shows what the job requires, with a "physical capacities analysis," which shows what a man *can* (not *will*) do, is a "simple matter" and is the crux of the placement function. When the data are sent to the employment office, there is no mention of the physical impairment which the applicant has suffered. "This fact was for hospital records only." [29]

29 This procedure is somewhat similar to the one mentioned in Chapter VIII where it was assumed that job referrals can be made quite mechanically after the primary and secondary occupational classifications are on file. It overlooked the function and values of the referral interview. The military procedure fails to recognize that the attitude of a man and the effect of his physical disabilities and rehabilitation on his personality are often more important than his physical capacities, and that the supplementary and interpretative values of the interview are recognized as a major placement technique.

The removal of NP (neuropsychiatric) from the records of "psychological" disability cases and the substitution of "not suitable for military service" has the same objective and is based on the same erroneous assumption: to conceal nonobservable disabilities and nonobservable evidences of rehabilitation from placement officials and employers lest knowledge of the facts militate against referrals and employment.

Doubtless in some cases there is justification for this fear. There are many undereducated, underexperienced placement officials in the United States Employment Service and many employers who, because of liability under the provisions of the workmen's compensation laws or for other reasons, would not, were they aware of it, employ rehabilitated cases. On the other hand, both veterans' counselors and placement officials, if qualified to hold such positions, recognize that "psychoneurosis" has a wide applicability and are making strenuous efforts to distinguish employables so classified from the unemployables; those who are in need of medical service from those for whom work is the only therapy needed. This is a not so "simple matter." Psychologists tell us that it cannot be accomplished by tests alone, although tests may reveal helpful clues. A quotation from Allport has been sent this writer by one of the "understanding" veteran counselors as an indication of his fear that psychologists will fail as counselors unless with their technical training they have "acquired the insight and experience which leads to understanding."

The psychologist delights in the use of recording instruments—galvanometers, kymographs, and scales of all kinds. Yet strange to say he discredits the most delicate of all recording instruments—himself. The human mind is the only agency ever devised for registering at once innumerable variables and for revealing the *relations between them.* It is the one and only instrument capable of comprehension. Failing to employ intuition the psychologist unduly limits his resources. Without it he starts with analysis and ends with conceptualization; on the way he sacrifices his chance to understand living people.[30]

On the employment phase of the problem, recent literature is replete with evidence that whenever possible employing concerns are more than willing to employ not only rehabilitated cases but also persons with permanent disabilities, provided they are not handicaps for the job under consideration. They expect the referring party to see that they are not deceived on this point.

This same problem of concealing physical, mental, and moral experiences from placement officials and employers was brought up years ago,

[30] Gordon W. Allport, *Personality, A Psychological Interpretation* (New York: Henry Holt and Co., 1937), p. 547.

and has been mentioned in this book, with reference to persons who had served time in penal institutions. Those of us who placed such persons soon found that the greatest protection a person so handicapped could have was the knowledge that his employer was supporting him in his efforts to re-establish himself in society and had confidence in his ability to do so.

This is such an important matter, and it requires such intelligent understanding of both the newer philosophy with reference to the employment of handicapped and rehabilitated cases, and of the responsibilities which this same philosophy, in practice, places on placement workers and employers, that a very simple illustration taken from the pioneering and model job study conducted at Oakland, California,[31] may help to clarify thinking:

N. A. B. was a carpenter. Amputation of his left foot prohibited his return to his former job. His "physical capacity analysis" indicated that he could not climb, jump, or run and that he should not work in wet quarters. He might be referred to any carpenter job if the "physical demand analysis" did not include climbing, jumping, or running, or that the work be performed in wet quarters. His medical record, as sent to the employment service, made no mention of the amputation.

Suppose there were to be an emergency in the plant which, for his own safety or for the safety of others, required that he run, climb, or jump—activities which were absolutely prohibited by a handicap which was unknown to others than himself and which could not be ignored even for a short period during an emergency! Let the reader decide!

If, however, experienced interviewers fail to receive all the available physical and mental data which would aid them in making satisfactory placements, most of them have long since acquired observational abilities which supplement their interview techniques to such an extent that much helpful information is secured through their own ingenuity. Emotionally unstable persons are apt to be frequent callers at employment offices and are easily recognized as such. That there was a considerable number of incipient cases in civilian life before the war and that placement workers were well acquainted with some of the "psychologically deficient" persons who were later classified as 4F's are evidenced by the records of employment services compared with the reasons for rejection at induction centers. As workers, such individuals tend to drift from job to job. Sometimes they are capable workers but are unsatisfactory employees because of

[31] Under the auspices of the War Manpower Commission co-operating with the permanent Foundations Hospitals at Oakland and the Kaiser Shipyard no. 3 at Richmond, the study mentioned was made and reported on in a 627-page publication.

their constant complaints, quarrelsomeness, irritability, tendency to shirk, and their proneness to harbor phobias of various types.

The best-prepared placement interviewers are separating, as they long have, the currently called "pseudoscientific flap-doodle" on emotional difficulties from the grain of truth which they need to know; they are keeping in touch with the findings of both lay and service psychiatrists and are constantly checking over their own knowledges, experiences, and techniques as they bear on the occupational adjustment of service-connected disabilities; and they are vitally interested in the self-rehabilitation cases which come to their attention. For example, one recently reported in the press:

C. A. S. was honorably discharged after long service in the Pacific. He returned to his home town but was restless, irritable, and difficult to get along with. He made his own "mental capacities analysis" and decided that a comfortable bed, clean sheets, and a pillow created conditions which handicapped his recovery. He longed for the foxhole bed to which he had become accustomed. Therefore, he dug one in the back yard and gradually reduced the number of nights per week of occupancy until he reacquired the ability to enjoy his normal sleeping quarters every night.

Practical suggestions on the handling of mentally disabled veterans are beginning to flow back into civilian circles, both from Army and Navy sources and from the Veterans Counseling Services. The Army and Navy recommend that, when mental discharges apply either for reinstatement in their former positions or for referrals to new ones, interviewers seek information from their prewar records on their performances and attitudes under normal conditions, rather than depend entirely on records based on combat conditions which are frequently such that any man might break under the strain. The best-trained counselors in the Veterans Counseling Service are pursuing this course and are finding that rehabilitation prospects are brighter and occupational adjustments more easily made when the disability is combat-connected rather than an intensification of a carryover from civilian life. Counselors are also confirming, what has long been known with reference to civilians, that it is more difficult for talented, brilliant, highly educated persons to face hard situations and make adjustments to them than it is for less able individuals on a lower educational level.

Of course, the rehabilitation of disabled men is not an employment service responsibility, but co-operation in rendering the best possible service to veterans is; and all agree that whenever employment is a therapeutic measure or an incentive to recovery the mentally disabled should be employed, provided this is possible without endangering themselves or others. Life pensions, which seem to be the alternative, too often close the door of hope and at best are a poor substitute for gainful employment.

(4) Classification on the basis of personality traits will reveal individuals whose characteristics do not permit their classification as "psychological disabilities," although at times the dividing line is not very clearly drawn. Since this topic has been discussed at length in Chapter VI, it will be sufficient, at this point, to note a few characteristics which have been commented on by veterans' counselors who have observed them during interviews. Some ex-servicemen reveal newly acquired courage, independence, self-reliance, and ambition. Perfectly conscious of the fact that their war record has increased their stature in the eyes of the community, they feel confidence in their own ability to become "master of their fate" and ask only that some way be found to stop the "veterans' runaround," [32] to cut the red tape involved in useless and cumbersome forms, and to give them the accurate information upon which they may make their own decisions and re-establish themselves in civilian life. Asking for the same sort of thing are veterans who were accustomed to taking the inconveniences of life in their stride before they entered the service, who have met the vicissitudes of war in the same fashion, and who are prepared to face the future in the same frame of mind. Both types have definite personality assets to offer employers.

Another type of personality may lack self-confidence, have no future plans, be lost without the military regimentation to which he has been accustomed, and come to the interview expecting, and wanting, "directive" or "prescriptive" counseling, or asking placement in a job rather than referral *to an opening* which requires some effort on his part if he is to be employed.

Some are asking for special privileges such as the waiving of college entrance requirements, or jobs for which they have no qualifications, and salaries which are nonexistent. Some brag of their service record and feel that it entitles them to permanent work of their own choosing; that had they remained at home they would be rich and should be well compensated for their loss. Such individuals frequently feel resentment against civilians and become very aggressive in their demands, or reveal the reformer attitude—they propose to clean up the country or their community. And always there will be the habitually disgruntled personality expressed in "crabbing," "griping," "grousing," or "grouching" according to the circle in which it takes place. The "world owes me a living attitude" is a definite

[32] Charles G. Bolté, "The Veterans' Runaround," *Harper's*, CXC (1945), 385–392.

personality liability. Insofar as undesirable personality qualities are service-incurred, and temporary, a little understanding and patience on the part of interviewers and employers is all that is necessary. But careful follow-up is necessary lest they be intensified and eventually contribute to the type of mental disability which disqualifies for employment.

(5) Classification on the basis of employability [33] will reveal that a veterans' service, no less than a general service, will register persons who exhibit all degrees of employability. *Unemployables* will fall into the lowest category. There will always be some, but the number and the point at which an applicant should be so classified are not static. They vary with the condition of the labor market. It is not necessary to labor this point since it is well known that many who were rated unemployable during the 1930's were quickly reclassified as employables when the war broke out. General placement services will be prepared for a considerable dropback among these war-made employables. Veterans' services may expect to find some in this group who enjoyed military life and rendered entirely satisfactory military service, but whose prewar occupational life was a series of misfits, failures, and the accumulation of habits and attitudes which forecast unemployability. Will release from regimentation and the excitement of war result in return to their former status, or will some type of rehabilitation salvage them before it is too late?

Marginal Employables rank low on any employability scale. Psychologists and psychiatrists have long been aware of their presence in civilian life, and placement officials have found them unable to hold steady jobs, "quits" or discharges being due to a variety of reasons. The inclusion of a considerable number of 4F's in this group has aroused the interest of the public and has led, here and there, to special rehabilitation efforts on their behalf.[34] Men released from the service because of inability to withstand the shock of combat participation have added to the number. Some, under expert treatment, will be able to take their places in normal occupational life; others will be productive under favorable conditions; while another group will never be able to hold steady jobs. The third category is not placeable by any regularly constituted government service. The first group is, and the second group may be.

The Difficult-to-Place will doubtless include some marginal workers.

[33] An interesting "Index of Employability" appeared in *Occupations*, XXII (1944), 477–483. The scale, which comprised 16 items, was developed at Syracuse University by Bernard S. Newer and was reported on by Mary Z. Casety.

[34] The Vocational Adjustment Bureau, 1790 Broadway, New York, after many years of successful effort with girls, has assumed responsibility for the rehabilitation of servicemen and men of draft age who are mentally or emotionally disturbed.

"Difficulties" are due to many causes, and the entire group which might legitimately be classified in this category is very large. Some difficulties are congenital; others have been acquired by the individual, or have been imposed upon him by our educational system, by military, social-economic, or other conditions. Two of the largest groups of both veterans and civilians which should be so classified are those who are mentally or physically handicapped, and those who are handicapped by age.[35] The physically and mentally handicapped group has already received its share of attention. Comparatively little attention has been given to those whose only difficulty is that they are steadily growing older, thereby intensifying an incurable handicap. Many who fall into this category are perfectly normal persons. Their only handicap is that they are "too old," and sometimes "too good," for the jobs which are available.

Among the ex-servicemen whom one may expect to find in this group are veterans of World War I who rejoined the service early in the war and those who were in the upper draft age when they were inducted. All levels of education and all occupational levels, from the uneducated laborer and the semiskilled worker to well-equipped professional men and able executives, will be represented. So will all ranks in the Armed Forces. The predicament of the lower level group may seem to be more serious than that of those on the upper level. In practice the reverse is often true. Both groups should be of concern to their communities. Appreciation of the fears which haunt both groups, and the problems which harass placement services which attempt to find openings for both, may be increased by recalling previous happenings to other similarly handicapped persons.

On August 31, 1938, there were 136 companies (25,973 men) of veterans of World War I enrolled in the Civilian Conservation Corps.[36] These were, for the most part, representative of the types of men who, in spite of all our veterans' services, had failed, during the interval between their discharge and the depression, to make permanent occupational adjustments. The personal qualities which made them hard-to-place were discussed time and again during the years of job scarcity. Forewarned should be forearmed, and those who share in the responsibility of demobilizing and remobilizing servicemen should make every effort to place these mature veterans at the earliest opportunity.

On the higher level the reabsorption of discharged officers, some of whose salaries have ranged from $3,000 to $7,000, will pose a somewhat

35 Those handicapped by youth and inexperience might be included, but since such handicaps are curable the writer has preferred to consider them in Chapter XI.
36 See the U.S. Office of Education's comments in *School Life*, XXIV (1939), 106.

different, but no less serious, problem. The depression years witnessed many examples of previously high-salaried professional men and experienced executives who, were they unfortunate enough to become unemployed at from 40 to 50 years of age, were unable to find any suitable employment. Unless strenuous efforts to prevent it are made, it looks as though, as more and more officers are released, the history of World War II demobilization might repeat the history of the 1930's depression. Some of these officers will have given up a lucrative business to enter the service. They will have had attractive salaries in the service, and they will come back to find keen competition staring them in the face, plenty of people interested in veterans, but no suitable work available, and no prospect of salaries of more than $3,000 to $4,000 even for unsuitable and frequently distasteful work.

Others who entered the service as privates will have won promotions which carry salaries of $2,500 to $3,500. This will tend to disqualify them for any type of job in the small towns in which they formerly held small jobs. The man who left home a retail clerk and returns a major, and the one who left as a janitor and returns as a lieutenant, are more than likely to prove discontented and inefficient workers in almost any position which their community can offer. Nor will they be any more contented or any more efficient if they have heard about the fabulous salaries which have been received in civilian life while they were in the service, or if they have taken at face value all the lavish promises which have been expressed in legislation. Disillusionment, dissatisfaction, added years, and increasing inefficiency may be fatal to such veterans.

Everyone seeks to place the blame. Naturally those who are unfamiliar with business organization and with business problems ask: Why shouldn't employing concerns welcome the chance to add veterans of recognized executive ability to their personnel? Why don't veterans' bureaus and placement services open up such opportunities? There are many reasons. Some are operative in small businesses, others in large concerns. The small businessman is often afraid to employ an experienced, high-salaried man, even were he able to offer the requisite salary. He has worked hard to establish his business and probably withdrawn from it, as his own salary, far less than the minimum which he would be obliged to pay such an assistant. It is not usually considered wise for an employer who earns $5,000 to employ a person who is accustomed to earning $10,000. Moreover, there are many cases on record, with which the entrepreneur is familiar although the public may not be, where an able employee has taken over the business of his employer just as soon as he has learned the "ropes" and established the necessary contacts. All things considered, the wise entrepreneur prefers to employ a young potentiality rather than an "arrival." The experienced job solicitor knows all about this and admits its validity, even though he may desperately need job opportunities.

The larger employing concerns have equally good reasons for wariness in adding executives, who have already attained distinction, to their personnel. Under prevailing systems of organization there are comparatively few openings for older men, whose status would outrank and whose salary would exceed, that of junior executives who are coming up through the ranks. They are apt to be regarded as interlopers, and discontent and jealousies follow unless the reason is apparent and the justice recognized. In other words, it upsets the business "apple cart." Therefore the best-organized business programs provide for a steady flow of junior executives from the bottom up, and their selective policy is in harmony with this objective. If for any reason the stream becomes stagnant, as was often the case during the depression, the organization eventually finds itself with an unfilled gap in personnel between the rank and file and its older and upper executives. Experienced job solicitors know all about this, too, and they also know that many concerns are holding opportunities open for their own junior executives who will be entitled to re-employment on two counts—as former satisfactory employees and as ex-servicemen.

Normal Employables who rate high on the scale of employability, who are easy to place and who usually make satisfied and satisfactory employees, will form a group as large, if not larger, than the hard-to-place. However, the number of veterans in this group who will seek placement assistance through veterans' services will probably not be a high percentage of the total number of veterans who belong in the group. Their situation will be very different from that of those who are difficult to place. Rarely does the cream of any group, which has attained and maintained a high degree of employability without incurring the handicap of age, seek positions through an employment service. When they do there is some special reason, and they use special services. All types of placement services are cognizant of this fact. They do not expect to register either the cream of applicants or the cream of employers' orders. They never have done so. Such applicants and such openings seem to have an affinity for one another. Middlemen are superfluous. As a rule, "arrivals" among professional and technical men, junior executives who have attracted favorable attention, and some young but potentially promising collegemen, will be fortunate enough to be sought by *the* job rather than to be seeking *a* job. Veterans will have their share of such men and such opportunities.

In addition to these superemployables there will be other employable veterans who will not seek the assistance of veterans' placement services: those who own or expect to establish their own businesses, those who return to their prewar positions or to positions which have been promised them upon their discharge,[37] those who elect further education, and those who prefer to use other than public employment services. All told, many employable veterans will return to our civilian economy without benefit of veterans' placement services. This most desirable employer-employee situation with reference to veterans constitutes, as it always has with reference to public services for civilians, a handicap to the pooling and distributing of all the available veteran supply and demand, and it renders referrals less effective than they otherwise might be.

The Referral. Although the fundamental principles and practices involved in referrals to job openings have been pretty thoroughly standardized, legislative enactments have rendered some of these principles and practices difficult with reference to veterans. Under the Selective Service Act Congress assured veterans that they were to be accorded "maximum job opportunity in the field of gainful employment." This phrase has caused much discussion. General Hershey has interpreted it in favor of veterans who compete with nonveterans for new jobs, and his interpretation is gaining support. The Veterans Placement Service Board maintains that the United States Employment Service is to give preference in referrals to veterans of *this* war, and the War Manpower Commission has advised its field offices to follow this policy.[38]

While this interpretation does not assume either that preference in referrals will be given to less competent veterans if more competent nonveterans are available, or that employers will hire the veteran if they think that they can do better, it does create a rather difficult situation. Every placement worker is anxious to see veterans receive priorities in employment. Therefore experienced placement workers who have built up employing clienteles on the basis of ability to select satisfactory referrals will be tempted to set aside the accepted rules which oblige them to refer the person best fitted for the job and to offer in his stead the veteran best qualified for the job. Such a practice antagonizes civilian applicants, who

[37] *Steel Facts* for August, 1944, reported that about 10,000 former workers in the steel industries had been discharged and had returned to the industry. Less than 2 per cent had come back with disabilities that required special handling. The industry had its own rehabilitation plans, educational program, and special interview procedures.

[38] A clear statement of this policy is given in the *United States News*, XIX (Aug. 24, 1945), 62.

regard it as an unfair discrimination,[39] tends to lose the support of employing concerns, which do not receive satisfactory referrals, and, most unfortunate of all, tends to put placement practices on a patriotic rather than on an efficiency basis and may increase turnover after one year of employment for substandard workers, deny superstandard workers the consideration to which they are entitled, and finally obliterate any special interest in the employment of veterans.

Discrimination in referrals is not a new employment topic, although it is currently a very live legislative topic. If one is sufficiently interested in the current discussion, he will be rewarded if he will turn back the pages of history and note the long list of factors which, at one period or another and for one reason or another, have controlled referral practices, and observe how, in theory, one after another has been eliminated as unworthy until "potential performance and satisfaction on the job" has stood alone.[40]

Between 1914 and 1920 discrimination in referral came to be regarded as a prime qualification of placement workers, with the extent to which they possessed this discriminative ability a major factor in determining the degree of their success. All the information on occupations and on individuals, all the job specifications, all the dictionaries of occupations, lists of job families, studies of positions open to the physically and mentally handicapped, all the researches in aptitudes and attitudes, and all the experiments to improve interview techniques came to a focus on the single objective—discriminative referrals. But discriminative ability was not, and is not today, exercised only under conditions in which degrees of fitness or of unfitness of applicants are concerned and are determinable. Placement officers faced, and face today, more difficult tasks when they were, or are, forced to choose between several applicants all equally well prepared. Then priorities in referral, or preference in placement as they were sometimes called, were likely to be challenged as "unfair" by applicants who considered themselves discriminated against. Placement workers began to ask, and are still asking: In the very nature of the case, is it possible to do effective placement work without discrimination *against* traveling hand in hand with discrimination *for?*

[39] Veterans are not entirely in sympathy with giving veterans absolute preference in the civil service. See the action of the Catholic War Veterans, Inc., at its eighth annual welfare conference in New York in April, 1945, on the proposed New York State constitutional amendment for this purpose. The amendment was characterized as "drastic" and "unfair" and "designed to wreck civil service" (*New York Times,* April 22, 1945).

[40] See Chapter II.

For each applicant the referral interviewer will have at hand a "profile," which will keep before him the various categories within the different classifications into which each applicant falls. It will indicate which qualities he shares with others in the same group, and which are "individual differences." And it will throw light on the extent to which he possesses any specific quality. Although such a profile is a major tool in conducting a referral interview and in reaching a conclusion as to the suitability of the applicant for referral, it must be regarded as a changing rather than a static picture and must always be subject to revisions.

A second major referral tool is the job specification. But referral interviewers, as well as job solicitors, should be alive to the fact that, during reconversion, manufacturing industries will offer fewer opportunities, while distributive and personal-service occupations will offer more. This knowledge is of immediate importance, since both veterans and employment services are either unaware of it or are ignoring it. Therefore, the one seeks an opening in a declining line which he assumes does, and always will, pay the highest wages and have much overtime work. The other acts on the same assumption. This is quite logical since public services have had a sort of monopoly of placements in war industries and have been charged with the responsibility of recruiting a sufficient supply of labor for such industries. If some "antibias" legislation is put on federal and state statute books, both the profile of the individual and the job specification will be shorn of certain items which have heretofore been very helpful to referral interviewers in bringing the right job and the right individual together.

This legal depletion of information constitutes one hurdle which referral interviewers must face. Two other legal hurdles have been set up: the congressional enactment, possibly an unenforceable one, which has been interpreted to give veterans of World War II preference in referrals but does not, and cannot, force the government's hiring pattern on employers; and the provision which forbids discharge of re-employed veterans, without cause, for one year after employment. In addition to these legal hurdles, the labor unions and the veterans themselves, or their communities, friends, and relatives, have set up a few, and will doubtless set up more. Among them are:

(1) The determination of labor unions to protect the employment rights of their members against the inroads of veterans. Until the courts settle the disagreements between the unions and the Selective Service Administration, placement officials and employers will be more or less bewildered as to what referrals, and what employments, are within the law.

(2) The demands of veterans for referrals to jobs for which they do not qualify, accompanied by charges of discrimination when referrals are not given.

(3) The demands of veterans for high wages and for salaries which do not exist.

(4) The inability of placement services to refer veterans to the type of jobs for which they do qualify and their consequent resentment against referral officers, employers, and civilians who are fortunate enough to hold such jobs.

(5) The demand of war-made executives for executive positions in civilian occupations with no realization of the fact that executive duties in civilian life differ markedly in character and are performed under entirely different conditions from executive duties in the service.

(6) The interruption of the normal, if sometimes slow, progress in the broadening of the occupational horizon of the Negro and in his absorption into full participation in our economic life has been intensified by well-meaning but ill-advised propaganda to such an extent that the placement of Negro workers may suffer a setback. General Hines has recognized this and regrets it.

(7) The competition of women war workers.

(8) The problem of referring disabled veterans to the type of positions which promise job security.

Over against these difficulties, for which veterans' interviewers must be prepared, are some very encouraging facts, especially with reference to the referral of handicapped persons. The occupational horizon of the physically handicapped, just as that of the Negro, has gradually broadened, while increased occupational opportunities for various types of handicapped persons and a change in attitude toward their employability has been due to researches and experiment under various auspices, and to the reports of employing concerns on their experiences in two wars.

During the last thirty-five years a personal defect or a personal handicap has been redefined in such fashion that, even though it may legitimately be considered a serious handicap from a general or a social point of view, it is no longer regarded as an occupational liability for any job which the individual can perform in a thoroughly normal and satisfactory manner. This means that any job may be a suitable job for a so-called handicapped person provided the individual is selected for his suitability for the work and his capacity to perform. If these qualifications are regarded as referral essentials, the applicant ceases to be classified as a handicapped person *on that job*.

Moreover, if the testimony of employers may be relied upon, not only is he not occupationally handicapped, but frequently the very qualities which formerly placed him in this category have come to be recognized as valuable vocational assets. Employers now generally concede that persons with physical handicaps make satisfactory and often valuable additions to the work force; that they do not need to be payroll liabilities; that causes for discharge are rare, labor turnover low, and attendance and accident records good; that they are conscientious workers and their productivity normal; that they are careful, orderly, and alert; and that they do not ask, or expect, favors. The deaf have been in such demand that war-industry orders could not be met, and the blind are proving efficient in an increasing number of occupations. Obviously handicapped persons have had better occupational chances during this war than during the last war, and better postwar opportunities than after the last war are anticipated by those who are charged with the placement of disabled veterans.

Other encouragements for referral officials are found in the changes in workmen's compensation laws which lighten the employer's liability for second injuries, in technological changes which improve opportunities for handicapped workers, and finally, but of great importance, in the fact that handicapped persons themselves are coming to realize that adversity may be a challenge, and a defect may be transmuted into an asset.

The discriminative judgment of the interviewer comes into play during the referral interview, and its quality is expressed in the decision to refer, or not to refer, to any specific position. If the primary and secondary occupational classifications have been made *with* the applicant rather than *about* him, and if the registration interviewer has been qualified to help him interpret and evaluate his assets and liabilities in terms of choice of a specific position, it may be comparatively easy for him to decide that he should, or should not, apply for the position under consideration. But, whether or not the applicant desires to apply, the final decision as to referral is a referral interviewer's responsibility.

No one who has given even cursory thought to the matter can fail to realize the responsibility to veteran, employer, and public which is assumed by referral officers in veterans' placement services. Everything seems to depend on their discriminative judgment. The future occupational success of veterans may be made or marred by the choice of positions to which they are given their first referrals. The willingness of employing firms to go along with a veterans' service after the enthusiasm of the home-coming is over will largely depend upon the extent to which the service refers veterans who prove their desirability as permanent members of the employing firm. Satisfactory placements lessen the danger of veterans becoming future unemployables, and they help the public to make good on some of its optimistic promises to veterans.

The guiding principles for the referral of veterans are much the same as for civilian referrals. Assuming—a utopian condition—that the interviewer's insight and technique have been developed to the point where he is able to discover in every veteran the latent capacities which can most effectively be put to work, and that he is able to distinguish the remediable and temporary attitudes and complexes, which might make his job tenure short, from those which are permanent and should receive the attention of experts, he will proceed very carefully lest he overstress deficiencies and throw into the occupational discard a well-qualified, although in some respects a handicapped, worker. On the other hand, he must not allow his patriotism or personal interest to refer a veteran when he knows that, if employed, he will be a handicap to the employer. If he carelessly refers those who are temporarily suffering from the noise of combat area to occupations which aggravate their nervousness and increase their irritability, he will cause labor turnover, delay the return of the victims of his bad judgment to normal mental stability, and lessen their chances for a second occupational opportunity:

J. B. C. was 26 years of age. He was discharged because of "combat fatigue" and returned to his home town. The placement office found him a position in a manufacturing industry where he became a machine operator. The work was monotonous and the machine noisy. The veteran was dexterous and very quick in his movements, but very nervous and high-strung. He had been at work about 10 days when his former teacher, passing through the public library at eleven o'clock one morning, discovered him in a quiet nook reading a book. "Why J.! why are you not at work?" she asked. "Because about ten o'clock this morning I felt as though if I had to see that machine make another motion or hear it say another 'word,' I should scream. I just got up and walked out and came over here."

Then there are the men who have suffered serious facial disfigurements or deformities of other types. Servicemen know what a facial disfigurement means to both their social and occupational future and are said to dread them more than almost any other physical handicap. Positions for them can be found, but no experienced placement worker would say that they are many or are easy to find.

How best to deal with applicants for whom referral is questionable, if not impossible, is something which no person can tell another: human insight and humane understanding guide the procedure in each individual case. Nothing is more legitimately labeled "mental cruelty" than are some of the thoughtless comments which callous, tired, and routinized interviewers sometimes make to persons who are suffering from some occupationally disqualifying disfigurement. Granted that there be no immediate prospect of a job and that it may be very difficult to secure one at any time, no interviewer should permit such an applicant to leave his presence with lessened hope and courage. Every interviewer should master the technique of steering a straight course between promising the impossible, thus laying the foundation for future bitter disappointment, and sending an applicant away hopelessly discouraged. Every veteran has a right to feel that he belongs in, and is a part of, his community, that the placement office has dealt fairly and properly with him, that he has lost no fraction of his self-respect by applying for assistance, that his needs are understood and every effort to meet them will be made, and that, pending some possibility of a job, his personal record is being honorably guarded.[41]

Other obligations placed upon referral officers are (1) that they refer veterans only to positions known to be open, or to standing orders, thus avoiding the possibility of one more "veteran runaround"; (2) that they refer only those whom they believe to be qualified for the work; (3) that they avoid pressure selling to either party; (4) that they strive for permanent, not one-year, placements; (5) that they refuse to allow irresponsible veterans, no matter what their war record, to cast a stigma on the office and on all other veterans who seek to use its facilities; (6) that they be exceedingly cautious about the use of radio as a medium for counseling or referring veterans to employers. (Soliciting jobs over the radio is another matter.)

Apropos of the last two points readers may recall the experience of a certain radio show which attempted to place "honorably discharged veterans" through this medium. The publicity which preceded the opening of the show stated that the records of the ex-servicemen, whom it would recommend, would be cleared through the Veterans Administration, the United States Employment Service, and the public-relations offices of the Army and Navy. Unfortunately this promise was not carried out, and before the deception was discovered the "Heroes for Hire" project had degenerated into what *Time*, February 12, 1944, described as a "beautiful example" of our tendency to convert any serious human situation "into some form of sales ballyhoo."

After the interviewer has decided to refer, the next step is up to the vet-

[41] For an excellent presentation of the problems involved, see W. F. Faulkes, "Rehabilitation and Placement of Handicapped Applicants," in *Proceedings of the Twenty-fourth Annual Convention of the International Association of Public Employment Services*, pp. 41–48.

eran. Does he wish to apply? If he does, and if he is employed, adjustment to the employment situation is primarily his job. But he should, if he needs and desires it, have help. Fundamentally it is a community responsibility to see both that he gets the right kind of help and is protected against the many spurious counseling and placement services which always spring up when the human harvest is ripe for exploitation.

This one more chance to be helpful has been discussed in Chapter VIII. It should be the privilege of the referral interviewers. A common need, among civilian as well as among veteran applicants, is a bit of help in overcoming deficiencies in job-getting ability or in moderating too aggressive sales abilities. Referrals will include inferior job getters who do superior work, and superior job getters who do inferior work. In one case the applicant is apt to lose his chance; in the other he may talk himself out of it, or fail to hold it after employment. There is no reason why an applicant should feel apologetic or act as though an employer were doing him a favor. It is not wise for him to boast about his service activities, argue with an employer, or criticize home-front activities. An applicant must always be prepared for refusal of employment and should accept it without resentment or discouragement. Both he and the referral interviewer will try again. If an applicant is employed and accepts employment, he is responsible for bringing the employment agreement to completion, and, for the sake of other veterans as well as for the sake of his own reputation, he should see that a placement is consummated by becoming a bona fide employee, or he should explain his failure to do so with proper apologies for the inconvenience which he may have caused.[42]

What about the prospect for jobs to which veterans may be referred? No one can be sure. Hopes are high. One thing is certain, job openings are going to depend largely on what sort of labor market prevails at the peak of service discharges. Before the fighting stopped veterans were readily absorbed in war industries or in positions left vacant by servicemen and war workers. If postwar American economy is good, the veterans will fare well, but it will be difficult, if not impossible, to guarantee exservicemen economic prosperity in a depressed economy. There is already some complaint from veterans regarding their inability to secure openings. All the evidence indicates that the older ex-servicemen, especially officers who qualify for executive positions with good salaries, are having diffi-

[42] In the summer of 1944, 1,206 former employees of the International Harvester Company applied for re-employment. Of these, 1,179 were re-employed and returned to work. Several were hired but did not appear for work; some were ill; and others, for various reasons, had changed their minds.

culty in finding suitable openings. Probably the difficulty will increase as more such persons are discharged.

With reference to a different level group, veterans' representatives in some public employment offices are reporting that a considerable number of those who are complaining about lack of opportunities have refused to apply for the openings which are available.[43] There are various reasons: some prefer to accept unemployment benefits while they shop around; some have exaggerated ideas regarding current wage scales; some feel that the trades which they have learned in the service or the technical skills which they have acquired warrant better salaries than have been offered; and others are unwilling to leave the city or town which has been their home. This situation is a repetition of that which prevailed after World War I. A period of disillusionment and readjustment seemed to be a necessity for some veterans before they could grasp the economic situation on the home front and settle down. It must be expected now, no matter how hard a community may try to anticipate and prevent it.

Should veterans' services provide employment supervision? The extent to which real employment supervision for all veterans is a function of the Veterans Placement Service is open to question. But there should be no question as to its follow-up responsibilities. The authoritative interpretations and directives which advise that veterans seeking new jobs shall have referral preference over civilians and over veterans of World War I obligate the Service to keep in touch with a considerable number of its placements for at least one year. Bona fide employment supervision, however, except in the case of inexperienced workers, which will be discussed in the following chapter, is usually more satisfactory, has a higher promotional value, and is more harmoniously carried out if it is kept entirely in the hands of the employing concern. Many large firms have set up special counseling services for their own veteran employees; labor unions have some supervisory functions; and veterans' organizations are interested in assisting ex-servicemen to make their adjustments in several areas of life.

Finally, how may a veterans' placement service evaluate its success? A very elaborate presentation of methods of appraisal, evaluation, and measurement in connection with programs for personnel services was included in a former publication [44] and the subject has been given some attention in Chapters III, IV, and V of this book. Duplication must be avoided;

---

[43] The *New York Times*, May 15, 1945, contains a good presentation of the problem of veteran placement from the practical point of view of the employment service.
[44] Reed, *Guidance and Personnel Services*, pp. 435–450.

hence only a few criteria, which are applicable specifically to veterans' services, are added. To what extent has the Service held the respect and confidence of veterans? To what extent has it held the confidence of, and increased its orders from, employers? To what extent has it been able to keep the confidence of, and give assistance to, veterans of World War I? To what extent has it been able to avoid antagonizing civilian applicants? To what extent has it realized that every procedure in the placement process should have educational implications and an educational objective? To what extent has it been able to convince its employing clientele that it has referred, and will refer, veterans who are worthy without serving as a "crime cloak" for the unworthy? [45] To what extent have its placements been permanent?

[45] During the current year there have been several unfortunate incidents which have caused the public to question the extent to which the United States Employment Service, acting under Social Security Regulation No. 1, of November 21, 1940, was protecting criminals against detection by the Federal Bureau of Investigation and by local police departments. The War Manpower Commission has explained that under the regulation the Employment Service is not allowed to give to crime-detecting authorities the names and addresses of dishonest employees referred through its service. This is a very serious matter which requires immediate modification lest the employing public lose all confidence in the United States Employment Service.

CHAPTER XI

Junior Placement Services

PLACEMENT services for juniors or placement services for inexperienced persons? Which title should be chosen? Which better represents the pre-vailing philosophy of placement? Which is better from the practical point of view? Is there any justification for special services under either title?

HISTORY OF YOUTH PLACEMENT SERVICES

The story of the occupational placement of youth in this country begins with the colonial pattern, which was imported from the Old World, and has been discussed in Chapter I. Placement was confined to children of either sex, usually at ten years of age, whose parents were unable to sup-port them or who were forced "to put them out to service" as a prerequi-site to securing poor relief for the rest of the family. These placements were made under the authority of the poor laws. They were usually made by overseers of the poor, whose sole qualification for the performance of their function was the ability to make employment contracts which caused the least possible expense to the town. Requirements for "masters" as to maintenance, treatment, and sometimes education were laid down. The objectives were clear-cut—to save public expense and to teach children habits of industry and thrift. The philosophy underlying both objectives was public service. The bona fide apprenticeship system was also in use during this early period, but it should be classified under education rather than under placement. Its objectives and philosophy were entirely differ-ent, and in no sense could it be considered poor relief, although it did sometimes give parents welcome relief from the support of the apprentice.

As the population increased and new industries were established, other methods of employing youth came into being. Two which should be re-called are the family system and the padrone system. The former was a re-sponse to the growth of factories in small towns, while the latter was a response to the needs of certain types of personal-service entrepreneurs in the growing cities.

When the character of the manufacturing processes and their products permitted, factories employed entire families or the mothers and the children. Here again, the children's tasks were performed outside of their homes, but they worked as a family unit rather than as individuals. The parents were the placement officers and were responsible both for the welfare of their children and for the efficiency with which they performed their duties. This system has continued in use down to the present time. Until forbidden by child-labor and compulsory-education laws, it was quite common in the southern cotton mills where employers frequently contracted with parents to bring in each child as soon as it had attained a certain age. Currently the remnants of the system are found in agricultural occupations where nimble fingers and limber backs are an asset in gathering or weeding small fruits and vegetables.

The padrone system brought the immigrant child into our American economic system as an independent work unit. The padrone was both the medium of importation and of placement, and the sole objective was personal gain. As parents and padroni found the exploitation of children increasingly profitable, both systems grew in popularity. In due course of time other businesses and industries, which were of such character that the employment of juveniles 12 to 14 years of age was profitable, were organized, and a considerable number of children entered the labor market entirely independent of the family unit.

The Influence of Social Reforms. Simultaneously, a nation-wide movement for social reform was crystallizing. It included a number of reforms for the benefit of children in different areas of life. Among those which bear most directly on the occupational placement of children are child-labor, compulsory-education, and continuation-school laws.

But the evils accompanying child labor, as it was legitimately called, were told in song and story long before the first legislative enactment. One readily recalls how effectively Dickens pictured child delinquency and child labor, and introduced us to an unforgettable type of parent in the person of Micawber, to problem teachers and the need for educational reform through the personality of Squeers, and to a not uncommon type of fellow worker in the guise of Mealy Potatoes. Many of his characters, through the art of the novelist, served to reveal the extent of child exploitation in both industry and education, and they remind us today that the unsolved problems of yesterday have reached maturity in our own time.

Charlotte Brontë was concerned with the problems of the laboring classes as they succumbed to inventions and the application of steam, and as technological change increased unemployment. She recognized these factors as contributors both to progress and to the intensification of the labor struggle, and she urged society to assume responsibility for opening new opportunities for displaced workers. She portrayed minority-group problems traceable to an alien creed and an alien race, suggested many modern problems expressed in "capital and labor," and protested against the harsh treatment accorded the orphan child. Her church school was an initial step toward modern social group work, a type of work which in the later years of the Victorian era was represented by Charles Kingsley and still later by Mrs. Humphry Ward.

Kingsley was influenced by the experiments of Robert Owen, who had introduced a practical program of schooling for child operatives in his cotton-spinning mills in Scotland. It was his son, Robert Dale Owen, who in 1835 obtained a charter for a manual-labor college in New Harmony, Indiana. Some have classified this "college" as our first progressive school. Mrs. Humphry Ward, as the dawn of the new century approached, became a major advocate of group activities—the great interpreter of the settlement-house movement—and, perhaps more than any other writer, she focused public attention on the unfolding story of the struggles of the poor, the evils of child labor, and the sufferings of the unemployed. The United States public was well acquainted with all these writers, and the rather complete picture of English conditions which they collectively presented touched in many ways the shores of this country and led to vocal and practical expressions of disapproval.

Other reform measures were expressed in the organization of public employment services, some of which made special provision for the placement of juveniles,[1] and the institution of a number of vocational guidance

---

[1] Juvenile services in connection with public employment offices have been mentioned in Chapter II. They were few until after World War I, and the following citations indicate the situation as it was, or as leaders thought it should be, before the war. In the program for the prevention of unemployment, which was based on intensive research during 1914, were included two recommendations on youth services. (1) Public employment exchanges should be divided into separate departments for men, women, and children. (2) There should be a special department for vocational guidance in cooperation with education. The researches on which the program was based revealed that four exchanges had "separate juvenile departments" and, "Vocational guidance is systematically carried on by the public employment exchanges in Massachusetts, and in three other states the beginnings have been made by interested superintendents" (*American Labor Legislation Review*, V [1915], 177–178).

In "Juvenile Employment Exchanges," *ibid.*, p. 204, Elsa Ueland called for the separation of juvenile and adult departments, and in discussing the facilities of the Boston exchange said, "Technically all minors under twenty-one are 'boys' and are supposed to be in charge of the clerk who places 'boys'" (p. 215).

Superintendent Sears of the Boston Service, at the first meeting of the American Association of Public Employment Offices, 1913 (U.S. Bureau of Labor Statistics, Bull.

bureaus under philanthropic auspices.[2] Although most of the applicants for employment at these bureaus were children in the biological sense and their chronological ages ranged from 12 to 15 years, the word "children" with reference to employment was supplanted by "juvenile"—a term in general use in Great Britain in connection with its juvenile labor exchanges established by law early in this century.[3]

Minimum-Wage Laws and rulings introduced the word "minor" into employment terminology. It applied to both sexes under 18, sometimes 21, years of age, and, with a single exception, all state laws applied to women and minors. No person unless he or she held a position which required the placement of women and minors under the vagaries of these early minimum-wage laws can form any adequate picture of their deleterious influence on the occupational success of the very groups which they were supposed to benefit. Just one large group profited by their provisions —mature, mediocre women who were usually employed but who received remuneration far below either a living wage or a value-of-service wage, and who were powerless to change their unfortunate situation.

Superior women lost out; substandard minors lost out. Average, and especially above-average, female minors lost out when the labor market registered a sufficient supply of male minors or of adult women who could perform the same services more satisfactorily at the same price, or when

---

no. 192, 1914) advocated nine departments in large exchanges, one of which should be for "minors, with a vocational counselor in charge."

Early legislative enactments, such as those in Ohio, Pennsylvania, and New York, uniformly used "juveniles" in the law and set the upper age limit at 16 or 18.

[2] The story of the early vocational guidance bureaus under both philanthropic and educational auspices has been summarized periodically and is available in too many easily accessible places to warrant the use of space, which should be given at this time to the presentation of new or less accessible material. A very complete history may be pieced together from the following:

Elsa Ueland, *op. cit.*, 216–223.

John G. Herndon, *Public Employment Offices in the United States* (U.S. Bureau of Labor Statistics, Bull. no. 241, 1918), pp. 60–64.

W. Carson Ryan, *Vocational Guidance and the Public Schools* (U.S. Bureau of Education, Bull. no. 24, 1918).

E. Gauthier, "Vocational Guidance," *International Labor Review*, V (1922), 707–722. This article summarizes the situation in all the countries of the world.

Reed, *Junior Wage Earners* (New York: The Macmillan Co., 1920), pp. 36–56, and *Guidance and Personnel Services*, pp. 1–29.

[3] About the same time educators came to realize that boys and girls of teen age resented being spoken of as "children" and suggested the universal use of "pupils." The writer, whose first Seattle study was entitled, *Seattle Children in School and in Industry* (Seattle: Board of School Directors, 1915), well remembers her discussion with Superintendent Frank B. Cooper over the title. Superintendent Cooper approved the title but was very emphatic in his demand that teachers speak of, and to, teen age groups as "pupils."

they attained adulthood and, had they not been controlled by wage laws, might have secured a competitive wage commensurate with their ability and experience. Male minors gained or lost with changes in the status of the labor market. In a depressed economy, when at 18 or 21 years of age they were released from the operation of the law and could make their own wage bargains, they frequently took jobs from women who were permanently controlled by the law. They just as frequently lost jobs to women when the economic condition changed. The seesaw back and forth, from minor to adult and from male to female in order to make the best bargain which the law allowed, tended to make the adult woman and minors of both sexes pawns in a most uncertain and distracting occupational game. It was also a prolific breeder of labor turnover. This writer had the fortune or misfortune, whichever way one looks at it, to have been engaged in personnel work in Seattle when the Washington Minimum-Wage Law was passed (1912) and for four years thereafter to have placed hundreds of adults and minors whose occupational opportunities were influenced, for better or for worse, by the requirements of this law; and her files still retain many of the cases which she recorded during that period.[4] They tell a sorry story of good intentions gone astray.

As social reforms gained momentum, age and grade requirements for leaving school and entering the labor market were stepped up from 14 to 15, to 16 to 17, and here and there to 18 years of age, and from completion of the sixth grade to an occasional demand for completion of the high school. Ad interim, the United States Congress attempted to pass and finally did pass and sent to the states for ratification, the so-called National Child Labor Amendment to the Constitution. This document characterized its beneficiaries as "persons under 18 years of age." The ill-advised use of the word "child" aroused anger, resentment, amusement, or pleasure as the case might be. "What," the general public asked, "is a child?" "What," the American youth asked, "does the Congress mean by calling us children?" The employer retorted, "We have no use for children; we employ young persons only."

It was logical to call upon the United States Children's Bureau for enlightenment. What age group was *it* organized to serve? And the Children's Bureau replied, ". . . the period of life from birth to the fifteenth

---

[4] For detailed information on the practical effect of these laws, see Reed, *ibid.*, *passim*; *Human Waste in Education* (New York: Century Co., 1927), pp. 110–115, which quotes from the earlier publication; and *Junior Wage Earners*, pp. 162–163.

A good summary of the provisions of minimum-wage laws in the various states, as they affect minors, is found in Paul T. David, *Barriers to Youth Employment* (Washington, D.C.: The American Council on Education, 1942), pp. 69–82.

birthday probably coincides as closely as any other with the years of child-hood," and again, "Persons under 15 years of age, the group which is usually thought of when children are mentioned. . . ." [5]

One other word which was in common use in connection with rulings under state minimum-wage laws has a bearing on the obsolescence of "children" and "juvenile" and on the choice of a title for this chapter, *inexperienced.*

Study of the texts of wage laws and rulings reveals that, as a rule, wage rates for minors and for inexperienced women were rather closely related, although sometimes there was a differential as between inexperienced minors and inexperienced adults. The point to be noted is, that under wage laws inexperienced women and inexperienced minors and experi-enced women and experienced minors were frequently placed in the same wage categories. This tendency may, or may not, have been influenced by certain early-day practices with reference to age and sex. The great major-ity of public employment offices placed women and girls, or women and juveniles of both sexes, from the same division, department, or office. Juveniles of both sexes were beneficiaries of the philanthropic vocational guidance bureaus, although one of the earliest of these bureaus, The Alli-ance Employment Bureau of New York City, was organized to place women and girls and later was "almost forced" to include boys up to 18 years of age because of pressure from the women and girls, who begged the bureau to include them.

Federal Interest in Youth Placement Services. Federal interest in special placement services for youth was first expressed in 1916 while the Commis-sioner of Immigration was still in charge of such employment services as were in existence. Two youth services, one for Women and Girls, and the other for Young Men and Boys, were among the special services recom-mended between 1914 and 1917. In the order creating these services, men-tion was made of the necessity for every precaution in helping girls and young women to make suitable occupational adjustments. No organiza-tion was perfected under this order.

The United States Boys' Working Reserve merits special attention not only because of its contribution to the solution of labor problems during the first World War and because it has served as a model for a similar agency during the current war, but because its organization, procedures, and results are full of suggestions for educators who are seriously con-cerned with methods whereby work experience may be made an integral part of education.

[5] *Handbook of Federal Statistics of Children,* pp. 8, 10.

The order of April 20, 1917, which established the organization provided for three units—an Agricultural Division, an Industrial Division, and a Vocational Training Division. The first unit was the only one which was perfected. The industrial unit which was planned to look after the placement and welfare of boys who entered war industries attempted to carry out its function by placing a junior counselor in each of the large public employment offices. All male applicants between 16 and 21 years of age were supposed to be referred to this counselor. The responsibilities of the counselor were concisely stated by the Director General in his *Report* for 1918:

This official, chosen for his capabilities through education or experience in handling boy problems, centers his efforts first upon persuading the boy applicant to return to or remain at school; if the boy's reasons for seeking industrial employment prove legitimate, the officer finds a place for him, if possible suiting any natural bent, with an eye to his future career, and at the same time enrolls him in the Industrial Division of the Reserve, with insistence upon compliance with its educational requirements of part-time or extension-school study.[6]

The plan was put in operation to a very limited extent and was not a success, although, when the Junior Division of the Employment Service was established and took over all of the youth activities, this writer found a few very competent junior counselors who had been employed to carry out its avowed objectives.

The Agricultural Division of the Reserve supplied hundreds of seasonal workers 16 to 21 years of age for farm service. It was generally reported to have made a major contribution to the salvaging of crops. In accomplishing its war service objective it was not unmindful of the physical and moral protection which is essential to the welfare of young wage earners. Scout leaders, workers in religious organizations, and educators were listed as camp supervisors, and every effort was made to counteract ill-advised schemes for the utilization of youth which would have disrupted educational programs and violated labor and education laws. Secondary schools gave active co-operation. In many instances, in order to recruit boys placement services were for the first time allowed to gain a toe hold in a public school. *Farm Craft Lessons*, an introduction to farm work, was prepared and used as a part of the preparatory training program in a considerable number of schools.

Boy Power, the official bulletin of the Reserve, began publication in 1917 [7] and is a valuable source of information on the operation of the Re-

[6] Page 13.
[7] Department of Labor, Washington, D.C.

serve in the various states. Arrangements for excusing Reserve registrants from school during critical crop periods were made. Here and there a state required preparatory farm training as a part of the school curriculum, and credit for work actually performed was optional, but common. Wages varied according to the locality. Sometimes they were paid by the state but usually by the farmer. Maine inaugurated a unique program: the boys were uniformed and were disciplined and trained in the simple elements of military behavior. They received wages from the state on the same basis as the soldiers—one dollar a day rain or shine. After nine days of preliminary training they were sent out to farms under supervisors. That their work was more than satisfactory is attested by the fact that farmers frequently gave them additional wages; some received as much as $3.50 per day additional.[8]

When the war was over the Reserve was no longer needed. It was abolished in March, 1919, and such of its activities as were feasible were transferred to the Junior Section of the United States Employment Service.

The Junior Section of the United States Employment Service represents the third effort to establish a youth placement service under federal auspices. It was organized at the close of World War I to aid in one of the most serious problems of reconversion—the replacement in school, or in civilian occupations, of young war workers.

The history of this first broadly conceived federal junior employment service has never been written and probably never will be in its entirety.[9] The writer was called to Washington by wire the day before the armistice was signed to take charge of the girls' division of a juvenile employment service which was about to be launched. Jesse B. Davis of Grand Rapids, Michigan, had consented to take charge of a similar division for boys. She left Seattle the following day, November 11, 1918. Upon arriving in Washington she found that Mr. Davis and William Edwin Hall had already drawn up a tentative draft of the order which was to create a Juvenile Section to place youth under 18 years of age. It provided for administration and operation on a sex segregation basis. She suggested three changes in the draft; that the words "child" and "juvenile" be eliminated and that "junior" be substituted in both title and text; that the 18-year age limit be raised to 21, and that a single service including both sexes be set up with Mr. Davis as chief and herself as assistant chief.

There was no dissension. The only objection came from the Women's

[8] *Boy Power*, I (June 15, 1918), 3.
[9] The National Archives report that there are no records on this agency in its possession and that it has no knowledge as to their "whereabouts." Probably such data as have been preserved are in this writer's files.

Division which protested against raising the age from 18 to 21 on the ground that the additional age groups belonged in the Women's Division. There was much justification for this claim. There was also some objection to the consolidation of services for both sexes, again on the ground that the chief of the girls' section should be responsible to the Director of the Women's Division or at least have dual responsibilities to that individual and to the Director General. This writer declined to serve under dual supervision and her objection was sustained by the Director General.

The three suggested changes were immediately made, but it was interesting to rationalize the why of this difference in approach to these specific items. Mr. Davis was a high-school principal, his avocational interests were in the Y.M.C.A. and in the Boys' Working Reserve. He was accustomed to regarding 18 years as the age of completion of high school, and he frankly stated that girls were not his major youth interest. Mr. Hall was a boys' man; his many philanthropic activities had always been focused on boys' problems and boys' needs, but the age limits for the Boys' Working Reserve, which he founded, were 16 to 21 years. Quite unintentionally, and entirely unconscious of the fact, both men were getting rid of any responsibility for the placement of girls.

On the other hand, the writer's interests had been equally divided between the sexes, her educational experiences had been in coeducational institutions, her occupational contacts had been made in the interests of both sexes, and her placement experiences had indicated the frequent feasibility of substituting one sex for the other when filling employers' orders. Why educate the sexes together in the public schools and segregate them for distribution in the labor market only to bring them together again in employment situations? Why should youth, who elected to remain in school, be the sole beneficiaries of taxation for educational purposes? Was there no educational return on work experience? Were not wage-earning youth entitled to their share of public money for education, and was not a junior employment service one method of securing a more equitable distribution of such funds among all youth under 21 years of age?

The order establishing the Junior Section was issued December 6, 1918. Mr. Davis, who was employed on a part-time basis, resigned February 10, 1919, and Mrs. Reed was appointed chief. Shortly thereafter the "Section" became a "Division" and the "chief" became "Assistant to the Director General in charge of the Junior Division." The program of the Division was planned to function in co-operation with public-school sytems and such other philanthropic and educational agencies as might be desirable. Providence, Rhode Island, in March of 1919 made the first co-operative agreement. Philadelphia and Pittsburgh followed.[10] Indiana was the first state to follow federal precedent by establishing a junior section in its free employment service (Sect. 5, S 306, approved March 15, 1919). The beneficiaries were "minors," and the law allowed the section to enter into agreements with schools for the purpose of establishing and maintaining local free employment services and for the extension of vocational guidance to minors (Sect. 4 d).

Under the provisions of this law some very interesting contracts were drawn up between the state service and school districts. Sometimes the Junior Division of the United States Employment Service was a third party to the contract, but as a rule Junior Division contracts were made with local school systems without the intervention of state services.

For approximately three years this junor employment service grew slowly but sanely along co-operative lines. An administrative officer in the co-operating school system was usually appointed, on the dollar-a-year basis, as superintendent of the local federal service.[11] Some contribution to the operating expense was made by the Federal Service and all appointments were subject to its approval. During the first two years the funds allotted to the Junior Division of the Service were sufficient to permit quite a substantial financial contribution to local services and to maintain a well-equipped supervisory force in the Washington office. As the appropriation dwindled, nothing except the franking privilege remained, but this in itself was quite a valuable financial asset.

Pittsburgh, under Mr. Leavitt, attained the highest degree of development. Two local offices were maintained: one in the continuation-school office, in connection with the work-certificate division, so that youth between 14 and 16 years of age could complete all school-to-work procedures in one office; the other a genuine junior placement service for youth from 16 to 21 years of age maintained in a conveniently located downtown business block. This second office was liberally supported and was used as an observation and training center for prospective personnel from other cities.

Periodically, the Washington office issued newsletters intended to assist local offices in the upkeep of their corps and to make suggestions on the

10 The most elaborate, and practically the only, account of the organization and early development of this agency is found in Reed, *Junior Wage Earners*, pp. 34–165. The principles which controlled its activities are discussed in *Guidance and Personnel Services*, pp. 304–307.

11 Associate Superintendent of Schools Frank M. Leavitt in Pittsburgh, Assistant Superintendent Richard D. Allen in Providence.

solution of problems which were causing difficulties in several offices. As examples, one of these newsletters contained suggestions for helping young people to meet the postwar depression situation which was resulting in the loss of many positions, and another dealt with Policies, Developmental Plans, and Analysis of Positions in the Junior Division. In 1920 *Junior Wage Earners,* which was prepared as a manual for the use of junior placement workers, was published. It was not a government publication, although it was approved by the Director General of the Employment Service and by the Secretary of Labor.

Two efforts to co-operate with universities in the recruitment and training of personnel for Junior Division positions were made. Five one-year scholarships of from $200 to $1,200, combining internship and university study, were granted; and, in response to requests from colleges and normal schools for an outline of the minimum essentials of an introductory course in vocational guidance and placement, an outline for such a course was prepared and distributed. This outline was no more satisfactory than any of the other outlines for similar purposes which have already been mentioned.[12] Failure seems inherent in their character, purpose, and method. The method of preparation of this Junior Division outline was somewhat different from the usual method, but that does not alter the fact that it was not a practical success. The outline was prepared in the Washington office by E. W. Weaver, Frank M. Leavitt, and George E. Myers, all members of the field staff of the Division, working in unison on each unit of the course with Emery T. Filbey and Anna Y. Reed of the office staff.

But the United States Employment Service, of which the Junior Division was a part, was a war emergency organization. It had no permanent status. When its appropriation was reduced to the point where it was impossible to maintain even a semblance of efficiency, and when political protégés of a new administration were foisted on what little was left of the Service, this writer and her professional assistants resigned.

Coincident with the appointment of Francis I. Jones as Director General, Mary Stewart was appointed Assistant in charge of the Junior Division and eventually she took over what remained of the Women's Division. Both these appointments were rewards for political campaign services, but Miss Stewart was a woman of much ability. She made a strenuous effort to master the problems involved in this new and unfamiliar field, and all

[12] A few years later the National Vocational Guidance Association attempted to prepare a similar outline. It was published and proved to be both a professional and a commercial failure.

the evidence indicates that a nonpolitical appointee would probably have been no more effective. She faced a difficult, even an impossible, situation. The Service had no public prestige, and the Congress repeatedly refused to make it a permanent agency or to give it other than the most meager financial support. Under a most incompetent Director General it was moribund for several years. The Junior Division died, and Miss Stewart was transferred to another federal department.

Federal Activities, 1933–1940, represent a fourth federal effort to establish special services for juniors. It was motivated by the late economic depression and the resultant predicament in which both unemployed youth and a socially worried public found themselves. After the passage of the Wagner-Peyser Act in 1933, with its emphasis on state responsibility for the operation of public services and its relatively liberal financial contribution to such services, there was a period of rapid growth in the size and scope of public employment services. This renewed activity included development in the provision for junior departments, although in some states juniors were preferably placed by special interviewers from the same office as were adults.

Junior services shared in the benefits of the intensive studies [13] and the qualitative improvements which took place between 1936 and 1940 and to which the earlier experiments in Minnesota, Rochester, and Philadelphia had contributed. Surveys and researches on the junior level, dealing specifically with youth problems, were also made by the American Youth Commission, the National Youth Administration, and the United States Office of Education. Those of special value for the immediate purpose are listed in the bibliography which follows this chapter.

During these same years two federal agencies were established to deal specifically with the adjustment and employment problems of youth:

The Civilian Conservation Corps, which was established in 1933, may be dismissed without discussion, since from the point of view of this book it cannot be rated as an employment service. Applicants accepted for admission were assembled in camps where they were assigned to some sort of public-works project. The ages for acceptance were usually assumed to be 17 to 23 years, but the previous statement relative to the registration of veterans of World War I indicates an elastic age policy. The agency was abolished in 1942.

The National Youth Administration was established in 1935 as a part of the Works Progress Administration, and the guidance and placement of

13 See the reading list for Part Two.

youth, 16 to 25 years of age, was delegated to the Division of Guidance and Placement, Mrs. Mary H. S. Hayes, Director. This agency made two types of contributions to the progress of junior employment services.

It co-operated with state employment services by furnishing junior employment personnel, who functioned under the direction of the state employment services. Agreements provided, among other things, that certain statistical reports be sent to the state directors of both state employment services and of national youth administrations. Junior units agreed to serve all applicants of the specified ages, regardless of race, color, or creed, and, while no organized effort to stimulate the employment of youth at the expense of older workers was permitted, efforts to conserve for young people the jobs which were typically theirs were allowed. This service was initiated in March, 1936, with 21 offices. On December 31, 1936, there were 49 units operating in 21 states and the District of Columbia. Approximately 50 per cent of the 65,701 registrants between 16 and 25 years of age were without previous work experience of any kind. Sixty per cent of the new applicants were between 18 and 21 years of age, 26 per cent were under 18; and 14 per cent were between 21 and 25; 41 per cent had completed high school, and about one per cent were college graduates.[14]

Since the age limits for the National Youth Administration were 16 to 25 years, while the upper age limits of most state employment services were either 18 or 21 years, competition between the adult and junior divisions was bound to occur with reference to both job orders and applicants. And again one must admit, as was noted when the Junior Division of the United States Employment Service, in 1918, raised the upper age limit from 18 to 21 years, there was considerable justification for the resentment of the adult divisions. Nor were the adult divisions the only objectors. Applicants objected. In some cases, for example in New York City, their objections resulted in the placement of counselors to deal with inexperienced applicants between 21 and 25 years of age in the adult offices.

The second type of contribution by the National Youth Administration was made possible by the financial assistance of the American Youth Commission. The latter agency was established by the American Council on Education in 1935. It was commissioned to (1) consider all the needs of youth and appraise the facilities and resources for serving those needs, (2) plan experiments and programs which will be most helpful in solving the problems of youth, and (3) popularize and promote desirable plans of action through publications, conferences, and demonstrations.

[14] National Youth Administration, news release, Jan. 17, 1937.

Under this mandate it co-operated with the National Youth Administration in conducting fact-finding studies into the problems and needs of youth and in establishing experimental youth counseling and placement centers which might serve as models for communities which desired to institute similar services. The major fact-finding research is the most recent contribution to the "Youth Tell Their Story" series of publications,[15] which was initiated by the survey of women and child wage earners in the United States authorized by Congress January 29, 1907,[16] and which has continued to receive thought-provoking contributions for almost forty years.[17]

Community demonstration projects were carried on in eight selected centers from January, 1938, through September, 1939. The story of these projects and the recommendations for community occupational adjustment programs which are based upon their experiences may be read in Howard M. Bell's *Matching Youth and Jobs*. Both of the national agencies engaged in these projects were emergency services, and both have been abolished, but their contributions, theoretical and practical, remain and will doubtless have permanent values.

The period of transition and change which presently prevails in all public employment service activities is, of course, due to the war emergency and to the fact that state dominance has been superseded by federal dominance. Moreover, transfer of the United States Employment Service back to the Department of Labor, of which until the President's reorganization plan of 1939 it was a part, seems imminent. It is also possible that some of the employment activities of the Veterans Administration may be assigned to the Department of Labor.

SUMMARY

This brief overview of the evolution of occupational placement services for youth contains certain factual information which should be useful to communities contemplating the institution of such services to meet the needs of present-day youth. It ties the story of the successes and failures of the past to the problems of the present, reveals dominant control factors which have influenced the past, and raises questions as to their permanent

[15] Howard M. Bell, *Youth Tell Their Story* (Washington: American Council on Education, 1938).

[16] *Report on the Conditions of Women and Child Wage Earners in the United States* (61st Congress, 2d session, Senate doc. no. 645; Washington, D.C., 1910–1913), 19 vols.

[17] For a rather complete analysis of the content of 148 of these surveys covering two periods of "surveying," see Reed, *Human Waste in Education. Guidance and Personnel Services*, pp. 331–335, discusses the over-all results of such surveys.

influence; and it suggests factors which are important in forecasting the future. It indicates what changes have taken place in the objectives, beneficiaries, methods of organization and administration, and in the selection of operating personnel. It helps to determine whether or not either term— junior or inexperienced—can be so defined that it will be accepted as a sufficiently determining variant to warrant the segregation of either or both groups in a special placement service.

The high points which have suggestive values for communities may be summarized as follows:

(1) Age has been a continual eligibility requirement for admission to youth placement services. Progressively higher, lower, and upper age limits have been noted—10 years, 14, 15; 16, 17, 18, 21, and finally 25 years. The occasion for this last raise was the large number of youth who, in the depression years, had passed the 18- or 21-year age limit without an opportunity to acquire occupational experience, plus the fact that employers frequently felt that the recent high-school or college graduate was a "better bet" than was one who had been out of school some time and was still unemployed. The accent was, therefore, shifted to inexperience, and the upper age limit was set at 25 years.

(2) The economic status of the family was for years an eligibility factor. But "poor relief," "economic pressure," and "underprivileged youth" were expressions which lost their eligibility significance as age limits were raised. Desire to work and capacity to work took their place.

(3) Since 1905 eligibility requirements have been markedly influenced by legislative enactments. Child-labor, compulsory-education, and continuation-school laws have determined what age- and educational-level groups might be registered for placement.

(4) Beneficiaries of youth placement services have been variously characterized as children, juveniles, youth, young persons, young adults, minors, juniors, and inexperienced persons. The obsolescence of "children" and "juveniles" in relation to employment has long been recognized, although some workers till use these terms.

(5) Youth placement services have been differently denominated as vocational guidance bureaus, juvenile exchanges, juvenile placement bureaus, vocational adjustment bureaus, junior placement services, junior personnel services, placement services for juniors and inexperienced persons, counseling and placement services, and college placement bureaus. Just at present there is a tendency, at least in educational circles, to overwork the term occupational adjustment service. Perhaps this is due to the recent activities of the National Occupational Conference and to the extensive

use of this term in the publications of the American Youth Commission.

(6) Youth placement services have been instituted and administered under a variety of auspices—poor commissioners, philanthropy, educational institutions, public employment services, and private enterprise. There is a growing feeling that responsibility for the occupational placement of youth should be shared by educational and employment agencies.

(7) As the scope of youth services has been enlarged to include an ever greater range of age and educational levels, it has become quite customary to set up two such services: one for the benefit of youth whose age and educational status keep them under the control of legislative enactments and make work certificates prerequisites to employment, and the other for young adults who are entirely free from the restrictions imposed by educational or child-labor legislation. The first-mentioned service usually operates under educational auspices, the latter under the direction of the state employment service.

(8) Types of registrants have changed materially. "Juvenile" workers are out of the picture except now and then for out-of-school jobs. Junior workers comprise the large majority of applicants. Two factors are responsible: restrictive legislation, which imposed an additional nuisance burden on employers, and the mechanization and other changes in business and industry which have made it unprofitable to employ youth under 17 or 18 years of age and more profitable to employ high-school graduates. College graduates, in small numbers, register in youth bureaus.

(9) Changes in types of jobs have, of course, paralleled changes in types of registrants. The machine performs many mechanical tasks which were formerly suitable work for young and nimble fingers. All types of positions open to college graduates, except those which require a combination of age, experience, and extensive education, are found in the employers' files by junior services and are competed for by experienced juniors and by inexperienced youth when the age limit is 25 years.

(10) Wage scales for young workers which, before the introduction of federal and state minimum-wage laws, were considerably lower than those of adults, now approach, if they do not equal, those which prevail on the adult level.

(11) Sex has never been a very important factor in setting up youth placement services, and it is a practically nonexistent one today except in situations where placement is one of several functions performed by an agency operating on a sex basis.

(12) The recent introduction of unemployment compensation requires all regular workers to register with the social security board and if unem-

ployed to present their claims with their registration number at the board office. They must also register for placement with the nearest United States employment office. This most recent legislation is tending to lessen the desirability of segregating junior and adult placement services.

Some of the decisions which must be made by communities before they establish junior placement services will be arrived at more intelligently if these historical data are used as the background upon which to understand present problems and the best methods for their solution. How may a community decide whether or not it is wise to institute a junior placement service? What should be the purpose of such a service? Who should be its beneficiaries? How should it be organized and administered? What should be the character of its operating personnel? What phases of personnel service should be included in its activities? Does the type of service determined upon have any justifiable claim to be rated as a special service? How are the outstanding facts in the history of youth services related to the summary of trends with reference to special services which was presented at the close of Chapter XI?

Reply to these questions by each community as a guide in determining upon a definite course of action is much more difficult than is reply to the same types of problems with reference either to a general community service or to a veterans' service. In submitting material which it is hoped will be helpful to communities, the original topic arrangement has again been followed. After some hesitation, the author has decided to avoid repetition by relying rather extensively on her recent book, *Guidance and Personnel Services in Education,* which was devoted almost entirely to junior services in connection with educational institutions. And, indeed, she has already written so extensively on junior personnel services that she cannot but wonder whether she has any further contribution to make in this area.

Preorganization Investigations and Decisions

Although preliminary investigations, the findings of which will be focused on decisions regarding the need for junior services and the best methods of introducing them, will cover much the same topics and seek replies to much the same questions as have been discussed under general services and under special services for veterans, the accent will be somewhat different; and the necessity for close co-ordination of any phases of guidance and personnel services which are already offered by the public-school system or by other agencies with those which may be contemplated for inclusion in a new service, will become a major preorganization responsibility. Topics which may advantageously be given special committee consideration prior to the institution of a junior service are Legislation, Community Surveys, and Community Co-operation.

Legislation. Guidance and Personnel Services, pages 109–117, discussed twelve legislative enactments and occupational restrictions with which counselors and teachers should be familiar, and it noted that, under present conditions, youth were daily passing from the jurisdiction of our educational systems into occupational life with little or no knowledge of the statutes and the labor restrictions which controlled their entry thereto, or which had been put on the statute books to protect them in the performance of their duties.

The laws mentioned related to compulsory school attendance and child labor; educational and personal requirements which control enrollment in federal, state, or municipal institutions of all types and admission to civil-service examinations; accreditment and licensure of private academic, trade, commercial, and other schools; vocational rehabilitation; entrance into occupations; conditions of labor; workmen's compensation; state and federal minimum-wage orders; the employment of aliens; the collection of wages and other personal matters; the employment of married women; and social security. If, in any given state, an antibias, antidiscriminatory, or fair-employment-practice law has been enacted, that, too, must be included in this list. And all rulings and enactments which have a bearing on the employment of veterans will be of value for junior employment services wherever the upper age limit is over 18 years.

The investigating committee will need to be familiar with all types of legislation, federal, state, and municipal, which affect the employment of youth if it is to decide intelligently upon either the desirability of a service or upon the type of service which will be most useful. Knowledge of the provisions of such statutes and of labor-union regulations will aid it in understanding the types of problems which will arise in connection with the age, educational status, and physical condition of junior applicants and their placement possibilities. Complete understanding of such problems will warn it that a junior employment service, under public-school, public-employment, or other auspices, which attempts to do placement work without this knowledge is doing youth, employers, and the agency responsible a grave injustice, as well as neglecting an opportunity for service of a type which is not usually offered to any other agency. If there are enough juniors in a community to warrant the operation of a special service for them, there will be enough juniors who need help in understanding the how and why of such laws, and enough employers who, if they agree to employ juniors, will expect, and perhaps demand, that the referring agency relieve them of the nuisance of checking on the legality of the applicant's employment and the danger of incurring legal penalties if they employ the referrals.[18]

The fact that the laws under only one of the categories mentioned are limited in application to persons under 16 or 18 years of age serves to emphasize the obsolescence of the words "children" and "juveniles" in connection with the labor market, and it reveals how very thin the line between the youth worker and the adult worker has become. If anything further is needed to emphasize the thinness of the line, it will soon be supplied by the return to civilian life of the "child" or the "juvenile" veteran. Ask any official in charge of recruiting and induction centers for the Armed Forces! Study such photographs as those which appeared in the *New York Times* May 19, 1944, which show boys between the ages of 16½ and 17½ filling out applications for the United States Maritime Service at 45 Broadway. Of the 500 youth who appeared the previous day, 150 were examined, 100 were accepted, and the remainder were sent home for parental consent.

Local committees may also be interested in tracing the changes which have come about in the objectives of child-labor legislation and in determining the extent to which they desire to give their support to its current objectives. The sole original objective of child-labor legislation was the welfare of "children." Beginning with the late economic depression its dominant objective—with temporary wartime reversion to its original purpose—has come to be the protection of adult workers from youth's competition for such jobs as may be available. And this new objective has received the endorsement of such social agencies as the United States Children's Bureau [19] and the National Education Association,[20] and of such practical agencies as the National Small Business Men's Association.[21]

[18] The United States Children's Bureau has several times warned youth under 20 years of age that "the war plants, which offer the favored opportunities, are all operating under Federal laws," and those who leave home seeking employment should carry with them a birth certificate or some other proof of age (news release, Feb. 14, 1944).

[19] The Chief of the Bureau urged the 1945 legislatures to enact statutes requiring 16-year standards as a means of cushioning "the transition to peacetime economy and lessening the threat of postwar unemployment" (*New York Times*, Oct. 29, 1944).

[20] Among the suggestions formulated by the seminars held at the 1940 convention of the National Education Association was: "Remove youth from the labor market by fixing a school-leaving age of 16 years, at least, in every state" (*Journal of National Education Association*, XXIX [1940], 173).

[21] The *New York Times*, Aug. 14, 1944, reports the Association's advocacy of a uni-

How will this back-to-school movement affect youth? It is not the first time we have tried it. Will youth be both willing and mentally able to continue their formal education? What inducements does the community offer if they are both able and willing to remain in school? If they prefer to do something else, and are ruled out of participation in the occupational activities of the community, how will they occupy their time and utilize their energy—in delinquencies, in social agitation, or how?

Many youth problems will come to the surface as the committee studies the impact of legislative enactments and labor-union regulations on the educational and occupational opportunities of youth, on their idleness, delinquencies, and final employability or unemployability. Revelation of such problems and understanding of the enactments which foster them will help the preorganization committee to realize that there are legal limitations within which a junior placement service must operate, and if need for a service be shown and if organization be consummated, it will provide information of great value to educators and will permit the placement service to protect both applicants and employers from violation of laws.

Community Surveys. An important factor in helping the committee to determine the need for a junior employment service will be the findings of a series of local studies, surveys, or investigations which deal with the number and types of applicants and the number and types of employing concerns who will probably desire to make use of junior employment facilities, plus an enumeration of such community resources as may be available to assist youth in the making of occupational adjustments.

Several publications on the methods of conducting such local investigations are available. Some have already been mentioned. Statistical summaries on many of the topics which are usually included in such investigations will serve as guides for communities which lack experience or may be largely dependent upon volunteer surveyors.[22] Allowance must always be

---

form national child-labor law "to forestall postwar job competition between school children and war veterans."

Harriet Ahlers Houdlette, "Straight Thinking on Services for Children," *Journal of the American Association of University Women*, XXXVII (1944), 152–155, writing on the objectives of child-care centers, notes that the first subordination of the welfare of children to the needs of working women occurred during the depression years, and that the welfare of children has again become of secondary importance because women were needed in war industries.

[22] Bell, *Youth Tell Their Story*, and Ruth E. Eckert and Thomas O. Marshall, *When Youth Leave School* (New York: The Regents' Inquiry, McGraw-Hill Book Co., 1938) include many topics which characterize young wage earners and their jobs. The author's

made for community variations in the character of applicants and of industries.

Investigations which reveal the number, age, sex, educational status, general and special preparation for occupational life, vocational interests and potentialities, and the personality characteristics, both assets and liabilities, of youth as they come directly from the schools and colleges into the labor market must rely largely on school records and teachers' opinions as sources of information. What percentage of the total prefer local employment, and what percentage will seek opportunities in other labor-market areas? [23] What proportion of the probable applicants are promotable material? How many youth with physical, mental, moral, or emotional handicaps are placeable through an employment service? What is the opinion of the school regarding the "readiness" of its product to assume the responsibility of occupational life? [24] How many veterans would probably use the service?

There should be no difficulty in securing all the necessary preorganization data on prospective applicants directly from the school census and school records. Information should also be available on former graduates and dropouts who are still in their home community and who are within the purview of the contemplated service. The educational system might well assume responsibility for all investigations bearing on the quality and quantity of an applicant clientele.

The job-opportunity survey should include all the employing concerns in the labor-market area. It should reveal entry jobs and their pre-employment requirements, the usual percentage of beginners for whom there are promotional opportunities, and the percentage which, after a period of induction and adjustment, will probably have to seek positions in other communities. It should ascertain which firms offer counseling services, in-service training, or apprenticeships, and what community serv-

---

compilation in *Human Waste in Education* summarizes survey topics and their findings over a considerable period of years.

Bell, *Matching Youth and Jobs*, Part II, deals with the broader aspects of all three types of investigations.

[23] Labor-market areas and school districts are not always geographically identical. This fact should be considered in making local studies and in determining upon the geographical area to be served by a junior employment service.

[24] Eckert and Marshall, *When Youth Leave School*, pp. 110–114, in a section entitled "Readiness for Vocational Responsibilities," report that almost 50 per cent of those who withdrew from the high school were denied job recommendations by the school authorities and that from 10 to 15 per cent of those who attained certificates of academic proficiency were considered unready to attain job proficiency. Reed, *Guidance and Personnel Services*, pp. 335–336, compares this statement with a similar teachers' estimate in 1907.

ices offer facilities which provide satisfactory additional or substitute services. Such a preliminary survey will allow the committee to estimate the probable number of openings which will be available and the quality of the applicants required to meet the demand. But teachers (other than vocational teachers), club-women volunteers, and student investigators are usually so grossly ignorant of the processes and problems of the occupational world that it is an insult to a busy employer to suggest that he assume the responsibility of educating them. A committee is more likely to win the hearty co-operation of employers if it delegates job surveys to those who talk the language of occupational life, understand its problems, and can secure its confidence.

Community Co-operation. All of the comments on community co-operation found in the voluminous literature of recent years, which has tried to impress the public with its responsibility for various services for youth, are applicable to establishing and operating junior placement services. If such co-operation is to be attained, the key which unlocks the door to success is found in the attitude of the board of education and of the school administration toward the responsibility of the educational system for the occupational distribution and adjustment of its product and by-product. If any given educational system refuses to recognize occupational distribution as an educational function, or if it makes cursory responses to the requests of public employment services, or other placement agencies, for the type of information necessary to service juniors adequately, it will not only lose its chance to broaden the vision of the school corps and to increase the value of its public educational services, but it will be a serious handicap to the success of any other agency which attempts to make up for its neglect. For, after years of wishful thinking and pussyfooting, it is now openly declared that junior employment service requires the assumption of a number of very important responsibilities by the public schools and colleges in the labor-market area. Therefore, decision on the single point as to how far both co-operation and genuine leadership may be expected from educational agencies becomes of first importance and will have a marked influence on the type of administrative setup recommended.

That educational administration has been unconscionably slow in accepting responsibility for the distribution of its product has long been recognized to everyone except educators themselves. This writer has elaborated it so many times that she is loath to add anything to her previous denunciations. Time and again other writers have noted that philanthropic and public employment services have been far in advance of education in grasping youth's occupational adjustment needs and in attempting to make provision for them.[25]

A wholesome change in educator attitude came about coincidentally with the organization and allocation to other than an educational agency of the liberally financed Civilian Conservation Corps and the National Youth Administration. The change became even more noticeable when certain war-training programs were assigned to noneducational agencies. Whether this improvement in interest in wage-earning youth is attributable to sincere repentance for the neglect of the past and a tardy recognition of present and future responsibilities, or whether it is due to the fear that other agencies will increasingly encroach on the educational preserves and usurp some of their functions and funds, is beside the point. For even though jurisdictional disputes which have accompanied these happenings may bring a smile to the faces of the living, and perhaps to those of the dead, who remember the unpopularity of that small number of educators who long ago envisaged the present situation, everyone will welcome the change and make haste to capitalize on it before there is time for a reversal in attitude.

What co-operation has the committee a right to expect from educational institutions serving within the labor-market area? Of course, education will be well represented in the membership of the committee. Quite possibly educators may have instigated the project and assumed leadership in the preliminary investigations. An educator may be chairman of the committee. But whether or not educators are prime movers, there are a minimum of functions which should be assumed by education. They reach back into pre-employment days and are concerned primarily with the preparation of a marketable product, labeled as accurately as is possible as to characteristics and quality, so that first-class applicants may be readily distinguished from irregulars, seconds, and damaged goods—for it must not be forgotten that the educational systems, as well as all other mass-production industries, do, in their "processing" procedures, damage some of their best raw material. This broader aspect of educational responsibility will be taken up in a later chapter. At this point it is necessary to mention only such functions as are closely related to the occupational

---

[25] This, of course, is a generalization. But as a generalization every study ever made confirms it as a fact. See Bell, *Matching Youth and Jobs*, pp. 72–73; Eckert and Marshall, *When Youth Leave School, passim;* Walter C. Eells, *General Report on the Methods, Activities, and Results of the Cooperative Study of Secondary School Standards* (Washington, D.C.: American Council on Education, 1939); and Edward Landry and others, *Occupational Adjustment and the School* (Bull. XXIV, no. 93; Washington, D.C.: National Association of Secondary-School Principals, 1940).

referral of the school product to the positions for which it is best qualified.

Now and then a writer on this subject claims that a junior placement service cannot function unless school and college curricula have included occupational information and tryout courses, and unless a testing program and cumulative records have been maintained. The writer has seen enough excellent placement work done by public employment services and other agencies, including commercial agencies, which have not had the benefit of such co-operation to be unwilling to agree to this dictum. But no one will deny that there are some educational contributions which are valuable aids to interviewers who are charged with the occupational referral of the school product, nor will anyone deny that occupational information and counseling are needed long before, and preparatory to, contacting an employment office.

The school's most important contribution to the readiness of the individual for immediate participation in occupational life is in assisting its charges to gain an understanding of the work world and to acquire right attitudes toward work; to know something of the purpose, problems, and methods of business and industry and how they differ from those of education; to know something of the various media through which positions are secured and how to evaluate and use them; and to formulate their conception of what they have a right to expect of themselves occupationally, what they may legitimately expect of an employer, what the employer has a right to expect of them, and what society's legitimate claims upon them are.

Co-operation with the referral agency centers around the furnishing of adequate information, which will assist interviewers in the job and other classification of each individual, and of the type of follow-up and training-for-promotion assistance which only educational agencies can render.

What co-operation may be expected from employing concerns? Concerns which employ juniors should be willing to furnish definite information regarding job requirements and entry qualifications; to indicate vertical and horizontal lines of promotion and the additional preparation required of those who seek advancement; to take an intelligent interest in junior adjustment problems, to know what they have a legitimate right to expect of junior employees, and to be reasonably patient with their lack of know-how and foolish blunders; to provide sympathetic employment supervision which can and will make suggestions for improvement; and to give the schools and the placement service the benefit of such information as may be useful in making educational curricula more practical and selections for referral more satisfactory.

Each public, or semipublic, community agency—public library, welfare council, health and recreation centers, service clubs, noncommercial employment services, and newspapers—has something of co-operative value to offer a junior employment service, and its interest should be enlisted. Contributions to the financial budget must be secured in order to establish and maintain the service; various types of publicity are needed in order to introduce it to, and keep it before, the public; a good word now and then before women's and service clubs is apt to fall on fertile soil; and there are many other ways in which community agencies can express their interest and willingness to co-operate.

EXTERNAL ORGANIZATION AND ADMINISTRATION

If the surveys and investigations have uncovered a need for a junior service and if the promises of community co-operation have been generous and there is reasonable expectation that they will be sustained, the committee may next turn its attention to what have been called "problems of external organization and administration." For the immediate purpose three topics are stressed: Objectives and Functions of the Service, Administrative Control, and Selection of the Operating Personnel. Decisions on these topics are so closely related that, no matter what order of presentation is chosen, it may seem to be illogical.

The Objectives and Functions of a Junior Placement Service. The primary objective of a junior placement service is exactly the same as is that of any other type of placement service—the effective distribution of applicants whom the committee has seen fit to classify as juniors. Again, the student of methods of effective occupational distribution will raise the same sort of questions as were raised with reference to special services for veterans: To what extent do special services for juniors, or inexperienced persons, meet the criterion set up by professional workers for the institution of special services? Is either "junior" or "inexperienced" a sufficiently determining variant to warrant a special service?

In considering these questions as they bear upon the objectives and functions of a junior service, the committee will need to keep in mind the story of the evolution of junior placement activities from services for children and juveniles to services for young persons under 21 years of age and/or inexperienced persons under 25 years of age. It will also need to remember that useless decentralization of the labor market is always a handicap to the effective distribution of workers, that it denies substitution in referrals, causes duplication in employer contacts, creates interdivision jealousies, and tends to lose the support of experienced juniors and of employing concerns.

However, if it is determined that special services for juniors are warranted, then, keeping in mind the disadvantages of a decentralized labor market, other questions will be given attention: What age and experience-status groups should be served? What types of applicants should be registered? What functions should be performed?

Preliminary investigations, in a typical community, will have revealed the number and characteristics of the probable applicant clientele in different age and experience groups, and the extent to which other agencies are attempting to serve the same groups. They will have provided many facts, uncovered many problems, and suggested several possible replies to the questions propounded. It may be difficult to secure committee agreement on a number of matters.

Some of the more significant survey findings, as they have been reported over the years, are recapitulated:

(1) Persons of working age under 21 to 25 years will usually comprise a considerable percentage of the total community labor supply.

(2) Such an age range includes approximately two to three years of biological adolescence and seven years of maturity.

(3) Persons who fall into the first category would be a minority group still under the control of child-labor and compulsory-education laws, and still obliged to secure work certificates in order to be eligible for employment.

(4) A considerable part of this group may not be definitely classified as either students or wage earners, and their employability is frequently handicapped by their educational objectives. High-school and college students who seek part-time, after-school, vacation, or other temporary employment may be classified in this minority group even though they do not require work certificates and are over 18 years of age.

(5) The character, number, problems, and needs of the majority group differ materially from those of the minority group, even though, as has been pointed out time and again, no sharp line can be drawn between the two groups on the basis of age.

(6) Classified on the basis of experience, many of the 18- to 25-year group belong in an adult division; others, as they continue to accumulate experience, are more in need of counsel for the occupational adolescent than are some members of the minority group. This is especially true of inexperienced college graduates.

(7) Classification on the basis of experience is bound to clash with

classification on the basis of age and to act as a complicating factor in the clarification of the objectives of the service. That is, the age range of inexperienced applicants may extend from 16 to 25 years; that of the experienced from 17 to 25; and some whose age still allocates them to a junior division may have had more experience, and have acquired greater occupational know-how, than have those who are approaching the 25-year age limit.

(8) The functions usually determined upon primarily for the minority age group—occupational and personal counseling, instruction in methods of approaching employers, how to choose an employer, and the like—are frequently just as essential for the older age group. And it will be remembered that experienced placement workers have long since recognized the desirability of including a qualified counselor in the personnel of adult offices.

(9) The functions performed by junior services have always depended somewhat upon the agency which administers the service.

(10) When an adult public service is in operation, the organization of a junior service registering applicants up to 21–25 years is usually regarded as an attempt to set up a rival service.

(11) Youth who have passed the compulsory-education age, and especially experienced persons and war veterans, have always resented classification with the law-controlled group and have refused to register in services which bore any of the earmarks of "juvenile." And, indeed, it is ludicrous to assume that persons who may have entered the labor market at 17 or 18 years of age and have been continuously employed for four or more years will register in other than adult divisions.

(12) That a very elastic age for youth has come about gradually and naturally, that it is in tune with the social-economic thinking of the day, that it is demanding a correspondingly flexible line between junior and adult placement services.

(13) That throughout the entire history of "juvenile" placement, neither public-school graduates nor dropouts (eighth grade in the early years) have ever shown any confidence in the occupational distribution ability of educators, and that they have rarely returned to the school office for replacement. Worldly-wise youngsters will not accept the referral decisions of occupational illiterates.

By the time the evidence is all in and is interpreted and weighed, the committee will probably have arrived at one very important conclusion: That it will be very difficult, if not impossible, to *pool* and *hold* a junior clientele up to 21 years of age unless the operational provisions are sufficiently flexible to permit experienced persons to register in an adult service. Therefore, it may attempt to iron out some of the troublesome incongruities arising in connection with age and experience factors by organizing a junior service in two operational units, closely articulated but quite independent of one another as to clientele, location, and administrative control.

One unit, reverting to the program of the early vocational guidance bureaus, would counsel and place youth whose employment is conditioned by certain types of legislation; it would be located in a school building and would operate under educational auspices. The other unit would register clients from 18 to 21 years of age, would operate in connection with, and under the same auspices as, other public employment services. If there was no local adult service, provision for a suitable location and for a policy-making board would conform to the principles laid down in Part Two.

Such a recommendation, if adopted, would put great additional responsibilities upon, as well as have far-reaching implications for, education. It would force it to determine degrees of employability for its charges, to analyze those who are occupationally as well as those who are intellectually standard, superstandard, and substandard, and to differentiate between those who are totally and partially employable. Analyses of all types of applicants, their readiness for employment, and their referral to, and supervision in, employment until they were transferred to the second unit, or to the adult service, would become functions of the public schools. Were such a project to be carried out, the community would be perfectly justified in giving an affirmative reply to the question, Is "junior" or "inexperienced" a sufficiently distinctive variant to warrant a special service for persons under 18 years of age?

Is it a sufficiently distinctive variant to warrant a special service for persons 18 to 21 or 25 years of age? That is an entirely different matter. The committee may decide that it is the function of an adult service to provide for this majority group and to see that a qualified counselor is available for consultation with any who desire to take advantage of such services. There is much statistical and experience support for such a decision.

The writer, as she reviews the progress of junior personnel services since, in 1918, she recommended that the Junior Division of the United States Employment Service fix its upper age limit at 21 years and give its registrants all the benefits of an educational and occupational counseling service under educational auspices, is forced to admit that it has turned out to be a questionable recommendation. She now believes that a local committee, if it takes into consideration all the facts which have been revealed during the last twenty-five years, will proceed very cautiously in stretching the objective of a junior service to cover the placement of persons up to 21 or 25 years of age.

Local junior division services, which collaborated with the Junior Division of the United States Employment Service immediately after World War I, usually organized on the two-unit basis, but both were operated under educational auspices. The minority unit was housed in a school building where it was in close touch with the school census and certification offices and any counseling program which might be offered by the schools. This arrangement did not materially enhance the effectiveness of the school counseling service nor has its continuance, even in 1945, resulted in winning the confidence of those whom it has attempted to place. On the other hand, the majority of school placement bureaus have shown utter incapacity to hold the patronage of either graduates or dropouts.

The service for the majority group was frequently housed in the downtown section and was generally more successful than was the service for the younger group, although sometimes both units were entitled to be considered successful. When the second group was effectively conducted, it was usually due to the fact that the educator manager was well versed in the ways of the occupational world. When it was not successful, the cause, or the causes, were sometimes inherent in conditions which were beyond the control of the educational authorities. Some of these inherent difficulties have been eliminated, and others can be if a local committee desires to advocate the inclusion of persons under 21 years of age in a junior service. But no matter whether the 18- to 25-year group is registered as juniors or as adults, the services offered should be more than mere registration and referral in their narrowest sense.

After it has been determined who shall be considered juniors and whether the service shall operate as two units or as one; after the committee has decided to what extent the placement function shall include counseling and to what extent the interview technique shall be supplemented by other tools and techniques, such as occupational information, records, tests, personal ratings, and teachers' and employers' comments; and after the location, or locations, have been chosen, the way is open to consider the administrative auspices under which the internal organization should be perfected and the type of operational personnel which is best qualified to carry out the policies of the committee and to realize on the objectives which have been set up.

Administrative Control. The distinction between an administrative board and an advisory board has been made clear in Part Two. The essentiality of the former and the questionable value of the latter has also been discussed and requires no further comment except to repeat that a junior service, insofar as it is administered as a part of federal or state services, is required to appoint an advisory board. If the service is administered as a part of the educational system, this regulation does not apply. If the service is operated as two units, the one under public-school auspices does not require an advisory board, whereas the one under federal or state employment auspices usually does.

The writer is not partial to advisory boards; some authorities are very partial to them. Her point of view, when she was director of the Junior Division of the United States Employment Service, was that, if a junior service was under the administrative authority of the public schools, the board of education automatically became the advisory board. Since it was usually an elected board, it was more representative than any appointed board. There was some controversy in Washington over the matter, but the final decision accepted her viewpoint and no junior divisions were instituted during her incumbency which had local advisory boards.

If the service has grown up under educational auspices, the question of an advisory board may never arise. But if it is the result of community interest represented by a committee, there may be some factions who would be quite unhappy were they to be denied a voice on an advisory board. Each community will have to weigh its own pros and cons.

The selection of a policy-making board is quite a different matter. No agency can operate effectively unless its policies are established with definite objectives in view, are clearly defined, and thoroughly understood by all who are to participate in their execution. The duties of the board will be quasi-professional and the fact that a member represents this, that, or the other will be of little weight. His most important qualifications for board membership should be his ability to grasp educational, occupational, and economic situations and their interrelation, to see when and where, as between units and agencies, co-ordination and articulation are needed to select executives capable of carrying out board policies and perfecting a satisfactory internal organization, and to evaluate results in broad outlines.

Selection of the Operating Personnel. Whatever concept the committee, or the policy-making board, may have regarding the qualifications of junior-service personnel, the formulation of its concept will serve both as a guide to the selection of suitable functionaries and as an expression of its philosophy of occupational placement in its relation to current philosophies of education.

Considerable attention has been given to this topic in Chapters IV and X, and *Guidance and Personnel Services,* pages 403–434, has covered the subject of selecting directors and other functionaries for educational personnel services in some detail. Therefore the reader is referred to these citations, and discussion at this point is limited to the major respects in which the functions of a junior-service director differ from those of an educational-personnel director and from those of an adult-employment-service director. These differences should be given consideration in the selection of operating personnel.

The duties of a junior director will fall about equally into two different but closely related fields—the educational and the occupational. Those of an educational director will lie primarily in the educational field, and those of an adult-service director primarily in the occupational field. The junior director will deal intimately and continually with four types of clients whose confidence he must win and hold—pupils, applicants, educators, and employers—whereas the contacts of the directors of the other two services will be mainly with either pupils and educators, or with applicants and employers. The junior director must understand his own functions in their relation to both school administration and employment management, whereas the directors of the other services are concerned chiefly with relationships to either school administration or to employing concerns.

The ability, skill, general and special knowledge, social culture, and experiences of a junior director should be commensurate with those of the persons with whom he must co-operate in both fields and whose activities he must co-ordinate. His organizing, executive, and public-relations abilities should be such that he can be of material assistance in selling the public schools to the community and the product of the schools to employing concerns. He must be able to collect, or direct the collection of, reliable occupational information and information regarding the occupational success of the institution's product, and to share it with both educators and placement officials.

Insofar as his assignment covers the under-18-year group, he will have an opportunity to make the transition period from school to work one of the most fruitful educational assets of youth's entire pre-employment career. If he deals only with the 18- to 21-year group, he will meet each new occupational recruit at the close of his formal educational career and will have an unexcelled opportunity to pool at its source and to distribute the entire oncoming labor supply. He will be able to counsel with each youth at the bottom of the occupational ladder and be able to respond to calls for assistance as each works his way upward. Should the junior director be given jurisdiction over both groups, he will need the patience of Job and the wisdom of Solomon in addition to any qualifications which anyone can enumerate. "Aim high" is a good slogan for those who are charged with the appointment of junior placement directors. The necessary salary will be public money well spent.

INTERNAL ORGANIZATION AND ADMINISTRATION

This topic, too, has been given so much attention in Chapters V and X and in the previous publication, pages 371–453, that, at first sight, it seems superfluous to offer any supplementary comments. However, a review of the problems involved in the operation of a junior employment service, in comparison with those common to either of the allied types of services which have been elaborated, reveals several which are peculiar to junior services, or which are of sufficient importance to warrant the emphasis of repetition. Among them are Centralized Control and Decentralized Execution, Location and Layout, and Publicity.

Centralized Control and Decentralized Execution. Pleas for the acceptance and utilization of the principle of centralized control and decentralized execution in connection with educational services were made, and are on record, from the very beginning of the guidance movement, and the principle has long been endorsed by public employment officials. Nowhere is its practical application of greater importance than in a junior employment service which covers the entire age range under consideration, with its activities reaching back into the educational system and forward into the occupational world. For, although a junior service is but one unit of a complete employment service, it occupies a strategic position midway between the educational system and the economic system and acts as a transfer agency from the one to the other. Its success depends upon its ability to co-operate with all the related units which precede and follow it and to co-ordinate the activities of all the units which lie within its own domain. In the final analysis its efficiency will be judged by the effectiveness of the total and broader services of which it is a part—educational or production, and placement or distribution.

It is peculiarly difficult to introduce the principle of centralized control

—even though decentralized execution be stressed—into a junior employment service, or into a unit of such a service, if it operates under the auspices of an educational institution. This fact and its causal factors have been noted by many writers and have been exhaustively dealt with in *Guidance and Personnel Services*. It has come about quite naturally and is due to three major causes: (1) the independence rather than the interdependence of the various operational units which constitute a school system or a university, (2) the lack of understanding on the part of educational administration of the value of a product-distributing agency in connection with a product-producing agency, and (3) the dearth of individuals who are qualified to direct the inauguration and development of a centralized placement service.

There are very obvious, and perhaps insurmountable, difficulties in any scheme of internal organization and administration which attempts to unify all the placement activities of an educational institution under centralized control, and there are equally obvious, and equally insurmountable, difficulties in attempting to operate a placement service without so doing. The situation today is chaotic, and it has been so for years. Educational administration seems to be either totally incompetent, or unwilling, to improve the situation.[26]

It would be impossible to enumerate all the unscientific, blundering, disintegrating placement performances which are carried on in a haphazard fashion under educational auspices. A few illustrations will be indicative of needed changes.

(1) In institution A each segmented administrative unit, each department, and each instructor who wishes places students. There is not the slightest effort to "clear" placements or to pool information regarding the employability of applicants.

(2) In system B six high schools allow any teacher who wishes to do so to solicit orders here and there for his own pupils utterly oblivious of the fact that duplicate solicitations annoy employers and discredit the operational efficiency of the public schools. Competition among schools, and even among teachers in the same school, results.

(3) In special-room C the teacher, who had become righteously in-

---

[26] This, of course, is not a universally applicable statement. There are many superintendents of schools and presidents of universities who, in every sense of the term, qualify as such. But there are many others who find a niche in Dr. Cubberley's portrait gallery of superintendents who have little or no idea what personnel work is all about—the mail-opening superintendent, the joiner, the publicity man, the man who sees only buildings, budgets, and reports, the superintendent who does everything himself, the board's errand boy, and the like. Junior placement directors have to fit into the administrative setups of all sorts of superintendents and presidents.

dignant at the legal enactments which force overage, overgrown, under-mentalitied, underinterested pupils to comply with school residence requirements which act as incentives to delinquencies, took matters into her own hands. She found suitable work for three of her charges in the school neighborhood and carried them on the daily register of the school while they were holding regular jobs. This teacher had no idea that she was encouraging dangerous law violations. She was salvaging the by-product of social legislation.

(4) In system D teacher-counselors from each of nine high schools drew up an agreement whereby they would divide employer visits among them. Each would blacklist concerns which they deemed unsuitable places for young workers, and the lists would be exchanged so that unworthy em-ployers who were denied workers from one school could not shop about until they secured employees. Not one of these teacher-counselors knew the legal significance of blacklisting, or whether there were antiblacklist-ing statutes in their state. The blacklist was written on the official letter-head of the board of education and signed by the teacher-counselor.

(5) In school system E a similar practice was in use with reference to furnishing high school and college girls as domestic helpers. In this in-stance the housewife was scrutinized, her housekeeping abilities noted, and the reputation of any male member of the family "investigated." Again, the blacklist was on the official stationery of the college and high school, and the reasons for ineligibility comprised such comments as "a dirty housekeeper," "morals of husband," "too closefisted," "regular old screw."

(6) University G, department X, decreased its registration by a practice which it had hoped would increase its enrollment. It refused to give a rec-ommendation to the central placement office for any applicant who had only a master's degree, provided one with a doctor's degree wanted a simi-lar position, or to give a recommendation to a B.A. when an M.A. was available. Registration declined, and the central placement bureau lost that particular type of clientele to commercial placement services.

(7) School H does not consider placement an educational responsibility. No one in the school is interested, and its sole "counseling" effort may be summed up in the frequently repeated admonition, "Stay in school; edu-cation pays."

(8) School K and college Y are sufficiently interested to permit a clerk to receive a telephone order and to post it on the bulletin board à la the early hostel and post-office notices.

(9) When decentralized placements are in vogue, teachers and depart-

ments, in large numbers of educational institutions, pick off and "place" the cream of their finished product, relegating to the central placement service the less desirable product and the entire by-product. No central service which is stripped of first-quality registrants can attract employing concerns which have positions for superior employees; therefore this custom denies the placement service the opportunity to secure, for second-rate applicants, the second-rate opportunities which are always available in first-class firms. Moreover, when it is practiced by academic teachers, it ignores the fact recorded in every youth survey from the earliest to the most recent—that teachers are unreliable judges of potential occupational efficiency and that in the world of affairs "school dull" often proves to be "life bright."

(10) It is logical to assume that vocational schools and colleges can make better selections for referral than can a central placement service. But what do the records show relative to the placement efficiency of these segregated units? Effective placement, on a national basis, requires that the total number of employable persons who wish to work be distributed to the best advantage in productive occupations. The same criterion obtains with respect to placement services operated under states and municipalities, and it also applies to educational institutions which purport to conduct placement services. But the surveys are unanimous in their revelation that only a small percentage of the graduates of such schools, and an even smaller percentage of the dropouts, have ever been placed by vocational schools.

Cases and comments, similar to those cited, were common years ago and are common today. Their occurrence in some institutions has cast unfavorable reflections on all forms of educational personnel services and will continue to do so until the administrative authorities are alive to the situation.

There are four conditions under which the principle of centralized control and decentralized execution may be applied to the organization and administration of a junior placement service.

(1) When it serves the under-18-year group and is operated under educational auspices, or when it serves a college group. The appointment of a single director of all institutional personnel services including placement would, were he qualified for such a position and were he allowed to delegate the performance of the various functions to appropriate subdivisions and to co-ordinate the activities of all, be a long step in the direction of progress.

(2) When it serves all youth under 21 and is operated by an educational

system. This situation, when it occurs, is usually nominal since, except in college services, youth over 18 years will register in the adult services or in commercial agencies.

(3) When youth under 18 are placed under educational auspices and those between 18 and 21 or 25 under public employment auspices. This situation poses many problems. Who shall be the director? No comment is necessary. Currently the gap between educational personnel and employment service personnel is "long and deep and wide." It is questionable whether educators would accept a director from the "outside world," while it is equally questionable if experienced employment interviewers would have much confidence in an educator director.

(4) When all youth under 21 are placed by state employment services. In this case the director would be an employment man with an educational viewpoint, and leadership in articulating the counseling activities of the schools with the placement activities of the employment services would be his responsibility.

No matter which of the four situations prevails, there is no one best source from which to secure a director and no one best way to distribute personnel functions. Too much depends upon the agencies involved, the attitude of their administrative authorities, and the facilities available for the breakdown of the service. But, in general, any junior placement service, whether it registers youth of one age or another and whether it operates under one auspice or another, should be expected to assume responsibility for certain functions: (1) pooling and distributing the entire junior labor supply of the community, (2) collecting and distributing occupational information and reports on the success which has attended the educational product, (3) forecasting changes in occupational opportunities and operational methods and anticipating legislation which might affect educational programs and placement prospects, and (4) suggesting to junior workers such educational opportunities as promise to enhance their occupational values.

Location and Layout. The custom of locating the placement unit for youth under 16 or 18 years of age in an easily accessible school building— board of education, central high school, vocational school, opportunity school, or continuation school—has been mentioned. This may be a very desirable arrangement. If so, just as careful attention should be given to the location within the building of the one unit as of the other.

Upper floors, basements, and attics in school buildings are, in some cases, taboo, and school authorities which have attempted to use them usually regret it. The best location is on the main floor opening out of a general reception room in charge of a clerk and shared with callers on the principal, school attendance officers, or other persons. A few of the new buildings have been so arranged and are proving very satisfactory.[27] Since placement offices should be open during school vacations, Saturdays, and until 5 P.M. on school days, there will always be sufficient protection against gossip if the clerk's or principal's doors open into the same reception room and all doors stand open whenever good judgment so suggests.

For the unit, or units, of the service which are located in the downtown district, the best location will probably be in connection with the adult service. Some layouts place the junior service between the men's and women's divisions so that it may use the files of both, and both may use its files. This plan makes substitute referrals easy. Sometimes the different divisions of the service are grouped around a central reception room, and but one set of files is used for all applicants and orders. Such a layout is especially desirable if the line between junior and adult is flexible enough to permit the receptionist to determine whether the experience of the junior warrants assignment to the adult division, or the inexperience of the adult entitles him, or her, to the benefit of the junior counseling service.

If the younger group, which during vacation periods sometimes includes boys as young as 14 or 15 years, registers in the downtown office, the reception room facilities become of great importance. Not long ago a group of young boys was found in a dark hall where, without any supervision, they were engaged in all sorts of disorderly conduct. In another office an amiable, fatherly man, somewhat past the age to deal with obstreperous youngsters, confided to this writer, "Those little fellers ought to be where somebody understands them better than we do. I can't do a thing with them. I have to call in the police almost every day." No matter where the junior service is located, all of its implications should be educational.

Publicity. Those who are responsible for junior employment publicity will need to be just as well, if not better, informed as to what constitutes desirable and obtainable publicity as will the publicity directors of any other employment service. The character, timing, and number of news releases are very important. Those who seek free newspaper publicity should remember that newspapers maintain both a news section and an advertising section. Since it is the function of the news section to print news, free space in that section should not be sought unless the copy is of

[27] Sometimes executive offices are located on the second floor and the same arrangement is possible.

such a character that it has news value, or is tied to some event of current interest, and is prepared in news form with no semblance of advertising or of personal publicity. Stories and pictures, fresh and hot, if they can be given to the public without offense, make good news material, but facts and good taste should never be violated. Rules for preparing news releases may be secured from several sources and if followed may be helpful in securing free space.

Radio quizzes, dramatizations, debates, and interviews create interest and, if properly prepared, have educative and informative values. But they reach large audiences, and destructive as well as constructive programs are to be heard over the air. Since citations which warn against undesirable practices are usually more effective than are those which commend desirable ones, a single illustration is given:

A junior service had been given free radio time in order to publicize the newly organized counseling and placement service. An interview was being held with a girl, who was currently employed as a "marker" in a department store. She had called to secure advice as to her promotional prospects were she to learn typing and office-machine operating. Quite spontaneously and with no apparent realization of the gratuitous slap in the face which, through her instrumentality, the placement service was administering to every office-machine operator and manufacturer who was listening to the station, the interviewer exclaimed; "Pound a typewriter all your life! What are you thinking of?"

Bulletins and sales letters to employers and potential applicants are always in order provided they are not too frequent, make no promises upon which the service cannot make good, and avoid causing a desire to change positions. Some junior employment services have had a flair for the right type of publicity. South Bend, Indiana, Pittsburgh, Pennsylvania, and Minneapolis, Minnesota, are among those which have issued very effective publicity over a considerable period of time.

JUNIOR PLACEMENT PROCEDURES [28]

Interviewing youth during the various procedures involved in the placement process is usually regarded as a special task requiring special qualifications, some special knowledges, and a somewhat different approach than interviewing adults. This is entirely logical since, although all qualified placement workers are prepared to offer some counseling in connec-

[28] Reed, *Guidance and Personnel Services*, pp. 311–327, discusses the various types of interviews involved in placement procedures under college and secondary-school auspices. The applicant's interview with the employer is included. A section on "Guidance Services for Beginning Wage-Earners" is found on pp. 331–340. Since the approach is somewhat different from that in this book, junior interviewers may find it profitable to read both presentations.

tion with placement interviewing, counseling is an indispensable element in the majority of junior interviews. The educative element is always in the foreground of the consciousness of the interviewer.

His knowledge of the educational world, of educational practices, and of educational opportunities for wage-earning youth must be broad and accurate enough to permit him to serve as an articulator between the school world and the occupational world. His knowledge of the work world must be such that he recognizes the obligations of the employer to youth and vice versa. If his experiences have been mainly in occupational life, he must avoid an interview approach which casts reflections on educational experiences or undervalues the continuous contribution which education can make to occupational adjustment and progress. On the other hand, he must avoid the very common error which is made by some junior counselors of responding to a request for assistance in securing employment by harping on the variations of the slogan, "Stay in school; education pays."

Young persons go to employment offices to get jobs, not to be advised to go back to school,[29] and if they get this sort of counsel they not only will not go back to school, but they will never go back to the employment office. Just as the schools have lost their chance to make school worth while educationally, so the placement service will lose its chance to make the placement service worth while occupationally.

Special Tools for Junior Interviewers. In addition to the tools mentioned in Chapter VI as essential for the use of a general placement office, there are certain other tools which are important, or more important, for junior services. Three are given consideration: school records, occupational information, and the registration card. The value of *school records* as tools in the successful conduct of job placement procedures has long been recognized by public employment officers who report many instances in which service to youth has been seriously handicapped by the lack of information upon which potentialities could be estimated and more profitable referrals be made. Recently the schools have acquired a new interest in record making and record keeping, and the future looks more promising. Three major happenings have acted as spurs to this increase of interest:

(1) The activities of the Education Records Bureau and its affiliated agencies have stressed the importance of educational measurements and

---

[29] King O. Bolton, *Employment and Welfare of Juveniles* (London, 1925). The top classes of some London elementary schools were questioned regarding further education: "About 70% had no further use for school at all."

personality appraisals as a means of guiding developmental growth, and of the periodic recording of individual achievements on a cumulative record as a means of determining to what extent and in what direction growth was taking place.

(2) The economic predicament of youth during the 1930's which led to a revival of interest in "Youth Tell Their Story" surveys and resulted in a broader understanding of youth's upstream struggle against the stupidity of the educational world and the vicissitudes of the occupational world.

(3) The short-lived co-operation between the United States Office of Education, the War Manpower Commission, the War Department, and other governmental agencies in the development and use of the Educational Experience Summary Record, 5,000,000 copies of which were distributed to the schools.[30] Each student at school leaving was supposed to receive a copy, and, since the items were pertinent to occupational as well as to military life, the procedure has established a precedent which should make for closer co-operation between the schools and the occupational life. The use of this particular card was soon discontinued by the Army, but further experimentation may be helpful to the progress of school placement services.[31]

Some special forms of *educational and occupational information* are desirable in junior offices. Since entry occupations will furnish many junior opportunities, Part IV of the *Dictionary of Occupational Titles,* which covers classifications for persons who are not experienced workers in any one job, should be available. Two publications of the War Manpower Commission [32] are valuable tools for helping young veterans to translate their service experiences into civilian jobs, and for assisting counselors and placement officials to determine the qualifications of the veteran for a civilian position in work similar to that which he has done while in the service. *The Manning Tables,* also prepared by the War Manpower Commission, are helpful in showing the relation between wartime and peacetime jobs and skills. All such informational data should be used in connection with the findings of local opportunity surveys.

Educational counseling, especially for young veterans, may be sought in connection with an employment service interview. Therefore, abundant

[30] See *Education for Victory* (U.S. Office of Education, vol. I, May, 1943).

[31] The Science Talent Search, going forward under Science Service, 1719 N St., N.W., Washington, D.C., also requires careful school records. For complete information, see *Science News Letter*, XLII, no. 4 (1942), and Harold A. Edgerton and Stewart Henderson Britt, "The Science Talent Search," *Occupations*, XXII (Dec., 1943), 177–180.

[32] *Special Aids for Placing Military Personnel (Enlisted Army Personnel) in Civilian Jobs* (Washington, D.C., 1944) and *Special Aids for Placing Navy Personnel in Civilian Jobs* (Washington, D.C., 1943).

information on all sorts of educational opportunities should be at hand, and counselors should be prepared to discuss long- and short-term programs, either in connection with immediate employment or in anticipation of some later position. Charts, showing entry positions with vertical and horizontal lines of promotion and indicating the necessary preparation to attain each step, are additional helps. Under the auspices of the American Council on Education, progress is being made in the translation of military training into educational terms and college credit,[33] while the tests given under the Armed Forces Institute are making a contribution along the same lines; and, supplemented by the individual record and evidence of achievement in related academic fields, they furnish the registration interviewer with basic counseling material.

If handicapped juniors, including veterans, are registered in junior placement services, all of the recent material on educational and occupational opportunities for such persons should be considered as essential tools for registration interviewers.

The *form and content of the registration card* for juniors may differ from that used in the adult service, either for all applicants or only for the inexperienced; but the purpose will always be the same—to secure a presently prevailing picture of a potential employee. Junior registration forms, as well as those prepared for the use of adult services,[34] will contain items which have recently been challenged as inviting unfair discrimination in the choice of candidates for referral without having any relation to success on the job, and there will be the same difficulty in determining whether such items are necessary in order to make satisfactory referrals, or whether they are to be used for unfair discriminations.

Recently, because of the demand that every employable person be utilized in war industries, attention has been called to the universal custom among employing concerns and placement officers of including in their job specifications and registration forms, respectively, certain items which indicate preference for, or status of the applicant as to, race, creed, color, age, or nationality. In a moment of enthusiasm for wiping out all individual differences in these respects, the citizens of a number of states have turned to that ever-present American remedy for all social ills—legislation.

Two or three states have already placed enactments on their statute

<hr/>

[33] American Council on Education, *Sound Educational Credit for Military Experience* (Washington, D.C., 1943), and Ralph W. Tyler, "Sound Credit for Military Experience," *Annals of the American Academy of Political and Social Science,* CCXXXI (Jan., 1944), 58–64.

[34] See Chapter VI.

books which prohibit the inclusion of certain items either on employment agency registration forms, or on employers' requisitions. For the
most part the items are race, creed, color, and national origin, but, to
complicate the matter further, one state is now considering adding "persons of advanced age."

The Ives-Quinn Antidiscrimination Law in New York State, effective
July 1, 1945, was the pioneer and has, therefore, attracted national attention. This writer would not attempt to interpret the provisions of this
bill, nor to prophesy how many snags will be encountered in its enactment, but legislation seems to her to be a questionable method of reaching
the problems which it is designed to solve. That there are problems no
one who has had any experience in placement work would think of denying, but the destructive results of such legislation loom large. When is
referral on the basis of any one of the items cited "unfair"? When is discrimination "based upon a bona fide occupational qualification"? How
shall it be determined whether or not such an item is the cause of refusal
to employ?

When the provisions of this bill are considered in connection with the
rules and practices of educational systems regarding personal data on their
registration blanks, it looks very much like another case of the left-hand
of the legislature not knowing what the right-hand is doing. What is the
result of this lame sort of teamwork?

A boy enters the public school at six years of age. Personal data, including pedigree, include all the objectionable items, and are recorded. School
census data, decreed by state and federal departments of education, and
school items which we are straining every nerve to make ever more complete and more accurate, once on a pupil's record, go with him clear
through college and are easily transferred to his occupational record. If
perchance he aspires to one of the many scholarships available through
the generosity of institutions or individuals, he not infrequently finds
himself discriminated *against* because of race, creed, color, or national
origin, while because of these same items another boy is discriminated *for*.
Take, for example, the Barbour Scholarships for Oriental Women at the
University of Michigan or the University of Pennsylvania scholarships
open only to sons of Pennsylvania Railroad employees, or the Rosenwald
scholarships open for Negroes—what fine chances for "unfair" discrimination! [35]

[35] It might be profitable to check through the entire list of scholarships and fellowships
listed in Ella B. Ratcliffe, *Scholarships and Fellowships Available at Institutions of Higher
Education* (U.S. Office of Education, Bull. no. 10, 1936) and note how many of them are
available on the basis of discriminatory items.

Turning to another aspect of the problem, observe how, over many years, Dartmouth College has kept its student personnel cosmopolitan by the use of quotas from the various sections of the country and from various groups. Other colleges have engaged in the same practices, and we have applauded them for making genuine contributions to the effectiveness of the "melting pot." And how about the quotas at the various International Houses?

Of course when one is discriminated against one is sorry. This writer was very sorry recently when a young college man of marked ability lost a coveted scholarship because, when he came to fill out the application blank, he found that the donor had limited recipients to youth whose parents were born in the United States. His were born in Canada.

Tacit admission that education needs this sort of information in order to perform its functions effectively, while placement services do not, reveals gross ignorance of the educational objectives of placement services and the educational implications of every step in the placement process.

Coding of items on placement and employers' registration forms is also taboo, the assumption being that the purpose must be sinister. In a previous chapter this writer has indicated that she practiced it to good advantage in her own office and secured much useful counseling material for herself and for the public-school teachers from employing concerns who practiced it. For example:

Having learned that it was a fairly common custom for employing concerns to code the reasons for refusal to employ applicants, she sought to ascertain what educative values these various coding systems might reveal. At her request, she was given access to all junior application blanks and was permitted to take as many as she wished to her own office for study. The items were decoded and reasons for refusal to employ were classified into a few categories. Those which dealt with educational deficiencies ranked first, those which were concerned with personality deficiencies including ordinary good manners came second, while carelessness, inability to follow instructions, and other undesirable habits ranked third.[36] This furnished excellent guidance material for school use, focused the attention of the Superintendent of Schools on educational needs, and helped the placement office to check on the assets and liabilities of referrals.

The Registration, Classification, and Referral. In some junior offices the purposes of both the registration and the referral interview will be accomplished by a single interviewer and in a single interview; in others,

[36] Group study of employers' application blanks is a good method of vocational guidance.

the registration interviewer will secure the information, make the occupational classification, and then file the card, or send the applicant to another interviewer who makes the referral. Since previous chapters have considered the registration and referral interviews separately and in some detail, it seems sufficient, in this section, to treat them as a unit with emphasis on the special problems involved and on the final outcome.

The age, ability, interests, aptitudes, and experiences of applicants who visit junior services will vary greatly. It is to be hoped that some arrangement will always be made which will give each group—the experienced, the inexperienced, and the school-attendance applicants—the type of special personnel best qualified to understand its problems and to make discriminatory referrals. For, no matter how many or how good the tools available for the interview may be, the ability to use them with discretion and skill, to determine when and what additional tools are needed to adapt techniques to individuals, to observe the personal qualities, and to infer the intangibles which contribute so much to accurate pictures of junior applicants is an indispensable qualification of the one who conducts the interview.

As the interview proceeds and the gaps in the picture are being filled in, the interviewer will need to keep in mind the many types of youth problems and the conditions to which they are due, to assume some counseling responsibilities which legitimately belong to the educational system, and to anticipate the possible outcomes of any number of decisions. Outstanding among the points to be remembered are:

(1) That the applicant is not a child and may not be treated as such. He is about to become a productive member of society, even though because of his inexperience and immaturity he may be deserving of special attention.

(2) That the placement interview is probably giving the applicant his first opportunity to subject the school theories and practices of guidance to the acid test of practicality.

(3) That both the immediate needs and the future welfare of the applicant require consideration and neither should be overlooked. Youth needs help to recognize the value of constructive planning and to make an intelligent effort in that direction.

(4) That many of the observable personality traits which have been mentioned with reference to adults are in their incipient stages in youth. Usually youth can more easily acquire desirable assets or eradicate the undesirable. But if desirable changes are impossible, the earlier in life occupations are chosen in which deficiencies are minor liabilities the better.

The interviewer will realize that choice of occupation is fundamentally an educational rather than a placement responsibility, but he will also realize that sometimes a placement interviewer can drive home more effectively the occupational significance of school achievement, attitudes, and behavior than can a teacher. Frequently, too, the placement office secures more and different information than do teachers. One explanation is that the placement interview is conducted at the moment of need rather than in anticipation of some future and quite uninteresting possibility.

(5) That there are many incidental opportunities, which must be taken advantage of without "preaching," to focus the attention of the applicant on the importance of personal appearance and of ability to take job responsibility, to be prompt and self-reliant, and to avoid drifting from job to job. Many youth who have been accustomed to automatic annual or semiannual school promotions have no knowledge of how promotions in occupational life are handled.

(6) That the placement office is the great detective agency for "life-bright" youth who present themselves labeled "school-dull," and for the discovery that many a youth whose school record pronounces him "uneducated" does in reality possess a very useful imitation of an education.

(7) That interest and ability are not synonymous but that it is possible to create interest which is in harmony with ability.

(8) That clothing and grooming are capital assets. Once lost they are hard to replace, and as age increases their loss tends to translate unemployed into unemployable. John, 18 years of age, knew this. During the depression he lost place after place, and his personal appearance became a definite liability. As he pled with the interviewer for help, he said, "If you only could have seen me before I got so ragged! I could have had a job several times lately if I'd only had a front." The sterling worth of this boy was so obvious that it was not too difficult to provide both the "front" and the job.

(9) That aggressiveness has been a characteristic of the wartime situation; that "killing" has been a major occupation and many youth have been trained for no other.

(10) That some young veterans are going to present serious discipline problems in occupational pursuits. Reports of such instances are already being heard, and in preparing for veterans' readjustment allowance must be made for the fact that they have experienced two periods of regimentation with no breathing spell between—in school and in the service. On the other hand, accuracy and neatness have been required, and the soldier

is never allowed to forget that war is a serious business—something which youth is rarely allowed to learn relative to education.

(11) That many part-time youth, who have lacked suitable employment supervision, have formed undesirable work habits and must adjust to entirely different work situations in peacetime occupations.

(12) That it is going to be very difficult to find openings for young women which, after their war experiences, will be satisfactory to them.

After the data on each junior have been collected and interpreted, the occupational classification is made. It is obvious that it must be tentative and without definite limitation, and again the classifier must keep certain points in mind as the work goes forward:

(1) That the types of applicants to be classified will range from the employable subnormal to the supernormal.

(2) That the occupational assets of inexperienced youth may not be appraised on the basis of past accomplishments. Therefore, the entry classification in which each is placed will depend upon the data contained in his school record plus the results of the registration interview. If there is no school record, the interviewer will have full responsibility for collecting the facts, making observations, and weaving both into the picture of an employee who is potentially successful in certain selected jobs.

(3) That, if the school record is available, test scores, rank in class, best and poorest subjects, school activities participated in, and dominant personality traits revealed in school situations are helpful in determining the range of the applicant's occupational possibilities and in suggesting definite job classifications.

(4) That although entry jobs are many and the average beginner will fit into one about as well as into another, the classification which results in a first job is of great importance and may determine the applicant's entire occupational career.

(5) That great discriminative ability is required to so classify the lower- and upper-level potentials that at maturity the former may not suffer the terrible disappointment and mortification which accompanies demotion from popular and promising entry occupations to the status of common labor, or that the latter may not be sidetracked in occupations, or in positions, which afford few promotional opportunities.[37]

When placement procedures have reached the referral stage, if employ-

---

[37] If teachers who are accustomed to grouping pupils in standardized categories make occupational classifications, they should be cautioned to remember that different jobs require different abilities and degrees of abilities, and that nature brews some queer, but often very desirable, mixtures of talents, deficiencies, desires, and abilities.

ers' orders are on file they may be canvassed immediately to see if a suitable opening is available, otherwise the applicant will be called in when he has been chosen to consider applying for a newly received order. Junior referrals will be selected by the same procedures as are adult referrals, but, as a rule, much more careful attention will be given to the choice of the concern to which each youth is to be referred, although the interests of the employer will be weighed side by side with those of the applicant. In spite of all the criticisms on the occupational efficiency of the school product, employers usually consider the public schools as the best source from which to recruit young workers. Frequently their job orders contain "your best boy" as the sole or major item of the job specification. But the placement interviewer knows that there is no such thing as the "best boy" in the abstract, and no such thing as a universally best job. It is his business to help each youth find *his* best job and each employer *his* most satisfactory employee.

In meeting these responsibilities, he studies and questions both the personal and job data which he has collected to guide him in arriving at decisions:

(1) Does this job order seek a youth who will be of immediate and temporary value, or does it seek one with developmental possibilities? The type of boy selected will depend upon the interpretation of the order.

(2) Does this order seek a youth who is qualified for, and headed toward, specialization, or is mediocrity in several related lines more desirable? This is an important point when school records are being studied for referral selections. In the light of the previously noted opinions of teachers regarding the "unreadiness" of the school product for occupational life, it is well to remember that mediocrity in several lines often makes a stronger sales appeal to a small business concern than does efficiency in a single line. Both employers and teachers sometimes need help to understand this, but the placement worker knows that it is a fact:

Mary was the daughter of a stolid, slow-moving, slow-thinking, honest, and faithful city employee. She registered in the stenographic course in high school. The teachers at once recognized her limitations and day after day pestered her with suggestions that she change to the home-economics course. The placement counselor called attention to the never-completely-met need for general office help, and Mary was willing to change to that course. She graduated at the bottom of her class and was its first member, in a depression year, to secure a position. Moreover, she had her choice of three openings all in small businesses where her willingness to dust the office, answer the telephone, send out bills, write a letter, wrap and mail packages was more important than was superior stenographic service.

And this incident calls to mind another:

A fine and very scholarly man was principal of a secondary school. An irate teacher of unusual ability resented the mediocrity of two or three girls who had been assigned to her classes. She pled with the principal to drop them as "morons." The principal replied, "There are a great many places in our American life where these dear little morons have a real contribution to make. It is our business to find out what that contribution is and then see that they are prepared to make it. Oftentimes this type of pupil is more credit to our educational efforts than is the brilliant mind."

(3) Is the mental and moral atmosphere of the concern, and the character of the associates with whom the applicant will be thrown such that he will be benefited by accepting the position? If these elements are open to challenge, are his habits and principles well enough established so that undesirable influences will not adversely affect him?

(4) If there is a clash in educational and occupational standards, how well prepared is this youth to deal with them?

Sarah was almost seventeen when she went to work in a beauty shop. When she appeared for her first continuation-school work she had been manicured, lipsticked, waved, and otherwise "processed" as good advertising for her employer. The teacher gave one horrified look. "Go to the lavatory at once and wash all that stuff off," she ordered. "Why, I can't," Sarah replied, "it costs money to put it on and it's part of my job." But she had to wash it off. Her employer was disgusted, and Sarah never asked the school to counsel her on any future problems.

(5) Will the teachers be satisfied with the selections for referral? No, frequently not. There are many reasons. Teachers are very close to their pupils. Daily contact with their vices and virtues often leads to biased judgments relative to their employability. Moreover their comparisons are between, or among, youth, whereas the placement office must look upon applicants as more or less in competition with adults.

When the applicant responds to the call-in card, the job requirements will be explained in detail and his willingness and ability to meet them will be determined. Other topics taken up in the referral interview will depend somewhat upon the type of preparation for occupational induction which has been afforded by the educational system. There are many possible topics which may profitably be discussed have they not already received sufficient attention: how to approach the employer, how the school atmosphere differs from that of the work world, how to select associates under the new conditions, how to get along with foremen, supervisors, customers, or others, how to play one's part in securing promotion, when to change jobs, how to meet refusal of employment, or discharge, and the like.

A few suggestions for anticipating youth's difficulties in meeting initial occupational problems covered by such topics, and a few instances which reveal the need for preliminary assistance, are given:

(1) Job shifting has always been a characteristic of young workers. Placement bureaus [38] and employers have both made studies of the amount and causes, and, over a period of years, there is some evidence that bright boys changed jobs two or three times a year, while "dull" boys either held their jobs until they had outgrown them physically or changed every few weeks with long periods of unemployment between. How long should a junior stay on a job? That depends on the junior and on the job. There is no standard answer. Some placement interviewers attempt to make it a personal matter by asking all inexperienced workers, who are tempted to quit, to consult with them before so doing. This is a good practice:

James was employed by a hardware concern. A day or two after he had entered upon his duties, a supervisor came around, had a friendly chat with him, and when leaving remarked, "Keep right at it and we'll have a promotion for you." Three weeks passed. It seemed like an interminable time to James, who began to feel that the promised promotion was a myth. He was ready to quit, but, since he had promised to do so, he came back to the placement office to talk it over. When he left he was in a happier frame of mind and had a much better understanding of the length of time required for occupational promotions.

College graduates are sometimes more illogical about "quitting" than are high-school youth:

Miss C. was a college graduate. Her first position was in a one-man office where she took the place, at the same salary, of a woman who had held the position for several years. Her employer was so busy for the first two days that he told her to do the best she could until he had a chance to help her "get on to things." On the third afternoon he was ready to help, and it was 5:30 P.M. before they had completed their talks. Early the next morning Miss C. telephoned the placement office for an evening appointment. Her sole question was, "Shall I quit?" Why? "Because, you see, I am supposed to go home at five o'clock." It did not take long for her to realize that she was receiving the salary of a woman who needed no help to do her work, and that in reality she had kept her employer after hours rather than being kept by him. She admitted that she had a fine position with good pay, but she had heard that one must not "start an employer wrong" and she didn't know what to do about it.

[38] *Trade School Girls in Massachusetts* (U.S. Department of Labor, Bull. no. 215, 1917) reveals the "curious fact" that self-placed girls retained their jobs longer than did the school-placed.

Frank's "quit" problem involved entirely different factors:

He was fifteen years of age working during the summer vacation as a water boy on a construction job. Prohibition was still the law of the land, and he soon discovered that he was a "beer and whiskey" boy rather than a water boy. He was instructed where to go to get the liquor, how to avoid detection, and where to put it when he returned. Innocently, he asked about the law and was threatened with dismissal if he complained to higher-ups or made any comments to anyone on the subject. Frank, too, reported back before quitting. His reason was approved, and it was not difficult to find him a new place which his reason for quitting was an asset in securing.

(2) The importance of ethical business practices is often overlooked by inexperienced workers. Stealing an employer's time and his supplies is worthy of mention if the schools have not covered the subject.

(3) Sometimes very promising beginners receive hints from their employers regarding certain steps which are necessary for promotion. This is one way of testing the promotional caliber of new employees. Youth who do not respond to such suggestions frequently close their own door to promotions.

(4) Failure to report for duty after the acceptance of a position gives a beginning worker a bad start. Request that entry on duty be postponed while the applicant enjoys some social pleasure queers an employee before he has a chance to prove his worth:

Martin was a college graduate but his fraternity house party still appealed so strongly to him that two or three days after he had accepted a position in a bank, he returned to request the personnel department to permit him to delay beginning work so that he could attend a week-end party at his Alma Mater. He attended the party, but he did not become an employee of the bank.

(5) Sometimes it is difficult for beginners to realize that a referral is not a placement. Therefore, there are several situations in which, due to embarrassment or to the discovery that there are other applicants competing for the position, they do the wrong thing and forfeit their chance for employment. If employers, as they sometimes do, want to interview several applicants, the interviewer should explain to each applicant that there are other referrals being made, that but one will be employed, and that he must not be disappointed if he is not chosen. It is also sometimes helpful to inexperienced youth if suggestions are given as to how to meet situations in which additional abilities or skills, not listed in the job specification, are inquired about. Three beginners were referred to similar stenographic positions on the same day. Each, just at the point when she was feeling pretty sure of employment, was asked if she could operate a

calculating machine. None could. The first said, "Search me. I never tried"; the second with a wave of her hand exclaimed, "Oh, good night"; and the third replied, "No, Mr. B., I'm sorry, but I can learn at evening school if you will give me a little time." The third girl was employed.

(6) Before inexperienced applicants leave the placement office the interviewer should be sure that they understand, and know how to comply with, all the legal preliminaries to employment, including the securing of a social security number.

(7) And finally, a few words, which will indicate to youth that each job he holds and the way he fills it make a chapter in his permanent occupational record, may be an additional incentive to keep his record clean and to make only favorable entries.

One must not assume from the emphasis which has been put upon the responsibilities of youthful applicants that there are no special obligations upon those who employ them. Nor that it is legitimate to assume that every concern is an equally suitable place for youth's occupational baptism. Every placement worker knows that there are some employers who have no conception of what they have a right to expect of youth, or of the personal responsibility which they assume when they bring immature persons into their organization. And every seasoned placement worker knows who the exploiters of youth in his labor-market area are and how to deal with them without antagonizing or blacklisting them, and without placing a tax-supported agency in the position of refusing to accept orders from any concern which has received the endorsement of the state labor department.

This writer received some such orders when she was doing junior placement work. The better acquainted she became with high-grade employers and the more nearly she came to pooling the entire junior supply and demand, the easier it was to deal with the lower type of employer without giving offence. Their orders were always accepted, but never filled. After two or three courteous notifications that no applicants were available for referral to their positions, it became clear to them that they were not going to receive referrals. Since the service approached a monopoly of the junior labor supply, it also became clear that they were not going to secure desirable juniors from any source. The usual result was a call at the office "to talk over the stuation," a frank admission of their undesirable features, proposals of changes, and invitation to visit and make suggestions, and sometimes an invitation to sit in on staff meetings. In due course of time referrals were made, and employment almost invariably proved to be satisfactory.

But the great majority of concerns which employ youth are well aware of the types of problems which come to work with them and are augmented by the new problems incident to occupational adjustment. And they are quick to recognize the potentialities of youth who not only meet their job specifications but are clever enough to supplement them gratuitously with "that little something more" which varies with position but which cannot be taught or requisitioned and is discovered only by the alert mind of a keen and willing youth.[39]

FOLLOW-UP AND/OR EMPLOYMENT SUPERVISION

The first step in follow-up or employment supervision is the securing of information as to whether or not a placement has been consummated. It is also the last step in the placement process. This information may be obtained by a report from the person referred, by notification from the employer, or by inquiry to one or both of the participating parties directly from the placement office.

If the reply is affirmative, one more placement may be added to the statistical record. But if follow-up consists only in recording a "hiring," the placement process, in its currently accepted sense, remains an unfinished business. If follow-up by the employing concern involves only the adding of another name to the payroll and seeing that the new employee reports to the foreman under whom he is to work, then, in the current acceptance of the term, an incomplete contribution to the company program for personnel service has been made. If the hiring of an inexperienced junior be involved then, in common parlance, the educational process remains an unfinished business.

Follow-up and employment supervision, especially the latter, are educational terms. They came into use in this country soon after the opening of the century and are supposed to have been suggested by the "aftercare" programs inaugurated by England and Scotland for the supervision of early employment experience. Changes in our economic life and in industrial processes and progress in understanding the importance of the human factor in the successful operation of the private enterprise system have broadened the area of their applicability to include all the educative, distributive, and productive facilities of the country as they are related to the human factor.

[39] Two recent pronouncements on the responsibility of employers for the selection, induction, and progress of youth are "Owen D. Young Urges Aid for New Workers," *Bulletin of the American Youth Commission*, IV (1940), and, John A. Scott, "Experience with Youth in Industry," *Executives Service Bulletin*, XXII (1944).

Since the educational implications of either of these terms are bound to dominate their discussion, irrespective of where they are used or what agency uses them, a complete presentation of their meanings and importance in connection with educational systems is not permissible at this time. Therefore a few brief statements regarding the purposes and methods of the follow-up of referrals to employment must suffice.

Follow-up is usually considered to be a more meaningful term when used in connection with the final responsibility of a junior employment service than is employment supervision. It is interested in both the personal and technical aspects of the occupational adjustment of those whom the service has referred to jobs. Its major purposes and the justification for its inclusion in junior placement procedures are:

(1) It is a tool which helps interviewers to appraise their referral efforts, and it serves as an evaluative criterion on the selective ability of interviewers and points out their comparative discriminatory abilities.

(2) It affords excellent opportunities to maintain friendly contacts with employers and to supplement services to them by co-operating in the occupational adjustment of juniors and in the development of their interest in preparation for promotions.

(3) It provides an opportunity to secure factual statistical data regarding the results of referrals: How many referrals never applied? How many who applied were not employed? How many who were offered positions refused to accept them? How many who were employed never returned to claim them? Such statistical data open the way for investigation into causes and remedies and have both immediate and future research values.

(4) It frequently acts as a check on useless and undesirable "quits." A little timely assistance in interpreting occupational requirements, customs, and traditions may remove causes of friction or disappointment and tide a junior over the initial period of adaptation to new situations.

(5) It affords an opportunity to study the problems involved in junior quits, layoffs, and discharges, and to weigh the causes of satisfaction or dissatisfaction on both sides.

(6) It is an excellent method of securing new occupational information, of keeping in touch with shifting occupational patterns, and of aiding educational systems to keep their vocational programs abreast of practical demands.

Methods of follow-up, as well as its purposes, have changed materially since the middleman system of placement first made some sort of follow-up an essential of the employment process. Telephones, letters, post cards, personal visits to employers, and personal calls on employees have all been used. In some offices an especial effort has been made to invite juniors to call at the placement office, and hours which would make the acceptance of such invitations possible have been set aside for this purpose. Conferences outside of their places of business give young wage earners a better chance "to blow off steam," and to give impartial consideration to such questions as, "Would you hire yourself?" and "Would you fire yourself?"

The timing of follow-up is important. Some junior offices have standardized their practices, and follow up all placements within a given period, which varies from one to six months for the first visit. This writer found that discouragement, for one reason or another, often overcame the good intentions and promises of youngsters who were serving their novitiate within the first three or four weeks, and many "quits" were salvaged by prompt and early follow-up.

Shall all juniors be followed up, or only a selected group? And if only a selected group, on what basis shall selection be made? This may seem like a silly question, but it is not. It is a decidedly pertinent one in the light of the current assumption that there are always educational implications involved in junior placements. Moreover, the reply is not uniform. There are junior services, some operating under educational auspices, which include in a "selected" group "those placed in permanent positions whom we think it worth while to follow up." [40] Further elaboration of practices reveals that such services do not feel that they can afford to bother with some of their placements because they had been so difficult to place originally that they might be discouraged and come back for replacement.

SUMMATION AND CONCLUSION

Part Three of this book has been concerned with Special Employment Services. The history of such services and their original *raison d'être* has been briefly reviewed. A number of bases of specialization have been revealed, which, since they have been closely related to our social, economic, and religious history, and to the various waves of immigrant nationalities, have been shifting rather than static. As public services have increased in number and prestige, two bases for instituting special services have superseded most of the earlier ones—types of occupations and types of applicants.

For a time specialization was very popular, and a considerable number of services were based on the combination of persons and occupations.

[40] Courtesy prompts the withholding of documentation. The implications are just as effective without it.

Divisions for men, women, and juniors, plus divisions or departments for different occupations which employed each type of persons were common. But even as differentiation into special services was approved and progressed, problems arose and dangers became apparent. Social legislation, which tended to break down the age barrier between junior workers and adult workers, and custom, which was gradually breaking down the traditional barriers between the professional and commercial opportunities open to men and women, warned experienced workers that continuous subdivision of the total labor supply prevented the substitute referral of one type of person for another and fostered the maintenance of an abnormal labor reserve in each service.

Obviously, some special services were necessary. What were they, and by what criteria could they be determined? Stocktaking began. A single criterion was formulated. A special service is warranted whenever the character of the work, the qualifications of the workers, or the conditions and circumstances of the work vary from the universal to such an extent that a special service, or a specially trained interviewer in a general office, is necessary to supplement usual placement procedures.

To what extent does the application of this criterion indicate that either or both of the special services which have been presented in Chapters X and XI, and are presently of considerable public interest, should become permanent special services in a complete, well-organized public placement service? Recapitulation will serve to bring the issues squarely before us:

Who are the veterans? Generally speaking, they are a rather complete cross section, occupationally and socially, of our entire male population between 18 and 50 years of age. Subdivided as to age, education, physical and mental condition, occupational experiences, and the like, they will fall into about the same categories and face approximately the same problems in securing suitable occupational openings, retaining positions, and finding new ones if they are unemployed late in life as do nonveterans.

Each group will include its quota of physically and mentally sound and of the physically or mentally unsound; each will register an occupationally desirable and an occupationally undesirable element; the malicious veteran and the antisocial nonveteran will be equally hard to place and to keep placed; the young veteran, who has never made his occupational adjustment, will face approximately the same situation as will the young college graduate who is about to begin his struggle with the occupational world; and men who are unfortunate enough to be seeking new positions when they are between 40 and 50 years of age will be in the same predicament whether they be veterans or nonveterans.

Who are the juniors? No authoritative pronouncement is possible at this time, and no effort to reply authoritatively has been made. What has been revealed, and is well documented, is that a chain of events has tended to lessen the number of youth below 16 years of age who are either proper subjects for a public employment service or are placeable by it. Hedged around as they are by legal restrictions and requirements, and endowed as they are with the faults as well as the attractive qualities of young adolescents, they are regarded by both placement workers and employers as occupationally undesirable, and can usually secure only part-time or vacation jobs. This underage group, plus a considerable number of the 16- and 17-year-olds fall just as legitimately into the hard-to-place category as do some of the overage veterans or nonveterans.

But there is another group of juniors, between 18 and 21 years of age, who to all intents and purposes are prepared to take their places in the occupational world and to compete with other experienced workers—veterans or nonveterans. Therefore, from an employment point of view they should be classified as adults rather than as juniors. They comprise both veterans and nonveterans, the physically sound as well as the physically handicapped. A fourth group of juniors is comprised of inexperienced youth 18 to 25 years of age. In this category there will be both veterans and nonveterans, the physically and mentally sound and the physically or mentally handicapped. Some because of their inexperience, immaturity of judgment, and ignorance of the requirements of occupational life will be exceedingly difficult to place.

When the composition, characteristics, occupational abilities and opportunities, and the personal needs of the groups which have been classified as veterans and as juniors are checked, the one against the other and each with a cross section of our employable population, in order to determine to what extent they meet the criterion for a special service, one is forced to conclude that there are only two types of persons included under these special services which can be better served by the maintenance of special services, although the use of a specially trained interviewer in a general office might be desirable for other groups.

(1) Juniors, 14 to 16 years of age, who are still under school and child-labor supervision and are primarily school pupils. Their wage-earning experiences will usually be limited to out-of-school hours and to vacations, and work certificates will be an eligibility-for-employment requirement. In some states this classification would cover youth under 18, if they are

still charges of the educational system. If the inexperienced applicants over 18 years of age comprise a large enough group to warrant a special interviewer, one might be allocated to the general service and be available to any who desired to consult on problems which are common to novitiates.

(2) Adults, over 18 years of age, who are suffering from physical or other handicaps which do not render them unemployable but which do affect their employability in competition with normal persons applying for the same types of work—in other words they are difficult to place.

For some years those who are experienced in the placement of handicapped persons have favored the subdivision of those who are suffering from physical handicaps in such fashion that all those whose handicaps permit satisfactory job performance under normal conditions be segregated from those whose handicaps prevent competition with normal workers. The former, including both veterans and nonveterans, it is argued, should not be penalized by being forced to register in special services, since this in itself tends to draw attention to their defects rather than to stress their assets, but should be placed through the same channels as are all other normal persons. The second group, also including both veterans and nonveterans, is thought to be in need of, and entitled to, special services manned by interviewers who are thoroughly familiar with the modern bases upon which the occupational services of handicapped persons are advantageously sold, and are good salesmen in their profession.

Were these recommendations to be carried out, it would mean that, after the initial period of adjustment, handicapped persons of all ages, both sexes, and veterans and nonveterans alike would fall into one or the other of the two categories mentioned; the one would be merged with the general employment service, and the other would share, with all other similarly handicapped persons, in the benefits of a special service or of a specially trained interviewer.

It would seem, then, that some reorganization in our practices relative to special placement services should be a part of the postwar reconversion program; and that one factor in the planning for such reconversion should be the desirability of minimizing "types of persons" as the bases for instituting special services, accompanied by the retention of "types of occupations" as the dominant control element in the subdivision of general services.

SELECTED SUPPLEMENTARY READING

Berry, J. A., and others. *The School Follows Through.* National Association of Secondary School Principals, 1941. An important reference for educators.

Breckenridge, Sophonisba P. *Guidance by the Development of Placement and Follow-up Work*. Washington, D.C., 1914. (U.S. Bureau of Education, Bull. no. 14.)

Culbert, Jane Fullerton, and Smith, Helen R. *Counseling Young Workers*. New York: The Vocational Service for Juniors, 1939. Testing in connection with counseling and placement is exceptionally well handled.

Davenel, George F. "How to Plan for Postwar Employment," *Personnel*, XXI (1944), 70–78. Concerned with methods of assisting war workers to make their occupational peacetime adjustment. Includes a helpful bibliography.

David, Paul T. *Barriers to Youth Employment*. Washington, D.C.: The American Council on Education, 1942. Concerned with the more conspicuous obstacles which frequently stand in the way of youth employment and the extent to which changes are needed in order to facilitate that employment.

David, Paul T. *Postwar Youth Employment*. Washington, D.C.: The American Council on Education, 1943. Discusses American economic development in relation to youth employment. Analyzes population changes, technological development, and industrial trends, and attempts a partial forecast of postwar occupational patterns.

Disabled Veteran, The. Annals of the American Academy of Political and Social Science, CCXXXIX (May, 1945). The entire issue. Includes articles on all phases of the subject by Walter V. Bingham, General Hines, William C. Menninger, and others.

Dougherty, N. F. *The Relation of the School to Employment*. New York: National Association of Corporation Schools, 1914. (Bull. no. 8.) Expresses the point of view of employers in 1914.

Eckert, Ruth Elizabeth. *When Youth Leave School*. New York: McGraw-Hill Book Co., 1938. (Regents' Inquiry, State of New York.)

Harrison, Shelby M., and others. *Public Employment Offices: Their Purpose, Structure and Methods*. New York: Russell Sage Foundation, 1924. Pp. 527–619. This is the most inclusive discussion of special services with which this writer is familiar. In the majority of cases attention is given to the relative values of general or special services for each group presented.

Hathaway, Katharine Butler. *The Little Locksmith*. New York: Coward-McCann, 1943. An autobiography of great inspirational value to youth who suffer from physical handicaps.

Hostetler, C. E., and others. "Reemployment of Veterans: A Panel Session," in *Reemployment of Veterans*. . . . New York: American Management Association, 1944. Pp. 13–50. (Personnel Series no. 76.) Topics include The Training and Placement of Disabled Veterans, Veterans' Employment Plans of the United States Employment Service, Selective Service Assistance to Veterans, and Plans for Reintegration of Veterans into the Organization.

Huntington, Emily H. *Doors to Jobs*. Berkeley: The University of California Press, 1942.

International Association of Public Employment Services. *Proceedings, the Twenty-eighth Annual Convention*. 1940. An unusually good report. Contains addresses on Special Training for Junior Counselors, Counseling and Testing at Registration, Principles of Organization and Veterans Placement.

Johnson, Mrs. M. F. "The Schoolhouse as Employment Office," *First National*

Conference on Civic and Social Center Development. [N.p.] 1911. One of the early expressions of social thinking on the subject.

Kushnick, William H. "A Guide to Personnel Counseling," *Personnel*, XX (1943), 132–153. This is a guide for establishing and conducting a counseling program. It was developed by the War Department and is applicable to most industrial organizations.

Michigan State Employment Service. *Manual on Junior Placement Procedures.* Detroit, 1939. (Mimeo.)

Mufson, Florence Adams. "Safeguarding Labor Standards in Vocational Training," *Occupations*, XXII (1944), 341–344. This article deals with the requirements of two federal statutes which influence wartime vocational training as conducted in the public schools: The Public Contracts or Walsh-Healy Act of 1936 and the Fair Labor Standards Act (the Wage and Hour Law) of 1938.

National Association of Employment Managers. *Proceedings of the First Annual Convention.* 1919. An important source of information for those who wish to compare the status of post-World War I employment problems with those of 1945.

National Education Association. Pupil Personnel in Part-Time Schools. Washington, D.C., 1926. An excellent and very inclusive survey made by a subcommittee of the Vocational Education Committee in the National Council of Education.

National Industrial Conference Board. *The Employment of Young Persons in the United States.* New York, 1925.

National Vocational Guidance Association. *Proceedings, Second Conference,* 1912. *Fourth Conference,* 1914. These early reports give considerable attention to the placement of youth. How much progress has been made since 1912?

New York State Education Department. *Youth: The First Year Out of School.* Albany, 1942. This is a study of the problems encountered by youth during the transition from school to occupational life.

Postwar Jobs for Veterans. Annals of the American Academy of Political and Social Science, CCXXXVIII (March, 1945). The entire issue.

Pratt, George K. "The Call of the Cradles; Some Psychiatric Problems of Demobilization," *Mental Hygiene,* XXVI (1942), 39–49. Suggests the possible results of building up a philosophy of dependency and the need for careful counseling on vocational adaptation.

Preston, George H. "Remobilization versus Demobilization," *Mental Hygiene,* XXVI (1942), 33–38. Warns counselors of young veterans that military service has often interrupted orderly growth and forced an unsuitable training program. The stage of development reached when these factors became operative is important.

"Report by Committee on Vocational Guidance," *Proceedings of the National Association of Corporation Schools* (New York, 1916), pp. 331–482. A survey of the movement with special reference to commercial firms.

Report of Osborn Committee of Postwar Educational Opportunities for Service Personnel. Washington, D.C. (78th Congress, 1st session, House doc. no. 344.) Emphasizes the importance of a counseling program in assisting service personnel to readjust to civilian life.

Rogers, Carl R. *Counseling and Psychotherapy.* Boston: Houghton-Mifflin Co.,

1942. The author characterized his method of counseling as "nondirective." Interesting to those engaged in child and parental guidance and in abnormal psychology.

Rogers, Carl R. "Psychological Adjustment of Discharged Service Personnel," *Psychological Bulletin*, XLI (Dec., 1944), 689–696.

Sher, David. "Government Efforts to Cope with Job Discrimination," *Personnel*, XIX (1943), 739–747. Written by a member of the New York Bar, this article reviews the principal statutes and decrees which are of interest to personnel workers. A good basic reference for students.

Spaulding, Francis T. *High School and Life:* New York: McGraw-Hill Book Co., 1938. (Regents' Inquiry, State of New York.)

Thorne, Frederic C. "A Critique of Nondirective Methods of Psychotherapy," *Journal of Abnormal and Social Psychology*, XXXIX (Oct., 1944), 459–470. This article is a criticism of Rogers' "nondirective" methods.

Time Magazine, Service on Postwar Information. *Reemployment of Veterans.* Revised ed. New York, 1945. This report comprises an extensive bibliography, abstracts from laws and other documents, and brief comments and interpretations. The coverage is broad and the material valuable.

U.S. Office of Education, Committee on Youth Problems. *Vocational Guidance for Those Out of School.* Washington, D.C., 1936. (Bull. no. 4.)

U.S. Office of Education, Committee on Youth Problems. *Finding Jobs.* Washington, D.C., 1936. (Bull. no. 5.)

Waller, William. *The Veteran Comes Back.* New York: Dryden Press, 1944. Offers some good suggestions but there is some criticism of his characterizations of veterans as "disgruntled" persons.

Ward, Edward J. "The Vocation Center and Employment Office," in *The Social Center.* New York: D. Appleton and Co., 1913. Pp. 271–282. Another early presentation of the topic.

Ward, Raymond S. "How to Use Part IV of the 'Dictionary,'" *Occupations*, XXII (1943), 39–41. Cites several ways in which counselors may use Part IV of the *Dictionary of Occupational Titles.*

Wecter, Dixon. *When Johnny Comes Marching Home.* Boston: Houghton Mifflin Co., 1944. A historical study of the treatment of veterans in the United States. Well documented.

Welfare Council of New York City. *The Manual of Clearance Practice.* New York, 1934. (Mimeo.) Describes the practices and procedures in 43 co-operating noncommercial services.

Woodward, Luther E. "Social Case-Work in Relation to Selective Service and the Rejected," *Mental Hygiene*, XXVII (1943), 370–389.

PERIODICALS

Occupations—The Vocational Guidance Magazine. Published monthly, October to May, inclusive, by the National Vocational Guidance Association, 425 West 123d Street, New York City. Primarily for educators.

Occupational Index, Inc. Published by New York University, Washington Square, New York City.

Vocational Guide. Published monthly during the school year by the Science Research Associates, 228 South Wabash Ave., Chicago. An annotated bibliography of selected materials on occupations.

PART FOUR

The Future of Occupational Placement

CHAPTER XII

Problems of Today and Tomorrow

THE military phase of World War II is about to take its place in the historic pageantry of the world. The peace ship is waiting in the offing for a pilot. Once again the confidence of our country in education has influenced some of us to declare that only the imposition of our educational system can nullify the Nazi philosophy and bring the peace ship safely into the harbor of One World.

Our domestic reconversion problems are stupendous, but, with full confidence in their ability to solve them, we are asking our industrial and business concerns to guarantee full employment and our educational authorities to provide education for all from the kindergarten through college. The twin problems of employment and education are challenging us on all sides.

In between these two agencies, one of which must produce the future workers while the other must absorb them into the productive life of the nation, stand our occupational placement agencies. If the expectations of the reconversion period are to be realized, these three agencies, proceeding co-operatively, their activities illuminated by the experience of the past, must accept the challenge of today and prepare for the responsibilities of tomorrow.

It is appropriate, therefore, to bring this study to its conclusion with a summary of the relationships of these agencies in the past, of their present status, and of their potential abilities to accept the responsibilities of tomorrow, and to ask what prospect there may be that the promises and programs of the last decade will be implemented by the type of considered action which will promote the educational and occupational welfare and happiness of millions of our citizens in the immediate present and in the years to come.

Placement services are only middlemen, although some forecasters feel that they should assume some of the functions of intermediaries. They are not the major recipients of the challenge of the future, nor are they the major actors in determining the course of the future, but they are the major topic of the discussion in this book and as such are entitled to the final accent. Therefore, it is permissible to stress the extent to which this intermediate agency has shown vision and imagination in the past, is able to offer suggestions for the present, and gives promise of more helpful suggestions in the future, and to ask: What of its philosophies and experiences, or of the results of its practices, have had worth-while educational implications? What have had worth-while occupational implications?

Among the facts and authoritative opinions which, over the years, have been accumulating in employment services and now have suggestions for the solution of present problems are:

(1) That placement has always had educational implications and placement personnel has always assumed some educational responsibilities. These implications and responsibilities were first recognized with reference to young wage earners, but gradually it was realized that the placement and continuous employability of adults also involved educational implications and required educational co-operation.

(2) That changing social-economic patterns always result in changing eligibility requirements for employment and that these changing patterns and requirements are registered in placement offices just as soon as they have crystallized sufficiently to reveal trends.

(3) That education, placement, and industrial relations, as concepts and as functions, are also subject to change; that sometimes an apparently unrelated series of events makes up the total picture of an era in transition.

(4) That all the members of the educational and occupational world are both buyers and sellers; that teachers, pupils, interviewers, applicants, employers, and employees, each in turn appraises the other and accepts or rejects his offerings.

(5) That placement services, in order to perform their social, educational, and economic functions, must keep their objectives and methods in tune with the social, educational, and economic philosophies of the time.

(6) That many of our present industrial relations problems center around the demand for a system which will guarantee workers a reasonable degree of economic security. Side by side with this demand a sort of creeping paralysis, in the form of a "security neurosis," has developed and may result in a philosophy quite foreign to the aggressive, confident thought and action which has been an outstanding characteristic of our economic life.

(7) That our country and our communities, although acting with the best of intentions, are not justified in creating false educational interests or unsatisfiable social desires.

(8) That "exploitation" in many forms and in many areas of life has characterized the history of our republic. Employment personnel has been in an excellent position to observe the educational, legislative, and economic exploitation of various groups and to note its motivations.

(9) That an effective placement service must be able to recruit workers who are qualified to meet the demand, and to exercise discriminatory ability in selecting and referring those who are best qualified to the positions open.

(10) That workers group themselves along lines of promotion in many ways. Each rises to a certain level, and then for one reason or another, at some point along the line, each falls into his own niche while his fellows continue on the main stairway.

(11) That workers subconsciously resent the fact that some individuals or groups are making profits from the labor of others. This is an educational problem. Its solution begins in the public schools where there is abundant material to study impartially the distribution of labor and the distribution of the profits of all the human and material contributions which are essential to carrying forward industrial and business ventures.

(12) That the steadily closing age gap between the junior and the adult worker, accompanied by substitution of experience for age as a major criterion of the employability of youth, has brought many college students and young veterans within the purview of a junior division and suggested the desirability of organizing such a division into two closely articulated units. Well-supported arguments are advanced for assuming that one unit, registering youth for part-time or vacation work, should become an educational responsibility and be so organized that work experience would become an integral part of our public system of education, while a second unit would place out-of-school juniors. Experienced juniors between 18 and 21 years of age would, if they wished, register in an adult service. Should educators find a practical method of implementing their recent pronouncements relative to the value of work experience, these arguments will be greatly strengthened.

(13) That every employee, in order to be available for advancement, must keep mentally alert, physically fit, and occupationally up to date.

(14) That federal and state wage laws have been set at adult levels with few exceptions for youth. This involves definite discrimination against youth and raises a question as to the intentions of the lawmakers. Is our country in process of organizing itself to exclude youth from sharing in the productive work of our economic organization?

(15) That in some cases where college and secondary education have

been used as substitutes for temporary employment relief, the recipients have been unfitted for work opportunities in which otherwise they might have been contented and effective.

(16) That follow-up of placements is an important employment service function, although certain phases of the complete process must be assumed by education and employing concerns.

(17) That prospects for the employment of the physically handicapped are constantly improving and that there is a growing tendency to classify as normal all handicapped persons whose disabilities do not interfere with normal job performance, with special services limited to those whose handicaps are of such a character that they rate as difficult to place.

(18) That legislation is making it progressively more difficult to place marginal or substandard workers.

(19) That there is a "distressing tendency" on the part of college men and women to ascribe to themselves executive abilities. One interviewer reports his inability to recall a single instance in which the applicant failed to make this claim. An equally "distressing tendency" on the part of able noncollege applicants to assume that college graduation is prerequisite to the attainment of high executive positions is also reported. Both types of applicants need factual information.

(20) That there is no future for a man or woman as a college man. Business will strip off his cap and gown, ignore his Phi Beta Kappa and his diploma, and get down to the fundamental problems as to what the paraphernalia mean in terms of what he is good for and what he can do.

(21) That high-pressure salesmanship in academic fields in which women recruits have been sought may have caused too much shifting into nontraditional fields, and may seriously complicate the future occupational adjustment of the sexes.

(22) That securing a position is a valuable part of the experience and information that constitute education; that youth learns something hunting a job, losing a job, being out of a job, and hunting another; and that guidance through the job is no less important than is guidance into the job.

(23) That the loss of a job need not be a serious handicap to a worker provided he is given proper assistance in interpreting its educational and occupational implications.

(24) That legislating youth out of industry has been very thoroughly tried and the results have not proved so satisfactory that it seems wise to attempt to end youth unemployment by "legislating out" the older worker. It would seem wiser to reformulate employment policies in such fashion

that provision for the equalization of occupational opportunities for youth and adult would result.

(25) That, in the occupational areas of life, there has always been a youth problem, that there is one now, and that there always will be one. The question always has been the same: At what point shall the youth stream be permitted to enter the main stream?

Since placement agencies must look to education to lay the foundation and pave the way for much of their success, it is logical that their interest in the attitude of educators toward placement should have increased as their own responsibilities increased, and that now and then they should have formulated suggestions for co-operation which they hoped might sometime be put into practice.

The story of educational co-operation, or lack of co-operation, in the occupational distribution of the school product and by-product is too well known to permit repetition. With perfect equanimity, prior to the recent depression, the leaders of education have, for the most part, been quite indifferent to the educational needs of employed youth. Throughout the years they have been content to work at cross purposes with youth —determined, with the help of the law, to keep him in school, whereas he, with or without the blessing of education, was interested only in how to get and keep a job.

During the early years of this century, while philanthropy was setting up guidance and placement bureaus for the "outcasts" of education, while the National Vocational Guidance Association, the American Association of Public Employment Offices, the National Society for the Promotion of Industrial Education, the American Federation of Labor, the National Association of Manufacturers, and the National Association of Corporation Schools were calling upon education to assume responsibility for assisting youth to make a more satisfactory transition to the work world, while here and there educators were uniting with local placement services in pleading for closer co-operation between the agencies which produce workers and those which distribute and absorb them, and while youth were repeatedly telling their own story, the great majority of our educational systems continued to muff one of the most important aspects of their job.

Then came the depression. Where the vision of the minority of their colleagues had failed to arouse the main body of educators, the changing pattern of our social structure laid the foundation for this accomplishment, while the institution, by the federal government, of agencies under other than educational auspices which were charged with leadership in assisting youth to meet their employment problems completed the task.

Educators organized for self-defense. They published youth studies and surveys, called conferences on youth problems and programs, prepared work-study plans, and the like. The American Youth Commission, the Educational Policies Commission, the National Association of Secondary School Principals, and the American Association of School Administrators have issued a plethora of studies, plans, pronouncements, and programs for the solution of youth problems. Placement services, employing concerns, and youth are now awaiting their implementation.

But the depression was not the only stimulus to a change in the attitude of educators. Additional stimuli have been provided by the criticisms of the Army and Navy on the methods and content of the education which prepared our armed forces for military service. The Army took over and became the largest educational agency in the United States, while "school" was relegated to second place. The latter is coming to realize that it is no monopoly but merely one of several competing educational agencies. Youth too has played some part in changing the attitude of educators. War has revealed the practical value of knowledge: mathematics, physics, geography, and other school subjects have proved their utility in world affairs. Alert young veterans are realizing that no compelling purpose gave character to or motivated their preinduction education, and they are challenging the education of today to furnish for the youth of tomorrow a substitute for the energetic and purposeful efforts of war.

Educators now seem to be agreed that youth must learn to work, and that experience in productive work is an excellent finishing school for the entire product of our public schools. Since they do not desire to turn over either this task or its supporting funds to another agency, they have given tacit approval to the incorporation of work experience in the school curriculum and have qualified their consent by adding, "this experience to be directed to educational aims." This qualification coming from an agency which has so long accepted compliance with legislated residential requirements without much reference to whether or not the resultant experiences were directed to "educational aims" puzzles some persons. But, on the whole, education is obviously moving forward, and closer co-operation in solving the occupational adjustment problems of youth seems imminent.

Specifically, what practical co-operative contributions do placement services, employers, and youth itself expect our educational systems to make to the occupational adjustment of youth and adult?

(1) That they recognize that vocational counseling is a long-term

educational activity, while placement is a specific service; that during the period of vocational counseling there are certain preparatory-to-occupational-success functions which no agency can so well perform as can education; and that no other agency is so well situated to assist adult workers in securing certain types of knowledges and skills which are essential to promotion.

(2) That every teacher should know the vocational implications of his subject and bring them out whenever possible, and that each should make some definite contribution to the development of "character collateral," which is such a valuable addition to job knowledge and skill.

(3) That teachers should study the abilities and capacities of their pupils, counsel on program choices in harmony with latent abilities, know the occupational range within which each can best use his talents, and develop interests along the lines in which each reveals potentialities.

(4) That teachers give conscious attention to the avoidance of creating prejudices against, or preferences for, any type of occupation which is approved by society for young workers. Carelessly made statements to the effect that there are no worth-while opportunities for youth are untrue and are often remembered by their hearers, furnishing plausible excuses for drifting about from job to job. It is also important that teachers cease accenting monetary motivation either as an incentive to reject occupational opportunities or to stay in school. Employers no longer need the help of inexperienced youth, but, if educators are to carry out their work-experience program, they will badly need the help of employers.

(5) That educators, while expounding our current philosophies regarding the enjoyment of the four freedoms and the rights to happiness and asking youth what they want to do, like to do, and prefer to do, remember that not only the labor market but the entire world is suffering for lack of men and women who understand the meaning of obligations and duties, who are able and willing to assume responsibilities, and who have in their youth acquired the moral and spiritual qualities which are in universal demand.

(6) That educators and social workers modify their tendency to assume that employers are reaching out to draw youth into the crucible of occupational life. That attitude on the part of employers is now ancient history. Under modern conditions employers find youth a nuisance rather than an asset, oftentimes an employment liability, while those responsible for securing job openings are glad to find employers who are willing to bother with them.

(7) Employing concerns are looking forward to reasonably permanent

employment. Therefore they are asking education to prepare men and women who will be able and willing to maintain employment standards and co-operate in the undertaking.

(8) That the educational systems follow up their product and co-operate in its occupational adjustment. The recent Occupational Adjustment Study of the National Association of Secondary School Principals has declared it to be the duty of school authorities to ascertain how the school product functions in occupational life, to know what problems are arising after induction which might have been prevented by different types or methods of education, and to suggest how educational programs may be altered in the interest of greater efficiency. Methods of procedure were included in the study and several practical applications of its instructions are on record.

The relationship of employing concerns to placement services has always been of major interest to placement workers. Whenever employers have failed to recognize the social disadvantages of certain of their employment practices, it has been a handicap to the maintenance of a balanced labor market and to the effective operation of public employment services. Their efforts to study the occupational aptitudes of different nationalities after World War I, to provide opportunities for older workers, to introduce counseling programs and in-plant educational facilities have been appreciated, and the difficulties which will confront them as they undertake to maintain postwar full employment are not minimized.

There has always been a sympathetic understanding on the part of placement workers of the problems which employers have encountered as they have struggled to keep their selective devices in tune with all the legislative reforms which have entered the employment picture since 1900, while placement services have regretted the extent to which such reforms have denied occupational opportunities to marginal and handicapped workers and have refused youth an opportunity to gain a foothold in the work world.

What, as postwar employment plans are being made, are the specific responsibilities which employing concerns are being asked to assume?

They are being asked to absorb all persons who are fit to work and wish to do so, and they are going to be invited to serve as a finishing school for the entire product of the educational systems. In meeting these all-inclusive responsibilities they are being asked to remember that both adult and youth bring their personal problems to work with them, and that many problems arise after workers are on the job which cannot be anticipated by either educators or placement services. Therefore, they are being asked to co-operate with education and placement services in a program of follow-up which shall include advice and assistance in meeting changing economic conditions and in preparing for promotion. Youth is asking them to be patient; to remember that, even if the educators do their very best, youth is unused to the type of discipline imposed by occupational life and that the great majority will backslide now and then as they pass from the irresponsibilities of youth to the responsibilities of maturity.

Finally, what is the prospect for public placement services in the future? It is not our privilege to read the scroll upon which the future functions, problems, and achievements of employment services are foretold. The road which such services have traveled thus far has been thorny. History has recorded that our public employment services have been born as emergency needs arose, as the pressure of each emergency lessened they have died, and then, as acute situations recurred, they have been born again.

It is difficult to estimate the permanent values of such intermittent services, but it is possible to cite some contribution which, during each period of activity, they have made to social progress. Therefore it is legitimate to expect that, as the machinery and personnel which the government borrowed from the states soon after Pearl Harbor is again returned to them, and as the United States Employment Service is reallocated to the United States Department of Labor, communities which are interested in establishing either general placement services or special services for veterans, juniors, persons hard to place, or others may secure the assistance and co-operation of both state and federal services as they face one or more of the following problems:

(1) What can be done with and for the average youth who will not go to school and who is not permitted by law to go to work? This is a constantly recurring problem. The New York City High-School Principals Association has recently (1944) pronounced this type of youth "far better off at work." But after many years during which youth has been "just worn out with school," and school has been just worn out with youth, millions of such youth without educational supervision still go out into the world where life itself makes up all the intelligence and achievement tests.

(2) Who shall market the product and the by-product of the educational system? In 1909 Dr. E. T. Devine raised this question. Others joined him in declaring that some agency must train to specifications and either the same or another agency must distribute to specifications. Should the educational setup include a sales department co-operating with its produc-

tion division, or was it wiser for some other agency to act as sales manager for education? The same question is before us today. If a sales department is to be installed, when shall the youth stream enter the main employment stream?

(3) How, the educator is asking, can he implement his work-experience program? How can the potential values of work experience be realized? Satisfactory solution is a gigantic undertaking involving many facts and factors. Occupational opportunities, suitable for the purpose, must be found without causing unemployment among adult workers. The operational aspects of the program, if educational aims are to be achieved, will require teachers and counselors who can give continuous assistance in the interpretation of educational activities in terms of their occupational significance, and vice versa. And it is very important that the transitional, rather than the compulsory, features of the program be stressed. Certain aspects of current part-time contracts will probably need revision, and the legislated stumbling blocks will be ever present. Finally there will be the problem of teaching personnel qualified to carry out a work-experience program.

(4) Popular indifference, ignorance, and prejudice must be overcome. The public, parents, teachers, and workers of all ages must understand that neither a utopia, a new deal, nor Providence itself has as yet been able to guarantee anyone against occupational failure, or to promise him occupational success, and that society may not impose any such responsibility upon either education, placement services, or employing concerns.

There are plenty of employment problems ahead of us, as our country moves into the reconversion period.

One thing is certain and perhaps only one. Unless educators, employing concerns, employees, and placement services work in harmony, supported by an intelligent public, it will not be possible to construct a satisfactory philosophy of placement based on the experiences of the past and the requirements of the present, and permeated by a perspective vision which will stimulate the creative imagination necessary to cut a pathway into the future.

INDEX OF SUBJECTS

INDEX OF NAMES